Richard

EMPEROR OF ROME

EMPEROR
of ROME

RULING THE ANCIENT ROMAN WORLD

MARY BEARD

Liveright Publishing Corporation

A Division of W. W. Norton & Company
Celebrating a Century of Independent Publishing

For information about permission to reproduce selections from this book, write to Permissions, Liveright Publishing Corporation, a division of W. W. Norton & Company, Inc., 500 Fifth Avenue, New York, NY 10110

For information about special discounts for bulk purchases, please contact W. W. Norton Special Sales at specialsales@wwnorton.com or 800-233-4830

Manufacturing by Lakeside Book Company

ISBN 978-0-87140-422-0

Liveright Publishing Corporation, 500 Fifth Avenue, New York, N.Y. 10110
www.wwnorton.com

W. W. Norton & Company Ltd., 15 Carlisle Street, London W1D 3BS

2 3 4 5 6 7 8 9 0

CONTENTS

THE MAIN CHARACTERS

JULIO-CLAUDIAN DYNASTY

 JULIUS CAESAR, after defeating Pompey the Great, became *dictator* of Rome 48 BCE; assassinated 44 BCE.

 AUGUSTUS (Octavian), adopted son of Julius Caesar. After defeating Antony and Cleopatra in 31 BCE, became sole ruler until 14 CE. Second wife, **LIVIA**.

 TIBERIUS, natural son of Livia and adopted son of Augustus, ruled 14–37 CE. Rumours that Caligula was involved in his death.

 CALIGULA (Gaius), great-grandson of Augustus, ruled 37–41. Assassinated by members of his guard.

 CLAUDIUS, nephew of Tiberius, ruled 41–54. Third wife, **MESSALINA**; fourth wife, **AGRIPPINA** (the Younger) – by whom he was rumoured to have been murdered.

 NERO, natural son of Agrippina, adopted son of Claudius. Ruled 54–68. Forced to suicide after army insurrections.

CIVIL WAR 68–69 CE

Three emperors ruling for just a few months each: **GALBA**, **OTHO** and **VITELLIUS**

FLAVIAN DYNASTY

 VESPASIAN, final victor in civil war. Ruled 69–79.

 TITUS, natural son of Vespasian. Ruled 79–81. Rumours that Domitian was involved in his death.

 DOMITIAN, natural son of Vespasian. Ruled 81–96. Assassinated in palace coup.

THE 'ADOPTIVE' EMPERORS – ANTONINE DYNASTY

 NERVA, chosen by senate. Ruled 96–8.

 TRAJAN, adopted son of Nerva, of Spanish origin. Ruled 98–117. Wife, **PLOTINA**.

 HADRIAN, adopted son of Trajan, of Spanish origin. Ruled 117–38. Wife, **SABINA**.

 ANTONINUS PIUS, adopted son of Hadrian. Ruled 138–61. Wife, **FAUSTINA** (the Elder).

 MARCUS AURELIUS, adopted son of Antoninus Pius. Ruled 161–80. Wife, **FAUSTINA** (the Younger).

 LUCIUS VERUS, adopted son of Antoninus Pius. Co-ruler with Marcus Aurelius 161–9. Death from plague (though rumours of poisoning by mother-in-law).

COMMODUS, natural son of Marcus Aurelius and Faustina. Ruled 180–92 (and from 177 jointly with Marcus Aurelius). Assassinated in palace coup.

CIVIL WAR 193

Four short-term emperors or usurpers: **PERTINAX, DIDIUS JULIANUS, CLODIUS ALBINUS, PESCENNIUS NIGER**

SEVERAN DYNASTY

 SEPTIMIUS SEVERUS, final victor in civil war, of North African origin. Ruled 193–211. Second wife, **JULIA DOMNA**, of Syrian origin.

 CARACALLA, natural son of Septimius Severus and Julia Domna. Ruled 211–17 (earlier jointly with Septimius and Geta). Assassinated while on military campaign.

 GETA, natural son of Septimius Severus and Julia Domna. Joint ruler with his father and brother, 209–11. Assassinated on the orders of Caracalla.

 MACRINUS, of equestrian rank, took power after assassination of Caracalla. Ruled 217–18. Overthrown by supporters of Elagabalus.

 ELAGABALUS, great-nephew of Julia Domna, of Syrian origin. Ruled 218–22. Assassinated by his guard.

 ALEXANDER SEVERUS, cousin and adopted son of Elagabalus, of Syrian origin. Ruled 222–35. Assassinated while on military campaign.

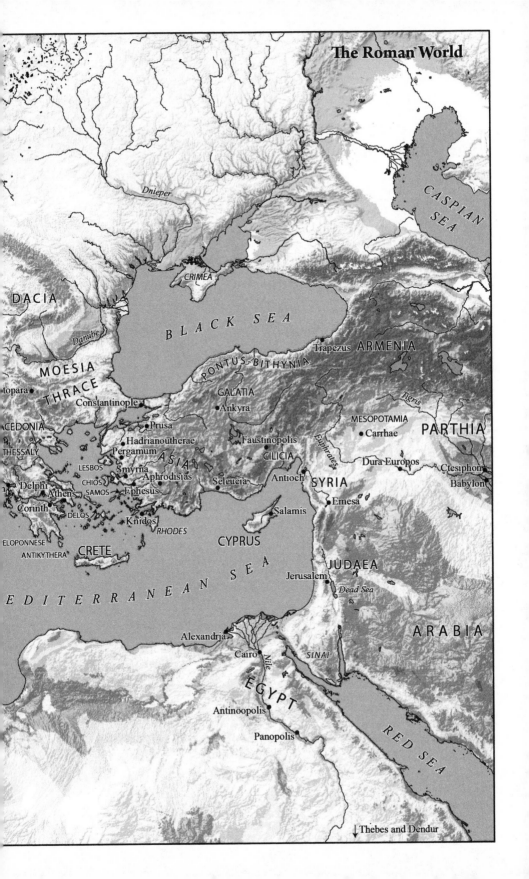

The Roman World

DACIA

MOESIA

THRACE

topara

CEDONIA

THESSALY

Delphi

Athens

Corinth

ELOPONNESE

ANTIKYTHERA

CRETE

Constantinople

Prusa

Hadrianoutherae

Pergamum

LESBOS

Smyrna

CHIOS

SAMOS

Ephesus

DELOS

Knidos

RHODES

ASIA

Aphrodisias

Seleucia

GALATIA

Ankyra

Faustinopolis

CILICIA

Antioch

SYRIA

Emesa

Salamis

CYPRUS

JUDAEA

Jerusalem

Dead Sea

Alexandria

Cairo

Nile

SINAI

EGYPT

Antinoopolis

Panopolis

BLACK SEA

CRIMEA

Dnieper

Danube

PONTUS-BITHYNIA

Trapezus

ARMENIA

MESOPOTAMIA

Carrhae

PARTHIA

Tigris

Euphrates

Dura Europos

Ctesiphon

Babylon

CASPIAN SEA

MEDITERRANEAN SEA

ARABIA

RED SEA

↓ Thebes and Dendur

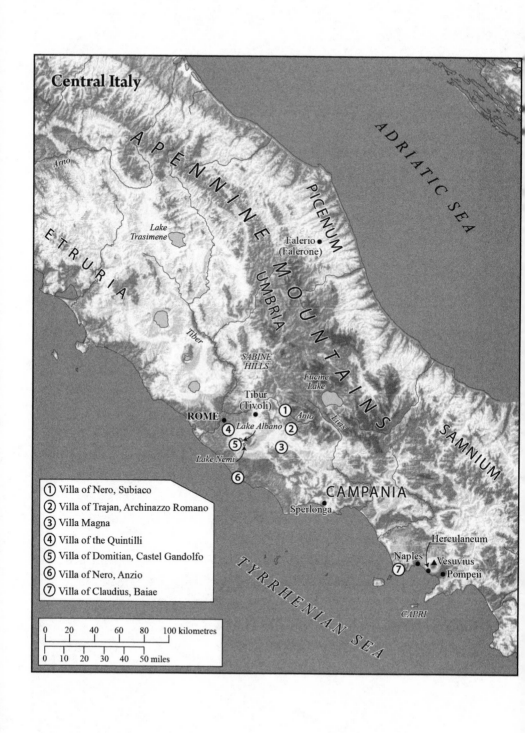

Central Italy

Arno

ETRURIA

Lake Trasimene

APENNINE

PICENUM

ADRIATIC SEA

Falerio
(Falerone)

UMBRIA

MOUNTAINS

Tiber

SABINE HILLS

Fucine Lake

Tibur
(Tivoli)

① *Anio*

Liris

ROME

④ *Lake Albano*

②

SAMNIUM

⑤

③

Lake Nemi

⑥

CAMPANIA

Sperlonga

① Villa of Nero, Subiaco

② Villa of Trajan, Archinazzo Romano

③ Villa Magna

④ Villa of the Quintilli

⑤ Villa of Domitian, Castel Gandolfo

⑥ Villa of Nero, Anzio

⑦ Villa of Claudius, Baiae

Herculaneum

Naples ▲ Vesuvius
⑦ Pompeii

CAPRI

TYRRHENIAN SEA

| 0 | 20 | 40 | 60 | 80 | 100 kilometres |

| 0 | 10 | 20 | 30 | 40 | 50 miles |

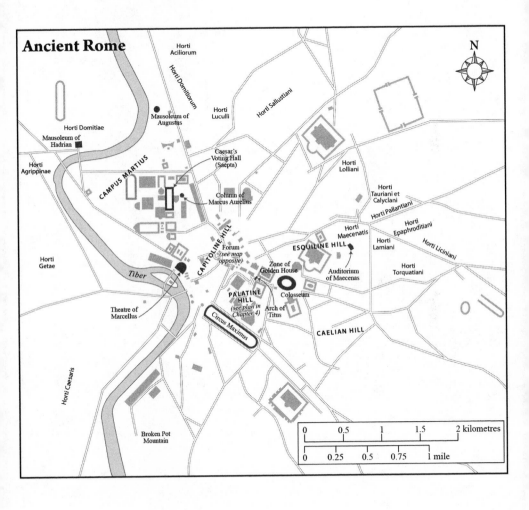

Ancient Rome

N

Horti Aciliorum

Horti Domitiorum

Horti Luculli

Horti Sallustiani

Mausoleum of Augustus

Horti Domitiae

Mausoleum of Hadrian

Horti Agrippinae

CAMPUS MARTIUS

Caesar's Voting Hall (Saepta)

Column of Marcus Aurelius

Horti Lolliani

Horti Tauriani et Calyclani

Horti Pallantiani

CAPITOLINE HILL

Horti Getae

Tiber

Forum (see map opposite)

Horti Maecenatis

ESQUILINE HILL

Horti Epaphroditiani

Horti Lamiani

Horti Liciniani

Zone of Golden House

Auditorium of Maecenas

Horti Torquatiani

Theatre of Marcellus

PALATINE HILL (see plan in Chapter 4)

Colosseum

Arch of Titus

Circus Maximus

CAELIAN HILL

Horti Caesaris

Broken Pot Mountain

| 0 | 0.5 | 1 | 1.5 | 2 kilometres |

| 0 | 0.25 | 0.5 | 0.75 | 1 mile |

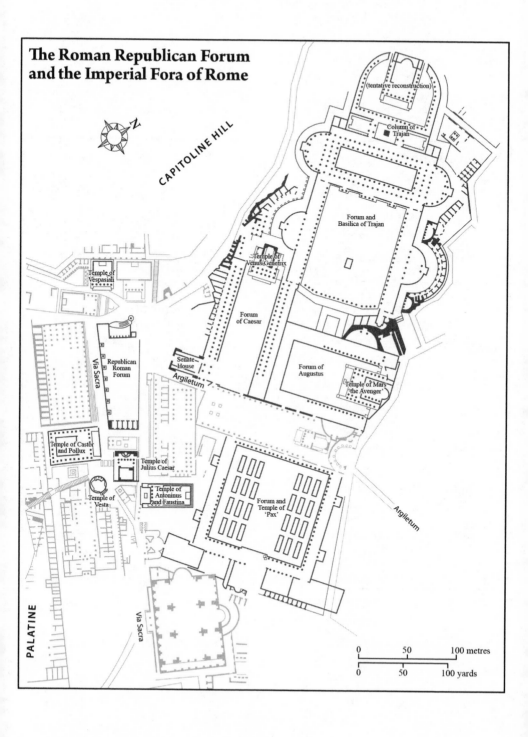

The Roman Republican Forum
and the Imperial Fora of Rome

CAPITOLINE HILL

(tentative reconstruction)

Column of Trajan

Forum and
Basilica of Trajan

Temple of
Vespasian

Temple of
Venus Genetrix

Forum
of Caesar

Republican
Roman
Forum

Senate-
House

Argiletum

Forum of
Augustus

Temple of Mars
'the Avenger'

Via Sacra

Temple of Castor
and Pollux

Temple of
Julius Caesar

Temple of
Antoninus
and Faustina

Temple of
Vesta

Forum and
Temple of
'Pax'

Argiletum

PALATINE

Via Sacra

| 0 | 50 | 100 metres |
| 0 | 50 | 100 yards |

WELCOME...

... to the world of the Roman emperors. Some, like Caligula and Nero, are even now bywords for excess, cruelty and casual sadism. Some like the 'philosopher-emperor' Marcus Aurelius, with his *Meditations* (or better, as I shall call them, *Jottings to Himself*) are still international bestsellers. Some are almost unknown, even to specialists. Who now recognises Didius Julianus, who in 193 CE was supposed to have bought his place on the throne for a few weeks, when the imperial guard auctioned the empire off to the highest bidder?

Emperor of Rome explores the fact and fiction of these rulers of the ancient Roman world, asking what they did, why they did it and why their stories have been told in the extravagant, sometimes lurid, ways that they have. It looks at big questions of power, corruption and conspiracy. But it also looks at the day-to-day practicalities of their lives. What, and where, did they eat? Who did they sleep with? How did they travel?

In the course of the book, we shall meet many people who were not, and did not aspire to be, emperors themselves, but who made the imperial system possible: wary aristocrats, enslaved cooks, diligent secretaries, court jesters – even a doctor who treated one young prince for his tonsillitis. And we will meet many women and men who brought their problems, large and small, to the man at the top, from lost inheritances to chamber pots falling from upstairs windows with fatal consequences.

My headline cast of characters, though, are the almost thirty emperors, plus their partners, who ruled the Roman empire from Julius Caesar (assassinated 44 BCE) to Alexander Severus (assassinated 235 CE). These had a relatively small part to play in my earlier book, *SPQR*, which told the story of the development of Rome, over the thousand years from the eighth century BCE to the third century CE. There was a very good reason for that. Once the system of one-man rule had been fully established under the first emperor Augustus in the first century BCE, not much changed on a grand scale for over 250 years: the Roman empire hardly grew in size; it was administered in more or less the same way; and political life in Rome itself followed the same broad pattern. But in this book, I want to put the emperors back in the spotlight. I shall not be going through their careers one by one, or be giving more than a nod to the likes of Didius Julianus. And I certainly do not expect readers to hold each individual ruler in their heads. No one does: so, for reference, there is a handy thumbnail guide to the complete line-up on pp. vii–ix. Instead, I shall be exploring what it *meant* to be a Roman emperor. I shall be asking some basic questions about how they actually ruled the vast territory notionally under their control, how their subjects interacted with them and whether we can ever recapture what it felt like to sit on the throne.

There are fewer psychopaths in *Emperor of Rome* than you might expect from the movie image of imperial Rome. This is not to deny that the Roman world was, in our terms, an almost unimaginably cruel place of premature death. Leaving aside the hundreds of thousands of innocent victims of plague, needless warfare or collapsing sports' stadia, murder was the ultimate way of resolving disputes, political and otherwise. 'The corridors of power', as well as many other humbler corridors in Rome, were always bloodstained. But the survival of the Roman empire as a system makes no sense if it was ruled by a series of deranged autocrats. I am more interested in how those stories of madness arose, in how the business of empire was really conducted, and in Roman fears that the rule of the emperors was not so much bloodstained (they expected that), but was a strange and unsettling dystopia built on deception and fakery.

No reign captures those fears of dystopia better than that of the occasionally resuscitated, but usually half-forgotten, Elagabalus. It is with him that we start *Emperor of Rome*.

Mary Beard, Cambridge, December 2022

DINNER WITH ELAGABALUS

The deadly host

Elagabalus was a Syrian teenager who was emperor of Rome from 218 CE until his assassination in 222 – and a memorably extravagant, inventive and occasionally sadistic party host. His menus, so ancient writers tell, were ingenious. On some occasions the food would be colour-coded, all green or blue. On others, it would feature delicacies that were exotic – or revolting – even by upmarket Roman standards (camels' heels or flamingos' brains, with foie gras served to his pet dogs). Sometimes he indulged his nasty, or juvenile, sense of humour by inviting 'themed' fellow diners: groups of eight bald men, eight men with one eye or with hernias, or eight very fat men, who raised a cruel laugh when they couldn't all fit on the same dining couch.

His other party tricks included whoopee cushions (the first ever recorded in Western culture), which gradually deflated under the guests so that they ended up on the floor; fake food, of wax or glass, served up to the least important banqueters, who would be forced to spend the evening, tummies rumbling, watching their betters eating the real thing; and tame lions, leopards and bears released among the revellers as they slept off the excesses of the night before, and such a surprise for some that, when they awoke, they died not from a mauling but from fright. Equally deadly, and capturing the imagination of the nineteenth-century painter Lawrence Alma-Tadema, Elagabalus once reputedly showered his fellow partygoers with flower petals in such over-generous quantities that the guests were smothered and suffocated (pl. 1).

The emperor's faults did not stop with these dubious tactics as a host. He was apparently so committed to extravagance that he never wore the same pair of shoes twice (an uncanny echo here of Imelda

1. A marble portrait bust of Elagabalus. The youthful emperor, no more than a teenager, is shown with long sideburns and just the hint of a moustache, hardly looking like the monster that he appears in the literary accounts of his reign.

Marcos, once 'first lady' of the Philippines, who was alleged to have had more than three thousand pairs stashed away in her cupboards). And with perverse and expensive bravura, he piled up his summer gardens with snow and ice from the mountains, and would only eat fish when he was many miles from the sea. Meanwhile he was said to have snubbed religious proprieties by *marrying* a Vestal Virgin, one of the most august Roman priestesses, bound to virginity on pain of death. In a further religious transgression, he reputedly initiated a subversive, though short-lived, revolution by replacing Jupiter as Rome's principal god with 'Elagabal' – who was the god of his home town of Emesa, modern Homs in Syria, and the source of the name by which the emperor is now almost universally known (snappier than the 'Marcus Aurelius Antoninus' as one version of his official title ran). Nor did he leave untouched the traditional norms of sex and gender. Several stories focus on his cross-dressing, his make-up and even his attempt to surgically transition. One contemporary writer, Cassius Dio, the author of a massive eighty-volume history of Rome from its origins to the third century CE, claimed that the emperor 'asked doctors to give him female private parts by means of an incision'. In our own day he has sometimes been heralded as a transgender pioneer, mounting a radical challenge to rigid binary stereotypes. Most Romans would probably have thought that he was turning their world upside down.

Ancient accounts of his reign devote page after page to an extravagant listing of the emperor's puzzling eccentricities, his disconcerting subversions and heinous cruelties – including, at the top of some lists, the human sacrifice of children. These, and other tales like them, are one focus of *Emperor of Rome*. Where do they come from? How well known were they to the ordinary inhabitants of the Roman empire? Who muttered, and why, about Elagabalus's parties? And true or not, what can those tales tell us about Roman emperors, or about Romans more generally?

Images of autocracy, then and now

Elagabalus, or 'Heliogabalus' in an alternative spelling, is not exactly a household name, even though his reported misdeeds (or, if you prefer, his desperate attempts to break the bounds of Roman convention) have inspired modern writers, campaigners and artists, beyond Alma-Tadema, from Edgar Allan Poe and Neil Gaiman to Anselm Kiefer. His crimes and misdemeanours far outbid better-known, and earlier, Roman imperial villains and their supposed villainies: whether Nero, who played his lyre ('fiddled') while the city of Rome went up in flames; Domitian, who relieved his boredom by skewering flies with his pen; or, from the end of the second century CE, Commodus, the anti-hero of the movie *Gladiator*, who took potshots at the audience in the Colosseum with his bow and arrow. The horror stories about Elagabalus are worse. How seriously should we treat them?

'Not very', is the usual answer. Even Elagabalus's Roman biographer, writing almost two centuries after the emperor's death – and the source of most of the lurid details of his party tricks and dietary fancies – conceded that some of the implausible anecdotes that he had just recounted were most likely inventions, concocted after the emperor's assassination by those who wanted to curry favour with his rival and successor on the throne. Scrupulous modern historians have trodden a very careful path through the tall stories. They try to sort the fiction from the fact, occasionally extracting a nugget of information that appears to have some independent support elsewhere (the fact, for example, that the Vestal Virgin's name is featured on coins minted under Elagabalus suggests some kind of connection between the two, even if not marriage). But what is left is often not much more than the dates of the reign and a few other very bare essentials. At the same time, they rightly warn of the prejudicial spin that can be given to relatively innocent activities. It would largely depend on your attitude to the emperor overall whether you presented the colour-coded

dinners as a despicable, self-indulgent luxury or – as is equally possible – the most deliciously refined form of haute cuisine. The bottom
line, however, must be Elagabalus's age. He was just fourteen years old
when he came to the throne, and eighteen when he was murdered.
Whoopee cushions, maybe; calculated religious policies, hardly.

Serious history, however, is about more than the bare facts. I am
trying to shine a light, from different angles, on Roman emperors
– whether benevolent elder statesmen or juvenile tyrants, would-
be philosophers or wannabe gladiators, famous or forgotten – and
trying to face such basic questions as why so many of them ended
up, like Elagabalus, dispatched by an assassin's knife or a poisoned
mushroom. In this kind of exploration, ancient exaggerations, fiction
and lies have important parts to play. The toolkit with which people
have constructed an image of their rulers, judged them, debated the
character of an autocrat's power and marked the distance between
'them' and 'us' has always included fantasy, gossip, slander and urban
myth.

The tales, for example, of Imelda Marcos's three thousand pairs
of shoes (of which, suspiciously, rather fewer have ever been tracked
down) are more about decrying a world of unimaginable and pointless privilege than about documenting a rich woman's passion for
footwear. On a more modest scale, the tales of Queen Elizabeth II's
pampered corgis, reputed to eat their dog food from solid silver bowls,
offer us a peg on which to hang the difference, in day-to-day experience, between a 'royal' life and our own, while also allowing a harmless
joke about the folly of conspicuous consumption in the palace.

The tall stories that fill the ancient descriptions of Elagabalus's reign,
whatever their origin, provide some of the most precious evidence we
have for how Romans imagined an emperor at his very, very worst.
These untruths and flagrant exaggerations operate almost as a magnifying lens, in exposing and super-sizing what seemed 'bad' about a
'bad' Roman ruler. Some of it may be predictable enough: the acts of

cruelty and humiliation, from the child sacrifices to the unfortunate fat men unsuccessfully squashed onto a single dining couch; and the gratuitous luxury (Elagabalus's dogs enjoyed tasty foie gras even if they didn't gobble it from silver dishes). But buried in the seemingly preposterous anecdotes of the emperor's eccentricities are some very different, and equally chilling, terrors of autocracy.

The terror of power without limits is one of those. The curious anecdotes about Elagabalus's decision to decorate his summer gardens with ice and snow, or to consume seafood only when far from the sea – or, as another story has it, to live and work by night, while sleeping by day – point to more than his quirky, and costly, self-indulgence (the 'man-who-has-everything' syndrome). They raise the question of where the emperor's domination stops, casting him as a ruler who tried to make nature itself bend to his will, disrupting the natural order of things (ice in the summer?), and rearranging time, place and, for that matter, the divisions of biological sex to suit his own pleasure. Elagabalus wasn't the first to raise these fears. Two hundred and fifty years earlier, one of his critics – the Republican politician, philosopher and wit, Marcus Tullius Cicero – joked darkly of Julius Caesar that he had forced even the stars in the sky to obey him.

But that was only one aspect of Elagabalus's dystopian world. It was also a nightmare of deception, in which truth and falsehood were repeatedly confused and confounded. Nothing was as it seemed. The emperor's spectacular generosity turned out to be lethal – his kindness could literally kill (that is one message of the extravagant shower of rose petals). And for those at the bottom of the pecking order, the attractive food on their plates at palace dinners proved to be no more than an inedible, if artful, replica. Conversely, fakes could morph into the real thing. In one odd aside, Elagabalus's biographer claims that, when adultery was represented on stage, the emperor insisted that it be carried out 'for real'. No doubt it would make for a raunchier show, live sex included. But the unsettling logic was that he turned fact and fiction upside down, creating a topsy-turvy world in which no one could know who (or what) was play-acting. A corrupt autocracy was all smoke and distorting mirrors. Or, as his Roman biographer summed up, Elagabalus had 'a fake life'.

The magnifying lens of these stories helps us to see clearly the anxieties that surrounded imperial rule at Rome. It was more than the capacity to kill. The power of the emperor stopped at nothing. It warped the senses, and it thrived in malevolent chaos.

A *history of emperors*

I shall be returning to Elagabalus from time to time in the pages that follow, not least to explain how a teenager from Syria came to occupy the imperial throne (one Roman answer, predictably enough, focused on the machinations of his mother and grandmother). And I shall also be returning to the fantasies (dystopian and other) that surrounded the ancient Roman court, scrutinising more tall stories that Romans told about their emperors. How Roman rulers appeared in risqué jokes and in satirical skits, as well as in such far-fetched anecdotes as clustered around Elagabalus, will come under my spotlight. We shall even find emperors appearing in various guises in their subjects' dreams (not always a good sign: 'to dream of being an emperor foretells death to anyone who is sick', as one dream-interpreter warned in the second century CE).

But these will only be a part of the book. Alongside the 'emperors of the imagination', I shall be exploring down-to-earth questions about the everyday life of these Roman rulers, about the sharp edge of politics, the demands of military security, and the routine, humdrum business of governing a vast empire, which often gets overshadowed in the glare of all those vivid anecdotes of cruelty and luxury. I shall be thinking about the paper-pushing and the admin, the balancing of the books, the hiring and firing. How far was the emperor himself involved in all this? Who were his staff and support network, from wives and heirs, secretaries and accountants, to cooks and clowns? And what if he was only fourteen years old?

We shall find another powerful, but very different, stereotype of imperial behaviour: the Roman emperor not so much as a dangerous libertine, but as a hard-working bureaucrat. Both will star in *Emperor of Rome*.

A working life

Elagabalus was the twenty-sixth Roman emperor, more or less (his exact place in the numerical order depends on which unsuccessful usurpers you decide to count). Emperors came and went, and many have been forgotten. Some have left a distinctive mark on Western culture. Caligula (on the throne 37–41 CE) has become unforgettable for proposing to give one top political office to his favourite horse; and Hadrian (ruling 117–38) for building his 'Wall' across northern England. But not many people now have heard of Vitellius (a notorious overeater who ruled for a few months in 69), or the disciplinarian Pertinax (with a similarly brief reign in 193), or even Elagabalus. Not all were long remembered.

These men (all men: no 'empress' ever occupied the throne) ruled a vast territory stretching, at its furthest extent, from Scotland to the Sahara, Portugal to Iraq, with an estimated population, outside Italy itself, in the order of 50 million. Emperors made laws, waged wars, imposed taxes, adjudicated disputes, sponsored buildings and entertainments and flooded the Roman world with their portraits, much as the faces of modern dictators are plastered onto billboards by the thousand. They personally owned and exploited large tracts of the empire, from commercial farms to papyrus marshes and silver mines, and some of them travelled widely to explore and admire it, not only in search of military glory and profits of war. Tourists now gather outside the town of Luxor on the river Nile to stare at a pair of colossal ancient Egyptian statues (dating back to 1350 BCE). They are standing in exactly the same spot as Hadrian and his entourage stood in 130 CE, also on a sightseeing trip. The emperor's party left their own appreciative reactions (in specially composed poetry) carved into the legs of one of the statues: 'I was here' elite Roman style (fig. 64).

Exactly how an emperor's control worked in practice is a puzzle. Apart from army units stationed in some 'hot spots', there was only a skeleton staff of senior administrators, spread very thinly across the empire as a whole (counting no more than senior staff, it was roughly one for every 330,000 or so inhabitants). So, for the most part, in comparison with some modern empires, the control must have been fairly light touch. And the vast distances involved, as well as the time – sometimes several months – that it would have taken for basic information or instructions to get from the centre to some of the more remote parts of the Roman world (and vice versa), would also have made day-to-day micro-management of the imperial territories impossible. That said, the closer we get to the Roman emperor himself, the busier we often find him to be.

Ancient writers refer to rulers apparently swamped in what we would call 'paperwork' (in their terms, wax tablets and papyrus jottings). Julius Caesar, dealing with his correspondence while watching the races, was said to have annoyed the rest of the audience, who took it as an insult to popular entertainments. Vespasian, one of those lucky emperors to die in his bed, in 79 CE, rose before dawn to read his letters and official reports. Elagabalus's successor, Alexander Severus, was apparently so wedded to the job that he kept a set of military records in his private apartments in order to 'go over the budgets and the troop deployments when he was on his own'. But the paperwork was only part of it. Emperors were expected to be accessible to their subjects, in person as well as on paper. That idea is summed up in a story of Hadrian, who was out on a journey when he was intercepted by a woman trying to ask for a favour. When he replied that he didn't have time, she sharply retorted, 'Stop being emperor, then' – and he let her speak.

We have to treat these stories with care. Some emperors must obviously have worked harder than others. All systems of one-man rule have their diligent George VIs (the father of Elizabeth II, and a dutiful, self-effacing family man) as well as their flamboyant Edward VIIs (with his string of mistresses and neglected obligations). But we should never assume that the tales of unglamorous administration are more trustworthy than the stories of glamorous excess. They too have a strongly ideological side in constructing an image of a perfect emperor. The story about Hadrian and the woman who stopped him is, in fact, told almost identically about some earlier rulers from the Greek world, suggesting that it reflected an ancient cliché of the 'good monarch'. Nevertheless, some of the most extraordinary documents to survive from ancient Rome back up that general picture. These are the records of decisions made by emperors in answer to requests, petitions and cries for help from their ordinary subjects, or from ordinary town councils, across the empire – sometimes inscribed on stone (presumably by a successful petitioner to celebrate a happy outcome), sometimes copied onto papyrus, or gathered together in austere ancient compendia of legal rulings. What is striking is how local or how trivial (though not, of course, to the parties concerned) so many of the problems that the emperor was expected to solve actually were.

'The case of the falling chamber pot' is just one example. In 6 BCE the emperor Augustus was asked to adjudicate a messy dispute in the town of Knidos, on the coast of modern Turkey. During a feud between two local families, one of the protagonists had ended up dead. Taking part in a nasty affray outside the house of his rivals, he had been hit on the head by a chamber pot, dropped from the upper floor by a slave (who may, or may not, have intended only to pour out the contents). The local authorities were minded to prosecute the slave's owners for unlawful homicide, but, according to the surviving text of his judgement, Augustus was of the opposite opinion: that, accident or not, the killing was legitimate self-defence. Almost exactly three hundred years later, the emperor of the day, travelling in the Danube region, was confronted with hundreds of personal dilemmas and disputes to resolve: from the case of a woman who wanted compensation for a cow she had leased out, but which had then been killed in an 'enemy invasion', to a tricky dispute involving financial liability after the collision of two river boats; and the complaint of a man who was suing for non-payment of the fee he was charging for prostituting his wife (happily, he got short shrift). Whether the emperor himself struggled with these legal niceties we do not know. Sometimes, he probably did; sometimes, he would merely have signed off on the judgements devised by his staff (I can't imagine the young Elagabalus doing more). But the point is that, whoever did the work, it was the emperor who was *seen* to be the arbiter.

These cases are a useful antidote to the nightmare vision of imperial power. They are a reminder that, while some may have seen emperors as the orchestrators of a dystopian and terrifying world, others looked to them as a solution to their problems – right down to their lost cow. They are also a reassurance that a book which focuses on the figure of the emperor will not just be about men in the uppermost echelons of the elite. Far from it. Paradoxically, perhaps, it is through the eyes of the emperor and his dealings with his subjects that we see with the clearest focus and in the richest detail the ordinary people of Rome and its empire, who so often remain invisible. *Emperor of Rome* is about rulers *and* ruled.

Imperial texts and traces

The records of emperors' decisions, and the striking view they offer of ordinary life in the Roman empire (and its difficulties), are just a few of the ancient texts and documents that I intend to set free from the lecture room and the research seminar. Of course, some of the best-known classics of ancient literature will guide our exploration too: above all, Tacitus, whose account of the rulers of the first century CE in his *Annals* and *Histories*, written soon after in the second century, has never been bettered as a cynical dissection of the corruption of autocracy; and, from roughly the same time, Suetonius, the palace insider (he was employed in the imperial archives and secretariat, under the emperors Trajan and Hadrian), whose colourful biographies of the first 'Twelve Caesars', from Julius Caesar to the fly-skewering emperor Domitian, have been a handbook to the period for historians over the last five hundred years. But I shall also be bringing into the limelight more curious and surprising works that are much less well known, and celebrating the richness of the literary material that has come down to us. The perilous process of copying and recopying, careful curation and, eventually, printing that has brought the words of ancient Roman writers from stylus and scroll onto the modern page or screen, has preserved a much wider range of material than we often imagine.

Some of this was intended to raise a laugh. We have a mini-collection of imperial jokes – Augustus, for example, teased his daughter Julia for picking out her grey hairs – and satires of various types. These include a skit on his predecessors by the fourth-century emperor Julian (in which Elagabalus has a walk-on part as 'the little lad from Emesa'); and a hilarious lampoon, written by Nero's tutor Seneca, ridiculing the whole idea that the emperor Claudius should be made a god after his death in 54 CE (we follow the slightly befuddled old emperor struggling up Mount Olympus to the home of the 'real' gods, only to be roundly sent packing when he gets there).

Some of it takes us behind the scenes, in unexpected ways. A handbook written by a Greek teacher of rhetoric gives advice on how best to address an emperor, should you need to. There are observations on life at court (including a chilling reference to soldiers working as undercover agents) from the philosopher Epictetus, who had once been the slave of Nero's secretary, while imperial doctors from the palace have left us descriptions not just of their celebrity patients' sore throats but of their tummy troubles and drug regimens too – two thousand years later we can still examine the case notes. And we can still read an edited collection of second-century CE reports sent back to the emperor in Rome from Pliny, an official posted hundreds of miles away on the Black Sea coast, explaining his problems with everything from some troublesome Christians to dilapidated bath buildings and a worrying overspend on a jerry-built theatre.

Other surviving writing is almost stranger than we could ever predict. The *Life* of Elagabalus, for example, with its wonderfully revealing fantasies and exaggerations about the lifestyle of the 'little lad', is one of a set of more than fifty biographies of emperors, including usurpers, heirs and other claimants, which run from Hadrian in 117 CE to a bloodthirsty nonentity who died in 285. Though many of these individual 'Lives' are very short (in our terms, these are 'profiles' rather than 'biographies'), together they stretch to several hundred modern pages and go under the title *Imperial History* (or *Historia Augusta*). This bills itself as a collaborative work penned at the very end of the third century by six different, rather grandly named authors: Trebellius Pollio, Flavius Vopiscus of Syracuse, and so on. Careful analysis of its language and style has shown that it was nothing of the sort: it was written by just one person (unknown), about a hundred years later than it claims. As such, it is one of the great mysteries of ancient literature. Why would anyone pull such a trick? Was it a forgery? A rather lengthy joke or satire? Or a radical experiment in pseudo-historical narrative? Whatever the

TEMPVSESTIAMTI CAESARGERMANICEDETEGERETEPATRIBVSCONSCRIPTIS
QVOTENDATORATIOTVAIAMENIMADEXTREMOSFINESGALLIAENAR
BONENSISVENISTI
TOTECCEINSIGNESIVVENESQVOTINTVEORNONMAGISSVNTPAENITENDI
SENATORESQVAMPAENITETPERSICVMNOBILISSIMVMVIRVMAMI
CVMMEVMINTERIMAGINESMAIORVMSVORVMALLOBROGICINO
MENLEGERE QVODSIHAECITAESSECONSENTITISQVIDVLTRADESIDERA
TISQVAMVTVOBISDIGITODEMONSTREMSOLVMIPSVMVLTRAFINES
PROVINCIAENARBONENSISIAMVOBISSENATORESMITTEREQVANDO
EXLVGVDVNOHABERENOSNOSTRIORDINISVIROSNONPAENITET
TIMIDEQVIDEMP CEGRESSVSADSVETOSFAMILIARESQVEVOBISPRO
VINCIARVMTERMINOSSVM SEDDESTRICTEIAMCOMATAEGALLIAE
CAVSAAGENDAEST INQVASIQVISHOCINTVETVRQVODBELLOPERDE
CEMANNOSEXERCVERVNTDIVOMIVLIVMIDEMOPPONATCENTVM
ANNORVMIMMOBILEMFIDEMOBSEQVIVMQVEMVLTISTREPIDISRE
BVSNOSTRISPLVSQVAMEXPERTVMILLIPATRIMEODRVSOGERMANIAM
SVBIGENTITVTAMQVIETESVA SECVRAMQVEATERGOPACEMPRAES
TITERVNTETQVIDEMCVMADCENSVSNOVOTVMOPEREETINADSVE
TOGALLISADBELLVMAVOCATVSESSETOVOD OPVS QVAMAR
DVVMSITNOBISNVNCCVMMAXIMEQVAMVISNIHILVLTRAQVAM
VTPVBLICENOTAESINTFACVLTATESNOSTRAEEXQVIRATVR NIMIS
MAGNOEXPERIMENTOCOGNOSCIMVS

2. Part of the bronze text found in Lyon in the sixteenth century, recording Claudius's speech to the senate, urging enhanced political rights for the Gauls. The unusually clear script makes the words quite easy to make out. The first line of this extract starts 'TEMPUS EST', 'now's the time'. See pp. 239–40.

answer, it pointedly straddles the boundary between history and fiction.

Thousands of original documents add to the richness and the variety of stories of the Roman emperors. Some were inscribed on stone and bronze for public display, others scrawled on papyrus, preserved in the sand of Egypt and dug out over the last century by modern archaeologists in huge quantities (many still unread). We have, for example, the text on bronze of a speech given in 48 CE by the emperor Claudius, arguing in favour of granting a bigger political role to men from Gaul, and treating his audience to a potted history of Rome at the same time. And we can still read on papyrus a transcript of the words of Germanicus, an imperial prince and father of the emperor Caligula, addressing the crowds in Alexandria, and saying among other things that he was missing his 'granny' (better known as Livia, the wife of Augustus, and with a more fearsome reputation than the word 'granny' would suggest). We are also offered glimpses of what went on behind the scenes: from the surviving epitaphs of a hundred or so of Livia's staff (including a masseuse, some dressers, a painter, even a window cleaner), to the disgruntled correspondence of an official in Egypt, who was having dreadful difficulties getting all the provisions together for an impending imperial visit.

We can enter the material world of the emperors too. It is still possible to walk around their palaces, not just on the Palatine Hill in central Rome (the origin of the word 'palace'), but also their suburban pleasure gardens and out-of-town residences. One of those, the villa of the emperor Hadrian, at Tivoli, about 20 miles from Rome – with its parkland, accommodation blocks, multiple dining rooms and libraries – covered almost twice the area of ancient Pompeii. 'Villa' is a glaring

3. & 4. Two surprising places to find an image of the emperor. On the left, a modern replica of an ancient pastry mould (possibly for making the cookies distributed at religious festivals), showing an emperor standing in a chariot on his triumphal parade (pp. 46–7), being crowned by the goddess Victory. See also fig. 12. On the right, the emperor on an earring (the hook no doubt originally angled so that the head did not hang upside down).

understatement. It is more like a private town. And we can also look their portraits in the eye. Those that survive amount to just a fraction of what there once was (one reasonable guess is that across the Roman world there were originally between 25,000 and 50,000 statues of the emperor Augustus alone). But thousands of them still line our museum shelves. They come in all sorts, shapes and sizes. Some inhabitants of the Roman empire even ate cookies decorated with figures of emperors (or that, at least, is what some surviving pastry moulds suggest). Around 200 CE, one Roman lady went one better: she had the head of the emperor Septimius Severus, one of Elagabalus's immediate predecessors, cast into her gold earrings.

There is, of course, a range of questions about the world of the emperors that we cannot answer for lack of evidence (what that world looked like to a woman, for example, or how in detail their finances worked). But I hope that, overall, readers will go away from this book not frustrated by *how little* we know about these rulers of two thousand years ago, but amazed by *how much*.

Which emperors?

Many emperors followed Elagabalus. In fact, if we concentrate on the eastern part of the empire, with its capital eventually established in Constantinople (modern Istanbul) in the fourth century CE, there was an unbroken succession of Roman rulers down to 1453, when the city fell to the Ottomans. *We* think of those later rulers as Byzantine. *They* thought of themselves as Roman. But, in this book, I shall not be looking much later than Elagabalus's cousin, adopted son and successor: Alexander Severus, the one who reputedly worked overtime on his military records and troop deployments. He was another boy emperor, coming to the throne at the age of thirteen or fourteen and ruling between 222 and 235. Starting the book with the architects of one-man rule at Rome (Julius Caesar, assassinated in 44 BCE, and his great-nephew Augustus who became the first emperor), I shall be dealing with a period of just under three hundred years, from the mid first century BCE to the mid third century CE, and just under thirty emperors.

All such chronological limits are to some extent arbitrary, and I shall occasionally cross the lines I have set (indeed I already have: those cases of the lost cow and prostituted wife date to the later third century CE). But there are powerful arguments for stopping where I do. Things changed dramatically after Alexander Severus. Over the rest of the century, emperors came and went rapidly, in a series of military coups and civil wars. Many of them now hailed from far outside the upper echelons of the Roman aristocracy, and the geopolitics were so changed that a good number never even visited the city of Rome during their short reigns. They *were* short. Plus or minus a few unsuccessful usurpers, as many men were emperor in the fifty years after the death of Alexander Severus as in the almost three hundred years before. The change of style and character is captured in a story told of Alexander's successor, Maximinus Thrax ('the Thracian'). It was said that he was the first emperor who could not read and write. This may well be a tendentious slur rather than an accurate observation. True or not, it points to a new world.

Between the reign of Augustus and Alexander Severus, the stability of Roman politics and geopolitics meant that you could have gone to sleep in, for example, 1 BCE and woken up two hundred years later and still have recognised the world around you. After Augustus, conquests went on being exuberantly celebrated, none more so than that commemorated by Trajan's column, erected in the early second century CE to blazon his victories over Dacia (in the region of modern Romania) and also to serve as the last resting place for the emperor's ashes. But most of these victories added little to Rome's territory, and were often more trouble than they were worth (Britain might aptly be dubbed

'Rome's Afghanistan') or the land won was quickly lost again. They were military 'vanity projects', as one historian has recently called them, though vanity which came at a terrible cost in human life.

Of course there were some underlying, long-term changes. Most importantly, as we shall see, there was an increasing geographic – and sometimes ethnic – diversity among the emperors. Trajan and Hadrian in the first half of the second century CE both had origins in Spain. A few decades later, Septimius Severus, 'the first African emperor', was born in what is now Libya (pl. 3). Elagabalus was the great-nephew of Septimius's wife, the Syrian Julia Domna, and it was through her family's influence that he came to the throne in a coup, no doubt masterminded by others. But, for all these gradual developments, Augustus and Alexander Severus were doing much the same job, and were judged by much the same standards and against the same stereotypes.

Historians, both ancient and modern, have often given accounts of these imperial centuries in minute detail, dissecting the palace rivalries, the quarrels, the clashes between one faction and another, the military campaigns and political showdowns. They have tried to delineate the different characters of the different rulers, from the grumpy and hypocritical Tiberius, Augustus's successor, or the flamboyant and irresponsible Nero, to the fusspot Antoninus Pius, or his successor, the philosophical Marcus Aurelius. Modern historians have tried carefully to guide their readers through dynasties, whose complicated family relationships, strategic adoptions (like Elagabalus's adoption of Alexander Severus) and multiple marriages are almost impossible to depict on a conventional family tree. And they have enjoyed the colour of many of the extreme anecdotes that were told about these rulers, while also distrusting their accuracy or searching out a more prosaic truth lurking beneath the surface (as we shall see in the next chapter, Caligula's threat to honour his horse with high office may simply have been a rough joke that backfired).

I too will be relishing the colourful stories of the Roman emperors, with all the quirky idiosyncrasies that have made them memorable ever since – though I will be using those stories to shed light on the Roman imperial system in a different way. Mercifully, this book is not a history of almost thirty individual rulers, one after the other. A lifetime of teaching and researching ancient Rome has convinced me that narrative detail of that type (whether it is of one ruler, or twelve or more) often conceals as much as it reveals. After all, one hastily contrived self-interested palace plot is usually much the same as any other, with a changed cast of characters but similar dodgy (or high-minded) motives. There is often not much to distinguish one errant prince or princess from the next. And the same shocking anecdotes that can seem so distinctive and characterful are regularly repeated in more or less the same terms about several emperors. I am certainly interested in why some emperors have gone down in history as sadistic monsters, others as decent men doing their best; some as generous benefactors and others as mean-spirited misers. But I am more interested in seeing beyond that to the bigger picture of what autocracy, and autocrats, in Rome stood for, and in how *similar* these rulers were, not just how *different*. In this, I am on the same side as Marcus Aurelius, who, in his *Jottings to Himself*, reflected that over the centuries one-man rule had not really changed: 'same play, different cast'.

So *Emperor of Rome* is as much about 'emperors' as a category, or '*the* emperor', as it is about any individual flesh-and-blood ruler. In that respect, it almost certainly reflects the view of the vast majority of the population of the Roman empire. The character of the man on the throne, his personal faults or his preferences, might have mattered a very great deal to those on his dinner list, or to those of the elite who carefully studied, or wrote, imperial biographies. Emperors were not all the same. But for most of those 50 million or so living outside Italy, and for a good many inside, it was 'the emperor' who was important, whichever one, of whatever name, that it happened to be at the time.

It was 'the emperor' to whom they appealed with their problems. It was 'the emperor' of whom they dreamed. When an emperor died, or was overthrown, one option commonly taken to accommodate the new regime was to re-carve or 'adjust' the marble portraits of the old man on the throne to fit the features of his successor. There might have been various reasons for this, whether saving the money that a brand-new sculpture would have cost, or a desire literally to obliterate the features of the predecessor. But the underlying message was that it took only a few hits with a chisel to turn one emperor into another (fig. 91).

5. A list of Roman emperors on an Egyptian papyrus, written in Greek, and headed 'Reigns of the *basileis*', that is of the 'emperors' or 'kings' (see p. 39). After the heading, Caligula should be third in the list, but he has been entirely omitted (so that Claudius directly follows Tiberius).

It is a fair bet that some of the inhabitants of the empire would not have been able to name the current emperor. That is what one philosopher, and Christian bishop, from North Africa suggested, when he wrote a little later, at the very beginning of the fifth century CE, that there were men in his part of the world who knew that there was an emperor on the throne because of the tax demands, 'but who he is, is not very clear' (and he went on to joke that 'there are people among us who assume that Agamemnon is still king', referring to the Greek commander in the mythical Trojan War). It is certainly the case that very many would not have been able to give anything like an accurate list of emperors past and present. Even the obviously diligent person in the mid third century, whose efforts at compiling such a list are preserved on a scrap of papyrus, made some serious mistakes, omitting several, including Caligula, and getting the lengths of other reigns wrong. I shall be introducing each of the emperors I discuss (not every single one of the nearly thirty) with the necessary details. But we don't need to worry if we can't always tell our Marcus Aureliuses from our Antoninus Piuses. Most ordinary Romans probably couldn't either.

The world of the emperors

Roman emperors bring us face to face with some of the most extreme images of ancient power, and with some of the most humdrum day-to-day realities of life in the Roman empire. More than that, right down to the modern world they have continued to provide a template for autocrats and a warning for politicians: from all those kings and dynasts depicted in painting and sculpture dressed in Roman imperial garb to all those prime ministers and presidents satirised in cartoons as if they were Nero, 'fiddling while Rome burns'. It is worth taking Roman emperors seriously and digging deeper into how the Romans themselves understood, debated and contested a vision of power that still hangs over us.

I have been trying to pin down these elusive, distant but strangely familiar rulers throughout my whole career. In *Emperor of Rome*, I am hoping to share those explorations of the world of the emperors, real and imaginary, from the lofty realm of the gods (to which many of them, not only Claudius, aspired) to the filthy waters of the river Tiber, where others, unceremoniously, ended up. While I am doubtful that so many of these men were the bloodthirsty or deranged psychopaths that they have often been painted, equally, I do not think it helpful simply to try to rehabilitate some of the worst 'monsters'. The various

BOLSO-NERO

6. Jair Bolsonaro, then President of Brazil, portrayed as an instantly recognisable 'Nero fiddling while Rome burns'. From Barack Obama to Boris Johnson and Narendra Modi, there is hardly a prominent politician in the world who has escaped this particular satire.

attempts to turn Caligula or Nero or Commodus into misunderstood reformers who simply had an unfavourable press have never really convinced me. It is hard now to walk that tightrope between distaste and sympathy.

Working on the Roman empire for so long I have come increasingly to detest autocracy as a political system, but to be more sympathetic, not just to its victims, but to all those caught up in it from bottom to top: from some of the ordinary men and women, living in the emperor's shadow, who puzzled about power and autocracy and who tried their best to get along, to the (probably equally ordinary) man on the throne. It is easy to forget that he too was no doubt puzzling about how to *be* an autocrat, and what it meant to be *Emperor of Rome.*

In the chapters that follow I shall track the emperor down, through the intriguing world of fiction and fact – from the imperial dinner table to the military frontiers, from his doctors' reports to his appearance in jokes, satires and dreams, from his office desk to his last words. But first, a long way from Elagabalus and his whoopee cushions, I shall set the scene, by moving to the politics and definition of one-man rule in the Roman empire. Autocracies come in many different forms. In the next two chapters I shall be pinning down some of the nuts and bolts of autocracy, *Roman* style – what the job description for a Roman emperor amounted to, how the system began, who these people were that we now call 'emperors of Rome', and how they ended up on the throne.

1

ONE-MAN RULE: THE BASICS

The emperor's job description

On 1 September 100 CE, a century or so before the reign of Elagabalus, Gaius Plinius Secundus rose to his feet to offer an extravagant vote of thanks to the emperor Trajan, in front of the senate. This was one of Rome's most ancient and prestigious political institutions, which by now had developed into a council, a court of law and a talking shop of some six hundred senators, including the emperor and other leading public figures. It was a mixed bunch of the rich Roman elite, from lackeys to discontents, old aristocracy to new money.

Pliny, as he is now usually known for short, was the pedantic administrator whose dispatches home from his Black Sea posting we can still read (pp. 216–19). He was also a rich and successful lawyer, and the author of the only surviving eyewitness account of the eruption of Vesuvius in 79 CE, watching as a seventeen-year-old from a safe distance. On this occasion in 100, he had been chosen to serve, through September and October, as one of the two consuls. Once upon a time the highest elected offices of the Roman state, these posts still carried enormous distinction, but they were now awarded not by the voting public but, in practice, by the emperor himself. For that reason, the custom had grown up that new consuls should give thanks to him, in a speech in front of the assembled senate. Pliny took the stage, standing next to his fellow consul and to Trajan himself, in the grandiose purpose-built 'senate house' sponsored by Julius Caesar in the heart of Rome – conveniently, for the emperor, a quick ten-minute litter ride from the main imperial palace.

Only rarely were these votes of thanks anything more than dutiful, dull and routine. Even Pliny conceded that there was not much in them to keep you awake, and the emperor had to sit through a lot of them. A few years earlier, in 97 CE, one such speech had won some unfortunate notoriety, when an octogenarian consul died from injuries sustained preparing it: he had dropped the heavy book he was consulting, bent down to pick it up, and – in a type of accident we still know all too well – had slipped on the polished floor, broken his hip and never recovered. Pliny's speech found a different kind of fame. For, after he had delivered it in the senate (where attendance might have been a little thin in the holiday month of September), he performed encores to his friends, reading it out over three sessions of private recitals on three successive days – a form of entertainment that was a staple among the Roman aristocracy, and not quite the exercise in vanity that it would seem now. Circulated by Pliny in written form as an exemplary piece of public speaking, it has come down to us under the title *Speech of Praise,* or *Panegyricus* in Latin. Let's hope that it was expanded from the version delivered to the emperor and senate. What we now read would, on my calculation, take over three hours to get through, even at a cracking pace. Yet it is still a precious record of one particular face-to-face encounter between subject and emperor and of the words spoken on that occasion. More than that, it almost amounts to a job description for the role of Roman emperor.

Modern readers have often found the obsequious, oozing, long-winded praise directed at Trajan almost as unpalatable an aspect of Roman autocracy as all those stories of capricious cruelty or perverted luxury. Each page of the *Speech of Praise* brings new hyperbole: the emperor, Pliny proclaims, is a model of perfection; an awe-inspiring combination of 'seriousness and good humour, authority and lightness of touch, power and kindness'; an idol for his loving subjects, who rush to catch a fleeting sight of him, carrying their little ones on their shoulders; a one-man stimulus to the Roman birth rate, for the simple reason that no one hesitates to bring children into a world blessed by such a benevolent ruler. How different, he insists, from the monstrous emperor Domitian, assassinated just a few years before in 96 CE, lurking in his bloodstained den, gorging on elaborate banquets with over-ingenious dishes and celebrating 'pretend' military victories he had not really won: 'a terrible arrogance on his face, rage in his eyes and womanly pallor on his flesh'. (The parallels – in fakery, effeminacy and cuisine – with the stories of Elagabalus are clear.) Contrast Trajan, urges Pliny, an emperor distinguished by his crime-free, welcoming palace, his simple suppers, his authentic war record, as well as his strong physique (with a touch of greying hair to add extra authority). 'While rulers in the past,' he fawns, 'had lost the use of their legs, and were carried above our heads on the backs and shoulders of slaves, it was your own renown, your glory, the devotion of your citizens and freedom that bore *you* along, far higher than they.' It may come as no surprise that one modern critic should have bluntly written off the whole speech: 'It has fallen, not undeservedly, into almost universal contempt.'

We are now, in general, less sensitive to the nuances of praise than many were in earlier generations. But, in the case of Pliny's vote of thanks, we should rein in some of our 'contempt'. The speech is more complicated than it may at first appear. For a start (though this may not make you warm to it any more), what is billed as praise of the emperor is also praise of Pliny himself. We learn, for example, how intimate he is with his dear friend Trajan (on kissing terms, in fact), and we share the familiarity of their long evenings together at the palace,

7. & 8. In their portrait sculptures the hero and anti-hero of Pliny's *Speech of Praise* – Domitian on the left, Trajan on the right – have a very similar image. Despite his reputed baldness, Domitian is shown with a good head of hair (unless we imagine he is wearing a wig).

dining from unpretentious menus and enjoying friendly conversation. We are also treated to some virtuoso displays of Pliny's own expertise (particularly hard going for a modern reader are several pages about the intricacies of Roman inheritance tax, on which he had a minutely detailed inside knowledge). The *Speech of Praise* is a claim to status by Pliny himself in front of the emperor and fellow senators.

But, even more to the point, embedded in the flattery are some clear lessons for the emperor to take home. As Pliny comes close to acknowledging, there is no better way of influencing a man's behaviour than praising him for the qualities that you *want* him to have, whether he has them or not. It is in that sense that the *Speech of Praise* adds up to a lengthy job description for the position of emperor, as drafted by a leading member of the Roman elite. Beneath the superficial compliments, it offers instructions on how to be a good ruler. Imperial virtues make a far less racy story than imperial vices, and to celebrate the qualities of a benevolent autocrat has a hollow ring for most modern audiences. But it is worth attending to Pliny's job description, as a counterweight to the fantasy horror stories of imperial power.

Pliny itemises a whole range of specific requirements. His emperor must be generous: he should give pleasure, in the form of shows, and practical support, in the form of food and cash, to his people. He must build, not for his own comfort or self-indulgence, but public monuments for the public good. He must conquer in war. In one chilling passage Pliny, the administrator who can so easily get buried in the details of taxation, and whose brief military service had been well away from enemy action, praises any emperor whose achievements rest 'on battlefields piled high with corpses and seas stained with blood'. But he also lays out more general principles to guide the emperor's behaviour. He must be transparent, not bolstering his position with false claims and fake achievements. Pliny's 'bad' emperors cheated even when they were out hunting for recreation, bagging animals that had been rounded up in advance specially for them to shoot. And – with a turn of phrase that reveals how embedded the language of slavery was in the language of Roman power – he must act like a father to his people not as a slave master (*dominus*), guaranteeing their liberty, not forcing them into servitude. To the senators, he must act like 'one of us' (literally, in Latin, *unus ex nobis*).

Throughout the rest of this chapter, on the origins and the 'basics' of one-man rule in Rome, Pliny's relations with Trajan will continue to act as a point of reference. So too will his construction of the ideal ruler – with all its high-minded moral earnestness, blinkered elitism (no ordinary Roman would ever get invited to a friendly dinner at the palace) and occasionally glaring self-contradiction. When towards the end of the *Speech of Praise* he thanked the emperor for '*ordering* us to be free', Pliny himself surely must have realised that, by Roman logic, it was only slaves who could be *ordered* to be free. Inadvertently, no doubt, he was exposing some of the double-think involved in being a citizen under an autocrat, benevolent or not.

The power-sharing Republic and the origins of empire

When Pliny, as a new consul, rose to speak in September 100 CE, Rome had been ruled by an emperor for more than a century. But the city of Rome itself was over eight hundred years old, and for the majority of that time, after a largely mythical series of seven early kings – starting with the founder Romulus and ending when Tarquin 'the Proud' was thrown out around 500 BCE – it was governed by a *sort-of* democracy, in what is now usually called the Roman Republic.

The 'sort-of' is important. To be sure, the major political officials of state, including the consuls at the top of the hierarchy, were democratically elected by all the male citizens, and those same citizens also had charge of making laws and taking decisions about war and peace. But it was a system dominated by the rich. Their votes in elections expressly counted for more than those of the poor, and they alone were allowed to stand for office and to command Rome's armies. Meanwhile the senate, consisting of several hundred ex-office-holders, was the most influential political institution of the state. Even if its precise formal power is, and was, hard to define, the senate's decisions were usually followed. It would be more accurate to call this government a *power-sharing* system rather than a straightforwardly *democratic* one. For apart from the senate, whose members sat for life, all political offices were temporary, held for just a single year, and always held jointly. There were always two consuls at any one time. Next below them in seniority were the 'praetors', concerned with the administration of law, among other things, who gradually increased in number so that there were eventually sixteen of them in post together each year. It was not simply that more officials were created in order to cope with a bigger workload, though that was a factor. The underlying principle of the Republic was: you never held power for long, and never alone.

This was the system of government under which – many years before it had an emperor – Rome gained its empire, dominating much of what is now Europe and beyond: 'staining the seas with blood', as Pliny put it. What drove them to this, and why they were so unnervingly successful in their conquests, especially during their major period of expansion between the third and first centuries BCE, has always been debated. The Greek historian Polybius in the second century was already wondering how Rome, a very ordinary mid-Italian town in the fifth century, had come to dominate most of the Mediterranean within a few hundred years.

It is too easy to put everything down to the Romans being aggressive and militaristic, or having superior discipline and expertise in battle. They *were* militaristic, but so were most of those they conquered. And the Romans also had their weaknesses in combat skills, their early inability in naval warfare, for example, being close to a standing joke. The best explanation (or guess) is that, somehow, aggression and militarism were combined with a hugely competitive ethos among the Roman elite in their hunt for military glory, with almost limitless resources of manpower at the Romans' disposal once they had taken control of most of Italy, and, most likely, with an element of simply 'getting lucky' – all of it resulting in vast, rapid and violent imperial expansion. But what exactly the combination was, and which were the real deciding factors, is quite uncertain.

What *is* certain is that this series of conquests had an almost revolutionary effect on the politics of Rome itself, in addition to the more obvious consequences for the victims. Part of the disruption was caused by the enormous profits of empire, which destroyed the notional equality that had previously existed between the power-sharing elite and had acted to mitigate their competitive rivalry. For the commanders, there were personal fortunes to be made out of war, especially against the rich kingdoms of the Eastern Mediterranean, and an increasingly large gap opened up at the top of Roman society between a few super-successful 'big men' and the rest. When one of those big men, the tycoon Marcus Licinius Crassus, observed that he would count no man rich who could not raise an army out of his own cash, he obviously revealed the level of wealth commanded by the fortunate few (he himself had inherited one fortune and made another largely out of property speculation). But he also hinted at the uses to which that wealth might be put. As it turned out, none of this did Crassus much good himself. He was killed in 53 BCE on what had promised to be a lucrative campaign against the Parthian empire (stretching east of modern Turkey), his severed head allegedly ending up as a gory prop in the performance of a Greek tragedy at a Parthian royal wedding.

Equally important were the pressures put on the power-sharing structures of Rome's Republican government by its growing imperial territory. Traditionally the same elected officials handled both the domestic business of the city and its external affairs – whether commanding the legions in front-line war, 'peace-keeping' or trouble-shooting. To begin with at least, the Romans did not aim at much hands-on, direct control of what they had conquered, beyond taking the tax revenue, exploiting the local resources (such as the Spanish silver mines), and getting their own way when they wanted. But even so, all the different roles became more and more difficult to accommodate within the framework of shared, temporary, annual offices. It might, after all, take a few months of a single year's office simply for a man to get from Rome to a trouble spot at the edge of the empire.

The Romans were not blind to this, and they made various adjustments in response. Office-holders, for example, began to serve in positions overseas for an additional temporary period, *after* their year in Rome itself. But, all the same, the crises generated by the empire sometimes required more radical solutions. If you wanted, say, to clear the Mediterranean Sea of 'pirates' (a word that had something of the ring of 'terrorists' to an ancient ear), you had to give authority and resources to a single commander on a potentially long-term basis, in a way that fundamentally flouted the temporary, power-sharing principles of traditional Roman office-holding. The empire, in other words, gradually destroyed the distinctive structures of government that had brought it into existence in the first place, paving the way for one-man rule. The empire created the emperors, not the other way around.

Prequels to autocracy

Through the early part of the first century BCE, Rome witnessed a series of prequels to autocracy. One of the big men of the 80s, Lucius Cornelius Sulla, marched with his army on Rome, installed himself as 'dictator' and imposed a programme of conservative political reforms, before resigning a couple of years later and then dying in his bed. It was, by all accounts, a very nasty final illness, but still perhaps a better end than he deserved, given the death squads he had let loose in the city. Just a decade later, Gnaeus Pompeius Magnus (Pompey the Great) took a slightly more subtle route to what was almost sole power. It was he who, by a citizens' vote, was given charge of getting rid of the pirates, with a huge budget and seniority over all other Roman officials in the Eastern Mediterranean for a period of three years. (In the event it took him only three months, and he followed it up with an even longer-term mandate, a bigger budget and greater power, to confront other enemies of Rome.) He went on to be made consul *on his own*, without a colleague, a flagrant breach of Republican principles, however unremarkable it might sound now. He ploughed money into grand public buildings in Rome itself, much as later autocrats did, and occasionally saw his own head on coins minted by cities outside Italy, a key indicator of monarchical power in antiquity, as it has remained.

The turning point, however, came in the mid first century BCE with Julius Caesar, who stood on the cusp between Rome's sort-of democracy and the rule of the emperors. Caesar's career started in a fairly standard way for a member of the Roman elite, despite later writers imagining that he had secretly harboured overweening ambitions from an early age. One apocryphal story imagines him, in his early thirties, standing gloomily in front of a statue of Alexander the Great (from whom Pompey borrowed his name, 'Great'), and lamenting his own slow start in comparison with the precocious Macedonian king. But after a successful (and shockingly brutal) military command in Gaul, which he managed to extend to eight years without a break, he followed the example of Sulla. In 49 BCE he marched with his army on Rome, 'crossing the Rubicon', the boundary of Gaul and Italy, en route, and making that a well-known phrase even now for 'passing the point of no return'. In the civil war that followed, his enemies were led by Pompey, who was now, for a change, playing the part of the conservative traditionalist and ended up decapitated on the shores of Egypt where he was seeking refuge. Caesar used his victory to take what was effectively sole control of Roman government. He was appointed 'dictator' by the senate, and in 44 became 'dictator *for ever*'.

Yet Caesar in some ways still looks back to the Republic. His career started within the framework of traditional short-term elected offices. Even his 'dictatorship' had at least tenuous links with an ancient temporary appointment designed to handle public emergencies, although, since Sulla, it increasingly meant something closer to our modern sense of the term. It is for those reasons that most historians recently have tended to treat Caesar as the last gasp of the old order. But when, in the second century CE, the biographer Suetonius (Gaius Suetonius Tranquillus, in full) was composing his *Lives* of the first Roman emperors, he chose to begin with Julius Caesar, as number one of twelve, the ultimate founder of imperial dynasty. Even more to the point perhaps, all Roman rulers after him took 'Caesar', previously just an ordinary Roman family name, as part of their own official titles – in a tradition that continued down to modern Kaisers and Czars. And that is exactly how Pliny addressed the emperor through most of his vote of thanks: not 'Trajan' but 'Caesar' (which he used more than fifty times, compared with 'Trajan' just once).

It is easy to understand why Caesar was cast in this founding role. Although there were fewer than four years between his victory over Pompey and his own death in 44 BCE (and although he was rarely in the city of Rome itself for more than a month at a time as he finished off other pockets of the civil war overseas), Caesar managed to change the face of Roman politics in radical and controversial ways that established the pattern for later emperors. Like them, he controlled election to high office, nominating some candidates who were then simply given the nod by the voters. He went further than Pompey in having his own head represented on coins minted in Rome itself, not just abroad (the first living Roman to do so), and he set about flooding the city and wider world with his portraits, in numbers never seen before: hundreds, if not thousands, were planned. And he exercised unprecedented power, in new areas, apparently unchecked. Cicero's wry quip

9. A coin of Caesar, minted just before his assassination in 44 BCE. Behind his head are symbols of the priesthood he held (a ladle and ceremonial staff); in front runs his name CAESAR IM<P> – for IMPERATOR (see p. 38).

about the stars in the sky being forced to obey him was a reference to his bold reform of the Roman calendar, changing the length of the year and of the months, and effectively introducing the 'leap year', as we still know it. Only all-powerful autocrats – or, as in eighteenth-century France, revolutionary cabals – claim to control time.

Caesar also set a pattern for the future in the manner of his death, assassinated in 44 BCE, shortly after he had been made 'dictator for ever'. This became both a warning to his successors and a model for political murder lasting into the modern world. (John Wilkes Booth chose the date of Caesar's killing – 'the *Ides* of March', the 15th of the month by our dates – as the code word for his planned assassination of Abraham Lincoln in 1865.) The truth is that, thanks to William Shakespeare and others, the assassins have been treated rather generously by history. They were a predictably mixed group of high-principled freedom fighters, malcontents and self-interested power seekers who ambushed and killed the dictator during a meeting of the senate, leaving him dead in front of a statue of Pompey. Marcus Junius Brutus, who emerges as an honourable patriot from Shakespeare's *Julius Caesar*, was probably one of the most self-interested of the lot. He had an appalling record of exploiting people in Rome's empire. Notoriously, he lent money to a city in Cyprus at a 48 per cent rate of interest, four times the legal maximum, and he had his agents blockade the local council chamber to recover what was owed, starving five councillors to death in the process. And within a couple of years of Caesar's assassination, despite his opposition to monarchy, he had his *own* head depicted on the coins that he minted to pay his troops.

But even more to the point, the assassins' success in eliminating their victim (which is often the easy bit) was overshadowed by their lack of any plan for what to do next. More than a decade of civil war followed, in which the supporters of Caesar first of all turned on his killers, and then on each other. By 31 BCE, it had come down to a clash between two main parties: on the one side, Caesar's henchman Mark

Antony, now in alliance (and more) with the famous Queen Cleopatra of Egypt; and on the other, Caesar's great-nephew, Octavian, who had also officially become his son, by posthumous adoption, in Caesar's will (a not uncommon Roman practice). Their final battle was fought at sea off the coast of northern Greece, near the promontory of Actium, just south of the island of Corfu. The Battle of Actium, as it is known, was celebrated extravagantly in later propaganda as the decisive and heroic victory for Octavian, and the glorious start of a new era. In fact, it was won more by desertion and disloyalty than by heroism. Antony's battle plans were leaked to the enemy by one of his generals, and, on the most plausible reconstruction, Cleopatra headed back to Egypt with her ships, and her treasure, almost before

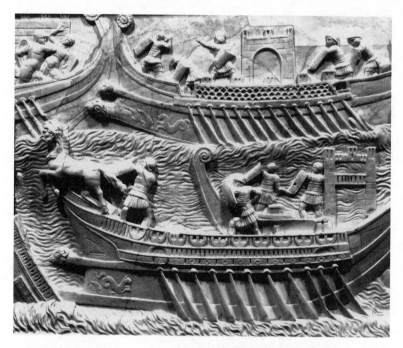

10. Section of a marble relief of the first century CE, found in Italy, depicting the Battle of Actium. The ship in the foreground has the image of a centaur (half man, half horse) decorating its prow, indicating that it is part of the fleet of Antony and Cleopatra.

the fighting had begun, quickly followed by Antony. Quite how ignominious a departure it was is still debated, but many ancient writers were keen to paint Cleopatra as a cowardly queen who couldn't take the heat and simply scarpered. Whatever the circumstances, though, Octavian was left as the sole leader of the Roman world, and soon to be the first *emperor of Rome*. To put it another way, the assassins had, indirectly at least, brought about the very thing they claimed to be fighting against: permanent one-man rule.

The emperor's new clothes

Octavian's record during the conflicts following Julius Caesar's death lies somewhere on the spectrum between illegal, ruthless and shockingly sadistic. Aged just nineteen in 44 BCE, he raised what was in effect his own private militia, and during his temporary alliance with Mark Antony they together initiated a reign of terror in Italy: a series of officially sponsored murders, with the combined purpose of punishing Caesar's enemies, settling old scores and raising money from selling the property of the victims. Hostile propaganda even alleged that on one occasion Octavian had pulled out the eyes of an enemy with his bare hands. How he managed to transform his image from that of young thug to responsible statesman, and the founding father of a system of government that (for better or worse) would last for centuries, is one of Roman history's biggest puzzles. But it was a transformation and a rebranding signalled by an astute change of name.

In 27 BCE, only a few years after the final defeat of Antony and Cleopatra, and after his return to Rome, Octavian was given – at his own suggestion, presumably – the name 'Augustus'. Several ancient accounts claim that he had flirted with being renamed 'Romulus', after the legendary founder of the city of Rome, but was dissuaded by the awkward associations (Romulus, after all, in killing his brother

Remus, was also the legendary founder of Roman civil war). 'August-us' was safer: an entirely new, and conveniently vague, made-up name, meaning something close to 'Revered One'. It stuck. Future Roman emperors included both 'Caesar' and 'Augustus' among their titles. And the Western calendar still commemorates them together, as July (from *Julius* Caesar) and August. The old Roman months of Quinctilis and Sextilis were renamed in their honour, and more than two thousand years later we are still living under their sign.

Big constitutional changes are almost always messier at the time than they are made to appear in retrospect. We have no clue what plan Octavian had worked out by the time he returned to Rome, but most likely it did not go far beyond stepping into the shoes of Julius Caesar while avoiding his grim fate. Stories of the new ruler wearing body armour under his toga – a bulky, hot and uncomfortable outfit – is one hint of his nervousness about assassination. We can only guess about any second thoughts he might have had (Roman writers suggest that there were occasions when he wondered about giving up one-man rule entirely), or about all the bright ideas that must have come to nothing, or were violently opposed and then conveniently forgotten. We do not even fully understand how Octavian/Augustus chose to describe his own position in the state.

We now refer to Roman *emperors*, harking back to the Latin word *imperator* or 'commander' – an ancient Roman title given to military victors and granted, as standard issue, to Augustus and his successors (whether they had actually been victorious or not). But there was a range of alternatives, with very different emphases, that were either more keenly adopted or were avoided. A Roman 'emperor' was much less likely to refer to himself as *imperator* than as *princeps*, the origin of our word 'prince', though in Latin it meant not much more than 'leader'. 'King' (or *rex*), however, was a more complicated matter. In the eastern half of the empire, where far more people spoke Greek than Latin, emperors were regularly called 'kings' (*basileis* in Greek).

But that was rarely the case at home, where Romans still prided themselves on having got rid of the last of their legendary early kings centuries before, and had no intention of welcoming any such tyrants back. From the beginning, most emperors were very keen to stress to their local audience that, whatever else they were, they were *not* *kings* (another good reason for Octavian to steer clear of the name 'Romulus', Rome's founder but also first king). That did not, however, stop some cynical ancient critics wondering if there really was much difference, beyond window-dressing, between a *princeps, imperator* or *Caesar* and a *rex*. As Tacitus darkly observed in the second century CE, in the first words of his *Annals*, a history of the early emperors, 'From the very beginning Rome has been ruled by *kings*'.

All the historians in the Roman world who looked back, cynically or not, to the reign of Augustus assumed that he had been working to some kind of master plan. Whether they were writing a couple of decades or a couple of centuries later (and no substantial narrative account survives from the period itself), they hid the messy processes of improvisation underneath the commanding image of a founding father establishing a new autocratic regime for the future. Cassius Dio, in whose massive history of Rome we read of Elagabalus's attempts at gender reassignment, even devoted the whole of one of his eighty books (that's about the length of a modern chapter) to a formal debate in which the new ruler decided how he would rule the state. Supposedly staged just a couple of years before the rebranding of Octavian as Augustus, this featured two of his friends arguing over the relative merits of democracy and autocracy (the virtues of equality versus the rule of the fittest), and comparing the practical pros and cons of one-man rule, which was of course the winning side. These range from financial planning and the need for good advisers (make sure they are not too young), to the personal anxieties of the ruler, the threat of conspiracy, and all that insidious and corrupting flattery. It is a revealing snapshot of how a senator such as Dio, in the early third century

CE, could evaluate imperial government, and one that Pliny a hundred years earlier would have instantly recognised. But, as an account of how the Roman system of one-man rule actually began, it is fantasy.

We shall probably never be able to reconstruct in any detail the improvisations, the backtracks and the U-turns by which Augustus and his friends and colleagues hammered out a role for an emperor within a new system of government. They were not, of course, re-inventing the wheel and they could well have read how earlier Greek political philosophers had defined kings and kingship, good and bad – though how much attention they actually gave to that is a mystery. But, thanks to one of those extraordinary, and lucky, survivals from antiquity, we do have a retrospective view of 'What I Did' from the pen of the emperor himself. It is a short 'essay' or 'manifesto', of a dozen or so modern pages, written immediately before his death in 14 CE aged seventy-five, and preserved in stone, inscribed all over the walls of an ancient Roman temple in what is now Turkey.

What I Did

Several books written by Roman rulers have come down to us. Julius Caesar's self-justificatory accounts of his campaigns in Gaul and his civil war against Pompey were circulated in ancient Rome, copied through the Middle Ages, and survived to be a school textbook in the modern world. Much the same happened to Marcus Aurelius's *Jottings to Himself* and to the writings of the fourth-century emperor Julian, which still fill several volumes. Julian's works include, along-side some frankly hard-core pagan theology, that deliciously ironic satire in which he hilariously characterised his predecessors on the Roman throne, from Elagabalus to Augustus himself, who was signifi-cantly described as an old 'chameleon' – changeable, wily and hard to sum up.

Augustus's own essay on *What I Did* (*Res Gestae* in Latin) has a very different history, for he wrote it to be publicly displayed, etched onto two bronze pillars outside his tomb near the centre of Rome. Those pillars, with their inscription, have long since been melted down, probably recycled into medieval weaponry. But the essay was widely copied, and the reconstructed text that we have comes mostly from the almost complete version found in Ankara, carved into the temple walls in both Latin and Greek (with a local Greek-speaking audience in mind), its letters originally highlighted in bright red paint to make them stand out. Large chunks had appeared from the six-teenth century onwards, but it was fully uncovered for the first time in the 1930s, under the sponsorship of Kemal Atatürk, the founder of the modern Turkish Republic, to mark the two-thousandth anniversary of Augustus's birth. Soon after, it was copied again, on the orders of Benito Mussolini, the Italian fascist dictator, who was keen to reinvent the emperor as the forerunner of himself. He had a complete Latin version, in bronze letters, set into the outside wall of a new museum he had erected, overlooking Augustus's tomb – where it still is, for all to see.

What I Did is a relentlessly egocentric first-person narrative, 'I did this …', 'I did that …'; first-person pronouns, 'I', 'me', 'mine', are repeated almost a hundred times in the short modern text. It is not an exciting read or a reflective autobiography, but at first sight a dry record of 'achievement' combined with sometimes misleading euphe-mism. The awful crimes of the civil wars are passed over in weasel words ('I liberated the state oppressed by the power of a faction' is the closest we get to any reference to the pogroms he had initiated). And several pages are monopolised by *lists*: of money spent, shows given, temples restored, population head counts or enemies brought to heel. But there is more to it than first meets the eye. To be sure, the document is a skeletal, retrospective and self-serving account of the emperor's more than forty years in power. But, as its public display suggests, it was also intended to act as a blueprint for the future, a lesson in what an emperor *should be*. In other words, like Pliny's vote of thanks, it was also a 'job description'.

Unsurprisingly perhaps – for Pliny must have had one eye on Augustus – there is a good deal of overlap between the two. Beyond the superficially dreary roster of facts and figures in *What I Did*, three particular requirements for an emperor stand out, as they do in Pliny's *Speech of Praise*: he should conquer, he should be a benefactor, and he should sponsor new buildings or restore those that have fallen into disrepair. We read of new lands brought under Roman control 'where no Roman had ever been before' and of foreign kings offering their loyalty, not to mention the boasts of massacres that almost rivalled Trajan's bloodstained seas. We read of Augustus's benefactions to the people on a massive scale (or bribery, as some might have seen it), in the form of entertainments as well as wine, grain and cash hand-outs to hundreds of thousands of citizens, sometimes amounting to the equivalent of several months of an ordinary person's wages. And, in what was very likely a prominent position on the original bronze pillars, there were the details of all Augustus's lavish schemes of building and restoration: from sparkling new shrines, porticoes and piazzas to the refurbishment of aqueducts, theatres and, in 28 BCE, of 'eighty-two temples of the gods in the city ... neglecting none that needed repair'. 'Eighty-two temples' was not far from the sum total of all the temples there were in Rome. My suspicion is that little more than a lick of paint can have been required, but it was certainly part of a post-civil war, 'Make Rome Great Again' campaign.

Emperors continued ever after to build themselves into the fabric of the city of Rome. Its ceremonial and public spaces (and I do *not* mean the slums and tenements where most of its million or so inhabitants lived) carried the marks, in concrete and marble, of one ruler after the next. Sometimes this was bombastic, and competitive, display. Trajan's column, for example, a triumphant exercise in securing maximum impact for minimum floor area, was outdone half a century later by the column of the emperor Marcus Aurelius, which was almost 5 metres taller. A century earlier, Augustus himself is reported to have boasted that he found Rome a 'city of brick' and left (some of) it 'a city of marble'. But these architectural developments were often part of a more significant project, to reconfigure the cityscape around the idea of the emperor, to make his presence seem inevitable, even 'natural'.

Of that, there is no better example than Augustus's brand-new Temple of Mars 'the Avenger', mentioned in *What I Did*, which was the centrepiece of the new 'Forum of Augustus'. Here Mars, the god of war, was celebrated for 'avenging' both the assassination of Julius Caesar and the disastrous battle against the Parthians in 53 BCE, in which Crassus literally lost his head. As we can tell from Roman descriptions of it and from the traces still remaining on the ground, the huge piazza in front of the temple building itself (the 'Forum') was lined with over a hundred statues. Some depicted the various mythical founders of the city, Romulus included. Many more celebrated the 'great men' of the Republic, from the national heroes who had saved Rome from Hannibal, to Sulla the dictator, right down to Caesar's enemy Pompey. At the centre of the forecourt, dominating the scene, was a statue of Augustus himself, standing in a gilded chariot. The conclusion was obvious: the political conflicts of the earlier age no longer mattered (even Pompey, after all, is welcomed to the line-up of heroes), and all Roman history had been leading up to Augustus.

The many portraits of the emperor erected in bronze and marble across the Roman world made a similar point. More than two hundred of Augustus still survive of the tens of thousands that there once were (see chapter 9) in addition to the millions of coins jangling around in Roman pockets and purses that carried his head. This went far beyond the example that Julius Caesar had begun to set in his short time in power, and it meant that it was next to impossible to be active in public, urban or commercial life in the Roman world without coming

11. The remains of the Temple of Mars 'the Avenger', the focal point of the Forum of Augustus. It contained the military standards lost by Crassus in 53 BCE, after his defeat by the Parthians at the Battle of Carrhae (p. 31), and recovered by Augustus, through diplomacy rather than military victory.

face to face with the image of the emperor on a daily basis. Whether most people outside Rome knew exactly who he was, or could pin the right name to the right face in a line-up of imperial statues, is another matter. But 'the emperor' as a figurehead was omnipresent. The text of *What I Did* is, of course, a further aspect of that. It is likely that relatively few people would – or, given low rates of literacy, could – have read it carefully enough to take in all the facts and figures. But the very act of copying and displaying the words of Augustus literally *wrote* him into the cityscape of Rome and its empire.

What I didn't say

Despite the detailed lists of his achievements, Augustus is notably reticent in *What I Did* about the hard-nosed political logic that underpinned his own rule and set the pattern for his successors into the third century CE. This was almost certainly not worked out in detail in advance, but we can reconstruct two important principles of power that developed over his reign.

The first is that this was *military* rule. I do not mean that Rome was full of men in uniform and march-pasts, as in the modern cliché of a military dictatorship. The fact is that the city of Rome itself was strikingly demilitarised even by the current standards of Western capitals. There were no regular ceremonies, such as Trooping the Colour or Bastille Day, which put the army on display in the city centre. Most soldiers were stationed towards the edges of Roman territory, with only a few urban or palace guardsmen (the so-called 'Praetorian Guard') in Rome itself. In any case, apart from their body armour and a few 'accessories', Roman soldiers didn't wear uniform in our sense of the word. But the key fact was that Augustus himself controlled all the armed forces in the empire, more than 250,000 of them, setting the pattern for the emperors who followed him. The significance of this was not lost on sharp-eyed Roman observers. One wry anecdote tells of a pedantic argument in the second century CE between the emperor Hadrian and a notable scholar about the correct usage of a particular Latin word (sadly, we are not told what the word was). The scholar gave in to the emperor, and was criticised by his friends for not standing his ground when he knew that the emperor's view was wrong. 'A man who commands thirty legions always knows best', was his apt reply.

This was a revolution, even if its importance is sometimes now obscured in apparently technical details of army pay and conditions, and in the fine-tuning of military appointments, as recorded by

Roman writers. Augustus must have been well aware of the dangers of rogue armies over the last decades of the Republic, whether in the shape of big men with their private legions (as he himself had raised following Caesar's assassination), or of troops who were simply more loyal to their own generals than to the state. His answer was, in our terms, to nationalise the army, as a volunteer force, with Roman citizens serving in the legions proper and non-citizens from the provinces enrolled as 'auxiliary' troops. He established, for the first time, regular terms of employment, with standard pay and length of service – and on retirement the soldiers in the legions (it was slightly different for auxiliaries) received a fixed pension settlement from central funds. The idea was not to improve employment practice. It was to bind the troops to the emperor and the state, and also to loosen their links with the individual generals, on whom they had previously depended for cash or land when they were demobbed.

At the same time, Augustus devised a scheme to ensure the loyalty of the senior representatives of Rome throughout the empire. This involved dividing the provinces into two groups: on the one hand those, such as Greece and the south of France ('Achaea' and 'Gallia Narbonensis'), that were largely peaceful; on the other, those where active fighting continued and where most of the army was stationed, such as Germany and northern France ('hairy Gaul', as it was sometimes nicknamed). He left it to the senate to select the governors for the peaceful provinces, while he chose the governors for the rest, to serve explicitly as his deputies, hiring and firing them at will. His aim was to keep tight control over anyone who could influence the soldiers, to ensure that they did not step out of line and to claim a monopoly on military authority for himself alone. He also claimed a monopoly on military glory, as the story of what happened to the traditional ceremony of 'triumph' sums up. For centuries, this had been the height of ambition for Roman commanders: a lavish victory parade through the city of Rome celebrated by the most successful generals, dressed up as the god Jupiter for the occasion. No longer. After the middle of the reign of Augustus, only members of the imperial family ever 'triumphed', regardless of who had actually commanded the troops on the ground. It was as if all victories had been won by the emperor.

Augustus could have congratulated himself for keeping the troops under the emperor's thumb. Until the third century CE, soldiers en masse intervened directly only twice in the power politics of the imperial regime: once in 68 at the fall of Nero, and again in 193 in the civil wars that followed the murder of the emperor Commodus. (I am not counting the several occasions on which individual members of the guard had a role in coups and assassination attempts – every ruler throughout history has always been at risk from his own body-guard.) But nationalising the army was also cripplingly expensive. The combination of regular pay and the pension pot for retiring soldiers

12. A more luxurious representation of a Roman triumphal procession than in fig. 3. This silver cup is part of a precious collection buried by the eruption of Vesuvius in 79 CE. It shows an earlier triumph of the future emperor Tiberius, step-son of Augustus, who stands in the chariot – while here a slave, not a goddess, holds a crown over his head.

amounted each year to a sum that was more than half the total revenue of the Roman state.

Augustus was soon forced to come up with extra sources of funding, introducing in 6 CE some unpopular 'death duties' to pay for the military pension arrangements. (It was on this inheritance tax that Pliny in his vote of thanks showed off his niche specialist knowledge.) And to judge from the reports of elderly, arthritic and toothless soldiers mutinying after Augustus's death in 14, some were kept with their units much longer than their fixed term of sixteen, or later twenty, years. As modern governments have also found, postponing the pension age was a convenient way of saving money, for it not only deferred coming up with the hard cash, but some of the potential beneficiaries would be certain to have died in the interim. The military underpinning of the rule of the emperors came at a very high price – for all concerned.

Augustus's second basic principle was to reconfigure Rome's sort-of democracy. Many things still *looked* the same, and that was presumably the point. The traditional offices that had been central to Republican politics – from quaestors (the most junior), through praetors, to consuls (at the top) – continued to be filled by some of the richest citizens. Ex-office-holders went on as before to become permanent members of the senate, and their perks and privileges were actually enhanced, including designated front-row seats at all public shows. In a way, Augustus used these old political structures as a framework for his new one-man rule, and he broadcast the slogan of *civilitas*. This meant literally 'behaving like a citizen', but was probably closer to the idea of 'behaving like *one of us*', when, as in Pliny's *Speech of Praise*, 'us' was the Roman elite. In this spirit, Augustus and his successors were active members of the senate and took part in its debates. They made a habit of refusing 'excessive' honours – *What I Did* blazons honourable refusals (of silver statues, a dictatorship, a perpetual consulship and 'any office that went against traditional custom') alongside the lists of achievements. They regularly became consuls in more or less the old way, as well as using the language of Republican politics to define and package their own position, referring, for example, to their 'power equivalent to a consul'.

But the emperor increasingly controlled who held the key offices, making popular democratic elections, even in Rome's 'sort-of' form of democracy, irrelevant. Pliny had no doubt that he owed his consulship in 100 CE to Trajan (hence the vote of thanks), and Roman writers referred casually to emperors 'appointing' these officials. In practice, they did. Augustus may at first have proceeded more cautiously than Julius Caesar – or so it would seem from the stories of him publicly canvassing for his favourites in the assemblies of the people and even introducing measures to stamp out bribery in elections (as if to give the impression that they were still hotly contested). But it was taken for granted that those he had, formally or informally, marked out for office would be successful. Immediately after his death in 14, Augustus's successor Tiberius 'simplified' things by transferring the ritual of elections (and by then it was little more than ritual) from the citizens as a whole to the senate itself. Tacitus reports, as a sign of the changing times, that there were only a few grumbles from the people at large, and that the elite were glad to be relieved of the bother of popular politics.

The slogan of *civilitas* obscures other major disruptions. For a start, Pliny was typical in holding his consulship for only two months, unlike the consuls of the Republic who served the full twelve. Appointing up to a dozen or so consuls each year, serving in pairs for a short term, was an easy way for the emperors to satisfy the ambitions for the top office of many more senators. But it was also a subtle way of devaluing it, turning what had once been a position of power into one of honour. But the decisive change was the end of popular voting, which – like the reform of the army – had the effect of breaking the links between leading Romans and the ordinary people, and so of preventing the rise of rival popular power bases. Elections might have been a chore that many in the higher echelons were glad to be rid of, but they had also formed the interface, the glue of mutual dependence, between them and the citizens more widely. Again, no longer.

Even the physical fabric of the old democratic institutions was repurposed. One grand building scheme started by Julius Caesar, and completed under Augustus in 26 BCE, was a new marble 'voting hall'. Only a few traces of it survive, but there is enough to show that it could hold well over 50,000 voters, as many people as would later squash into the Colosseum, constructed a century afterwards. This voting hall was a white elephant almost before it was finished. Already in Augustus's reign it was being used for politics of a new kind. Among other things, it became a place where the emperor hosted gladiatorial shows for 'his' people. It *was* a proto-Colosseum.

Emperors vs senators?

Did the old Roman elite simply lie down and accept all this? One answer is: no. The fraught relations between senators and emperors – a political fault line running through the almost three hundred years of history covered in this book – have always been a major theme in the accounts of imperial rule. They have produced some of the most chilling, memorable and occasionally (to us) hilarious tales of senatorial opposition and imperial caprice and cruelty – of which Elagabalus and his whoopee cushions are only one tiny part.

At the extreme, there was bloodshed on both sides. Emperors were conspired against and assassinated. Hit squads from the palace eliminated – or forced to suicide, which was more the Roman way – awkward or supposedly disloyal senators. So-called 'treason trials' ended up with sentences of death passed on senators for crimes that, later at least, were presented as trivial (casual criticism of the emperor, damage to an imperial statue, and the like). The prosecutors in these cases were senators and the jury was the senate itself, and it is hard not to suspect that there was sometimes an element of senators settling old scores against one another, or ultra-loyalists eagerly doing the emperor's dirty work for him. But not always. Augustus himself was probably behind the judicial execution of one rich senator who had gained popular support by funding the first semi-professional fire brigade in the city – evidence of the rudimentary level of Roman public services as well as of the emperor's anxiety about potential rivals exploiting their popularity with the people. And the philosopher Epictetus's story of soldiers acting rather like modern Stasi-style undercover agents makes the same point. Pretending to be ordinary civilians, they encouraged people to bad-mouth the emperor ('they speak ill of Caesar, then so do you') – and then hauled them off under arrest.

There were few emperors without any blood on their hands, as the *Imperial History* implies by treating it as noteworthy that young Alexander Severus had put not even a single senator to death during his reign. Contrast the emperor Claudius, almost two hundred years earlier. Whatever the emperor's avuncular modern image (largely, I'm afraid, a creation of Robert Graves's *I, Claudius*), Suetonius claims that a total of thirty-five senators, out of roughly six hundred, were put to death under his rule – whether guilty, in Roman terms, or not.

Much more often, though, it was a question not of bloodshed, but of Elagabalus-style humiliation, calculated insults and micro-aggressions. Pliny looked back to the emperor Domitian belching in the faces of his upmarket dinner guests and throwing at them the food he didn't fancy himself. Caligula is supposed to have 'joked' with two consuls that 'it would take only a nod on my part and both of you could have your throats cut here and now'. Over a hundred and fifty years later, Cassius Dio describes how he sat as a spectator in the Colosseum in 192 CE when Commodus was taking his turn as a wild-beast hunter in the arena (the unfortunate animals were penned up to make it easier and safer for him). Once the emperor had successfully decapitated an ostrich, he came over to the special front-row seats assigned to senators and waved the head at them, as if to say, 'you next'.

In their turn, senators resisted and fought back. Laughter was one response. Dio boasts that he and the others almost got the giggles (nervous ones, I should imagine) at the sight of Commodus and the ostrich, and that they had to stuff laurel leaves from their garlands in their mouths to stifle what might have been a dangerous outburst (pp. 253–4). Non-cooperation was another. Senatorial refuseniks ostentatiously staged walk-outs or simply stayed at home – like the elderly gentleman who, according to Dio, could not bring himself to show up for Commodus's antics in the Colosseum (though he prudently sent his sons in his place). Others used faux naivety or two-edged flattery to put the emperor on the spot. On one occasion in 15 CE, for example, when the verdict was being given in a treason trial, Tiberius's hypocritical pretence of equality with other members of the senate was exposed by a man who begged him to cast his vote first, 'because if you vote last, I might find that I have voted the wrong way by mistake'. (If it was a clever way to ensure that the defendant was acquitted, it worked.) There was plenty of bloody-minded, low-level defiance too. It is this that some modern historians have suggested lies behind Caligula's infamous threat to make his favourite racing horse a consul. If the story is true, they argue, it was most likely an exasperated, ironic response to the surly non-cooperation of the senators. 'I might as well make my horse a consul as any of you lot' was the emperor's point.

These tales, as they have come down to us, are all told from the point of view of the senators, whether as noble victims or as heroes (we can only speculate what might really lie behind Caligula's threat about his horse, or what Tiberius felt about his own performance in the senate). One-sided though they are, they point to an awkward mistrust, combined with an equally awkward mutual dependence, between elite and ruler: senators powerless in the face of imperial whim, and an emperor hostile or fearful in the face of the senators, who were his most likely rivals, but on whose cooperation he relied simply to get the business of running the Roman world done. And they point to some of the destabilising double-think that was embedded in one-man rule at Rome from the very beginning, and in such catch phrases as *civilitas*.

For the story about the senator who asked Tiberius to 'please vote first' was highlighting more than the hypocrisy of one particular emperor. It was puncturing the very notion of *civilitas*, and exposing the fact that – whatever his parade of participation alongside his fellow senators – no emperor could ever be 'one of us'. An even starker example might be the behaviour of Augustus when he entered or left meetings of the senate. He is reported to have stopped to greet, and bid farewell to, each senator in turn, by name. If he ever really did this (and it is certainly hard to imagine that he did it often), the whole rigmarole, assuming a reasonable senatorial turnout, would have taken at least an hour and a half, on entry and on exit. For all the carefully choreographed courtesy, it was a very clear sign that Augustus was *not* an ordinary senator. It was more a pageant of power than a recognition of citizenly equality.

By and large, Augustus seems to have 'got away with it'; or so later Roman writers believed. Many of his successors were not so successful at the elaborate political dance required to manage the perilous balancing act with the elite, and partly for that reason have gone down in history as 'bad' emperors. For historians in the Roman world, drawn from the elite almost to a man, 'bad' was often synonymous with 'bad from the perspective of the Roman upper crust'. Even with Augustus there are lines of connection with the exaggerated, partly fictional, dystopian world of Elagabalus. In relations between the emperor and the senate, things were never quite as they appeared. On both sides, people rarely meant exactly what they said, and that disjunction, between appearance and reality, fuelled mistrust.

The other side of the story

But there are other sides to the story of emperors and senators. Historians, writers and artists have almost always been drawn to the rebels and dissidents. Some of the emperors' victims have remained the stuff of heroic legend into the modern world. Lucius Annaeus Seneca, for example, philosopher, playwright, satirist, and the man with the perhaps unenviable task of being tutor to the emperor Nero, was implicated in an unsuccessful plot against his former pupil in 65 CE and was instructed to kill himself. Many artists, from the Renaissance onwards, have recaptured the scene as the old man was placed in a hot bath to help release the blood from his veins, while he (histrionically, it must be said) imitated Socrates in dictating philosophy until he eventually died (pl. 2).

Even now, those of us who rarely put our own heads above the political parapet still tend to side with people we see as the principled and plucky opponents of corrupt autocrats. Their stories are more exciting than those of the 'collaborators', and anyway, it goes against the grain for us to invest our sympathies in the plight of a ruler threatened with assassination or just driven to distraction by the 'awkward squad' (though we should probably take more seriously than we do the emperor Domitian's complaint that no one believed in conspiracies against the emperor until he was dead). In our sympathy with the rebels, it is easy to forget that – despite the loud protests against the crimes and misdemeanours of individual rulers, or the discontent with some aspects of one-man rule – there is hardly any trace of significant resistance to one-man rule *as such*.

The last moment at which we catch any glimpse of resistance to the imperial system was in 41 CE, less than thirty years – and only two emperors – from the death of Augustus. Just after Caligula, the second of those two, had been assassinated by some disaffected members of his guard, a rousing speech was delivered in the senate, demanding a return to the 'liberty' of the old Republic. It was too little, too late. The time for any return to the old order was gone. Claudius had already been proclaimed the new emperor, and the speaker's eloquence was quickly undermined when he was found to be wearing a signet ring bearing Caligula's head. How un-Republican was that? Beyond the fantasies of a few unrealistic philosophers, or of nostalgic dreamers who kept portraits of Brutus and Cassius, Caesar's assassins, on their mantelpieces, that is the last time we ever hear of any practical call for the overthrow of one-man rule at Rome. The system established by Augustus endured for the rest of Roman time.

It is also easy to forget that not all senators under the emperors were engaged in this war of words, or worse. Tacitus, with characteristic cynicism, identified two main groups in the senate: on the one hand, the largely ineffective dissidents, full of noble sentiments and grand gestures but not much action or political good sense; and on the other, the cowards, the flatterers and those who readily traded their freedom for wealth and political success. Pliny himself has often been painted by modern historians as one of these craven bootlickers (and some imperial boots were certainly sometimes licked by craven senators). But he might equally be seen as a man getting on with his life and career in the only political system he had ever known. No doubt he was happy overall in his role in the senate and in the administration of empire, and delighted to be awarded a two-month consulship. Very likely he was proud to count himself a friend of Trajan, skilled at walking the tightrope between flattery and frank talk, and capable of adjusting to the comedy of manners that surrounded the emperor – while also pointedly reminding him of what an emperor should be (and do).

It is difficult to know how many men like Pliny there were, partly because they have generally been overshadowed by their noisier, more discontented and to us more glamorous colleagues. But my guess is that the majority of senators were prepared, or pleased, to cooperate with the *princeps*, whether 'good' or 'bad', most of the time. There is obviously a fine line between 'cooperators' and 'collaborators', between the polite and the obsequious. But for better or worse, and whatever the double-think sometimes entailed, it was partly thanks to the Plinys of the Roman world that the system established by Augustus worked – and lasted.

2

WHO'S NEXT? THE ART OF SUCCESSION

Heirs of Augustus

Almost as soon as he arrived back in Italy in 29 BCE after the Battle of Actium and the defeat of Antony and Cleopatra, Octavian, as he then was, began building a vast mausoleum near the centre of Rome. It was the biggest tomb the city had ever seen, and is still standing now, not far from the river Tiber, 90 metres in diameter. (In the early twentieth century, it had been repurposed as one of Rome's premier concert halls, the 'Augusteo', with almost four thousand seats, until Mussolini stripped away the modern additions and converted it back into an 'ancient monument'.) It was an uncompromising symbol of autocratic power, and the engraved text of *What I Did*, which was eventually displayed at its entrance, underlined that point. The size alone almost insists that the tomb was intended to hold not only the emperor and his immediate family but a line of successors too. This mausoleum acted as a guarantee, or warning, that emperors would not stop with Augustus, and was a very large boast of dynastic continuity.

Yet, despite that boast, 'succession planning' was the single, most glaring weak spot of the Augustan system. Who should follow Augustus? Or, more generally, how should any successor to the Roman

13. Augustus's mausoleum, constructed at the very beginning of his reign, was one of the most glaring symbols of his dynastic ambitions. Here, at the main entrance, his *What I Did* was inscribed on two bronze pillars, almost as a manifesto for one-man rule.

throne be chosen, by whom, on what principles, and from what group of candidates? After Augustus's death, over the next two hundred years or so, and over the next two dozen emperors, the transition of power was almost always debated, fraught and sometimes killed for – from the notorious dish of poisoned mushrooms, allegedly served up to the emperor Claudius in 54 CE by his fourth wife, Agrippina, to the humiliating end of Caracalla in 217, attacked by an assassin while he was having a pee. But regime change at Rome did not only produce moments of uncertainty and conflict. As we shall see, it also produced moments when history was reinvented, past emperors' reputations were made or broken, and men like Pliny were faced with some uncomfortable readjustments. There are curious and almost unfathomable intrigues involved here and sometimes a sprawling cast of characters. But it is the *pattern*, not the details, that is important. Succession, and its problems, was at the very heart of the imperial story, and of how Roman rulers are still judged and remembered.

In this respect the usually lucky Augustus had an unusual run of bad luck. First, although he and his wife Livia both had children by previous partners, they had none surviving together. So, in looking for heirs among his descendants, he had to turn to the family of his only daughter Julia or of his sister Octavia, and to Livia's sons by her first marriage: hence the hybrid title 'Julio-Claudian' now usually given to this first dynasty, from the 'Julii' of Augustus's family, and the 'Claudii' of Livia's previous husband, Tiberius *Claudius* Nero. Even so, one by one, all his chosen heirs died – until the last man standing was Livia's son, Tiberius, who was formally adopted by Augustus and came to the throne, as the second emperor, on his death in 14 CE (pl. 5).

Some Roman writers, like modern novelists, speculated that Livia had been scheming for this all along, and – thanks to her special skills in poisoning – had been instrumental in Augustus's 'bad luck'. One rumour even claimed that she finally got rid of Augustus himself, with poison smeared on his favourite figs, to smooth the path for Tiberius. Who knows? In the ancient world it was impossible to distinguish a nasty case of appendicitis from a nasty case of poisoning, or the effects of doctored figs from the effects of dysentery; and we can only guess what combination of conspiracy theory, gossip, misogyny or well-founded hypothesis lay behind these allegations. It *is* clear, though, that Livia was the first of a long line of imperial woman who were credited or blamed for easing their own sons, or grandsons, onto the throne. Agrippina's poisoned mushrooms were supposed to ensure the succession of her son Nero. It is usually said that the succession of Elagabalus in 218 CE followed a similar pattern, engineered by his grandmother and mother, in league with some disaffected

The Family Tree of the Julio-Claudian Dynasty

It is almost impossible to plot in a diagram the inter-relationships among the descendants of Augustus. But this (simplified) family tree captures the complexities and difficulties of succession in the first imperial dynasty.

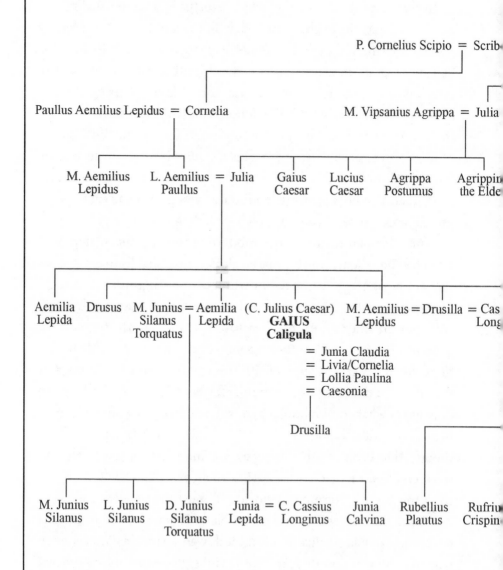

C. JULIUS CAESA

P. Cornelius Scipio = Scrib

Paullus Aemilius Lepidus = Cornelia

M. Vipsanius Agrippa = Julia

M. Aemilius Lepidus   L. Aemilius Paullus = Julia   Gaius Caesar   Lucius Caesar   Agrippa Postumus   Agrippin the Elde

Aemilia Lepida   Drusus   M. Junius Silanus Torquatus = Aemilia Lepida   (C. Julius Caesar) **GAIUS Caligula**   M. Aemilius Lepidus = Drusilla = Cas Long

= Junia Claudia
= Livia/Cornelia
= Lollia Paulina
= Caesonia

Drusilla

M. Junius Silanus   L. Junius Silanus   D. Junius Silanus Torquatus   Junia Lepida = C. Cassius Longinus   Junia Calvina   Rubellius Plautus   Rufriu Crispin

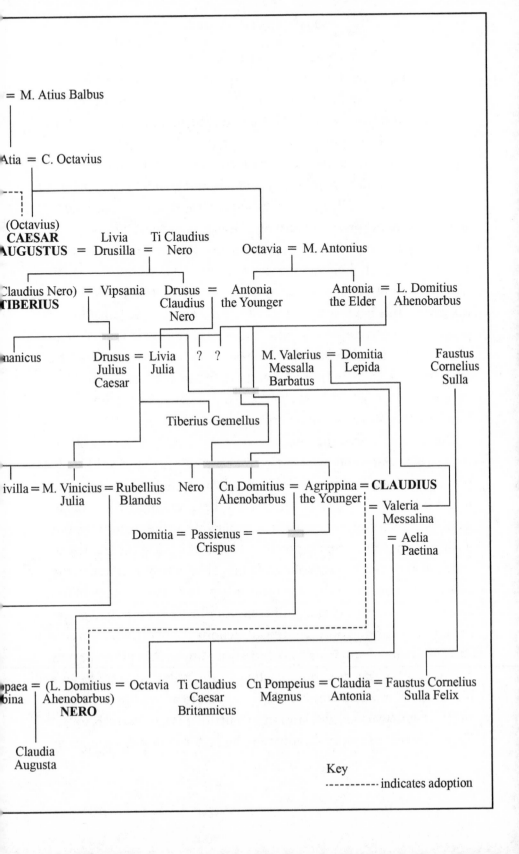

= M. Atius Balbus

Atia = C. Octavius

(Octavius)
CAESAR   Livia   Ti Claudius
AUGUSTUS = Drusilla = Nero   Octavia = M. Antonius

Claudius Nero) = Vipsania   Drusus = Antonia   Antonia = L. Domitius
TIBERIUS   Claudius   the Younger   the Elder   Ahenobarbus
                Nero

manicus   Drusus = Livia   ? ?   M. Valerius = Domitia   Faustus
         Julius   Julia   Messalla   Lepida   Cornelius
         Caesar   Barbatus   Sulla

Tiberius Gemellus

ivilla = M. Vinicius = Rubellius   Nero   Cn Domitius = Agrippina = **CLAUDIUS**
      Julia   Blandus   Ahenobarbus   the Younger   = Valeria
                                                  Messalina
           Domitia = Passienus =   = Aelia
                 Crispus   Paetina

paea = (L. Domitius = Octavia   Ti Claudius   Cn Pompeius = Claudia = Faustus Cornelius
bina   Ahenobarbus)   Caesar   Magnus   Antonia   Sulla Felix
      NERO   Britannicus

Claudia
Augusta

Key
---------- indicates adoption

soldiers, to get one of their own family back on the throne, after the brief rule of an 'interloper'. True or not, it has been a cliché of ancient and modern history writing, that behind the scenes, from Livia on, women could be kingmakers.

There was, however, something much more fundamental than bad luck, poison bottles or ambitious mothers and grandmothers behind the controversies of Roman succession and the fractures it opened in the structures of power. Modern European monarchies have tended to follow a system of the 'succession of the first born', or 'primogeniture' as it is technically known. That is to say, the oldest child (or traditionally the oldest *male* child) automatically inherits the position of the father. This has the advantage of ensuring a smooth transition of power, for everyone knows who comes next and there is no debate about it. The disadvantage is that the heir may be wholly unsuited, by temperament, ability or political support, to take the throne. You have to put up with what you get, whether a dutiful but dreary administrator, a lascivious spendthrift or a transgressive teenager.

The Roman system had no such fixed rule, either in family inheritance (big estates did not simply end up with the eldest son), or in political succession. This allowed much more flexibility over who might inherit power and position, with the advantage that it was in principle much easier to bypass the unsuitable or the unpopular. But it came at enormous cost: a potential fight every time power changed hands or, more often, years of rivalry and jockeying for position in the race to take over. Augustus's reforms may have removed much of the threat of rival armies backing different candidates for the succession, but they did not stop the infighting of factions. And even when an heir had been marked out, it was not entirely clear who actually *made* him emperor. It became common practice for the ruling emperor to give his favoured successor the title 'Caesar', and to award him a consulship earlier than usual, plus any number of other honours and baubles. Two of Augustus's short-lived young heirs, for example, were given the title *princeps iuventutis*, 'leader' – even 'emperor' – 'of the Roman youth'. But once the old ruler was dead it was others who could turn, or refuse to turn, the implied promises of succession into reality.

For that reason, most reigns started with the new or would-be ruler throwing money at the palace guard, at the other troops and at the population of the city, and throwing promises of deference and *civilitas* at the senate. In return for this, if all went well (and it didn't always), the senators formally ratified the transfer of power, the people were at least compliant, and the soldiers enthusiastically acclaimed their new emperor. Even then, there often seems to have been a concerted campaign of what we would call 'spin', devoted to making him seem the obvious, the inevitable, or – best of all – the divinely chosen man for the job. That was the point of all the omens and prophecies dredged up, or more likely invented, that we can still read in the ancient biographies of emperors: the eagle (a classic symbol of imperial power) that had one day landed as if by chance on Claudius's shoulder; or the priestess who 'mistakenly' addressed the future emperor Antoninus Pius as *imperator* long before there was any suggestion of him coming to the throne. The basic rule is that the flimsier the claims to power, the more insistent and extravagant the signs and portents had to be. Vespasian, who became emperor in 69 CE in the civil war after the death of Nero, an outsider with no direct links to earlier rulers, was even credited with performing miracles in almost biblical style. In Egypt, on his way to Rome to take up the throne, he is said to have restored sight to a blind man with his spit, and to have made a lame man walk with his touch. It was one way of compensating for a lack of imperial connections.

Routes to the top

Over the first two and a half centuries of one-man rule at Rome, emperors came in many different shapes, sizes and colours. They were all drawn from the upper echelons of the elite, and all but one were either senators themselves or the sons of senators. The single exception was Elagabalus's predecessor, Macrinus, who ruled for just over a year after the coup that had ignominiously dispatched Caracalla in 217 CE in mid-pee. Even Macrinus was a successful lawyer, high-ranking administrator and commander of the imperial guard, not a career soldier from the ranks, taking his chance at the imperial throne. But these emperors were increasingly diverse in origin, so that by the end of our period men had occupied the Roman throne who counted North Africa, Spain or Syria as 'home'. Trenchantly, if not entirely accurately, one Roman historian in the fourth century CE claimed that after the death of Domitian in 96, 'all emperors were foreigners'.

Behind this change was the increasing diversity of the Roman elite more generally. One of the distinguishing features of Roman social and political life was that the ruling class of the provinces was gradually incorporated into the ruling class of the metropolis itself. By the end of the second century CE, there were senators who traced their family origins back to Greece and Spain, Gaul and North Africa. (The backwater province of Britain is the only one that, so far as we know, produced not a single senator, ever.) And as the elite became more diverse, so too did the men on the throne – while the division between who counted as 'Roman' and who as 'foreign' became increasingly blurred. Trajan and Hadrian, in the early second century, were the first rulers whose origins lay in Spain, both from Italian settler stock, rather than 'native' Spaniards. Half a century later, Septimius Severus, the first man from North Africa to become emperor, was a senator and soldier, and the son of an aristocratic Italian mother and a wealthy local man from the town of Lepcis Magna. His wife, Julia Domna, the great-aunt of Elagabalus, was a member of a princely and priestly family from Emesa in Syria. In one of those (no doubt retrospective) predictions of future power, it was said that her horoscope showed she would marry a king.

The traditional aristocracy did not always welcome this diversity. There is a strong hint of prejudice in the story of other senators laughing at Hadrian, before he came to the throne, for his 'rustic' or 'provincial' accent, which prompted him to take elocution lessons. And much the same is found in the claims that decades later Septimius Severus always 'sounded African' and was very partial to eating a particular type of African bean (a sneer at his native cuisine not unlike the disdain the British elite might show for a prime minister whose favourite food was reputed to be mushy peas and pork scratchings). It was even said that his sister could hardly speak Latin, and that Severus 'blushed' for her when she visited him at Rome and sent her back home promptly. No doubt similar attitudes also lie behind some of the tales about Elagabalus's 'exotic' religious innovations, which exaggerated as well as deplored his Syrian roots. Although he certainly held priestly office at Emesa, he was not (as the stories would have us believe) plucked directly from a lifetime of seclusion in an Eastern temple to become Roman emperor, but had already spent much of his childhood in Italy and the West. As often in history, xenophobia and cultural prejudice at Rome went hand in hand with ethnic diversity and an openness to the outside world. But one thing's for sure: these rulers in the flesh were far more diverse, and increasingly so, than you would imagine from all those line-ups of lookalike, white marble imperial busts that we now see on museum shelves.

The stories of how exactly these men ended up on the throne are as varied as their origins. A few lucky ones did slip directly from the role of chosen heir to that of incumbent ruler, but by no means all. Very occasionally they were the 'last contender standing' in a civil war. That was what happened to Vespasian in 69 CE and Septimius Severus in

193. Or they were simply the right man in the right place at the right time, as when Claudius in 41 was discovered hiding behind a curtain by the palace guard after the assassination of his nephew Caligula. He was declared emperor as there was no other plausible candidate to hand. It was a variation on the same theme that brought the elderly Nerva to power half a century later, following the assassination of Domitian. After several other candidates had said a firm 'no, thank you' to the conspirators' advance offer of the throne (perhaps thinking that acceptance was too risky should the plot fail), Nerva was the first and only to say 'yes'. But perhaps the grubbiest succession of all was when, in the civil war that ended with the victory of Septimius Severus in 193, the very short-term emperor Didius Julianus is supposed to have paid cash for the position. Not content with a generous handout from the new emperor after the event, the palace guard decided to auction off their support to the highest bidder.

It was not even a question of only one man on the throne at a time. We now think of the Roman emperor as a *one-man* ruler. That is how I have been referring to him, and will continue to do so. But it can be a misleading shorthand. For there were a number of occasions in this period (and it became even more common later) when two men were on the throne together, holding imperial power jointly. Already in the early first century CE, one report implies that Tiberius planned to make his great-nephew, Caligula, and his young grandson, Tiberius Gemellus, his joint heirs. If so, the plan did not come off. Caligula became emperor alone, and the grandson did not survive much longer (pp. 113–14). It did, however, come off in 161 after the death of Antoninus Pius, when Marcus Aurelius and Lucius Verus ruled as co-emperors until Verus died in 169 (probably in a great pandemic, unless you prefer the story that his mother-in-law got rid of him with a dish of poisoned oysters). Again, towards the end of his reign, Septimius Severus ruled jointly with his son Caracalla, and at the father's death in 211 Caracalla and his brother Geta proceeded to share the throne, albeit briefly. In this case, joint rule was not the easy answer to family disputes. Within a year Caracalla is said to have had Geta murdered as he clung to their mother's lap.

In all these different routes to imperial power, it was certainly seen as an advantage to be the natural son of a previous ruler. It was for that reason that the leaders of the coup that put Elagabalus on the throne in 218 CE spread the rumour that he was the illegitimate son of his predecessor but one, Caracalla (reinforcing the point by dressing the poor lad up in clothes that they alleged had once belonged to his 'father' and changing his name accordingly). A few years later the supporters of Alexander Severus made exactly the same copycat claim for their own candidate for the throne, though, so far as we know, without the dressing-up. But there was no expectation that imperial power would necessarily be transferred by direct blood line and, in many cases, there was no biological heir. It was not until 79, after more than a hundred years of imperial rule, that a biological son actually succeeded his father, when the emperor Titus followed Vespasian. It did not happen again for another century, when in 180 Commodus succeeded his biological father, Marcus Aurelius.

My stress on *biological* is crucial here. For the mainstay of imperial succession was always a system of adoption, which allowed a wider choice of heir beyond the emperor's closest family while still presenting the transmission of power in family terms. From as far back as we can trace, adoption at Rome had a different function from most adoptions today. It was a means of ensuring the continuity of property and family name when there were no surviving sons by birth (this was a world in which half the children born did not live to reach the age of ten). The majority of those adopted were not babies or young children but adult men, often with their birth parents still living.

Adoption was built into the system of one-man rule from the very beginning. The first Roman dynasty was launched by Julius Caesar's adoption of his great-nephew Octavian in his will, while Augustus designated the series of ill-fated nephews, grandsons and other prince-lings who were to be his heirs by adopting them as his sons. In just the same way, more than two centuries later Elagabalus – instructed by his minders, no doubt – tried to shore up his own position and secure dynastic continuity by adopting his cousin Alexander Severus (even though the boy was only about four years younger than his new 'father'). Adoption, in other words, was always the favoured mecha-nism by which close associates or relatives who were not the natural sons of the ruling emperor were marked out for succession, and so placed above potential rivals in the inner circle. This reached its logical (and absurd) conclusion when Septimius Severus, after gaining power in the civil war of 193, turned the process on its head. In order to bolster his right to the throne, he retrospectively proclaimed that he was the adopted son of the last emperor but one, Marcus Aurelius, who had died more than a decade earlier. 'I congratulate you, Caesar, on finding a father', was the reaction of one wit to this 'self-adoption'.

But for over eighty years, from the very end of the first century CE and through most of the second century, adoption was used even more systematically. Starting from Nerva, one childless emperor after another adopted his successor from a much wider family group or from outside it entirely. Part of the driving force in this must have been necessity: the lack of any close natural heirs, suitable or not. But even if it was, at some level, a cosmetic exercise to mask the absence of biological sons or near relatives, for decades (and for almost a third of the period that is the focus of this book) adoption became elevated to a guiding principle at the heart of imperial succession, and was even advocated as a means of establishing an imperial meritocracy. In Pliny's vote of thanks, he explicitly praised the way in which Trajan – Nerva's choice of son and the first in this series of 'adoptive' emper-ors, as they are now sometimes called – had come to the throne. He presented it as a matter of pride that 'the man who is going to *rule* over all citizens should be *chosen* out of all of them'. Choice is a better

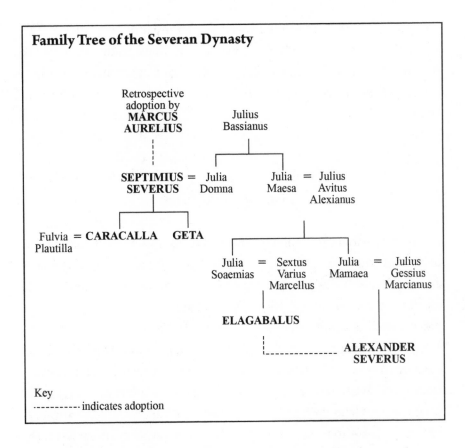

Family Tree of the Severan Dynasty

Retrospective adoption by **MARCUS AURELIUS**

Julius Bassianus

SEPTIMIUS SEVERUS = Julia Domna

Julia Maesa = Julius Avitus Alexianus

Fulvia Plautilla = **CARACALLA**   **GETA**

Julia Soaemias = Sextus Varius Marcellus

Julia Mamaea = Julius Gessius Marcianus

ELAGABALUS

ALEXANDER SEVERUS

Key
---------- indicates adoption

guarantee of a good emperor than mere accident of birth or, as he put it, than whatever a wife produces.

It is not hard to detect, again, the characteristic blindness of the Roman elite to the overwhelming majority of citizens, who had no earthly chance of being picked as emperor. For Pliny, 'all citizens' meant 'all citizens *like me*'. But his point is clear: biological heredity is an unsatisfactory way of selecting a man to rule the Roman world. Edward Gibbon in the eighteenth century would no doubt have agreed. In his *Decline and Fall of the Roman Empire* (and, to be honest, with as much selective blindness as Pliny) he chose the reigns of Nerva and his 'adoptive' successors down to Marcus Aurelius, who died in 180 CE, as the period in the whole of world history when 'the condition of the human race was most happy and prosperous'. This 'happy' period ended when a natural son, Commodus, survived to follow his natural father, Marcus Aurelius, onto the throne. It was in the sequel to the assassination of Commodus that Septimius Severus returned to a principle of adoption, with his bizarre new retrospective twist.

A culture of suspicion

Modern historians have always enjoyed dissecting the 'official version' of the various succession stories, and the propaganda of the new regime that was designed to paper over some of the uncomfortable cracks in the new ruler's rise to power. I am not the only one to have had my doubts about just how innocent, or taken by surprise, Claudius really was when he was conveniently discovered cowering behind that curtain. Was it not just as likely to have been a clever piece of theatre, staged to make it *look* as if he had nothing to do with the murder of his predecessor Caligula? And – despite Pliny's high-minded sentiments about choice – there are strong indications, if you read between the lines of ancient accounts, that Nerva was having the Roman equiva-lent of a gun held to his head in 97 when he adopted Trajan.

Sometimes those writers expressed even more open doubts about what went on behind the scenes when power changed hands. The author of the *Imperial History* reports one allegation of outright faking when, a couple of decades after he himself had been picked by Nerva, Trajan supposedly adopted Hadrian as his son and successor. The story was that after Trajan had died, his wife arranged for someone to imper-sonate him, announcing his choice of Hadrian as heir in a faint voice, as if from his deathbed (and presumably from behind a curtain). In much the same spirit was the Soviet-style news management suppos-edly masterminded by Livia after the death of Augustus. According to the historian Tacitus, she continued issuing optimistic bulletins about the dead emperor's health until her son Tiberius arrived on the scene and the death of the old emperor and the accession of the new could be proclaimed simultaneously, with no inconvenient gaps.

True or not, and I don't imagine that they all are, stories of this kind point to the anxieties and uncertainties surrounding the moment of imperial succession. So too do all the stories of the murder of the old emperor to make way for the new. To take just the first dynasty, of the Julio-Claudians, from Augustus to Nero, there is not a single emperor for whom there is *no* allegation of an unnatural death, or at least a hastened end. I don't just mean the semi-public assassination of Caligula or the forced suicide of Nero in the face of army rebellions. As well as the rumours that Augustus was killed by Livia or that Claudius was finished off with mushrooms, the other member of that dynasty – Tiberius – is reported by some Roman writers to have been smothered on his sick-bed by one of his successor Caligula's henchmen. The same is true of the Flavian dynasty that followed, even if the only allegation about the death of Vespasian by foul play is mentioned in Cassius Dio's *History* in order to be firmly dismissed. Gibbon would very likely point out that (apart from the case of Lucius Verus, co-emperor with Marcus Aurelius) there were no such allegations, so far as we know, surrounding the deaths of the series of 'adoptive' emperors, as if to suggest that the more radical system of adoption had somehow solved the problem. I doubt it. For a start, rather less evidence, gossipy or otherwise, survives for the lives and deaths of the second-century emperors compared with their predecessors in the first. But – whether or not Trajan's wife really did pull off any such trick with the adoption of Hadrian – it does not look as if allegations of foul play or double-dealing came to an end. Rather they shifted, from the circumstances of the death of the ruling emperor to the machinations behind the choice of adopted heir. Whoever the key players were, Roman imperial succession was always mired in a culture of suspicion.

History written by the winners

Matters of succession had an impact far beyond the corridors of the palace or the bedrooms of dying rulers, and still partly determine how we judge the rulers of Rome. It is impossible to understand the history of the Roman empire without thinking hard about the conflicts and controversies of regime change. These help us to explain how Roman emperors have been remembered ever since, and how their colourful, if two-dimensional, reputations as 'good' or 'bad' – from the monstrous Caligula or Nero to the virtuous Trajan or Marcus Aurelius – were created. Of course, those stereotypes are as misleading as they are convenient and commonplace (the *Imperial History*'s biography of Elagabalus opens with a list of past emperors 'good' and 'bad', leaving no doubt where the 'little lad from Emesa' belonged).

In real life, emperors did not fall into such simple categories, any more than modern monarchs, presidents or prime ministers do. No ruler pleases everyone: good *in whose opinion*, we should always ask; or bad *by what criteria*? Nonetheless, the stereotypes originated at the very heart of Roman imperial culture, not so much as an accurate reflection of the qualities of the men on the throne but of the interests of those telling their story. One factor here, as we have already seen, was how well the emperor in question had got on with the class of people who wrote the histories. Whatever their popularity among the poor or among the rank-and-file soldiers, those rulers who successfully managed the potentially tricky relations with the metropolitan elite were likely to be given a positive spin. The interests of their successor and the circumstances of the succession were even more influential. The conventional story of the Roman emperors is a very particular type of 'history written by the winners'.

One basic rule is that emperors who were followed onto the throne by their own chosen candidate ended up with a broadly favourable reputation. For the new ruler was almost bound to invest heavily in honouring the man who had put him there, and on whom his right to rule depended. Sometimes this investment extended to ensuring that his predecessor was worshipped as a god, complete with temple, priests and offerings (a particularly difficult aspect of Roman imperial society for many modern observers to take seriously, which I shall attempt to make better sense of in chapter 10). More generally, it was a question of managing the old emperor's image and reputation. That does not necessarily mean anything quite so crude as hiring tame historians to write sympathetic accounts of him, though there might have been a little of that. It usually involved a more subtle combination of careful commemoration, selective memory, and a favourable spin placed on some of his more dubious actions. To give a simple example, all (or very nearly all) Roman emperors used the death penalty, murder or enforced suicide to remove some of their enemies; successful image management ensured that this was seen as a legitimate and proportionate response to treachery rather than a reign of terror.

And so, the 'good' emperors emerged. Vespasian in the first century CE was followed, peacefully, by his son Titus whom he had marked out to follow him. However well or badly Vespasian may have ruled, Titus's position rested on being the worthy son and heir of a worthy father, and he had an enormous interest in promoting, even creating, the positive image of Vespasian. By the same logic, the series of adoptive emperors in the second century were almost inevitably committed to bolstering the reputation of the man who had officially 'chosen' them to succeed, however fudged or faked their adoption might have been. When Gibbon pronounced that period the happiest and most prosperous in the whole of human history, he was not only ignoring the ordinary inhabitants of the Roman empire, not to mention most of the rest of the planet, he was also overlooking just how invested those emperors were in making the rule of each of their predecessors *seem* happy and prosperous.

It was exactly the reverse when an emperor was assassinated or was the victim of a coup. Assassinations, both ancient and modern, happen for many reasons: from principled opposition to personal grudge or self-seeking ambition. Throughout history, 'good' men as well as 'bad' have been murdered. But whatever the circumstances, or the rights and wrongs in each case, anyone who owed their place on the throne to open conflict, coup or conspiracy (I am not talking here of stealthy, behind-the-scenes application of poison to figs), was bound to justify their right to rule by insisting that their predecessor had deserved what had happened to him. In the most extreme version of this, the new regime presided over the destruction of the fallen emperor's statues and the striking out of his name from public documents. Sometimes, convenient omens were later circulated, apparently 'foretelling' the assassination and giving it divine approval (in 96 CE, for example, a talking crow is supposed to have perched on the roof of the main temple of Jupiter in Rome and helpfully squawked out what was taken to be a prophecy of Domitian's death). Almost always, gossip, spin and allegation became 'the official version': each unexplained death of a prominent senator was attributed in retrospect to imperial sadism; each act of generosity reinterpreted as prodigality; and each wry joke or sharp irony, such as Caligula's quip about his horse, turned into an exercise in malicious humiliation or a sign of madness. The impression we are meant to take away is that emperors were assassinated because they were monsters. It is equally likely that they were made into monsters because they were assassinated.

It is important not to fall into a modern revisionist trap here. I am not for a minute suggesting that all those emperors who ended up with a dagger in their back were actually upstanding statesmen who have been woefully misrepresented (the victims of undeserved *character* assassination as much as the real thing). Some of them may well have been very nasty pieces of work, and in the dystopian world of the imperial court it is hard to imagine that any emperor was 'good', still less 'nice', in our terms. My point is that, whatever the conduct of these rulers during their lifetime, whether in the wheeling and dealing behind palace walls, in the tricky politics of the Roman elite, or in the treatment of the rest of the empire's population, much of their post-humous reputation was always determined – and overdetermined – by their successors, and by the sometimes messy circumstances of the succession. In the following chapters, we shall be wondering what the

14. Erasing the names. On this dedication to the goddess 'Fortune' (visible in the first line) the name of the emperor Geta has been chiselled out after his murder. This is not just about *forgetting* the fallen ruler; the obvious gash across the centre of the stone almost celebrates his fall.

stereotypes of imperial vice and virtue can tell us, and why they take the form they do, and we shall enjoy puncturing, or looking beyond, a few of them (the people who regularly decorated Nero's tomb with flowers in the years after his death presumably did not see him as the tyrant that he is often assumed to be). But the bottom line is clear: the man who followed an emperor onto the throne, and by what means, was absolutely crucial in how his predecessor has been remembered and represented in the historical tradition over the centuries.

The art of readjustment: Pliny's past

There is more to all this, however, than the question of how history was written, and rewritten, and more to it than the immediate dangers faced at moments of transition by the innermost circles of anxious rulers, artful poisoners, ambitious heirs, loyal and disloyal servants. The difficult readjustments that came with regime change Roman-style, the new versions of the past that replaced old orthodoxies, had a powerful knock-on effect on almost all those involved in politics and administration, at least in the capital. The circumstances of succession did not impinge very much on the ordinary people in Rome or in the provinces, beyond bringing to some a welcome cash handout. Who had reached the throne, and how, hardly mattered to the local population of darkest Britannia. But in the city of Rome itself, and in the corridors of power more widely, there was a ripple effect that caught even the more distant ranks of the elite in the messy consequences of succession.

As one reign gave way to the next, loyal or collaborative senators like Pliny – and they, as I have suggested, were probably most of them – had to reinvent themselves, to fit in with the new emperor and sometimes to distance themselves clearly from the old. Cassius Dio explained how in 193 CE, when he went up to the palace to greet one of the new short-term emperors, he 'moulded his face' to conceal the grief he felt for the man's predecessor (so successfully no doubt that the new man on the throne had no inkling of Dio's ambivalence). But we can see this reinvention in action more vividly, and some of the compromises, half-truths and desperate readjustments it involved even more clearly, if we return once more to the *Panegyricus*. Delivered against a background of two recent regime changes, it tells us almost as much about the transfer of power from one emperor to another as it is does about Pliny's views of the ideal ruler.

The emperor Domitian, the last of the Flavian dynasty, had been killed in 96 CE, just four years before Pliny delivered his vote of thanks, in a plot involving palace staff and the emperor's own wife, with probably a few senators on the sidelines too. It was not a universally popular assassination; *no* assassinations are universally popular at the time. One apocryphal story tells how a travelling philosopher, realising that some soldiers were about to mutiny in protest at the killing, jumped naked onto a convenient altar and denounced Domitian, and so prevented the uprising. Apocryphal maybe, but it is just one hint among several that there were conflicting reactions to the coup, while also revealing a more colourful side to Roman oratory than we often imagine. (Were the troops swayed by his arguments or distracted by his performance?) Domitian's successor, the elderly and childless Nerva, was quickly ratified by the senate, though his reign of just fifteen months might be seen as little more than an interregnum. By the time of his death, Nerva had survived at least one attempt to oust him, and had been leaned on (it is not quite clear by whom) to adopt Trajan, a successful senator and soldier, as his heir. It was only a couple of years into the new reign, and four years after the assassination of Domitian, that Trajan became the main focus of Pliny's *Speech of Praise*.

But here he shared the limelight with Domitian, who is almost as much the memorable *anti*-hero of the speech as Trajan is the hero (figs. 7 & 8). Pliny's Domitian was an arrogant tyrant, a cruel cheat, a thief and a murderer, laying his greedy hands on 'every pool, lake or meadow' in other men's estates and positively revelling in the elimination of the most distinguished characters in Rome. No senator, or their property, was safe. They all lived in terror of the invitation to dinner in the monster's lair, of the charges trumped up by his secret police, and finally of the ominous knock on the door. It is obvious enough that the *Panegyricus* was part of the process of readjustment I have been describing. Whatever praise of Domitian circulated during his lifetime (and some admiring poetry does still survive, often now hastily dismissed as 'empty flattery'), Pliny's condemnation was intended to obscure anything of the sort, and to create the new orthodoxy in which the tyrant Domitian was deemed rightly killed – and, more to the point, Nerva and Trajan were deemed a rightful and legitimate new deal.

But what of Pliny's own relations with Domitian? It would be easy to get the impression, from a quick reading of his speech, that he himself had been a victim of the tyrant, a paid-up member of the 'opposition'. It is certainly an impression that comes from some of his highly crafted, and no doubt much-edited, 'private' letters, which he collected and put into public circulation, and which have come down to us by that usual process of copying and recopying. It is one of these that contains his famous description of the eruption of Vesuvius in 79 CE, and of the death of his uncle, who got too close to the volcanic action. Others are more overtly political. They refer to how his 'friends' had been put to death or exiled under Domitian, and – looking back from the safety of the new regime – they claim that there had been 'reason to suspect that the same fate hung over me'. One even goes so far as to state that a document was found on Domitian's desk after his death with charges against Pliny that would have led to a trial for treason. We are meant to suppose that he had escaped by the skin of his teeth.

Not a bit of it. An unusual amount of evidence survives for Pliny's

15. A gold coin of the emperor Nerva. His head is surrounded by his formal titles IMP(ERATOR) NERVA CAES(AR) AUG(USTUS) etc. On the other side is the goddess of 'public liberty' – no doubt intended as a symbol of Nerva's new deal after the reign of Domitian.

career, both from his own writing and from the lucky find of his full CV, originally displayed in his home town of Comum (Como) in north Italy, but – in one of those complicated stories – reused to make a tomb in Milan in the Middle Ages. Never mind his claim to dissident credentials. From these sources it is absolutely clear that he did very well indeed under Domitian, climbing up the political ladder and holding major offices in the emperor's gift. In the closing section of the *Panegyricus*, he himself admits as much, though he wriggles out of his embarrassment by suggesting that his career was put on hold during the very worst part of Domitian's reign, in its final years. It is as if part of the purpose of this speech, and its later written version, was to reposition Pliny himself in the light of his own collaboration with the assassinated emperor, to reinvent himself in the post-Domitian world.

Scholars have debated endlessly how harshly Pliny should be judged for this. How hypocritical was he? How economical with the truth? Can we support his claim that he had no involvement with some of the worst aspects of the reign, even if we have to re-date slightly some of the offices he held? Was Pliny a cynical collaborator who later tried to cover his tracks, or a man doing his best in a suboptimal (but no worse) regime? He has recently found both passionate detractors (he 'would have made a career under any ... despotic regime'), and more sympathetic appraisers of the tightrope he trod. But the bigger point is that Pliny was not on his own. This was not merely a personal predicament.

The historian Tacitus was also promoted by Domitian during his reign, and later performed the same volte-face, becoming a fierce critic of the emperor once he had been overthrown and almost giving the impression that he had always been one of the opposition. The senators who were Pliny's original audience must have faced the same dilemma too. For the great majority of them had not been in any particular danger under Domitian, nor been the victims of any treason trials that the emperor may have used to attack his enemies ('traitors', as he would have put it). They had actually been the judge and jury, complicit in the whole procedure, however reluctant they would no doubt later claim that their participation was. If they knew that Pliny was being economical with the truth, they were not likely to call him out – because so were they. There are some similarities here with the tricky political choreography of mid-twentieth-century Europe, where some one-time Nazi collaborators managed to concoct (and shelter behind) an undercover career in the resistance. In Rome, everyone in the political hierarchy was busy realigning, cooking up excuses, adjusting to the changed circumstances, until normality was restored, with more or less the same cast of characters albeit under a new emperor. From the very beginning of the empire, the problematic business of imperial succession had often been followed by the awkward business of realignment.

Dinner with Nerva

Exactly that point is brought out in some clever repartee at a small dinner party hosted by the emperor Nerva in 97 CE, described in a letter by Pliny himself, who must have been one of the guests (though he does not explicitly say so). The conversation, he explains, turned to a Roman senator, Catullus Messalinus, who had recently died. Messalinus had been blind, extremely successful (he had held the office of consul twice) and was notorious as one of Domitian's 'enforcers'. The Latin word for that, *delator*, is a slippery term, a shorthand covering anything from unofficial 'secret police' or 'informer' (with all the modern connotations of terror) to a private prosecutor, ready to do the emperor's dirty work for cash.

At a certain point Nerva asked the diners, who were deep in gossip about Messalinus's bloodstained record, 'What do we think would have happened to him if he were still alive?' To which one of the assembled company, Junius Mauricus, who had been exiled under Domitian, quipped, 'He'd be dining with us'. Pliny praises Mauricus's reply for its bravery, particularly as there was at least one man with the same kind of reputation as Messalinus among the dinner guests. But the emperor's question has usually been dismissed by most modern critics as hopelessly naive.

I suspect not. It is easy enough now to think of Nerva as a lame-duck ruler, who lasted for little more than a year on the throne and was more manipulated than manipulating. But Nerva was actually one of the first century's great survivors. He himself had been a useful informer to the emperor Nero in the face of the attempted coup in 65 CE (in which Seneca had been implicated); he had family connections with Otho, one of the short-lived emperors of 69; and he had been consul twice, under Vespasian and Domitian. He knew exactly what the answer to his question was. And the guests knew that the answer applied to them all. Mauricus was not being brave. He was smartly summing up a central truth about Roman regime change, and how to survive it – and he was doing that to a group who *had* successfully survived, including the emperor himself.

And he was doing it at dinner, which is the one place where we can see the emperor in more vivid detail than anywhere else, where the tensions of imperial rule were most starkly on display, and where we can still almost savour the pros and cons of imperial generosity. So it is in the dining room – not in the senate house or on the battlefield – where we will now take our first close-up look at the emperor in action.

3

POWER DINING

A black dinner

A few years before Pliny's cosy supper with the emperor Nerva, his predecessor Domitian, in the late 80s CE, had hosted a dinner for a selection of prominent Romans, described in detail by the historian Cassius Dio. Domitian is one of the emperors whose habits at table ancient writers tell us most about, from various angles. Dio conjures up a picture of him that is very different from the surly 'belcher' of Pliny's account, tossing around the food he did not fancy. But it is more chilling.

The story was that when the guests arrived they found the emperor's dining room completely redecorated in black. Even the dining couches on which they reclined were painted black, as were the naked male slaves who attended them, and their places were marked out by imitation tombstones, with each of their names carefully inscribed. The food served, according to Dio, was the kind usually given as an offering to the dead, presented in black dishes, while the emperor himself talked only about death. At the end of the evening the guests were allowed to return to their own homes. But when, shortly after, there was a knock on the door, each assumed that his last hour had come. Nothing of the sort. Waiting outside was a posse of porters sent by Domitian, one bringing each man's imitation tombstone (which was made of silver), others the precious dishes that had been set on the tables. And, as a final gift, in came the slave who had served them, the black paint washed off and now beautifully dressed.

Where Dio, who was writing a couple of centuries after the event, got this story from, or how far it is imaginative fantasy, we do not know. But it is richly revealing. A modern audience is likely to be struck by the casual commodification of the slaves. There can hardly be a better sign of the dehumanisation of these 'boys' than the fact that they can be wrapped up, as it were, and sent off as a present from one owner to another. It was an act of post-prandial 'generosity' said to have been tried a few decades later by Lucius Verus, Marcus Aurelius's co-ruler, when the 'gorgeous boys' who did the serving were given away to the diners, along with the precious plates, goblets and glasses, and some (live) specimens of the exotic (dead) animals that they had eaten. But for Dio, the story is all about the humiliation of the guests and an object lesson in how terror did not necessarily depend on literal bloodshed, but could even be dressed up as generosity. How frightening was it to dine at the palace? Just how badly *could* an emperor behave at dinner?

There is no culture in the history of the world where communal dining – especially, but not only, when hosted by kings, aristocrats and other bigwigs – has not played a part in the conflicts of power, or has not put under the spotlight all kinds of anxieties, social, political and hierarchical. There is always a clash between the notional equality implied by the simple fact of eating *together*, and the inequality acted out by the pre-eminence of the host and the subtle, or not so subtle, distinctions of the menu and the seating plan. The person put at the very bottom of the table rarely feels the equal of those at the top. Elagabalus was not the first Roman said to have served inferior, or inedible, fare to his less important guests (and – let's be honest – as a professor, when I have dinner at my own Cambridge college, I sit at the 'high table' and am given better food and wine than the students 'below').

Being a host has its risks too. Prestige can be lost as well as won. Roman emperors were neither the first nor last to discover that hostile observers might interpret their splendid generosity as vulgar overspend, or their simple suppers as a sign of stingy meanness. The excesses of imperial dining were a predictable ancient cliché: whole fortunes blown on a single party; napkins woven with gold thread (reputedly an innovation of Hadrian); or dinner plates so pricey that the next man on the throne auctioned them off to pay for military campaigning, to demonstrate, in the process, his own commitment to business over pleasure. But Tiberius looked like a penny-pincher, as well as prudent, when he served up leftovers at the next day's feast, and had *half* a boar cooked, rather than a whole one, to minimise waste.

I have already returned several times to emperors at table, because that is the context in which they were so often imagined by Roman writers, and so often judged. Their qualities, good and bad, were assessed as much in the dining room as in the senate house. And their behaviour – as host, companion, gourmet and party animal – was interpreted and reinterpreted as proof of their virtue or depravity. Whatever the truth behind Domitian's black dinner, it takes only a little reflection to see how differently the story *could* have been spun: whether as the tale of a stylish and witty fancy-dress party, or as an exercise in the practical philosophy of facing mortality. In fact, Nero's tutor (and ultimately victim) Seneca, in one of his mini philosophical essays, stressed the importance of rehearsing for death, and referred to one Roman senator who every day had turned his dinner into a theatrical performance of his own future funeral, complete with eunuchs singing 'He has lived. He has lived'. Even Seneca thought this was going a bit far. But if that was Domitian's point, then it has got completely lost.

Imperial dining is a particularly revealing lens onto the world of the emperor, and onto some of the biggest themes of this book, from sadism to generosity, luxury to terror. The imperial dining room was a site of danger as well as pleasure for the emperor and his fellow diners (poisoning has an uncannily close relationship to cookery). It was also a place where the social order of Rome was both on display and uncomfortably subverted. We find a range of vivid, intriguing and important detail buried in sometimes funny, sometimes disturbing ancient anecdotes: from the guest who couldn't resist filching some of the tableware to the unfortunate slave who broke a precious crystal goblet and nearly ended up thrown into a pond of man-eating eels. Many of these stories are probably no closer to the literal truth than the modern myths of royal or celebrity dining that are the stuff of tabloids and magazines. Suspiciously similar tales are told about different emperors, harping on the same underlying issues and conflicts. That is why they offer some of the best evidence we have for how 'the emperor' (rather than any individual) was *imagined*, at dinner or elsewhere.

But what makes the dinner party an even better place for a dive into the life, and lifestyle, of Roman rulers is that we can go beyond ideology and imagination to see the emperor as he really lived. It is possible still to visit some of the lavish entertainment suites where he played the host, and to match up the archaeological remains and a few eyewitness descriptions with the rulers who partied there. In some places we can confidently say 'Nero' – or Domitian, or Hadrian – 'ate here', or even 'the empress Livia ate here'. The brilliantly naturalistic paintings of plants and wildlife often referred to simply as 'Livia's Garden Room' were part of the decoration of a dining room at one of the suburban villas of Augustus's wife (pl. 4). But more than that, we can occasionally see past the emperor, his family and his upper-crust guests, to some of those who made all this hospitality possible: the imperial cooks and food tasters who recorded their occupations on their tombstones, as well as a whole host of dinnertime entertainers. This is an opportunity to put the emperor back into his habitat and to ask about the other people in the palace whose work underpinned his regime. The emperor's world starts in the dining room.

Where Romans ate

Almost every film that is set in ancient Rome includes a familiar scene of a banquet: men and women together (mixed dining distinguished Rome from many other ancient cultures, and some modern ones too), reclining rather uncomfortably on long couches, propped up on their elbows, being served food and drink – usually grapes, with the occasional roast dormouse – by slaves. For once, Hollywood is not entirely wrong, at least for the rich (the poor were much more likely to take their food sitting at a table in a bar, and would have reclined to eat no more often than most of us now enjoy a full-blown silver-service banquet). The best-preserved ancient versions of this arrangement are found in the city of Pompeii, buried in the eruption of Vesuvius

16. A garden dining room in the 'House of the Ephebe' in Pompeii.
The masonry couches (presumably softened by cushions when
in use) are arranged in front of a fountain on the back wall. A
pergola, originally covered with plants, provided shade.

in 79 CE. Some of the interior decoration there features paintings of joyous and drunken dining, Roman-style (pl. 11), and in many larger houses the distinctive dining rooms still remain. Some were built for warm weather, in the open air at the edge of gardens, featuring three fixed masonry couches arranged in a U shape, with space for three people to recline on each, and in the most lavish set-ups surrounded by pools and fountains. The Roman elite, as we shall discover, liked nothing better than a good dinner to the accompaniment of the sight and sound of lapping or falling water. Others were inside the house, equipped with portable wooden couches, or *klinai*, whose standard position, again in a U shape, might be marked on the mosaic floor (it's those markings that can now help us to identify the main purpose of an otherwise anonymous room). All these dining spaces were commonly called *triclinia*, which means literally 'three couches'.

The super-rich in Rome itself and elsewhere outdid the local aristocracy of Pompeii in the scale, grandeur and ingenuity of their dining arrangements, while following the same basic scheme. Multiple *triclinia*, or multiple sets of couches in the same room, ensured that the host could give dinner to more than just eight other people, and there were many different levels of luxury in what was provided. One grandee, who was a contemporary of Julius Caesar, is said to have had a series of graded dining rooms, each with its own name (the one we know about was called 'Apollo', the others perhaps, equally, pretentiously, called after other deities). He had to tell his staff only in which room he would eat, and they would instantly know the quality of, and the budget for, the food to be provided. A century or so later Pliny, describing in a letter the layout of one of his out-of-town properties, shows how extravagantly water features could enhance the dining experience, if you had the money – and, some might now say, a taste for pointless display. In part of his grounds he had a summer dining area, shaded by a trellis of vines, under which was a slightly different layout of couches: a semi-circle, rather than a U shape, facing onto a series of fountains and directly overlooking a pool that was fed from water spouting from underneath the couches themselves – 'as if,' Pliny explains, 'it was forced out by the weight of those reclining on top'. It was from this pool that the diners helped themselves to some of the tasty delicacies, which were launched by slaves on the far side onto little plates in the shape of boats and birds and then floated across to the guests. Presumably someone had a way of rescuing any plates that ended up becalmed and out of reach, though Pliny does not seem concerned with such practicalities.

Dinners at the palace

Emperors outdid even the super-rich. Roman palaces were built for dining, with not just one but multiple entertainment suites, including some weird and wonderful places to eat, which went far beyond the rather squashed couches and conventional settings of the movie versions. Archaeologists have never managed conclusively to identify any traces of Nero's famous dining room, which, according to Suetonius, added the wonders of engineering to simple luxury by 'continually rotating like the earth day and night'. (Not for want of trying: the most recent attempt to identify its remains, and reconstruct its working, has focused on what is left of a tower-like structure that may, or may not, have incorporated a rotating dining room on the upper floor, and a hydraulic mechanism underneath.) But they *have* been able to identify – and it is still possible to access – one place among the imperial properties on the Palatine Hill in Rome where Nero certainly entertained his guests to dinner. Although it is now little more than industrial brick and concrete, enough traces of decoration survive, or were recorded by its first excavators, for us to reconstruct in some detail the luxury that surrounded the emperor and his friends as they lay on their couches, from fountains and marble floors to painted ceilings.

It is a room preserved by chance in the foundations of later palace structures built above it, and dated archaeologically with little doubt to the first part of Nero's reign, before the great fire of Rome in 64 CE, and the even more dramatic building schemes that followed it, notably the 'Golden House' (pp. 138–44). After its rediscovery in the early eighteenth century, it was often known romantically, but wrongly, as the 'Baths of Livia', after Augustus's wife, because of all the water piping it contained. But it was built half a century later than the heyday of that empress, and the water was, as in Pliny's villa, nothing to do with bathing at all but was the setting for dining. For this was a *triclinium* located in a sunken courtyard, open to the sky but pleasantly out of the sun.

17. People explore the now slightly gloomy underworld of Nero's dining-suite, on the day it was re-opened to the public in 2019. This shows what remains of the elaborate 'stage' onto which the main diners looked from their pavilion. A small section of the marble façade, on top of the brick, has been reconstructed at one end, giving some idea of the original appearance. Water would have poured (or trickled) down from the opening in the wall above. The start of one set of steps leading up to ground level is just visible in front of the visitor.

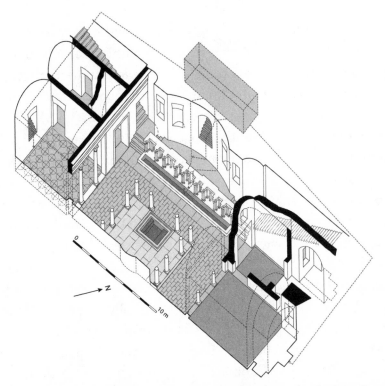

18. A cutaway reconstruction of Nero's *triclinium* (fig. 17). The 'stage' at the centre is fed with water from the tank above. Some of the water is then channelled into the main dining pavilion, surrounded by columns, where three couches would have been arranged around the small pool. Subsidiary rooms on either side, richly decorated and also fed with water, accommodated other diners. There were two access stairways, one at each end.

You entered down one of two staircases, which led to a pavilion supported on purple porphyry columns, where the main dining couches were placed. These looked onto an elaborate façade of multicoloured marble, made to imitate the back wall of a theatre, incorporating a narrow 'stage' on which poetry, music, stand-up or even philosophical disputations could have been performed. The permanent centre of attention, though, was a tumbling cascade of water above the stage, intricately constructed so that the overflow ended up in a basin at ground level, and some of it was then channelled into a further pool that lapped between the diners under the pavilion. On either side of the central dining space were other rooms, with their own mini waterfalls, where more couches could have been placed for larger dinner parties. The whole area was some 30 metres from end to end, but not much more than 10 metres wide.

Its decoration was top-of-the-range, though so little remains on the site now that, when it is open to modern visitors, they are given virtual-reality headsets to help recapture the atmosphere. The paintings from one of the sets of side rooms were removed in the early eighteenth century, and by a circuitous route ended up in the National Archaeological Museum in Naples, while some of the marble facing discovered at the same time was taken by the Duke of Beaufort to his country house, Badminton, in central England, but it was never used for the 'Marble Room' he had planned there. (Ironically, some of the stone from Nero's dining room might, years afterwards, have been used to decorate Badminton's chapel.) Much of what was found in later excavations has been stripped from its setting and deposited in the nearby museum. But, if you imagine, it must have been a dazzling display, the gilded capitals on the columns, twinkly glass 'gems' set into the ceiling, exquisite decorative marble floors and precious wall inlays (including a charming frieze of multi-coloured, miniature dancing marble figures – hinting perhaps at another party activity of the revellers). The painted panels, showing scenes from Greek mythology, and the intricate ceiling decorations became favourite models for European artists in the eighteenth century (pl. 18). The idea that the stories depicted were, as some archaeologists have argued, carefully coded references to the history of Nero's court, may be pushing things too far. But it is clear enough that some scenes – such as Hercules installing Priam as the king of Troy – could be understood as a mythical analogy for Roman imperial power and succession.

We can only guess what combination of apprehension, privilege, wonderment and anxiety Nero's guests might have felt as they walked down the stairs to dinner in this precious grotto, or what they would have made of the decoration on the walls. No eyewitness account, no ancient description survives. But not far away are the now less impressive remains of what was once an even more lavish imperial dining suite, for which we do have a contemporary response. This is a poem, almost seventy lines long, written towards the end of the first century CE, by Publius Papinius Statius – the leading poet of the day, well connected in court circles, and the 'modern' equivalent, so he himself boasted, of the Greek Homer centuries earlier, and of the Roman Virgil, who a hundred years before had been sponsored by the emperor Augustus. Statius had been invited to dinner with Domitian, and his poem describes that occasion, which took place in the grandest wing of the new palace that had, by then, been built on top of the earlier Neronian levels. It was the first time, he claims, that he had ever been a guest at a palace party and he revels in it.

This was no intimate soirée among friends, but a huge gathering of leading Romans, the equivalent of a state banquet. Statius may well have been exaggerating when he wrote that a thousand tables were set out, but it gives some idea of the imperial scale. The location must have been one or more of the vast display rooms whose traces can still be made out on the Palatine Hill (p. 148, nos. 10, 11, 12, 14). Here very little of the decoration has survived, not even hacked off and removed. The rooms are now reduced largely to the outline of their ground plan, a few sections of pavement, and the bare brick core of some of the walls. One of them (no. 14), roughly 30 metres square, flanked by the inevitable fountains, and (according to a recent reconstruction) originally standing more than 30 metres tall, matches a design for large-scale dining rooms given in a Roman architectural handbook. The others could easily have had multiple sets of couches installed, even if they probably had other functions when not in use for banqueting.

Statius's verses help us to picture these rooms as they once were, full of diners. The poem is a highly crafted mixture of awe, flattery and self-promotion, with occasional flashes of irony. Some of the praise of the host and the surroundings may sound, to a modern ear at least, awkwardly contrived or horribly insincere even for court poetry: 'I feel I am reclining with Jupiter among the stars/ ... The barren years of my life have passed./ This is the first day of what I was born for, here is the threshold of my life./ Is it you, ruler of the earth, and of the subject world/ mighty parent, .../ on whom I feast my eyes from my couch?' All the same, Statius does give us a sense of the occasion. The emperor was the centre of attention: neither Pliny's 'belcher' nor Dio's sadistic fancy-dress host, but an almost divine presence, presiding in isolation, in front of the assembled diners and under their admiring gaze.

The overwhelming vastness of the surroundings and the lustre of the walls provided a fitting backdrop to the event. What is now

19. This unglamourous lump of brickwork was once part of the water features of the vast dining room in Domitian's palace. It would originally have been faced in marble and delighted the diners with the sound of running water. It is shown on the bottom right of the reconstruction, fig. 20.

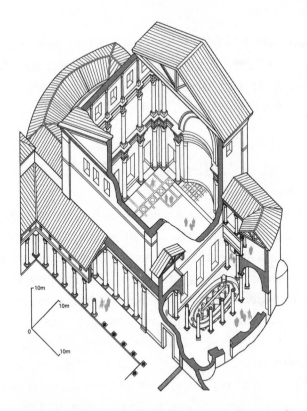

20. A cutaway reconstruction of the most imposing room for dining (and, no doubt, for other things) in the Flavian palace, trying to envisage the upper levels and roof, which no longer survive (p. 148, no. 14).

disappointingly dull brick was originally clad in marble of different colours, black and pink, blue and watery green, from all over the Roman world, a virtual map of empire. 'There,' Statius writes, pointing to two of the varieties, 'the mountains of Libya and of Troy sparkle in rivalry' – hinting also, in one of those flashes of irony that save the poem from complete sycophancy, that the competition here extended beyond the marble decoration. Statius and his fellow guests too were 'sparkling in rivalry', all looking their best, out to impress, and trying to attract the notice of the emperor among the crowd.

Maybe that is exactly what the poet managed to do, for some modern critics have guessed (and it is little more than a guess) that parts of this poem had been prepared in advance, and that Statius got up and recited it to the 'mighty parent of the subject world' at the end of the evening: an exercise in self-advertisement combined with an over-the-top thank-you letter.

Eating otherwise?

Grand as it was, the palace in Rome was only one relatively small part of imperial hospitality. Throughout Italy and beyond, in city and countryside, we can still identify the remains of dozens of dining rooms where the emperor once played host. Occasionally these were in the ancient equivalents of royal yachts, like the two luxury pleasure barges that Caligula built on Lake Nemi, a beauty spot some 25 miles outside Rome, which were floating restaurants, complete with sleeping accommodation, party and dining areas, mosaic floors and on-board bathing facilities (pl. 6). But no regular out-of-town imperial residence on dry land was complete without its lavish, often multiple, entertainment suites. In Hadrian's sprawling private town at Tivoli, these were constructed in all kinds of ingenious architectural settings, from an artificial island in the middle of a lake to a 'stadium garden' designed on the model of a racing track. Most famous of all, and now the most photographed spot on the whole site, was the so-called 'Canopus' – a long pool of water surrounded by choice pieces of sculpture, designed to evoke (so a passing reference in Hadrian's biography in the *Imperial History* has been taken to suggest) the famous Canopus Canal on the Nile Delta in Egypt (p. 162 and 163, no. 9). At one end of the 'Canal', shaded by some grandiose architecture, the emperor and his friends reclined on a complicated arrangement of couches on different levels, alongside yet more cascades of water. Diners received some of their food in the way Pliny described, floated across to them on little boats. At the sides there were three convenient toilets, with running water, ostentatiously decorated in marble and mosaic, so no one had to go far to relieve themselves.

Sometimes the emperor looked beyond his own property and simply commandeered other places to host his parties. Not even trees were safe from his grasp, if we believe the story that Caligula hosted a dinner party for fifteen, plus waiters, in the branches of a plane tree, which he called his 'nest'. Certainly, show-piece buildings in the city could be temporarily repurposed for imperial dinners, and that included the Colosseum. Visitors to the monument now imagine it packed with a baying crowd, screaming over the massacre of the poor human and animal victims in the arena. So it may sometimes have been (though not necessarily with that much 'baying', as we shall see in chapter 7). But, on one occasion at least, it was used by the emperor

21. The most striking dining room on Hadrian's estate at Tivoli, perhaps inspired by one of the landmarks of ancient Egypt, the Canopus canal. Here we look across a pool of water, surrounded by sculpture, into the shaded area where the emperor and his guests would have dined. See also fig. 40.

to host a dinner for thousands of grateful citizens: imperial banqueting hall rather than killing fields.

The occasion in question was another party hosted by Domitian, following a long tradition, going back to the Republic, of big men demonstrating their generosity by giving mass dinners to the people. Julius Caesar, for example, is said (slightly implausibly) to have given a public feast, somewhere in Rome, consisting of 22,000 *triclinia*, which – assuming nine people at each of these sets of three couches – would amount to 198,000 diners. Domitian's was on a more modest scale, 50,000 places being a reasonable estimate of the Colosseum's capacity. But the idea was that, however they were chosen, Romans of all ranks, from lofty senator to the man in the street, came to the amphitheatre to enjoy a meal, served in their seats (rather than on couches), and paid for by the emperor, who presided over the proceedings. The food was accompanied by shows on the arena floor: not gladiators or wild beasts, but – maybe almost as unpleasant to modern eyes – staged battles between rival teams of women and dwarfs, and sometimes risqué performances by musicians and entertainers. When darkness fell (this was happening in December), the whole place was lit by torches: night turned back into day.

The one description of the event comes from another poem by Statius, who implies that he was there. He marvels at the logistics of it all and at the seamless organisation: 'Look, through all the sections of seating/ comes another crowd [of waiters], splendid to look at and smartly turned out, /as many of them as there are seated guests. / Some bring baskets of bread and white napkins and elegant edibles. / Others offer generous portions of intoxicating wine.' And he captures some of the more spectacular stunts. The starters – of nuts, pastries, fruit and dates – literally rained down on the guests in their seats from nets and ropes stretched high above their heads (a banqueting trick, captured on a more modest scale in paintings at Pompeii, pl. 7). Not that Statius's wonderment prevented him from making a few wry jokes about it all. The shower of goodies at the very beginning was impressive, he insists, but it had its dangers too. For some of the falling fruit was unripe, and it made an uncomfortable hit if it caught you as it came down (a real 'bash', he says – *contudit*, in Latin). There are similarities here with the later stories of the dinnertime showers launched by Elagabalus, though also a happier outcome. Gently falling from the ceiling, Elagabalus's rose petals smothered his guests to death. Domitian's hard apples and pears just left some nasty bumps and bruises. But it was still a case of imperial generosity, from on high, rebounding.

On the menu?

Even in Statius's fulsome account, it seems fairly clear that the food offered in the Colosseum was not much more than an upmarket picnic, nibbles plus wine, with the clever stunts perhaps making up for the lack of quantity. It is hard to see how it could have been more than that when the guests numbered in tens of thousands. On other occasions what was served on the imperial table must have ranged from Trajan's simple suppers to more extravagant 'display food'. The stories we read of the most lavish dishes on the menu reflect the ideas of complicated haute cuisine the world over. They involved ingredients that were expensive and difficult to source, and they were often combined in a way that made them look like something they were not ('the swan made entirely out of icing sugar' trick, to give a modern equivalent). That was the case with many of the reported delicacies favoured by Elagabalus and other bons viveurs on the throne. The signature dish of the emperor Vitellius, for example, was known as the 'Shield of Minerva' on account of the enormous platter it occupied, and it supposedly combined pike livers, pheasant and peacock brains, flamingo tongues and lamprey innards, specially imported by warship from Parthia in the east and from Spain in the west. Openly fictional versions of such concoctions are among the highlights of a lavish dinner, hosted by Trimalchio, a colossally rich ex-slave, which features in the *Satyricon*, a first-century CE Roman novel written by Petronius, a one-time friend and later victim of the emperor Nero. Among the delicacies is a dish that looks like an elaborate melange of fish, goose and other kinds of birds. The joke is that it is actually made entirely out of pork.

Much of this was more fantasy than reality, reflecting no doubt the occasional blow-out, but wildly exaggerated by the typical dreams of outsiders about what was consumed inside the emperor's apartments. There are good reasons for supposing that for most of the time cooking in the royal kitchens was more down-to-earth. Leaving aside the spectacular tricks that the fictional cooks pulled off in the *Satyricon*, it is hard to see how dishes of anything like this intricacy could regularly have been prepared in the Roman palace. There were no kitchens on the scale of the huge catering suites of, for example, the Topkapı palace in Istanbul. To be fair, kitchens can be elusive in the houses of the elite in any part of the premodern world. The smell, noise and smoke sometimes ensured that they were located at a considerable distance from the main dining rooms, even if that meant decidedly tepid food on the dining table. And more cooking and preparation could have been done out of doors, barbecue-style, than we might imagine (Petronius's vignette of one of Trimalchio's slaves shelling peas while sitting on a doorstep points in this direction). It is puzzling nonetheless that no substantial cooking facilities have yet been identified on the Palatine. Even those discovered in some of the out-of-town imperial residences hardly match up to the supposedly elaborate dishes. All the kitchens firmly identified at Hadrian's villa at Tivoli, with its vast entertainment areas, are pokey little things. And although several ovens all in a row in Tiberius's villa on the island of Capri do suggest cooking for large numbers, there is no likely place nearby, no convenient surfaces, for all the pounding, the stuffing, the chopping, the mixing, the rolling out and the flavouring that any complicated dishes would have required.

The way the food was consumed only adds to my scepticism about some of the complex concoctions. What kind of meals could diners easily eat, with just one hand, while half-lying down, and without the benefit of a modern fork – even with practice? My guess is that, somehow, large and elaborate dishes were prepared every now and then, and brought in with great ceremony to impress the diners. That is the scene suggested by Vitellius's 'Shield of Minerva', if it is not wholly fantasy. But, after that grand entrance, almost everything must have been cut up into bite-size chunks before it was served to the guests, or floated across to them on those little platters. If so, the style of the imperial Roman banquet was more tapas than meat and two veg.

Below stairs

However lavish these dinners really were, we can get a surprisingly clear picture of some of the men and women who made them possible: not the guests who walked down the stairs into Nero's entertainment suite, with all their anticipation or anxieties, but those who struggled down those same steps, loaded with trays of drink and delicacies to serve to the assembled company and struggled back up again afterwards with the dirty dishes. To say that elite Roman dining, whether hosted by the emperor, or by men like Pliny, was based on the exploitation of hundreds, if not thousands, of slaves, who far outnumbered those who reclined on the couches, is obviously true. As we shall see, almost every aspect of the working of the Roman palace depended on slave labour, and on the labour of ex-slaves, all those men and women who had been given, or bought, their freedom but remained 'on the staff'. But we can go further than that, and can fill out something of the organisation behind the emperor's meals, the different jobs involved, and even a few details of the life stories of some of these enslaved people themselves. This is partly thanks to the occasional glance in their direction by the likes of Statius, who kept half an eye on the 'smartly turned-out' waiters in the Colosseum, and the 'squadrons of slaves' in the palace dining room. It is even more thanks to the small nuggets of information that they, or their families, chose to record on their tombstones, which almost allow us to hear a snatch of their own voices.

The overwhelming impression that comes from these commemorations is one of a hierarchical and micro-specialised world of palace catering, and a crowd of servants who were often unseen (either because they remained literally below stairs or because they were present but socially 'unnoticed'). Memorials survive to cooks, catering managers, butlers, waiters and sommeliers within the emperor's household, and also to master bakers of particular kinds of bread, food tasters, and the people in charge of the invitations or of the table napkins (a reminder, perhaps, that enjoyment of Roman-style dining depended on being able to wipe your face and hands). We even find the commemoration of peculiarly esoteric after-dinner performers, quite different from the musicians, poets or star philosophers often associated with upmarket Roman dining. Plenty of 'jokers' (practical and otherwise) are referred to by Roman writers as part of the amusements, including some pranksters known by the name of *copreae*, which means, literally, 'little shits'. Most curious of all is a man, known only from his commemorative plaque in a communal grave, who was an imperial slave (his name is now missing) and one of 'the emperor's players'. As the text goes on to say, his claim to fame was that he was a 'mimic' in the household of the emperor Tiberius, 'who first discovered how to imitate barristers'. It is hard to avoid the conclusion that Tiberius's dinner parties (where else would these performances have taken place?) were enlivened by an enslaved man raising a laugh with his imitations of free, posh lawyers.

This kind of specialised infrastructure, with its minutely defined responsibilities – going right down to the keepers of the linen or the niche comedians – was in part a boast of the emperor's power, and was mirrored on a smaller scale in other rich Roman households, both real-life and fictional. In the *Satyricon*, for example, Trimalchio comically divides his own slaves into ranked 'divisions', and threatens one with demotion from the 'cook division' to the 'messenger division'. But the tombstones also bring some of these often-forgotten characters into our spotlight for a moment; and they suggest that some slaves and ex-slaves in the imperial household, whatever their justified anger at their own exploitation, found an identity in this hierarchy of labour.

Titus Aelius Primitivus, an ex-slave in the imperial court in the mid second century CE, seems to have been one of those. The elegantly inscribed memorial that he and his wife Tyche (another ex-slave of the

22. The memorial of T(itus) Aelius Primitivus, described as 'archimagirus' or 'chef de cuisine', and of his wife Aelia Tyche. The phrase 'Aug(usti) Libertus' in the first line indicates that he was an 'ex-slave of the emperor'. The second part of the text is concerned with violations of the tomb, referring to the role of the 'college of cooks' ('collegium cocorum', clearly visible on the right-hand side).

DIS·MANIBVS
TI·CLAVDI·AVG·LIB
ZOSIMI·PROCVR·AT
PRAEGVSTATORVM
CLAVDIA·ENTOLE·CONIVNX
VIRO·BENE·MERENTI·
ET·CLAVDIA·EVSTACHYS·FILIA
PATRI·PIENTISSIMO

23. This substantial epitaph was put up in Rome to commemorate the
ex-slave Ti(berius) Claudius Zosimus, who had died in Germany with
Domitian. His place in the hierarchy is spelled out in lines 3–4, 'procurat(ori)
praegustatorum', 'manager of the tasters'. His wife and daughter, who
commissioned the memorial, are named in the last four lines.

emperor) commissioned for themselves does not describe him as a
plain 'cook', a *cocus* in Latin. It celebrates him instead as an *archimagiros*,
a rare Greek word for 'head chef', with all the culinary glamour of borrowed French terms in the English language: the equivalent of *chef de
cuisine*. Tiberius Claudius Zosimus was another, an ex-slave whose job
was defined as taster (*praegustator*) of the emperor's food, to check it
in advance for poison rather than quality. He had commemorations in
two places. One was in Germany, where he died accompanying Domitian on a military campaign. Wary emperors went nowhere without
this first line of defence against assassination (though Zosimus, so far
as we know, didn't die from poisoning). The other was put up to him
in Rome, as a 'well-deserving husband' and 'loving father' by his wife
and daughter, Entole and Eustachys. Both texts stress that he was not
just an ordinary 'taster'. That was the job of lower-ranking slaves such

as Coetus Herodianus, described on his memorial merely as a 'taster of Augustus' (and whose second name suggests that he was another of those 'human presents', this time from Herod the Great, of biblical fame, to the Roman emperor). Zosimus was a cut above that: his memorials insist that he was the '*manager* of the tasters'.

These commemorations also lift the lid a little on the community of the workers in the imperial dining rooms and kitchens. Some of the texts refer, for example, to a *collegium* (something between a staff organisation and social club) of cooks or to a *collegium* of tasters. A few even hint that they had some form of financial holdings. The regulations spelled out on the memorial of Primitivus suggest that violation was punished by a fine, to be paid to the *collegium* of Palatine cooks. But, beyond that, it is hard to get much sense of the atmosphere of daily life below stairs in the palace kitchens. The most colourful glimpse is found in Plutarch's second-century CE biography of Mark Antony, the rival of Octavian, eventually defeated by him at the Battle of Actium in 31 BCE. It is a story not set in Rome at all but in the palace that Antony shared with Cleopatra in the Egyptian city of Alexandria – where the cooking facilities were, it seems, anything but pokey.

Plutarch explains that his information comes from his own grandfather who had a friend who had once actually visited the palace kitchens. There he had seen no fewer than eight wild boar roasting on spits. 'Why so many?' he had asked. Was there really such a large number for dinner? 'No,' one of the cooks explained, 'just twelve.' But, as it was impossible to know exactly when they would want to eat, the cooks started roasting each boar at different times, so that one would be bound to be perfectly done whenever the meal began. It is a story that may be meant to celebrate the hyper-professionalism of the catering operation, as well as hinting at the plentiful leftovers for those toiling in the kitchen. It is also, of course, a cliché of royal over-consumption and waste. It appealed to William Shakespeare, who referred in his *Antony and Cleopatra* to 'Eight wild boars roasted whole ... and but twelve persons there! Is this true?' And it has a similar appeal even now. One story that used to be repeatedly told about the then Prince (now King) Charles, and repeatedly denied by Buckingham Palace, was that he had seven boiled eggs cooked at breakfast, with slightly different timings, to ensure that one of them was perfectly runny, just as he liked it. And so the myths of royalty continue.

Once again we are on the boundary that separates the day-to-day practical realities of the emperor's food and the imaginative fantasies about dynastic dining. That boundary is of course fuzzy, and there is an uncertain 'no-man's land' between fantasy and reality (spanning all kinds of exaggerations, half-truths and gossip). So, it is to the *ideology* of eating that we now return, as it emerges in the fact, semi-fact or out-right fiction (impossible as those are to distinguish) of the stories told about the emperor at table. Some of those I am about to retell cannot be literally true, but they open up different kinds of truths about impe-rial dining, and how it was imagined.

A theatre of power

One idea behind the imperial banquet was to put the emperor on show, to make him the centre of a spectacle. Even when he was dining 'in private', the setting of the *triclinium* – as at the Canopus in Hadrian's villa – often implied that the emperor was at least on *virtual* display. (Modern tourists, in a way, get the message of this Canopus right, when they turn it into their prime photo opportunity.) The same theme shaped Nero's underground *triclinium*. Its stage set may liter-ally have provided a place for the acts of after-dinner performers but, as a major part of the decoration, it also signalled the *theatricality* of the dining room itself.

On some occasions the emperor really *was* a spectacle. It is easy to imagine crowds on the shore of Lake Nemi watching Caligula at dinner on his barges, much as crowds of well-heeled visitors in the seventeenth century turned up at Versailles to watch the banquets of Louis XIV (in such numbers that the local pickpockets turned up too). And that idea of display must lie behind Domitian's conversion of the Colosseum, one of the city's prime locations of public shows, into the *spectacle of a banquet*; or, indeed, behind the story of Nero's conversion of one of the city's theatres into a floating restaurant-cum-nightclub. He is supposed to have had the building flooded somehow and a raft for himself and his fellow diners constructed in the middle of what was now an artificial lake. Emperor and guests stuffed themselves, as they lay on purple rugs and cushions, while round about, presumably at the water's edge, others visited the pop-up taverns and brothels that had been erected, or they simply gawped. The chances are that much of this is a lurid fantasy, including the claims of a large death toll, as both men and women in the assembled crowds were said to have been crushed in the melee. But fantasy or not, the point is that the emperor at dinner was framed as someone *to be looked at*. Alexander Severus in the third century CE knew what he was talking about when he complained that hosting a major feast made him feel as if he was eating in a theatre.

But it was more than the emperor himself who was on display. One vision of the social, political and even 'bodily' order of the Roman world was being put on view too, and also being debated and questioned, in stories of imperial dining. That is the obvious point of Suetonius's insistence that Augustus never entertained ex-slaves at his dinners. Apart from public occasions of mass eating, the emperor's table operated a strict divide between the invited guests, who were freeborn, and the menials and waiters, who were slaves or ex-slaves. It was a division of humankind into those who *served* and those who *were served*.

A similar point is underscored by some of the 'entertainments' laid on at dinner. A curious dining room recently excavated at a country estate of Antoninus Pius and his adopted son Marcus Aurelius, about 40 miles outside Rome, seems to have offered the elite banqueters a special vista in the wine-making season. For it looked directly onto an area used for treading grapes, slightly elevated, as if the work was happening on a stage. This emphasised the distance between elite diners and enslaved workers, who were themselves now turned into an object of spectacle *as workers*, while also reminding the boozy partygoers where their wine came from and (rather self-consciously) bringing a traditionally earthy agricultural atmosphere right up close to the elegant dinner. More often it was dwarfs and the disabled, including those who were deaf or blind, who performed at the emperor's table, as was 'fashionable' centuries later in European courts. Treated as figures of curiosity, or of 'fun', they now seem to us the victims of a peculiarly distasteful joke. But what was their point? In part, they too were doing an important job in the hierarchy of dining. The anomalous bodies of these marginal, déclassé characters were helping to define the bodies of those they 'entertained' – emperor, king or courtiers – as perfect by contrast. The real-life bodily imperfections of the elite were obscured by the presence of those deemed even more imperfect. In the imagination, at least, to dine at the imperial table defined you as freeborn, endowed with a finished, cultured and, in Roman terms, 'normal' body.

Of course, 'bad' emperors got all this the wrong way around, but the stories of how they *broke* the rules reveal the same basic principles. As well as supposedly inviting his favourite horse along (no 'normal' human body there), Caligula is also claimed to have had some of the most distinguished men of the city wait on him at table. The Latin in Suetonius's biography is not entirely clear, so we cannot be sure whether these senators-turned-waiters 'had napkins in their hands' or were 'wearing their tunics hitched up' in an embarrassingly revealing fashion. But, either way, this was more than a humiliation of the elite. By reversing the roles, it confounded what was supposed to be the social order of the banquet. Role reversal of another kind was signalled in those tales of Elagabalus lining up on his dining couches eight men with hernias, or with one eye, or whatever. It was a nasty practical joke, for sure. But it also undermined the notion of the bodily perfection that was supposed to define the guests. These stories, often now taken to reflect only the crazed caprices (fact or fiction) of some imperial psychopath, actually have a symbolic logic within the framework of 'power dining'.

It is a logic also found in some of the tall stories, which purport to show 'bad' emperors not so much flouting the principles of imperial dining but pushing them to the extreme, and in the process raising questions about how strongly the social rules could, or should, be enforced. Few are taller than the story of the emperor Commodus at one party displaying 'on a large silver dish two twisted hunchbacks smeared with mustard'. More than a dining-room version of a cruel freak show, this took to its absolute limit (even for Roman readers) the idea of the anomalous bodies at the feast. It was one thing to have the disabled acting as dinnertime entertainers. It was quite another to put them on show on a platter and covered in relish, as if they were actually food to be consumed. Other stories, in a similar vein, question the proper limits of the emperor's power by brutally exposing his abuse of power *as host*. Caligula, for example, was criticised for the sadistic punishment of a slave who had been serving at one of his public banquets. The slave was supposed to have stolen a strip of silver from one of the couches. As punishment, the emperor had his hands cut off and hung around his neck, and he was led among the guests with a placard held up in front of him explaining his crime.

The boundaries of cruelty were very different in the Roman world, and some regular forms of ancient punishment and retribution are shocking by most modern standards. But that does not mean that there were no boundaries at all. These dinnertime stories, or dark fantasies, were one of the ways of debating quite how far it was legitimate for the emperor to go. Total power, we are meant to conclude, might be better reined in, or at least veiled.

Much the same point was said to have been made by the emperor Augustus at another dinner, in a famous incident featuring those man-eating eels. This was not an occasion hosted by the emperor himself, but one at which he was the guest of a fabulously wealthy friend, Publius Vedius Pollio, at a villa on the Bay of Naples. Entertaining the emperor – 'inviting him back' – often had its downsides. It could be ruinously expensive. One story had Nero making one of his friends give a dinner at which all the guests wore silk turbans. It cost four million sesterces, which would have amounted to the combined fortune of a couple of ordinary senators. Even if it was an exaggerated and partly symbolic figure ('millions'), it symbolised a very large spend indeed. The inconvenience could be almost as bad. After he had entertained the dictator Julius Caesar in 45 BCE, who had shown up with two thousand soldiers and assorted hangers-on, Marcus Tullius Cicero, the Republican politician, observed with wry understatement that the party and conversation had been delightful, but that he wouldn't be doing it again in a hurry: 'Once is enough.' Augustus would not have come with such a retinue, but Pollio would certainly have been out to impress.

The story was that, at the banquet, one of Pollio's slaves dropped and broke a precious crystal goblet. The punishment that his master instantly imposed was death, by being thrown into a fish pond with the deadly eels – Pollio's favourite form of torture for disobedient slaves. But on this occasion the victim managed to wriggle away from those holding him and begged the guest of honour for a kinder death. The fact that no eels could eat a man to death, and that the story must in part be an urban myth, only increases the force of the moral. For Augustus's reaction was to order the slave be freed, to have all the rest of Pollio's crystal-ware smashed in front of its owner's eyes, and the fish pond filled in. 'If one of your goblets is broken,' he said to Pollio, 'is that an excuse to have a human being's guts torn out?' Augustus himself did not have an entirely unblemished record of modest dining habits. One fancy-dress banquet at which he was supposed to have sacrilegiously impersonated the god Apollo was notorious. But here he is presented as the (all-powerful) voice of moderation, of keeping the pleasures of the table in proportion.

The anecdote also takes us back to the conflicts between emperor and elite around the dinner table. As we have seen with the stories of fake food, guests were not all equal. The imperial dinner party was where many Romans pictured the power of the emperor most vividly in action – and where ruler and aristocrats were imagined facing up to each other. In this case, Vedius Pollio was put in his place.

Death by eating

We should not be *too* macabre about this. For every senator who shuddered at an occasion like Domitian's black dinner (whatever the truth behind it, or its intention), there were probably several like Pliny keen to boast about their companionable evenings at the palace, whoever the emperor might be. Suetonius claims, for example, that Vespasian in his younger days, long before he gained the throne in the civil wars of 68–69 CE, had got up in the senate to thank Caligula for an invitation, and presumably to make sure that his fellow senators knew all about it. There was also a story of one outsider, a 'provincial', trying to buy a place at an imperial dinner (told as a sign of the emperor's vanity in being flattered by the man's keenness as much as to show the value of a place at the table). The point was that eating with the ruler, especially on an intimate scale, must have made the guests feel at the centre of power, and allowed them to bend his ear, not unlike eating with political leaders now. There is a modern ring to some of the ancient allegations that prestigious jobs went to those who were the party companions of the emperor, or that big decisions were made around the banqueting table. One classic case of such dinnertime lobbying concerned the golden statue of himself that Caligula planned to erect in the Temple of Jerusalem, shamelessly offending Jewish religious sensibilities. According to one version of this complicated story, which was finally resolved only by Caligula's death, it was over an expensive dinner hosted in Rome by Herod Agrippa, then king of Judaea and well-connected to the Roman imperial house, that Caligula was persuaded to think again about the statue.

But the image of the imperial dinner party was also indelibly one of high risk. It was almost as much the classic Roman crime scene as the country house is in modern British fiction (daggers in the library, etc.), whether that was Claudius dying from his plate of doctored mushrooms, or those rumours of Lucius Verus being finished off by poisoned oysters. The mere presence of the ranks of 'tasters' was one part of it. They might have protected the emperor and his closest family from the threat of poison, but they simultaneously reminded everyone present that, unless they were careful, what they ate could kill them. They underpinned a culture of suspicion. Occasionally this has a slightly comedic tone. Commodus, for example, was reputed to have had human shit mixed in with some of the most expensive dishes (not deadly, though not so funny if you were one of the guests). But there were many stories in which – despite the tasters' best efforts – dinners *were* deadly.

The most revealing story is that of the death of the young prince Britannicus, thirteen years old, at a palace dinner, in 55 CE. It was at the start of the reign of Nero and, as the natural son of the emperor Claudius, the boy was a potential rival for the throne, best eliminated by the new regime. The historian Tacitus captures the scene in vivid and no doubt imaginative detail (born the year after the events, he was certainly not present, and we have no idea what kind of reliable information about it he could have had). Britannicus, he explains, was sitting at the children's table, set slightly apart from the couches of the adult diners. To avoid the tasters, Nero's poisoners had squirted their toxin not into his hot drink, which *was* pre-tasted, but into the jug of cold water used to cool it down, which was not (no one suspected plain water). The boy collapsed immediately, and Nero's explanation was that it was an epileptic fit. Maybe it was – and that would certainly be one way of cutting through the fantasies of foul play with the water. But the explanation was rather undermined by the fact that the funeral pyre had been prepared in advance. Or so claimed Tacitus, who had no interest in diminishing the darkness of the occasion.

Perhaps the most chilling side of all this, however, was Tacitus's account of the reaction of the other guests. Some of them betrayed their suspicions by rushing around in panic, others stayed in their places, but were still unable to keep their eyes off Nero. The only person who got it right was Britannicus's older sister, Octavia, who had also become Nero's wife, in a blatantly dynastic marriage. She showed not a flicker of emotion, but – it is implied – simply went on eating as if nothing had happened. Tacitus is insisting here that the menace of the imperial dining room lay partly in the fact that you could never let your true feelings or suspicions show there, even if your brother had just collapsed in front of you.

It was by revealing her suspicions too obviously that one imperial princess got it wrong in the reign of Tiberius. Locked in conflict with the emperor– whom she believed had played a part in the death of her husband – she was just a little too hesitant in biting into an apple he had offered her, giving the impression that she feared the fruit had been tampered with. She was never invited to dinner again, and before long was in exile. The story may be too good to be literally true. Something suspiciously similar is told of young Tiberius Gemellus, who, having been mooted as his possible co-ruler, might have had reason to be wary of dinner with the new emperor Caligula. According to Suetonius, the lingering smell of what was actually cough medicine on his breath was interpreted as the smell of poison antidotes, which he was presumed to have taken to counteract whatever might be sprinkled on his food. It was enough for him to be given orders to kill himself. True or not, the point is that the imperial banquet was so easily imagined as a site of self-incrimination, with fatal results.

Good hosts and bad

But the dinnertime relationship between emperor and elite – whether that was the gratitude, bonhomie and flattery of the silent majority, or the resentment, covert sadism and capricious cruelty stressed by most writers, modern and ancient – did not simply come down to death and bloodshed. Terror in the *triclinium* did not require that anyone was actually killed. As the story of Domitian's black dinner showed, it rested also on nasty (or backfiring) jokes, micro-aggressions and calculated (or perceived) humiliations. There are dozens of ancient anecdotes, often dressed up in colourful and apparently specific detail, but all focusing on the same basic questions, transferable from one ruler to the next. How far was the imperial banquet an occasion of (at least) *notional* equality? How far was the emperor at dinner 'one of us'? What made the emperor a good, or a bad, host?

Good behaviour on the part of the emperor sometimes involved exactly the same courtesy as was paraded in those stories of Augustus saying hello and goodbye to every single member of the senate by name. Whatever his nasty grudge over the suspect apple, Tiberius was praised for greeting the consuls at the door, and for standing in the middle of his dining room and bidding farewell to everyone personally at the end of the evening. Others received a good press for their tolerance, or witty punishment, of minor offences committed by their guests. When, for example, one of them pinched the golden cup from which he had been served (a common modern misdemeanour in hotels and restaurants), Claudius's 'moderation took a comic turn', as Plutarch put it. When the same man showed up for dinner the next day, he found that he was the only guest being served out of earthenware. In a similar vein, Julius Caesar is said to have punished his baker for making higher-quality bread for Caesar himself than for his guests – so neatly combining the exercise of power over the 'menial' with the assertion of equality between host and fellow diners.

But at the same time, it was at dinner that emperors were reputed to rub the noses of the elite in their own subservience. Sometimes this amounted to little more than those calibrated differences in food and drink, as when Alexander Severus consumed five goblets of wine to his guests' one (there was some wine snobbery in Rome, though less than now: it was quantity that really counted). But there were higher stakes too. The same Tiberius who was so careful about the formalities of meeting and greeting was supposed to have broken off relations with a man who discovered the key to his after-dinner quiz game (and later forced him to suicide). The emperor had a penchant for setting his guests questions on whatever he himself had been reading that day, and the unfortunate victim had tried to upstage him by finding out Tiberius's reading list from the palace staff in advance. Others were said to have turned political power into sexual power. Caligula, for example, was reported to have taken to bed, mid-dinner, the wives of the male guests, and then to have humiliated both the woman and her husband by making unfavourable (or favourable) comments to the assembled company on the woman's 'performance'. If true, it must have felt, especially to the women, like one of the downsides of the apparent equality of mixed dining.

The most memorable anecdotes, however, focus on laughter and joking, not as a sign of tolerant good humour, but as a weapon in the hands of the emperor against the elite (laughing *at* them, rather than laughing *with* them). Caligula's quip at dinner that he could slit the consuls' throats any time he chose was a sign both of his own overweening excesses and of the potential vulnerability of the senators. Even more uncomfortable was the story of a distinguished Roman whose son was put to death before his very eyes, also on the orders of Caligula. Later that day, after the execution in the morning, he was invited to dinner by the emperor, who with a tremendous show of affability forced the poor man to laugh and joke (as if he could control even those most 'natural' human responses and emotions). Why on earth did the bereaved father go along with this? Because, one Roman writer sharply observed, 'he had another son'.

The power relations in these stories are more complicated than they might appear. For whatever their origin, and whatever the real-life abuses were, their target – as they have come down to us – is of course the emperor himself. They are not so much evidence for the emperor's behaviour, as part of a case against him, and a warning to ruler after ruler, as they circulated and were told and retold, of how *not* to behave. While sympathising with the father who had lost his son, readers are actually deploring the power that an emperor could in theory choose to wield. And the stories are made more complicated by superimposing the image of a potentially abusive host over that of a potentially abusive emperor (and vice versa).

Some of those complexities are summed up in one final imperial dining room in a spectacular seaside setting, and decorated with a lavish, but disturbing, set of sculptures. It is hard to imagine that many could have eaten there without reflecting on the problematic relationship between host and guest, between emperor and fellow diners.

Polyphemus's cave

This dining room was rediscovered in 1957, on the coast near Sperlonga, a small village between Rome and Naples. Even more daring than the water features we have looked at already, this took the form of a platform for couches set on an artificial island in the sea, which faced a natural cave where archaeologists unearthed thousands of fragments of sculpture. Many of these have now been pieced together, to reconstruct a series of marble statues that once decorated the cave's interior, based on themes drawn from the mythical Trojan War and Homer's epic *Odyssey* (as big a classic among the elite in ancient Rome as it was in ancient Greece). The idea must have been that the diners were taken by boat onto their island, where the food was floated across to them, and from where they could admire the statue-filled grotto, dramatically illuminated as the sun sank down behind them to the west.

There is a strong chance that this was the place where, in 26 CE, the emperor Tiberius had a very lucky escape at dinner. He was eating in a natural grotto in a country residence called *Spelunca* (or 'cave') on

24. The grotto at Sperlonga. In the foreground is the base of the dining area and couches; beyond, the natural cave which the diners faced, containing groups of sculptures illustrating themes from the Trojan war and Odysseus's travels.

his way to the south of Italy, when some of the rocks at the entrance collapsed killing some of those present. The name itself (*Spelunca/ Sperlonga*) makes the connection very likely. But even if that is not the case (and the statues themselves could anyway be later), it is overwhelmingly plausible to imagine that this state-of-the-art dining grotto, which is attached to a very grand villa, was part of an imperial property.

But what exactly did the statues depict? There were various 'epic' scenes, including Odysseus carrying the body of Achilles off the battlefield at Troy, and the monstrous Scylla, who threatened to destroy Odysseus's boat on his way back from Troy to his home on the Greek island of Ithaca. But the focus of the composition was another of Odysseus's homecoming adventures: the blinding of the

25. The focal group of sculptures in the cave at Sperlonga depicted the story of the blinding of Polyphemus from Homer's *Odyssey*. It has been hard to piece together the fragments of marble from the shattered figures (broken when the cave collapsed), but this reconstruction – part original, part modern – gives a reasonable idea of the composition: men of Odysseus's party drive out the eye of the drunken, sprawling giant.

one-eyed cannibal, and giant, Polyphemus. The story in the *Odyssey* was that, during their long travels, the Greek hero and his companions had landed on Polyphemus's island and set themselves up in the cave where he lived, while he was out tending his sheep. Returning to find the intruders, he literally made a meal out of some of them – until, to prevent the loss of more of his men and to enable their escape, Odysseus got the giant drunk and, when he had passed out, blinded him by skewering out his single eye with a hot stake.

It is a rich story of cultural conflict and the ambivalences of 'civilisation'. Whose side are we on? The cannibal whose home has been invaded, or the leader who resourcefully saves his crew's lives? What lies between the supposed 'barbarity' of Polyphemus and the Greek 'civilisation' of Odysseus? And it was a great visual conceit to use an actual cave to recreate the mythical cave of the story. But for those looking at this scene from their island *triclinium*, there was even more to it than that. Central to the myth of Odysseus and Polyphemus are precisely those questions about host and guest that were raised by so many stories of imperial dining. For this was a tale that exposed the risks of hospitality, in which murder was on the menu, the food was tainted, and in which the drink ended up destroying the host himself, who was as vulnerable as he was deadly. It was the mythical dinner party from hell.

The cave at Sperlonga was the most imaginative imperial dining room to feature the Polyphemus story, but it was not the only one. In a way, the scene became a brand for palatial dining. A statue of Polyphemus was at one stage installed in the Canopus suite in Hadrian's villa. There was another, in a room probably used for dining, at a villa owned by Domitian outside Rome (p. 129). There was yet another on the coast of the Bay of Naples in a luxurious entertainment area in a villa developed by the emperor Claudius, where guests reclined around a pool in what was effectively a man-made cave, at one end of which were placed statues of Odysseus offering wine to the giant – before blinding him. This was fully excavated from under water only in the 1980s, and one recent theory has suggested that this was the very dining room in which Nero entertained his mother Agrippina to her last dinner, on the night that he had her killed.

If so (and it is an optimistic theory, but not impossible), we can only wonder whether she reflected on the dangers these statues signalled. Even if not, the designers of these rooms offered the diners plenty of food for thought. Some might have felt reassured that their own banquets represented a civilised sophistication that those in the epic story so clearly lacked. The more observant would have seen some of their own tensions, dilemmas and anxieties reflected back at them. The dangers of the dinner, real and imaginary, were here summed up in the decoration of the dining room itself. For us, Sperlonga especially is a reminder of the complex amalgam that was an emperor's dinner: from

26. An underwater archaeologist rescues one of the sculptures from the Polyphemus group in Claudius's dining room at Baiae on the Bay of Naples; it is the figure of one of Odysseus's companions.

the organisational challenges (imagine getting all those little boats propelled across to the diners, especially on what was almost open sea); through the pleasures of those guests flattered to be invited to the emperor's table, floating or not; to the dark subtexts of imperial power that the hospitality of the emperor, like that of Polyphemus, revealed.

We can see that on a wider canvas if we now move beyond the dining room, to the palace as a whole.

4

WHAT'S IN A PALACE?

Caligula's grand designs

In 40 CE the emperor Caligula was asked to adjudicate between warring factions in the city of Alexandria in the Roman province of Egypt, where a combination of xenophobia, anti-Semitism, disputes about local civic rights, and a provincial governor who was (advertently or inadvertently) making things worse had led to violence between the Greek and Jewish communities. Both sides sent delegations to Rome, to win over the emperor. We can learn something of what went on when the different parties appeared in front of him, thanks to a vivid, if self-serving, eyewitness account of the proceedings by one of the Jewish delegates. He was the learned philosopher Philo, probably better known for his discussions of the Hebrew bible and tricky points of theology than for his encounter with Caligula.

It cannot have been a comfortable occasion for either of the rival delegations, who had been asked to show up at the same time to make their respective cases. The emperor had kept them waiting for months before he gave them an audience and they had already had one abortive trip to try to catch up with him in the south of Italy (the inconvenience of all this, the expense, and the inside knowledge or connections required to fix up a meeting, are issues to which we will return in chapter 6). There is no sign that he had made his decision before he was assassinated early the next year. In the short time they were actually face to face with him, the Jews became the butt of Caligula's hostile banter or, as Philo presented it, the victims of his tyrannical menace. The emperor grilled or needled them with questions about their religion and dietary rules. 'Why won't you eat pork?' he asked at one point, causing the Greeks to burst out laughing rather too heartily, for they were firmly reprimanded by some of the imperial staff. Philo claimed, without much direct knowledge, I suspect, that even a smile was dangerous in the emperor's presence, unless you were a close friend. But the judicious reply of the Jews hardly helped their cause. When they had patiently explained that different cultures had different customs and prohibitions, a lesson in elementary anthropology that the emperor may not have appreciated, one of their delegation pointed out, as a good example, that many people chose not to eat lamb. This now drew a laugh from Caligula himself, obviously no fan of the meat, and probably also determined to trivialise the issue: 'I'm not surprised,' he retorted, 'it really doesn't taste very nice.'

An extra insult, to both sides, was the fact that the emperor's mind was not entirely on the job, and he made it quite clear that his priorities lay elsewhere. This was not a formal hearing, and the two delegations were made to trail around after him as he inspected his property – the different pavilions, the men's and women's rooms, the ground and upper floors – identifying necessary repairs and suggesting a range of home improvements. In the middle of one intervention by the Jews, he cut them short to give instructions for the windows in a large room to be 'glazed' with transparent stones, 'so as not to obstruct the light, but to keep out the wind and the blazing sun'. In the next room, he cut them off again, when he turned to order some 'original paintings' for the walls. In recording these detours, Philo is obviously criticising Caligula for concentrating on the fripperies of interior decor rather than on the serious grievances of the Jews in Alexandria. But his account also gives us a rare chance to connect the emperor directly to the fabric of one of the buildings in which he lived, and to get a hint of his grand designs. In fact, a small section of this particular imperial estate was excavated at the beginning of this century, not far from what is now the main train station, and a museum recently opened on the site displays some of the finds and almost lets us follow in the emperor's footsteps.

This chapter widens our focus from the imperial dining rooms and explores the royal properties more generally, from the service corridors to the ornamental lakes, from the pricey artworks to the curious bric-a-brac collected from all over the Roman world, not to mention any number of surprises (few people now realise that what may be the earliest surviving representation of a Christian crucifixion was discovered in the quarters of some of the emperor's slaves on the Palatine Hill in Rome). One question is where did the emperors live and what did they call 'home'. As well as spotlighting the remains on, and in, the ground, I shall try to reconstruct what a Roman palace originally looked like and what happened there, and how imperial residences changed over time. Was the residence of Augustus anything like that of the emperors a century later? When did the idea of a 'palace' start?

There are questions too that go beyond the bricks and mortar. What did the palace say about the emperor and his power? What kind of ambitious claims, beyond boastful display (or equally boastful modesty), were built into its structure? What conflicts did these buildings provoke? ('Get out of here, citizens. Rome is turning into one man's house', as an anonymous ancient graffiti artist, quoted by Suetonius, satirised Nero's vast new pile in the city.) How did the emperors themselves see it? Was Domitian alone in sensing the danger at home when he had the walls of the private colonnades where he walked lined with a special reflecting stone, allegedly so that he could see what was going on – and who was coming up – behind him? As our final port of call, at the end of the chapter, we will visit one imperial residence that almost doubled as a carefully constructed microcosm of the Roman empire as a whole, a miniature replica of the emperor's world.

Homes and gardens

The building that Caligula was busy redesigning was not the palace (or *palatium*) in the centre of Rome, called after the Palatine Hill on which it stood. Most monarchs throughout history have moved among several residences, and the Roman emperor was no exception, with dozens of imperial properties scattered throughout Italy. Caligula's encounter with the rival delegations from Alexandria actually took place in one of the numerous suburban pleasure gardens (*horti*) owned by the emperor on the edge of town, a couple of miles from the city centre (p. xiii, 'Ancient Rome'). More than just parkland, these estates included chalets and pavilions, sleeping quarters and entertainment suites, and, of course, banqueting halls and elaborate water features. They were also full of works of art. The 'original paintings' and translucent windows that the emperor was planning to install in 40 CE were part of that. But archaeologists have for centuries been unearthing hundreds of sculptures and other treasures from the site of these *horti*: delicately cut crystals; gilded inlay and jewels once set into walls or furniture (pl. 20); statues that must already have been antiques when they came to Rome, collected or looted from Greece and Egypt; and some of the most extravagant portraits of Roman emperors themselves to have been discovered anywhere (fig. 56). The purpose of these gardens was to provide a more leisured and expansive style of life than was possible in the centre of the city, while also being within easy reach of the heart of the metropolitan action: a convenient combination of rural estate and urban powerhouse.

Most of the *horti* had originally been established by super-rich Roman aristocrats living at the end of the Republic or during the reigns of the first emperors, and they continued to bear the name of those early proprietors. It was the *horti Lamiani*, for example, that Caligula was intent on improving when he should have been concentrating on the disputes of the Alexandrians. These were called after their first owner, a friend of the emperor Tiberius, Lucius Aelius Lamia. But by the second half of the first century CE all the estates of this kind had 'fallen into the emperor's hands', to use the standard euphemism, which covers everything from generous gift to outright theft. In the process, in addition to the palace in the centre, the city had become almost entirely encircled by imperial *horti*, covering acre upon acre of prime real estate. Maybe there was some semi-public access to parts of this, allowing the great unwashed a brief sight of green spaces and luxury developments. But in a city of a million people, where the majority lived in cramped accommodation or squalid slums, or slept rough, the enormous size of the emperor's 'footprint' on the urban landscape was one proof of his power.

The imperial pleasure gardens were only the start of a network of residences that stretched down to the Bay of Naples and the emperors' private island of Capri, which was even more upmarket in the ancient world than it is now. In a way, this followed the pattern of landowning among the aristocracy more generally. Pliny had at least four country estates, as well as a house in Rome. But the imperial holdings were on a larger and grander scale, increasing over time as each emperor apparently inherited the properties of his predecessors, even as he went on to build more. Thirty or so imperial residences have been identified in the area around Rome (modern Lazio) alone, dwarfing even the landholding of the British royal family at its most opulent.

The remains of some of these have been tourist attractions for hundreds of years, from the eighteenth-century 'Grand Tour' or even before. Hadrian's villa at Tivoli is one of those. So too are the multiple imperial villas on Capri, where Tiberius notoriously retreated in 26 CE, for the last decade of his life, with all the later fantastic rumours

27. A Greek statue from the fifth century BCE, found in one of the imperial pleasure gardens (*horti Sallustiani*): the figure of one of the children of Niobe (who were put to death as divine punishment because their mother boasted she had had more children than the goddess Leto). How or when it came to Rome – war booty or the antiques trade – is unknown.

of sex games in the swimming pool, and enemies eliminated by being thrown from the clifftop. According to Suetonius, the emperor's main residence on the island included bedrooms covered in erotic paintings and a library of sex manuals, in case his flagging partygoers should need inspiration. Down-to-earth modern archaeologists have been less interested in the supposed orgies than in the cisterns, and have marvelled instead at how the imperial engineers managed to supply enough water for the gardens, the pools and the baths on what was little more than a rocky waterless outcrop with a great view.

Others are less celebrated or now harder to access, but equally remarkable in various ways. For size, one of Commodus's properties, just outside Rome a few miles down the Appian Way, rivalled

28. An aerial view of what survives of Tiberius's largest villa on Capri, originally covering more than 7,000 square metres. The apse at the top commanded a view across the Bay of Naples, the main cisterns are located in the centre of the building visible here.

Hadrian's estate at Tivoli – so huge that it was once believed to have been a whole town ('Vecchia Roma' or 'Old Rome', just as Hadrian's villa was called 'Vecchia Tivoli'). It is now known as the Villa of the Quintilii, because it only 'fell into Commodus's hands' after he had eliminated its wealthy owners, the Quintilii brothers. For dramatic setting, one of Nero's country houses takes the prize. It was built in picturesque hills some 50 miles outside the capital, near modern Subiaco, and the emperor's architects enhanced the atmosphere – and the view from the villa – by damming a gorge to create an artificial lake. Not far away, Domitian's most famous and ostentatious rural 'hideaway', one of several he owned, was constructed in a similarly scenic spot, on huge man-made terraces overlooking Lake Albano, and complete with every Roman amenity that imperial money could buy, down to a grotto with a sculpture featuring the one-eyed Polyphemus. Until recently this was more off-limits than most other imperial properties since it lies largely within the boundaries of the Pope's private summer residence at Castel Gandolfo, the hierarchy of the Catholic Church since the Renaissance having found the same delights in the local landscape as did the Roman emperors. But the grounds of the residence and ruins have now been reopened to the public.

There were many more, including a range of luxury seaside villas, from Tiberius's at Sperlonga, Claudius's on the Italian riviera at Baiae, to the sprawling mansion developed by Nero overlooking the beach at modern Anzio (now better known for the Anzio Landings in the Second World War than for a Roman imperial residence). The historian Cassius Dio, writing in the third century CE, saw that there was more to these estates than simply rich country retreats. He explained that, by his day at least, the title *palatium* was given to wherever the emperor happened to be living at the time. The peninsula of Italy, in other words, was full of palaces.

The reason that we can now identify many of these so confidently is partly because of their size and luxury (though emperors did sometimes choose to parade a more modest lifestyle, and very occasionally, as the Villa of the Quintilii shows, other rich landowners might build on a massive scale). It is partly because some remains can be tied into a description in surviving ancient literature (it is plausible enough to link the accounts of Tiberius's life on Capri with the most palatial villa on the island). But the habits of ancient manufacturers and builders have also helped us to pin the name of particular emperors to particular ruins in an unexpected way. For, almost as if they had the interests of future archaeologists in mind, they sometimes stamped onto bricks and lead water pipes not only the precise date of production but also the name of the property's owner, the official responsible for the installation, or the proprietor of the manufacturing works – making in some cases an imperial connection absolutely

29. A pope pokes at the Roman ruins. Pope John XXIII examines some of the Roman remains, from Domitian's villa, at his summer residence at Castel Gandolfo.

30. Lead piping from the *horti Lamiani*, with a stamp that almost
certainly identifies the commissioner, or maker, of the pipe as
a slave or ex-slave of an emperor of the Claudian family. We
read here the words: of 'Claudi Caes(aris) Aug(usti).

certain. It is, for example, because of the names on the piping that
we can firmly identify a vast mansion excavated in the hills about 50
miles east of Rome, not far from Nero's scenic retreat at Subiaco, as a
country property of Trajan.

What happened where

Things are much murkier, however, when we turn to the internal layout
of these residences, and try to work out what the rooms were used for,
to reconstruct the lifestyle, or – in our imaginations, at least – to put
the people back in. There are no surviving annotated plans or detailed
guides, such as those that help us to decode Versailles and other
modern palaces. And in only a few cases can we deduce the function

of a room from its ruined form. Dining rooms with built-in couches, or marks on the floor, are one example where that is often possible, as we saw in the last chapter. Bathing facilities and lavatories (easily recognisable) are another. These sometimes lead to more significant conclusions than you might anticipate. The distribution of single-seater versus multi-seater lavatories at Hadrian's palace at Tivoli, for example, has helped identify areas used mostly by the emperor and his elite guests and those used by staff, who did not get the same privacy as their bosses. And everything is made more complicated by the fact that many modern assumptions about domestic architecture cannot be applied to the ancient world. There is no point in looking for 'the emperor's bedroom' for the simple reason that Roman houses didn't have bedrooms. The Roman elite might well have slept on a couch in what was called a *cubiculum*, but it was not a 'bedroom' in our sense of the word, although that is how it is often translated. It was a room of privacy and intimacy, whether for sleeping, sex, entertaining your closest friends, plotting, or, if you were emperor, conducting particularly sensitive legal cases.

So in this chapter I shall often use names that have traditionally been given to parts of imperial palaces and are too well established to be thrown over, but that are at best optimistic guesses – at worst, hopelessly misleading. An extreme example is a pavilion surviving on the site of one of the imperial *horti*, probably those originally owned by Augustus's friend and adviser Maecenas, and bequeathed to the emperor in his will. Ever since it was rediscovered during building works in the 1870s, this pavilion has been known as the 'Auditorium of Maecenas', thanks to what appears to be a semi-circle of tiered seating facing an open room or performance space. Maecenas was a well-known patron of the arts and is sometimes now treated as the emperor's unofficial 'culture minister'. It was very tempting to imagine that this was where he showcased some of his literary protégés, even perhaps where Virgil might have presented to a select audience highlights from the *Aeneid*, his great epic on Rome's foundation, written under Augustus's patronage. Very tempting, but probably wrong. What looks like tiered seating was almost certainly the setting for another of those cascades of water, and the 'performance space' was probably a dining room with movable couches.

In the pages that follow I shall be navigating misidentifications of this kind, and attempting to do better where I can. My starting point is the original 'palace' on the Palatine Hill in Rome, and the story of how it developed from little more than a compound of loosely connected individual houses (not a 'palace' at all in our terms) to a labyrinthine mansion of more familiar palatial style. I shall end with a closer look at Hadrian's estate at Tivoli, the most overblown Roman imperial residence there ever was, going from the hundreds of pieces of sculpture

31. The interior of the 'Auditorium of Maecenas' as it is today, with another variation on the theme of performance. Here at a recent meeting of an 'art forum', what was originally a water feature at the far end is being used as a stage, while the audience sit in the space where the dining couches would have been arranged.

that have been excavated there to its network of underground passage-ways and even its flower pots.

A house on the Palatine

The history of the Palatine tells us a lot about shifts in Roman power. It was one of the seven (or more) hills on which the city of Rome was built, and in the middle of the first century BCE, before the rule of the emperors, it was home to most of the big men of Roman politics. Here the rivals who competed for power, influence and the votes of the people in Rome's sort-of democracy lived as next-door neighbours, in properties that changed hands for ridiculous sums of money and were sometimes inconveniently close together (it was all too easy to block your neighbour's light with some lofty home improvements). From the outside they would not have looked particularly impressive, at least to modern Western eyes. Traditional Roman houses faced inwards, built around internal courtyards, and relatively little effort was put into the exterior. But their rivalrous owners competed in architecture almost as much as they did in politics. How many columns you had in your internal porticoes, whether they were of expensive imported marble or of plain local stone, or whether you decided to make a show of rejecting luxury with your modest style of life – all of this mattered in the race for prestige.

The attraction of the Palatine was partly its closeness to the political action of Republican Rome. The Forum and the senate house were no more than a few minutes' walk away down the hill (or litter ride, if you preferred). Cicero had proudly boasted that from his house on the Palatine he could see the whole city and – no less important – that the whole city could see him. These houses both gave their owners a good view and put them prominently on display. But the Palatine also had important mythical and historical associations. It was here that the founder Romulus was supposed to have established the first settlement on the site of Rome (and a wattle and daub hut still visible in the fourth century CE – a symbolically important fake – was claimed to be where Romulus himself had lived all those centuries before). It was also on the Palatine that the Romans established the Temple of the Magna Mater or 'Great Mother', who was reputed to have saved them from defeat against Hannibal at the end of the third century BCE. This revered goddess was imported, on the instructions of a divine oracle, from what is now Turkey, accompanied by her notorious eunuch priests, self-castrated, so it was said.

Within a century or so of the beginning of one-man rule at Rome, by the end of the first century CE, the Palatine landscape had changed dramatically. The historic monuments and temples remained (it is rarely pointed out that for most of imperial history a group of religious eunuchs lived near the emperor's back door). But the aristocratic houses were gone, and most of the hill was occupied by a single palace. In one of the most vivid marks of the new political order, the emperor – thanks to strategic purchases, expropriation, theft, or merely a 'hostile environment' – had pushed the old aristocracy out of its traditional, prestige quarters. The symbolism of the change was obvious, but it was also gradual. The elite began to cede the residential quarters of the hill to the imperial family almost immediately, starting under Augustus (Julius Caesar has no responsibility for this). But the palace, in the terms we now understand it, was not built overnight.

Roman writers had plenty to say about the Palatine properties of the first emperors, usually in an attempt to align their living arrangements with their character and reputation. Augustus was credited with a parade of old-fashioned traditionalism, cleverly combined with significant markers of autocratic power. He is said to have occupied an 'ordinary' house, that had once belonged to an 'ordinary' member of the Roman elite, with no luxury marble decoration or elaborate floors, and simple furniture to match. (Suetonius insists that he slept in the same room for forty years, winter and summer, on the same low, plain couch.) Not so ordinary was the house's 'forecourt', which – according to Augustus's own *What I Did* – was decorated with laurel wreaths and other such honours, and even inscribed with the words 'Father of his Country', rather at odds with the plain decor inside. Half a century later, the supposed excesses of Caligula were matched by those of his Palatine residence. These went far beyond the new windows for buildings in the *horti*. Suetonius claims that the 'forecourt' of Caligula's house was somehow constructed out of the venerable old Temple of Castor and Pollux, which stood in the Forum just at the foot of the Palatine. It was a sign of his megalomania and impiety combined, for he would often sit, it was alleged, between the statues of the two gods in the temple, expecting to be worshipped.

The problem has always been how to match up any of these accounts, or ideological projections, with the remaining archaeological evidence. The early imperial levels of the Palatine are especially difficult to explore. That is largely because the foundations of the later Roman palace, or palaces, have more or less obliterated what was there before (Nero's dining room is one of the rare pockets of survival). But the presence on part of the site of the Farnese Gardens – a jewel of Renaissance landscaping – has understandably prevented extensive modern excavation. Leaving aside a few ingenious but unconvincing attempts to find traces of Caligula's 'vestibule' in the Forum, attached to the surviving Temple of Castor and Pollux, most of what we can say with certainty is negative. Particularly disappointing is that the remains of the splendidly decorated houses of the first century BCE – now known as the 'House of Augustus' and the 'House of Livia', and a star attraction on the visitor route around the Palatine – cannot possibly be where Augustus lived. He almost certainly had come to own these properties at the beginning of his take-over of the Palatine, but he had them destroyed and backfilled to make way for a brand-new temple of the god Apollo that was completed in 28 BCE (before he had even adopted the name Augustus). What we now visit are not the emperor's reception rooms, as we are usually told, but the basement accommodation of some Republican grandee's house over which the platform for the new temple and its surrounding porticoes was constructed.

The fact is that all physical traces of Augustus's own residence or residences are probably lost forever under the later buildings. But one revealing hint of how the emperors were housed in those early days of one-man rule survives in an unexpected source: that is, an account of the assassination of Caligula on the Palatine in 41 CE, written in Greek at the end of the first century by the Jewish historian Josephus. He makes it clear that, at least at the time of this murder, we should not be imagining a grand single mansion at all (whatever the story of the 'temple turned vestibule' might imply), but an expanding estate that gradually took over most of the earlier houses on the hill. Some of these were rebuilt, others knocked together or connected with tunnels (a few traces of these do survive), but for the most part they were left as independent buildings.

Caligula was killed, Josephus says, in a 'quiet alley' within the estate, a short cut to the private imperial baths where he had been heading when he was pounced on. As soon as the deed was done the assassins ran away via 'the nearby House of Germanicus, the father of the man they had just killed'. Then, presumably for the benefit of those readers (now including us) who were unfamiliar with the layout of the place, he goes on to explain a bit more. 'For though the palace was a single site,' he writes, 'it was made up severally of the buildings belonging to each member of the imperial family, named after their builders.' And in a variant on the more familiar story – that Claudius was discovered by members of the guard cowering behind a curtain (p. 66) – Josephus says that the new emperor had taken refuge down another quiet 'alley', and up a flight of steps.

It demands some effort now to imagine the residence of Augustus and his immediate successors not as a unified structure but more as a 'compound', with individual members of the extended imperial family having their own houses and households. However grandly decorated these various buildings were (some, no doubt, very grandly indeed), whatever symbols of power distinguished their façades, however many burly guards policed the entrances and dark passages, it was a complex of loosely connected properties, not the kind of single edifice that came later and is familiar from movie sets as well as from more austere archaeological reconstructions (pl. 9). Nero began to change this arrangement early in his reign. Although the archaeology is again hard to interpret, the elegant dining room we have already explored is almost certainly part of his first attempt at a radical redevelopment, as are some remains buried under the Farnese Gardens. Confusingly, this is called the *Domus Tiberiana*, 'the Tiberian palace', because it probably had nothing at all to do with the emperor Tiberius (except that it might have been on the site of his family house in the early compound). But the great fire of Rome later in Nero's reign, in 64 CE, was the crucial turning point. For this devastated much of the city, including the Palatine, presumably destroying any private houses that remained there and so clearing the way for the construction of the first brand-new, purpose-built, central city 'palace'. This prompted new questions about how an emperor should live, and it became a model of how an imperial residence should *not* be.

Living like a human being

This building was Nero's Golden House, or *Domus Aurea*. According to Suetonius, it was so large that it occupied land from the Palatine itself to the Esquiline Hill, almost a mile away, housed a statue of the emperor over 35 metres tall, and included in its grounds an artificial lake that was 'more like a sea'. One of the 'wings' of this palace – preserved on the Esquiline in the foundation levels of Roman public baths that were later built over the top and firmly dated thanks in part to the stamped bricks – has been a highlight of archaeology and tourism in the city for more than half a millennium. In the early sixteenth century the artist Raphael and his pupils crawled into the ruins through passages dug through the ceilings from above, carefully drew what they saw, and occasionally left their names scrawled over the paintings they so admired. Modern visitors have an easier time. The debris and in-fill have now been largely cleared away and you can walk in from the ancient ground level, put on a hard hat, and wander around the display rooms and corridors, which survive more or less up to their original height.

This still *feels* like a palace. True, most of the luxury decoration has gone (though again, modern visitors are given virtual reality headsets to help recreate the marble facing that once covered what are now bare brick walls and the sculptures that adorned the now empty rooms).

32. Hypothetical reconstruction of parts of the Domus Aurea seen from the south. 1. The main entrance to the Domus Aurea from the Forum; 2. The vestibule with the colossal statue of Nero; 3. The lake (future site of the Colosseum); 4.Neronian buildings on the Palatine; 5. The surviving wing of the palace; 6. The Temple of Claudius; 7. Circus Maximus.

The surviving stuccoes and painting are rather less dazzling than they were when Raphael saw them. And, apart from the dining suites and water features, it is hard to know what most of the rooms were used for, well over a hundred of them in the section that has been unearthed. But some are on a scale that is striking, even without their luxurious embellishment. One huge octagonal room, very likely intended for dining, has rightly been hyped by modern architectural historians as an absolutely revolutionary structure, and a daring development in the use of brick and concrete that set the scene for Roman construction for centuries. Most of us now gasp in greater wonderment at the long, high corridors, which feature some of the decoration that impressed the sixteenth-century artists. In reality, most of these were service passages.

This is the only substantial section of Nero's Golden House to survive, though a few archaeological traces have been uncovered on the Palatine and elsewhere. For any more detail we rely on the disapproving accounts written after the emperor's death, almost all dwelling on the luxury and the perverted ingenuity of the place: from the elusive revolving dining room to the hidden pipes that showered perfume on guests, or the tracts of artificial countryside (with woods, vineyards, fields and animals) that surrounded the artificial lake. Occasionally the evidence on the ground undermines those accounts. Suetonius, for example, describes the 'lake', almost as if it were a Neronian version of a modern rustic conceit, sheep and all, in the garden of an eighteenth-century English country house. And he hints at some dystopian upturning of the natural order of things, in the style of Elagabalus: the countryside implanted in the midst of the metropolis by imperial whim. The reality was not remotely like that. The few fragments that have been excavated make it almost certain that this 'lake' was not an imitation of some natural feature, set in a verdant landscape, but actually a formal, rectangular, urban pool in a stone basin, surrounded by marble porticoes.

33. The octagon room in the Golden House, once the setting for
Nero's dinner parties. The lighting came mainly from the opening in
the ceiling. One of the smaller adjacent rooms contained the almost
obligatory fountain. The original decoration included stucco, glass
mosaic and perhaps canopies draped over the dome itself.

Overall, many questions remain unanswered. We have little idea
how extensive this palace was. All the written evidence, including the
graffito about Rome becoming 'one house', stresses its size and take-
over of the city, but its boundaries are unknown. Modern estimates
range from a large 40 hectares (roughly twice the extent of Buckingham Palace, house and gardens combined) to an implausibly vast 160
hectares. Nor do we understand how it was arranged. It was clearly not
one huge single building. But how the parts on the Palatine related to
the surviving section on the Esquiline, and whether there was some

34. A glimpse of the palatial scale of the Golden House –
with a restorer at work on the frescoes that so impressed
the sixteenth-century artists who explored it.

public access to certain areas of the property, is anyone's guess. It was
not even finished by the time of Nero's death. The fire that cleared
the land for the project broke out in the summer of 64 CE and Nero
was forced to suicide within four years, which would mean impossibly
speedy construction work if everything had been completed. A few of
the dated bricks that survive confirm that some building operations
were still ongoing after Nero, into the reign of Vespasian.

This palace was something entirely unprecedented in the cityscape of Rome, but it was almost certainly a little less extravagant
than Roman writers make it seem. Significantly, perhaps, the emperor
Vitellius – who briefly lived in some part of the Golden House during

the civil wars in the year after Nero's fall – is said to have derided it for its poor accommodation and mean facilities (though that report may well have been intended more as a criticism of Vitellius's ridiculous expectations than of Nero's low standards). But, accurate or not, the hostile accounts of the palace written by Suetonius and others point to fundamental conflicts and controversies about how and where the emperor should live. The stress on its vast size raised the question of who *owned* the city, the emperor or the Roman people – a question underlined by the allegations that Nero himself had started the fire in 64 CE to clear the ground for his new living accommodation and by the rumours that he planned to rename Rome Neropolis (or 'Neroville'). What kind of residence was appropriate for a Roman autocrat anyway? How could you draw the line between the (faux) modesty of an Augustus and the (hyped) luxury of a Nero? And what did the house of an emperor reveal about imperial power? When Nero is quoted as saying that the Golden House made him feel that 'at last I am beginning to live like a human being', it was not only an indication of unselfconscious megalomania. The underlying question was what kind of 'human being' *was* the Roman emperor.

Vespasian, the first ruler in the dynasty that followed Nero in 69 CE, answered some of those questions by sponsoring a new building of a very different type. On the site of Nero's lake, and using the enormous profits he had made from putting down a Jewish rebellion and destroying the Temple in Jerusalem, he constructed what was then known simply as the 'Amphitheatre'. It was only later called the Colosseum, after the colossal statue of Nero that continued to stand nearby for centuries after the Golden House had disappeared (pp. 358–61, 362–3). Vespasian's message was clear. The city space that Nero had made his own private property was being returned to public use and public pleasure: 'Rome has been restored to herself', as one supportive poet crowed, to celebrate the Colosseum's official opening in 80, after a decade of building. Whatever had really been in Nero's mind, it suited the next dynasty to present him as an emperor who had stolen Rome from the Romans.

Nero's successors did not, however, immediately abandon the whole of the Golden House. Whatever their views, there was no other central city palace for the emperor to live in. Vitellius put up with its 'substandard' facilities for the short time he was in the capital. Vespasian let it be known that he preferred to be based in the imperial *horti* on the edge of town and made the grand gesture of turning Nero's lake into a popular entertainment venue, yet he finished some of the unfinished sections of the Golden House and no doubt used parts of it. But within a couple of decades most of it was gone or incorporated unrecognised in later developments. Vespasian and his sons, Titus and Domitian, had begun to establish a new palace on the Palatine, which crucially did not extend into the city beyond, though in its extravagance it was no more the residence of a ruler who was 'one of us' than was the *Domus Aurea*. Completed under Domitian, who is usually seen as the main mastermind behind it, from the late first century CE this would be the emperor's signature residence for the rest of Roman history, and it was repeatedly and extravagantly hyped by Roman writers (it left the pyramids in the shade, claimed the same poet who had heralded the opening of the Amphitheatre: 'there's nothing more splendid in the whole world'). This was where Statius came to dinner and these are the remains that visitors can still see, and in parts explore, on the Palatine Hill.

What happened on the hill?

We know more about what went on within, or just outside, the walls of this palace than almost any other building in the whole of the ancient Roman world (the senate house in the Forum, where Pliny gave his vote of thanks, is its only real rival).

It was here that many of the headline events of imperial history happened: emperors were raised and deposed, plots were hatched, declarations delivered. In 96 CE, Domitian was fatally stabbed in a *cubiculum* of his palace, murdered by some of his own staff, in the building he himself had commissioned. A hundred years later, Pertinax, who ruled briefly in the period of civil war in the 190s, was also stabbed to death 'at home', by a large group of angry soldiers who had forced their way in. According to the *Imperial History*, they 'went through the palace porticoes, until they reached the spot called "Sicilia" and "Jupiter's dining room" (*Iovis cenatio*)', and from there tracked down the emperor in 'the inner parts' of the residence – where his 'long and serious speech' did nothing to win them over. (One of Pertinax's problems had always been that he just didn't 'get' the mood of the soldiery.)

35. Much of the main part of the Palatine palace is very ruined and hard to decipher on the ground. The most striking feature in this view is, in fact, the Renaissance garden lodge (the Casino Farnese).

On a happier occasion, in 98, when Trajan came to the throne, his wife Plotina stood on the 'steps of the palace' and addressed the crowd. In a parade of modesty that would have gone down well with traditionalists (and in a rare example of public speaking by a woman, which would not have gone down so well), she promised not to be changed by her husband's power: 'exactly as I have arrived here,' she said, 'so I hope one day to depart – the same woman.'

But Roman literature also gives some hint of the more everyday business within the Palatine palace: from the regular dinners (not 'everyday' to the majority of the guests, I am sure) to the controlled 'open house' that took place most mornings. This occasion – technically called the *salutatio* or 'greeting' – was not an invention of the emperors. The big men of the Republic had often started the day by holding court to their friends and dependants, and the aristocrats of the city continued to do so under imperial rule. The emperors, though, gave this institution a new spin and a new scale. Their 'greetings' were usually restricted to select members of the Roman elite who, in coming to pay their respects, had the opportunity (or obligation) to show how well they could reconcile citizenly equality and deference to the ruler. But sometimes, in theory at least, any number of ordinary people were allowed to 'greet' the emperor, and presumably to try to bend his ear for whatever help or favour they wanted (pp. 221–2, 231).

These mass gatherings were probably a tough assignment for the emperor concerned. The elderly Antoninus Pius, in the mid second century CE, is said to have stuffed himself with his favourite dry bread in advance, simply to build up the stamina to manage it. And for the crowds who turned up, a lot of waiting must have been involved, even if they were eventually among the lucky ones to get admitted. One polymath, also in the mid second century, described occasions when he was among the people hanging around outside the palace ('in the Palatine Square', *in area Palatina*) or in the forecourt (*in vestibulo*): 'men of almost all ranks, waiting for their chance to pay their respects to the emperor'. Some of the intellectuals in the crowd, our polymath included, passed the time ostentatiously discussing knotty points of Latin grammar or the history of Roman law. We know the type.

Despite these rich and sometimes quirky descriptions of the Palatine palace, what we now see on the ground can seem like archaeology at its most frustrating. The detailed plan is even trickier to decode than appears at first sight. That is partly because some key areas have not been thoroughly excavated, and there are missing pieces in the jigsaw. It is partly because it is now hard to know what the upper storeys of the building, long ago destroyed, might have been like. ('What happened *upstairs?*' is one of the trickiest questions in the whole of classical archaeology.) But mostly it is because the palace was always a 'work in progress'. Over the centuries, it was improved, extended, repaired and rebuilt around the same basic plan. The fire of 64 CE was not the last to damage the buildings on the Palatine. In 192, for example, large sections of the palace, including the archives, went up in smoke. And it was repeatedly adapted to new, and unpredictable, requirements. In the early third century – so one story went – the whole building was divided into two separate halves in order to cope with the mutual hatred of Septimius Severus's sons, Caracalla and Geta, who had succeeded to the throne as joint rulers. In a bizarre case of multiple occupancy, they are supposed to have used the same front entrance but to have blocked the inside doors between the two sides. The result of all this is that we now see an almost impenetrable composite of structures, and adjustments, of different periods – a mass of walls, as Lord Byron despaired in the early nineteenth century, a feeling echoed by many other visitors since.

It is perhaps not surprising, then, that some modern accounts of this palace seem to come down to a list of what we *don't* know, or get stuck in the usually unbridgeable gap between what ancient writers tell us and what we can pinpoint on the ground. It's not simply that we cannot identify the *cubiculum* in which Domitian met his death, or plot

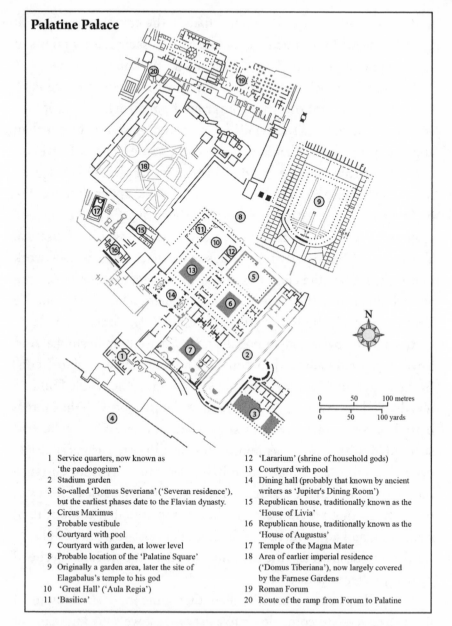

Palatine Palace

1 Service quarters, now known as 'the paedogogium'
2 Stadium garden
3 So-called 'Domus Severiana' ('Severan residence'), but the earliest phases date to the Flavian dynasty.
4 Circus Maximus
5 Probable vestibule
6 Courtyard with pool
7 Courtyard with garden, at lower level
8 Probable location of the 'Palatine Square'
9 Originally a garden area, later the site of Elagabalus's temple to his god
10 'Great Hall' ('Aula Regia')
11 'Basilica'
12 'Lararium' (shrine of household gods)
13 Courtyard with pool
14 Dining hall (probably that known by ancient writers as 'Jupiter's Dining Room')
15 Republican house, traditionally known as the 'House of Livia'
16 Republican house, traditionally known as the 'House of Augustus'
17 Temple of the Magna Mater
18 Area of earlier imperial residence ('Domus Tiberiana'), now largely covered by the Farnese Gardens
19 Roman Forum
20 Route of the ramp from Forum to Palatine

This simplified plan conflates different periods and irons out many uncertainties, but it still captures the complexity of the layout. The plan's key uses some of the conventional names for parts of the building, but the function of the different rooms is largely a matter of guesswork.

the path taken by the assassins of Pertinax ('Jupiter's dining room' was very likely part of the suite where Statius's dinner was served, but the spot named, or nicknamed, 'Sicilia' is a complete mystery). We do not even know where exactly the main entrance of the palace was, reluctantly shared by Caracalla and Geta, or the 'Palatine Square', where those pretentious scholars waited, or the steps from which Plotina addressed the crowds. So how the formal *salutationes* were actually organised is more or less a matter of guesswork. It seems plausible that, for the mass occasions, some of the large 'display rooms' (at other times doubling as dining rooms) were used for the 'greeting'. But most modern attempts to reconstruct the choreography of the ritual – how the people entered the presence of the emperor, or vice versa – have envisaged what is at first sight an implausibly circuitous route around the building, up and down narrow passageways and staircases. Even more of a mystery is where any of the administrative or service functions of the palace were carried out. Where did the slaves live? Where did the secretaries or the accountants or the laundry staff work? What about the storerooms, the transportation department or the stables? Were there 'offices' in our sense of the word? If so, where?

Yet to be overwhelmed by these questions we *cannot* answer is to miss the point of what the remains of this palace *can* tell us. First is its location. We have already seen that the emperor effectively ousted the old aristocracy from their favourite area of the city. But the position of the palace had an even greater symbolic impact than that. On one side of the Palatine Hill it overlooked the Forum, the old political heart of the city, where the senate house stood, where citizens had once gathered to vote, and where Republican big men had addressed the crowds. If you had looked up from the Forum as you walked out from the senate house, at any time after the late first century CE, the view would have been dominated – much like it is today – by the residence of the emperor towering above. There could be no doubt where the power now lay.

On the other side of the hill the palace overlooked an equally important monument in Roman cultural life and imagination: the Circus Maximus. For us, this Circus, where from the earliest days of the city regular chariot races took place, has tended to be eclipsed by the Colosseum (pp. 267–71). But if you were looking up to the Palatine from the south, you would have seen both palace and Circus together. The link between them was a crucial one with a clear message: the emperor was at home with the people, at the centre of popular entertainment. There was even what appears to be a small-scale racetrack within the grounds of the palace itself. This was not where the emperor enjoyed chariot-racing in the privacy of his own home. It was actually a garden, with porticoes and colonnades, flowers and fountains, all built *on the plan* of a stadium. These 'stadium gardens' were part of the more general repertoire of elite Roman landscape design. Pliny was proud of his version, with its roses and manicured box hedges, at one of his out-of-town villas, and the emperor Hadrian had something similar, equipped for dining (p. 96). But here on the Palatine, the miniature circus must have been a reminder of the real site of popular entertainment just a stone's throw away.

The second point is the sheer complexity of the palace layout. Even if the composite plans and the mass of walls of different dates now give an exaggerated impression of the impenetrable confusion, it was still a maze: laid out on different levels, with sunken courtyards and towering display rooms, dead ends and twists and turns, a mixture of open spaces, internal gardens and a dark warren of passageways. This is frustrating for those of us now trying to make some sense of the plan. But it served a purpose. Royal palaces across the world have often used unfathomably intricate layouts as a security device. One European traveller to Japan in the eighteenth century reported that Tokyo's royal palace of Chiyoda Castle had 'so many intersections, different moats and ramparts that I was unable to work out its ground plan'. It is much the same to this day with Buckingham Palace. In ancient Rome, too, the architecture was presumably meant to disorient outsiders, who simply would not have been able to find their way around the place independently, whether they were up to mischief or not. We know that an influx of people coming to greet the emperor in the morning was recognised to pose security risks. Claudius was not the only one to have had the visitors frisked for weapons hidden in their togas. One Roman dissident reported that Augustus too had senators patted down and – in conflict with the image of the emperor as 'one of us' – only allowed them to approach him one by one. And if the 'implausibly circuitous' route that has been suggested to bring them into the emperor's presence at the *salutatio* is correct, my guess is that it was intended as a strategy of disorientation rather than as an opportunity (as one archaeologist has rather desperately suggested) to show off the palace's splendour.

But there is another side to this. This maze imprisoned the emperor

36. The Palatine stadium garden was originally lined with shady porticoes, decorated with sculpture and enhanced with fountains: the setting, we imagine, for walks and talks, exercise and idling.

almost as much as it confused and controlled his visitors. It put him at the mercy of his family, his slaves, his staff and his guards, whether they were loyal or disloyal. Claudius may have been concerned about the danger of outsiders when he had them frisked. Domitian was much more likely thinking about the danger of insiders when he had the walls of his porticoes lined with reflective stone, to see who was coming up from behind. The palace was where emperors were proudly on display: receiving guests, hosting banquets or private suppers, parading before those who came to pay their respects. It was also the most dangerous place they could ever be. The murder of Julius Caesar in public, at a meeting of the senate, was almost a one-off in the period. Most emperors who fell victim to assassins were killed at home. This was not only where the poison was surreptitiously added to their food. This is where the daggers came out too: from the murder of Caligula, who was jumped on by a couple of disaffected guardsmen as he made his way around the palace compound, through Domitian and Pertinax, to the dispatch of Commodus in 192, strangled in his bath (or his bed; accounts differ) by his personal trainer. The most extreme case, though, was said to be the murder of Geta in 211. Ancient writers told a lurid story that, when the multiple occupancy arrangement in the palace finally broke down, Caracalla had his soldiers stab his brother to death in their mother's quarters on the Palatine, as he clung to her for safety. True or not, it captures the idea of the palace as a gilded cage for the emperor, where no one could be trusted.

There is just one place on the Palatine where you can still almost feel this atmosphere. It is the access ramp, built in its present form under Domitian, leading from the Forum up to the top of the hill and to the palace itself. It consisted of a narrow corridor, about 11 metres tall, which zigzagged up the slope, originally in seven twists and turns. It is easy to imagine how intimidating this could have been for the average visitor: you couldn't see who or what was coming round the corner, and armed guards must have been stationed on every bend (the latrines along the route were presumably for their use). But the emperor did not know who was coming round the corner either, and his safety in any such location depended on those armed guards remaining loyal. The fear that we sense here is an important counter-weight to the excitement of Statius at his banquet in the palace, the enthusiasm of Pliny for Trajan's generous open house, or Plotina's judicious speech on the steps.

37. The twisting zigzags of the ramp leading from the Forum up to the Palatine palace. A guard standing at every bend could control who went up and down.

The art of reconstruction

This ramp would not originally have presented quite so industrial an image as it now does, looking more warehouse than imperial residence. Again, the bare brick that we see today would have been faced in marble or covered in stucco, creating an altogether more lavish, if no less awe-inspiring, impression. That is just one reminder of the work of the imagination needed to picture the Palatine palace as it was in ancient times. Many archaeologists and illustrators have tried to help with the problem, offering careful reconstructions, scrupulously based on the surviving evidence, of parts of the building far less well preserved than the ramp (pl. 9). But how accurately do they capture the atmosphere, style or impact of the original? How good an impression of the emperor's palace do they give?

Like most archaeological reconstructions, they are rather short on people, from the emperor to the cleaners, whom I shall be trying to bring back into focus in the next chapter. Here we see, at best, a few diminutive figures completely dominated by the building. But the grand architectural context itself – a combination of fascist dictatorship, postmodern aesthetic and Hollywood movie – is also seriously misleading. It is a vision of the public, display areas of the palace (no one yet has been much interested in recreating 'below stairs') as furniture-free and clinically spotless, when there is very good reason to suppose that, for all their lavish luxury, even these parts would have been much messier and more cluttered. It was more an Aladdin's cave than a series of echoing, empty chambers.

It is relatively easy in your mind's eye to reclad the bare walls with plaster, paint and marble. It is also relatively easy to reimagine the paintings, sculptures and precious *objets d'art* that must have been on display. The archaeological discoveries in the *horti* and, as we shall see, at Hadrian's property at Tivoli give some hint of the sculptural richness and decorative style of the palace, from inlaid floors and exquisite mosaic panels to the best masterpieces Roman money could buy. And some smaller works of art now on museum display across the Western world almost certainly once belonged to imperial properties, even if we cannot pin them down exactly. Museum labels rarely make it clear quite how many of the surviving Roman masterpieces were the property of an emperor. But where else do we imagine that the outsized cameo (over 30 centimetres tall), depicting the family of the emperor Tiberius, would have been at home? It might have moved around a bit under different regimes, but it surely belonged somewhere on the imperial estate (pl. 17).

Ancient writers help us fill out the picture with their lists of treasures owned by particular emperors. The uncle of the consul Pliny – a learned encyclopaedia writer now usually known as Pliny the Elder to distinguish him from his nephew – records that the famous sculpture of Laocoon the Trojan priest being strangled by snakes once stood in the palace of the emperor Titus. He also notes that Tiberius was particularly fond of a painting by the fourth-century BCE Greek artist Parrhasius that he kept in his *cubiculum*, depicting a self-castrated priest of the Great Mother (just like those who lived next door to him on the Palatine). What this looked like, or how he had acquired it, we do not know – like most ancient paintings, it has long since been lost. But it was valued at six million sesterces in Roman money, well over the total wealth of many senators. It was a passion, or greed, for great works of art that rebounded on Tiberius. He was so keen on one antique Greek statue (dating back to the fourth century BCE) that stood outside a set of public baths in Rome that he removed it to his own residence, substituting another in its place. But after a demonstration in the theatre, where the audience shouted 'Give us back our sculpture', he was forced to return the piece. This is the 'Golden House Problem' writ small: how far could, or should, the emperor claim *private* ownership of the *public* art of the city? It was presumably to defend themselves against accusations of the same type that other emperors are supposed to have made a show of transferring some of the jewels of the palace, and the gold and silver plate, to public temples. The story went that Alexander Severus had disposed of so much precious tableware that, for a large dinner party, he had to borrow from his friends.

To recapture the original appearance of the palace, however, we need to think beyond the art treasures and the luxury. We need to put back the furniture, the lighting, the incense burners, the soft fabrics and the wall hangings (the internal doorways in the excavated part of the Golden House show no trace of hinged doors, implying that they were 'closed' with curtains). We need to have in mind rather more idiosyncratic elements of design. There were the constellations, replicating the stars under which he was born, that Septimius Severus had painted onto one ceiling in the palace, and the royal aviaries that were Alexander Severus's pet project, housing – according to one unreliable overestimate – 20,000 doves, as well as ducks, hens, partridges and so on. Augustus's animal mascot seems rather modest in comparison: a favourite goat, with deliciously sweet milk, which is supposed to have gone everywhere with her master. We also have to remember the collection of bric-a-brac, souvenirs, trophies and wonders from all over the empire that ended up in the palace, and made it the equivalent of a monumental 'cabinet of curiosities'.

Some of these were the spoils of war. After Roman forces under the future emperor Titus had destroyed the city and Temple of Jerusalem in 70 CE, his father Vespasian had all the treasures deposited in his new Temple of 'Pax' ('Pacification' gets the sense better than the usual translation of 'Peace'), except for 'the Law', probably the Torah scrolls, and the purple hangings from the Temple, which were placed in the palace. It is certain that some of the masterpieces of Greek art that had originally come to Rome, centuries before, as the loot of conquest, would have ended up there too. But other 'curiosities' were marvels of nature, or fakes passed off as such marvels. Emperors themselves actively collected the wonders of their empire, while their subjects donated any number of curious specimens, no doubt in the hope of a generous reward.

There are references to such weird and wonderful things in various imperial properties. At his villa on Capri, Augustus curated what has recently been called 'the world's first paleontological museum', or, as Suetonius described it, a collection of 'things notable for their antiquity and their rarity, such as the huge bones of beasts of land and sea, known as the "bones of giants"'. In one of the imperial gardens on the outskirts of Rome a large tusk was kept, said to have been from the monstrous 'Calydonian boar' (killed, back in the mists of time, by the mythical Greek hero Meleager). This had been taken by Augustus from a shrine in Greece, and by the second century CE was under the care of the emperor's (significantly named) 'keepers of the wonders'. But some of these things ended up in the Palatine palace itself. One particularly colourful example, discussed in an ancient compendium of all sorts of 'marvels', compiled by a man who had been a slave of Hadrian, was supposedly a centaur, a half man/half horse. According to the compiler, Phlegon, it had been captured by a local dynast in the hills of Arabia, and sent to the province of Egypt as a gift for the emperor, presumably to be transported onwards. Whatever it really was, the poor creature died, and had to be embalmed before its body could be forwarded to Rome, where at first it was displayed in the palace. By the second century CE, ragged at the edges, I would guess, if not a bit smelly, it had been relegated to the imperial cellars or storerooms (where Phlegon saw it, slightly disappointed that it wasn't quite the size he had imagined). It was as if the wonders of the empire, and its surprises, converged on the imperial palace.

But for us, the biggest surprise of the palace decoration is not this range of natural, or mythical, curiosities, from tusks and teeth to alleged centaurs, but a strange graffito found in one of the few parts of the Palatine palace where plaster – and what was scratched into it – survives on the wall. This is a set of rooms, around a courtyard, overlooking the Circus Maximus, used from the late first century CE on and covered in more than 350 surviving graffiti. It is hard to know what exactly these rooms were for, but they certainly belong to the 'service' rather than the display side of the palace. The phrase found more than a dozen times, 'so-and-so has left the *paedagogium*' (*exit de paedagogio*), has suggested that this might have been a 'slave training school' (one possible meaning of the word *paedagogium*) – and that these particular graffiti are then a record of a slave's 'graduation' from the school. But other less plausible guesses about its function include a slave prison, a hospital, a barracks and the palace wardrobe department (thanks to another graffito that lists items of clothing). Its claim to fame is, in any case, something quite different and much clearer: a scratched drawing parodying a scene of Jesus's crucifixion. This is not a total surprise. St Paul, for one, claimed that the emperor's household was a hotbed of Christianity. But here we see striking evidence of that: a human figure with a donkey's head pinned to a cross, with a man in

38. A parody of a Christian worshipper scratched in plaster (on the left), with a reconstructed line-drawing (on the right), found in service quarters on the Palatine. The 'joke' is written in rough and ready Greek, starting with the target's name, Alexamenos, and continuing with 'worship your god', or perhaps 'worships his god'.

prayer below. The caption, in Greek, reads 'Alexamenos, worship your god'. It was presumably intended as a joke on a Christian among the slaves (non-Christians in the empire are known to have called Jesus 'donkey-headed'), and if it dates to the end of the second century, as is the usual guess, it is one of the earliest representations of the crucifixion, perhaps *the* earliest, to have survived from anywhere in the world. There is a certain irony that, when so many of the expensive decorations in the palace have disappeared with hardly a trace, one of the most striking survivals is a roughly scratched graffito, probably by a slave taking a potshot at another who was a member of a minority radical sect that eventually emperors themselves would join.

Hadrian's world

Another irony is that some – probably many – Roman rulers spent relatively little time on the Palatine. Despite the significant events that took place there, from accession to assassination, despite its key position in the political geography of the city, and despite the extravagant praise lavished by loyal poets on both the Palatine palace and its occupant, it was almost a Roman cliché that most emperors had other favourite quarters well away from the city centre, ones they had inherited, remodelled to their tastes or built from scratch. Tiberius's retreat to his villas on Capri for the last decade of his reign is only the most notorious example of an emperor who based himself elsewhere. Vespasian, as well as preferring the suburban *horti* when in Rome, opted to spend the summers in his family house in the Sabine hills. In the third century CE, Alexander Severus came at the end of a long line of emperor-builders, constructing for himself a brand-new seaside palace at the resort of Baiae, near Naples, calling it, or so it was said, after his mother, Julia Mamaea (as if to underline his reputation as a bit of a 'mummy's boy').

Part of the appeal of these out-of-town residences was practical. People with money have always abandoned Rome for the hills or the coast during the heat of the summer. But part was, no doubt, the different lifestyle that could be enjoyed outside the city, away from the gilded cage of the Palatine. Sometimes that itself raised suspicions. When Tiberius decamped to Capri, one assumption was that he was looking for a place to indulge his monstrous habits away from prying eyes (as well as insulting Rome by his prolonged absence). But an altogether more wholesome picture of imperial life in a country villa is given by the young Marcus Aurelius, in one of a collection of letters between him and his tutor Marcus Cornelius Fronto (pp. 210–11). The future emperor, still in his early twenties, writes from the very estate that had incorporated the view of the grape-treaders into its dining room, describing how he had spent his day: rising early to read a treatise on agriculture; gargling for a sore throat; attending a sacrifice conducted by his adoptive father, Antoninus Pius; some grape-picking; a long chat with *his* 'mummy', sitting together on a couch; a bath followed by dinner, against a background of 'yokels squabbling' over their treading; and then bed. Where exactly this stands on the spectrum between serious country business and Marie Antoinette playing at milkmaids is hard to know.

It would, in any case, have been different for the ruling emperor, Antoninus Pius, himself. Imperial business, from the *salutatio* (albeit on a smaller scale) to matters of law, continued wherever the emperor happened to be, even on Tiberius's Capri, where sex in the swimming pool probably took second place to routine administration. These other residences were 'palaces' in the business sense of the word, not merely private hideaways. Young Marcus Aurelius refers to 'paying his respects' (*salutare*) to his father in the morning, on the country estate. And Pliny explains in a letter how much he enjoyed a visit to one of Trajan's seaside estates, where he helped the emperor and other advisers resolve some tricky legal problems. It took them three days (followed by more of those simple suppers) to judge the cases: that of an army officer's wife, who had had an affair with one of the lower ranks, but had apparently been forgiven by her husband (she was exiled nonetheless); a dispute over a forged will, where a former slave of the emperor was one of the accused (Trajan bent over backwards, Pliny claims, to show him no favour); and some unspecified trumped-up allegations against a man from Ephesus, who had travelled all the way from his home town on the coast of modern Turkey to defend himself (allegations dismissed).

Meanwhile, copies of imperial decisions or official letters written by emperors, permanently inscribed on stone and publicly displayed in cities across the empire (hence their survival), often included details of *where* the decision had been made or the letter sent from. These can amount to a virtual imperial address book or diary. On 22 July 82 CE, for example, it was 'in Albano' – at his villa in the Alban hills, at modern Castel Gandolfo – that Domitian adjudicated a land dispute between two neighbouring Italian towns. Just over forty years later, at the end of August or beginning of September 125 (only part of the date survives), Hadrian wrote to the Greek city of Delphi and its priestly council to acknowledge the receipt of a letter brought by an embassy. The emperor's reply, fragments of its inscribed copy still preserved in Delphi, explicitly says that it was written at his villa 'at Tibur'.

The emperor's villa 'at Tibur' is what we now know as 'Hadrian's villa at Tivoli' (Tibur being the ancient place name), about 20 miles from Rome. This private town, with its theatres, baths, colonnades, libraries, gardens, residential blocks, slave dormitories, multiple dining suites and more, extended originally over 120 hectares, and was never covered with later buildings, unlike most of the urban imperial properties. The modern archaeological site occupies only about 40 hectares of that, with traces of almost a thousand rooms still visible. The rest of it lies, largely unexcavated, under the neighbouring fields. This was no 'work in progress', gradually expanding over the decades or centuries. In an extraordinary feat of integrated design, capital invest-ment, coordinated supply chain and human labour, it was built to a single master plan in just a few years of Hadrian's reign, as the dated and stamped bricks make clear. It continued to be used as an impe-rial palace after his death in 138 CE (how else to explain the portrait statues of later emperors found on the site?), but the original concep-tion never seems to have changed. This was a complete creation of Hadrian on an almost parodic scale, although – largely because of his many travels (chapter 8) – it is not clear how long, or often, he was in residence even here.

No less striking than its size is the quantity of sculpture and other works of art that swamped this estate, and that were apparently forgot-ten when the place was abandoned in the fourth century CE. Many of the classical masterpieces of museums in Europe and America were later dug up here: from the exquisite mosaic of doves in a birdbath, one of the highlights of the Capitoline Museums in Rome (pl. 10), to eight large Muses, once owned by Queen Christina of Sweden and now in the Prado in Madrid, and a rather dreamy marble Hercules who now takes pride of place in the Getty Villa Museum in Malibu. Altogether we know of more than four hundred reasonably well-preserved statues from the site, not to mention the fragments of hundreds of others piled up in the storerooms at Tivoli, and more still being excavated. The vast majority of these were newly made according to a single grand design, often copies or versions of earlier masterpieces, not precious antiques or loot from the empire. It was artistic production on an industrial scale.

To delight the diners around the 'Canopus canal', for example, the sculptural highlights included four exact replicas of caryatids from the Athenian Acropolis, a couple of wounded Amazons (female warriors) based on famous fifth-century BCE Greek prototypes, a clutch of clas-sical Greek gods (Ares, Athena, Dionysus), not to mention a marble crocodile that doubled as a fountain (water spewed out of its mouth).

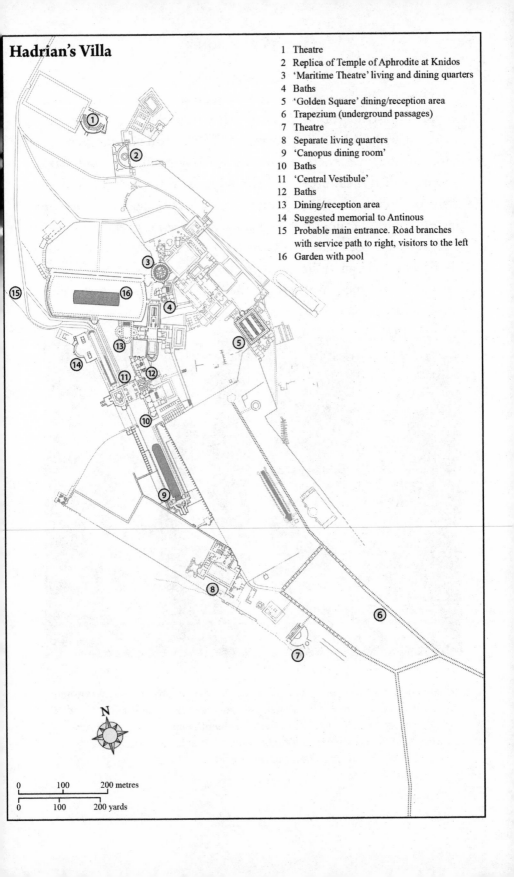

Hadrian's Villa

1 Theatre
2 Replica of Temple of Aphrodite at Knidos
3 'Maritime Theatre' living and dining quarters
4 Baths
5 'Golden Square' dining/reception area
6 Trapezium (underground passages)
7 Theatre
8 Separate living quarters
9 'Canopus dining room'
10 Baths
11 'Central Vestibule'
12 Baths
13 Dining/reception area
14 Suggested memorial to Antinous
15 Probable main entrance. Road branches
   with service path to right, visitors to the left
16 Garden with pool

N

0   100   200 metres

0   100   200 yards

One prominent design theme on the estate as a whole was the art of Egypt, with statues of Isis and other deities, of Egyptian priests and worshippers, and lookalike pharaohs. Hadrian had visited Egypt, as a tourist, and it was there that his beloved boyfriend, the young slave Antinous, had died, drowning mysteriously in the Nile while they were 'on holiday' in 130 CE ('did he fall or was he pushed?' was the big question). It cannot be a coincidence that some of the dozens of images of Antinous that Hadrian commissioned for the villa after his death depicted him in the guise of an Egyptian god – whether as an aesthetic preference, an allusion to the place of his death, or proclaiming his immortal status (fig. 41).

39. Two of the Muses from Hadrian's villa, discovered around 1500. Originally decorating the stage of a private theatre, they are now in the Prado in Madrid. They were heavily restored in the seventeenth century and given new attributes to make them individually identifiable: here on the left, Urania, the Muse of astronomy; on the right, Erato, the Muse of lyric poetry.

In a sense, Tivoli was a Golden House in the country. That is certainly what artists and collectors thought, who from the Renaissance on explored it for the genuine undisturbed remains of the Roman world, or for the chance to get their hands on those ancient treasures that we still admire in our museums. (One of Raphael's pupils, Giovanni da Udine, who scratched his name on the walls of the Golden House, also left his signature in the stucco at Tivoli.) But even though his villa was almost as big as the most implausibly exaggerated estimates of the size of Nero's palace, Hadrian got away with it. That was because – as well as Hadrian's good fortune in having a successor, Antoninus Pius, who was invested in giving him a good press – his architectural megalomania was safely out of sight, not in the city of Rome itself. Or he *almost* got away with it. There were some critics who saw in this a version of the 'Tiberius problem'. As one later Roman writer reported, it was Hadrian's retreat to the countryside, and his devotion to luxury there, that 'gave rise to dark rumours that he abused young boys'. The ancient logic is that emperors who avoided the gaze of their fellow citizens, whether on Capri or at Tivoli, were likely to be up to no good.

For us, the archaeology of Hadrian's villa has revealed all kinds of intriguing details of the day-to-day management of the emperor's housing and home life, right down to the techniques of the imperial gardeners, who recycled old containers of wine and oil (*amphorae*) to use as planting pots. One of the most surprising discoveries has been a three-mile network of underground tunnels (it has been estimated that just one section of this – the 'trapezium' – involved digging out 20,000 cubic metres of solid bedrock). The main purpose of these tunnels was presumably to allow the slaves to move around out of sight of the elite residents above, just as the main entrance to the whole estate seems to have had a separate 'staff track' at a lower level, unseen by the upmarket visitors who entered by the upper and grander route (p. 163, no. 15). But other more ingenious uses have also been proposed, from ice house to underground car park. Parts of the network are certainly wide enough for wheeled transport, and could have allowed access for, and possibly storage of, visitors' carriages.

Even at Tivoli, despite the enormous amount of material that survives, it remains next to impossible to figure out how the residence *worked* more generally, or (once again) what most of the rooms were for. The single ancient description of the place that we have – in the biography of Hadrian in the *Imperial History* – says only that the emperor called the different parts of his villa after famous places in the world: the Lycaeum (Aristotle's philosophy school in Athens), the Academy (Plato's), the Canopus, even a Hades (the underworld), and so on. Yet this account was written over two hundred years after Hadrian's death, by an author who was not immune to fantasy, and no amount of scholarly effort has ever managed convincingly to match

40. A line-up of four caryatids (supporting columns in the form of women), based on the figures from the fifth-century BCE Erechtheum on the Acropolis in Athens. Hadrian must have seen these on his travels (pp. 296–9), but at his villa these sculptures originally from a sacred shrine are turned into the lavish adornment of a dining suite.

41. A portrait of Antinous found in Hadrian's villa (now in the Louvre).
The young man is shown in Egyptian guise (with the distinctive
headdress). There may be a parallel intended here – as elsewhere
– between Antinous and the Egyptian god Osiris, who according
to Egyptian myth drowned in the Nile and was then reborn.

any of the names to surviving buildings – apart from the link between
the Canopus and the dining suite that we have already explored (and
some archaeologists are dubious even about that). For the rest, there is
a long modern history of identification, re-identification and dispute.

What earlier generations of scholars liked to think of as libraries
(believing Hadrian to be a bookish type) have often been re-cat-
egorised as entertainment areas. Barracks for the emperor's guard
have been reinterpreted as guest rooms, or vice versa. Even newly, and
carefully, excavated areas are contested. One mock-Egyptian building near the main entrance to the residence, discovered only at the
end of the twentieth century (complete with traces of the date palms

42. Part of the network of underground passages that provided service routes underneath the display rooms and entertainment suites of Hadrian's villa – keeping the underclass and the infrastructure out of the sight of the emperor and his circle.

originally planted there to match the architecture), has been seen by some archaeologists as just a rather grand part of the 'Egyptianising' decorative theme, and by others as the burial place of Antinous himself, his body fished out of the Nile and brought back to rest in his lover's villa. That itself points to wider questions about this place. Was it, despite the size, fairly 'ordinary', or at least the kind of residence that any member of the Roman elite might have built if he had had limitless cash and resources? We know of other rich Romans, Cicero and Pliny among others, who occasionally gave their garden features the names of 'exotic' places in the Eastern Mediterranean. So, was it then no more than an overblown *reductio ad absurdum* of a Roman villa? Or was it an intensely individual, idiosyncratic project, recreating Hadrian's life and passion in brick and marble, including the burial of his beloved Antinous? Was it, as one archaeologist has recently called it, *the emperor's dream*? Or was it a bit of all three?

After years of puzzling over Hadrian's 'villa', I am sure that something else is at stake. We have already seen in the dining rooms of the Palatine palace that the marble decoration, quarried all over the Roman world, was one way of evoking the geography and wide expanse of the empire at its very heart. The marvels of nature from distant provinces that ended up on display in the imperial residences were another. The emperor's palace at Tivoli takes that idea even further. That is what the author of the *Imperial History* suggests when he refers to parts of the estate being named after all those famous places. But it is also implied by the reproductions of famous masterpieces with which it

43. The replica temple in Hadrian's villa that is believed to copy the shrine of Aphrodite at Knidos, with a version of the famous nude statue in the background.

was stuffed: the wonders of Egypt, the highlights of fifth-century BCE Athens, even a walk-in replica of the famous Temple of Aphrodite at Knidos on the coast of modern Turkey, complete with a lookalike of its even more famous statue, by the Greek sculptor Praxiteles – the original famous for being the first ever full-sized nude statue of a woman in the classical world.

Hadrian had probably seen many of these masterpieces on his travels. But there is more to this than simply tourist souvenirs. And there is more to it than a rich man's theme park, even if it is hard entirely to banish the comparison with Las Vegas or Disneyland (right down to the underground world of staff quarters and supply corridors, as at Disney, designed to service the fantasy world above). Hadrian's villa was a microcosm of Hadrian's empire. The point he was amplifying at Tivoli was that the emperor belonged at the centre of the Roman world. The empire was his palace, the palace his empire.

5

PALACE PEOPLE: THE EMPEROR IN HIS COURT

The father of Claudius Etruscus

One man who knew the corridors of Roman palaces better than almost anyone is the subject of another extravagant poem by Statius: not, this time, a member of the imperial family or the grand host of official banquets, but a man who was born a slave and, after decades of service to one Roman ruler after another, became the head of the emperor's finance division (the *a rationibus*, as he was called in Latin, or 'chief accountant'). We do not actually know his name. Statius's long poem, of more than two hundred lines, is addressed to his son, Tiberius Claudius Etruscus, in consolation for his father's death in 92 CE. He is known to us simply as 'the father of Claudius Etruscus'.

In florid style ('through twice eight lustres the fortunate genera-tions flowed', and so on) and loaded with mythological allusions that would have been arcane even to most Roman readers, Statius reviews the father's career – starting from his origins as a slave in Smyrna, on the coast of what is now Turkey, followed by his sale into the household of Tiberius in Rome, where he became 'bosom compan-ion' of succeeding emperors. He was with Caligula on campaign in 'the Arctic icelands' (better known as Germany), was promoted by

Claudius, until he eventually became head of finances under Vespasian (controlling, as the poet extravagantly hypes, 'all that Spain spews out from its gold-bearing mines / ... whatever in the African harvests / is gathered... / everything the North wind, the violent East or the cloudy South / brings in'). At the same time, he climbed the ladder of social status: freed from slavery by Tiberius, married to a woman from a senatorial family, and formally given 'equestrian' rank by Vespasian (the next rank down from senators in the Roman hierarchy). Success seems to have followed success, until things went wrong under Domitian. Although Statius tries to dress it up as if it were a lengthy seaside holiday, this successful palace administrator and long-term survivor was dismissed from his post and exiled from Rome to south Italy in 82 or 83 CE. Allowed back seven or eight years later, he died soon after, aged nearly ninety.

The father of Claudius Etruscus takes us behind the scenes of the imperial palace. It is a world, in one sense, of social mobility. Here, a man born into slavery could – thanks to his closeness to a series of emperors – end up in the ranks of the Roman aristocracy, even if ousted from the court itself. But it was social mobility with strings. At the start of the poem, Statius openly calls his honorand's low birth a 'defect' or 'disgrace'. And he never once names him. It is almost as if the father never quite shook off the lack of *social existence* that was a defining feature of Roman slavery. Despite his promotion and celebrity, and despite his starring role in the poem, he still remained (and remains) a 'nobody'.

It was also a world of risk and danger. The lesson that most modern historians have drawn from this life story is just how insecure life at the Roman imperial court could be. A loyal retainer or the emperor's pal could any minute find themselves banished from court or capital, when rulers changed, internal politics took a different turn, or personal grudges came out. That is, as we shall see, absolutely true. The orbit of the emperor was always a perilous place to be. But there are other lessons too in the father's story. Suppose he had died a decade or so earlier, before his exile. We would then be focusing on the continuity of service he represented, working for ruler after ruler, even as one dynasty gave way to the next. And our image would be of a loyal palace functionary who could be lauded in terms almost as extravagant as the praise of the emperor himself. The fact is that the imperial palace was *both* a dangerous den of vipers, a lair of backstabbers, *and* a place where hundreds of men and women, enslaved and free, lived out their lives, got on with their jobs, made friends and found partners, whether they railed against their own exploitation or took pride in their work (or both).

I want to put back into our picture of the imperial palaces some of the *people* who lived or worked there, or those who regularly got past the front door. The men doing what we would call 'office jobs' (if only we knew what a Roman 'office' was like), working in the emperor's finance department, his libraries, his secretariat, his archives, were just one important part of it. The palace population stretched from the emperor himself to the humblest hairdresser or floor sweeper, from poets on the make to the power brokers who commanded the imperial guard or, almost as important, supervised the city's water supply. Only some of these grabbed the attention of Roman observers and commentators, in particular, the slaves and ex-slaves who in the view of the traditional elite used their closeness to the emperor to 'get above themselves'; the women of the emperor's family, repeatedly painted as devious plotters or poisoners, manipulating power behind the throne; and the others who shared the emperor's bed, from devoted companions to exploited victims. How close can we now get to any of these people and to what they did? And how closely can we look the emperor himself in the eye? Can we ever see a human being through the spin, the propaganda, the praise and denunciations?

The goings-on inside the Roman palace were often treated by Romans themselves as a mystery behind closed doors, and their lurid fantasies about palace life thrived in part because of that. But we actually have a surprising range of eyewitness perspectives on the emperor 'at home', and from bottom to top of the social hierarchy. One Roman writer of moral tales – a poet and adaptor of the better-known Aesop, by the name of Phaedrus – had very likely once been a slave in the imperial court, and his *Fables* (*the* classic literature of the underdog) featured emperors and their acolytes, sometimes thinly disguised as animals. The philosopher Epictetus had been the slave of an ex-slave of the emperor (in one of those complicated Roman networks of exploitation), and he drew on examples from his own palace experiences when he theorised on the nature of power. Higher up the pecking order was the imperial biographer Suetonius, who had spent years working in the secretariat of Trajan and Hadrian, and knew the gossip in the corridors of power first-hand – while the imperial doctor Galen, medical adviser to Marcus Aurelius, Commodus and Septimius Severus, preserved the case notes of his emperors' bodily frailties, and a glimpse of the contents of their imperial medicine cabinets. At the very top, in his *Jottings to Himself*, Marcus Aurelius offered some choice meditations, and occasionally improbable musings, on life at the palace, claiming, for example, that he wanted to dispense with 'bodyguards and flashy clothes' and live as close as possible to the life of a private citizen.

Court culture

Royal courts have often had a bad press, regularly deplored as hotbeds of rivalry, hypocrisy and insincere flattery, or – worse – plotting, conspiracy and murder. They can be self-obsessed microcosms, where proud inclusion in the inner circle, or humiliating exclusion from it, counts for everything; where elaborate rules of etiquette are designed to mark out, or trip up, the inexperienced or the unwary ('using the

44. The bronze statue of Marcus Aurelius, now in the Capitoline Museums, but until recently it had been on public display in the open air – in different locations – since the second century CE. See pp. 306 and 356.

wrong knife and fork' would be a very minor case of that); where no one ever quite means what they say; and where only one thing matters – how close you are, and are publicly *seen* to be, to the ruler himself. Their courtly conventions are some of the mechanisms by which the monarch controls those closest to him, and his rivals.

Yet there is another side to this, even if it is one that captures the historical headlines more rarely. For the court also enables autocracy to operate successfully. It provides the advisers, sounding boards and friends who help the monarch to govern (no one can govern alone), and who act as a filter, or as a system of brokerage, between him and the outside world (access to the king is policed by the personnel of the court). Its elaborate etiquette provides a set of rules to constrain the ruler as much as his subordinates. And its pomposity and flummery are always vulnerable to satiric barbs from inside and outside the palace walls.

The mixed assortment of people who surrounded the Roman emperor 'at home', and comprised his court – his *aula* in Latin – fits into that pattern. There were hundreds and hundreds of them. To return to the latrines, a forty-seater lavatory excavated near (but not directly connected with) the luxurious dining room of Nero is just one vivid indication of how many people must have milled around the palace. And they were *very* mixed. Marcus Aurelius at one point in his *Jottings* lists some of the people who made up the court of the emperor Augustus more than a hundred years earlier. The list goes from the emperor's family ('his wife, daughter, grandson, stepsons,

45. The multi-seater lavatory in Nero's (pre-Golden House) palace on the Palatine – presumably for the use of slaves and other staff, rather than elite guests. The channel in front of the seats carried clean flowing water, in which the users would have washed the sponges on sticks, with which they wiped their bottoms.

sister, son-in-law Agrippa, and other relatives') through his 'household staff', his 'friends' (Areius, a resident philosopher, and Maecenas, his cultural guru, get a special namecheck), down to his 'doctors' and 'diviners'.

Marcus Aurelius need not have stopped there. He could have gone on to mention any number of other fixtures of the emperor's circle, from the dwarfs and jesters, astrologers and fortune-tellers, military officers and bodyguards (perhaps all covered under the capacious category of 'household staff') to whole classrooms of youngsters – whether the troupes of naked slave children that some imperial ladies liked to have following them around, the offspring of foreign royalty, held in Rome as hostages and trophies, or the sons of select members of the Roman elite who lodged there. As a boy, long before his father was a claimant to the imperial throne, the emperor Titus, for example, had been raised in the palace during the reign of Claudius. Then in 55 CE he was an eyewitness to one of the most notorious crimes within the 'inner circle'. He was actually there at dinner, sitting right next to him on the special children's table, when his young friend Britannicus keeled over and died, allegedly poisoned on the orders of his stepbrother Nero (pp. 112–13). This was a world of toddlers and teenagers, as well as grown-ups and greybeards. Indeed, Epictetus cynically concluded that some of the greybeards, in pursuing crumbs of the emperor's favour, were not so very different from toddlers.

Of course, those within the court were not all treated in the same way. The slaves who lived on-site (wherever their lodgings were) would obviously have had a very different experience of palace life from the likes of Pliny, or any of the other high-ranking 'friends-cum-functionaries', who turned up in their litters to pay their respects in the morning or to dine in the evening (this was not a residential court in the way that Versailles was – the elite courtiers did not live on-site). But many of the surviving Roman comments on court culture reflect those standard views about life in a monarch's orbit that you find in almost every autocracy in the world. Key questions were, as always, 'who was *in* and who was *out*?', and 'how was the favour or *dis*favour of the emperor marked?'. Thrasea Paetus – senator, moralist and one of the awkward squad – was given a very clear message when he was explicitly forbidden from turning up with other senators to congratulate Nero on the birth of his daughter. Occasionally just a single word was enough. Earlier, in the reign of Augustus, a friend of the emperor who had been unguarded in passing on information about plans for the imperial succession, arrived one morning to pay his respects and said, as usual, 'Good morning, Caesar'. Augustus simply replied 'Goodbye, Fulvius'. One point of the story was to demonstrate the emperor's wit, but the dismissal was said to have been barbed enough for the (former) friend to take the hint, go straight home and kill himself.

The elaborate codes of etiquette offered a subtler way of calibrating status and favour. Everyone in the palace knew, or soon learned, who should stand up and who should sit down, and when. Tiberius won a nod of approval for simply getting to his feet to bid farewell to his dinner guests. The rituals of kissing were more nuanced. It was standard Roman practice, at least among men of the elite, to use a kiss as a friendly greeting, and there was so much kissing at court that at one time it had to be banned to prevent the spread of a nasty outbreak of infectious herpes. At its most basic, the key question was *whether* you exchanged kisses with the emperor, and could boast of the intimacy which that implied. Pliny was careful to remind listeners to his *Speech of Praise* that he was on kissing terms with Trajan, while Nero was assumed to be insulting senators when it was reported that he did not kiss them when he left for a visit to Greece, or again on his return. *Oscula* (kisses) counted.

But *how* you kissed, and in particular where on the body, added further levels of meaning. A kiss on the mouth or cheeks signalled (more or less) equality. For the emperor to offer his hand to be kissed, rather than his face, was taken as a display of his superiority. It was said that one of the reasons that Cassius Chaerea, an officer in the guard, was driven to assassinate Caligula was that he had been asked to kiss the emperor on the hand (though the fact that Caligula simultaneously made a rude gesture must have added to the insult). Kisses on the knees and feet were even worse. For Romans, they pointed to Eastern despotism, and were one of the standard charges levelled at, or that helped to define, 'bad' emperors. Again it was Caligula who was criticised for extending his foot to be kissed by a man he had just pardoned for his involvement in an alleged conspiracy, though (as a sign of how difficult these gestures could be to interpret) the emperor's supporters claimed that he simply wanted people to admire his fancy gold and pearl slippers not to offer kisses. Almost two hundred years later, Maximinus Thrax ('the Thracian'), who came to the throne in 235 CE after the assassination of Alexander Severus, may well have accepted kisses on his knees, but he drew the line at anything lower down: 'God forbid,' he is supposed to have insisted, 'that any free man should plant a kiss on my feet.'

Of course, some free men were imagined to have done exactly that, convicting themselves of fawning subservience at the same time as showing up the emperor as a tyrant. The most embarrassing story, which took subservience to even greater depths, turned the spotlight onto Lucius Vitellius, the father of the emperor Vitellius who reigned briefly during the civil wars of 69 CE. Described archly by Suetonius as 'a man with a stupendous talent for flattery', Lucius is supposed to have tried sucking up to Claudius by carrying around the shoe of the emperor's wife, Messalina, and from time to time getting it out and kissing it.

If all of this – whether literally true or revealing fantasy – now seems to us faintly ridiculous, Romans too enjoyed sending up the affected conventions of some aspects of palace life, as well as the insincerity that underpinned it. Pliny may have written proudly in his *Letters* of travelling to one of Trajan's country properties to help the emperor decide on those tricky legal cases. But at roughly the same time, Juvenal, Rome's star satirist – who coined the phrase 'bread and circuses' (*panem et circenses*) to sum up the limited ambitions of the Roman people – turned his ridicule upon another such gathering of the emperor's advisers. He was looking back to the reign of Domitian and to one, totally imaginary, occasion when a group of associates of the now dead emperor were summoned to a meeting at his villa over-looking Lake Albano. In the poem of more than one hundred and fifty lines, Juvenal describes them nervously scuttling along, in answer to the emperor's call, to offer their advice on the big problem his majesty had on his mind. It was not a major issue of war, peace, law or politics, but how to cook a giant fish (a turbot) that had been caught in the Adriatic, transported across the mountains and presented to him at his country residence outside Rome.

In part, this is a parody of the high-flown banality of 'life at the top'. (What on earth *do* you do with a mammoth turbot? Answer: get a very large pot made and, for the future, always keep a resident work-shop of potters in the imperial palace.) But it also takes aim at the unctuous hyperbole that comes from the mouth of the courtiers. One member of the company imagined at the Alban villa is Catullus Mess-alinus, who a few years later was the subject of Nerva's dinnertime reminiscences (p. 81). His contribution to the turbot debate perfectly summed up its vacuity. Though one of the most eloquent in his admir-ation of the great fish, he was completely blind and could not see what he was praising or even where it was (Juvenal depicts him looking to the left as he hailed the great beast, which actually 'lay to his right'). This is a moral lesson in the deceptive speech of the imperial court. As we saw in the palace of Elagabalus, nothing was as it seems, and here the praise was literally blind. It is hard not to suspect, however, that in this slippery poem Juvenal is also turning some of the satire on himself. For he is also reminding his readers that 'free speech' is easy after an emperor is dead (in fact, he fast-forwards to Domitian's bloody assassination in the poem's last few lines). Free speech to the face of – or about – a living emperor, whoever he was, good or bad, was always a trickier matter.

But what Roman writers deplored most of all about the workings of the court was the fact that power in the state was now determined by degrees of closeness to just one man, the emperor himself. Inevitably, as they saw it, corruption followed. 'Selling smoke' became the colloquial Roman expression for peddling your influence with the man at the top, with the strong implication that more promises were made than delivered. Underlying this, though, was the sense that the old social and political certainties of Roman life had been even more radically overturned.

In the days of the Republic, power and prestige, formally at least, had been in the hands of a male elite, who were elected to office in public by free male citizens, and who came together in the senate for open debate. Some of those traditional institutions continued under imperial rule, even if awkwardly in the shadow of the emperor himself. The palace, however, now represented an alternative source of power, where many suspected that the really important political decisions were taken in private (however much emperor after emperor claimed to respect the senate's authority). It is true that there was considerable overlap of personnel. Wearing a different hat, as it were, the majority of senators were also courtiers, or fancied themselves as such. The path from the senate house in the Forum up to the Palatine, and back down again, must have been a busy one. But around the emperor, power came to be calibrated very differently: according to who had access to him, and who could bend his ear. This was the power of proximity, which could (and sometimes did) favour the emperor's wives, slaves or lovers, over any senatorial grandee. You might even argue that one function of the elaborate rules of etiquette and the court flummery was actually to mask the relative powerlessness of the traditional elite (a point hinted at in Juvenal's turbot poem too: all that ceremony and serious discussion for a *fish*?) – while the emperor's barber, say, had twenty minutes a day, one-to-one, to raise his pet concerns directly with the man in charge.

There are dozens of occasions when Roman writers describe (or imagine) the influence at court of those at the 'wrong' end of the traditional political ranking. Suetonius, for example, claimed that he had eyewitness evidence of a mere dwarf jester at a palace dinner pushing Tiberius, with a well-timed quip, to get on with the prosecution of a man accused of treason, which he then did (though Suetonius's account that Tiberius at first reprimanded the jester for speaking out of turn suggests that there might have been another way of telling this story). But most of the outrage about power in the palace was focused on two groups who still feature prominently in modern discussions of the emperor's entourage: on the one hand, some of his slaves and ex-slaves; on the other, his wives, female relatives and the women and men who shared his bed. Behind many emperors the sinister figure of an overweening ex-slave was supposed to hover, dominating his master, wielding far too much power, and gaining far too much money and renown. Behind almost every throne, so it was said, was a scheming woman, sometimes murderously pulling the strings.

A slave society

Roman palaces, in Rome itself and elsewhere, were slave societies. They were populated, staffed and managed by thousands of slaves (some 'home-bred', to put it in stark Roman terms, others acquired in the ancient traffic in human beings), and by at least as many *ex-slaves*. It was a distinguishing feature of Roman society, thought to be extremely odd by some ancient observers from the Greek world, that Romans freed so many slaves, domestic ones at least (the enslaved workers in the fields or the mines were treated very differently). But these *ex*-slaves, or *freed*men and women as they are now often known (the *d* is crucial), usually remained tied in some form of dependence to their one-time masters. In the imperial court, slaves and freedmen together provided the basic infrastructure of palace organisation, outnumbering the freeborn residents or visitors many times over.

Ancient literature, like Statius's praise of the father of Claudius Etruscus, occasionally shines the spotlight onto these men and women. They have also left their own words, much less elaborately scrawled on walls or inscribed on their tombstones. There are, for example, those 350 or so graffiti surviving in the Palatine slave quarters where the parody of the crucifixion was discovered. These include a few more cartoons and a predictable sprinkling of Roman phalluses, but they are mostly just 'signatures' with occasionally a note of their jobs: 'Marinus ianitor' (Marinus, doorkeeper), 'Euphemus opifer' (Euphemus, first-aider), and so on. We can be confident that most of these *were* slaves (the giveaway is that they have just a single name, occasionally two, whereas free citizens normally used three), but some even make a point of noting the writer's origin, with an added abbreviation, 'VDN', standing for 'verna domini nostri' ('home-bred slave of our lord/emperor'). But there is nothing on the Palatine quite so evocative as the graffito written on the wall of a latrine in a large house in the town of Herculaneum, shortly before the eruption of Vesuvius in 79 CE: 'Apollinaris medicus Titi imp(eratoris) hic cacavit bene', or, to capture the tone of the Latin, 'Apollinaris the (slave) doctor of the emperor Titus had a good crap here'. It is vivid evidence of the travels (and humour) of one slave of Titus, unless – as some modern academic killjoys have wondered – it was a Roman lavatorial joke, an ancient 'Kilroy was here', not written by the emperor's doctor at all.

Much more information can be gleaned from their tombstones. The memorials we explored in chapter 3 to those who worked in the kitchens and catering department are just a tiny handful of over four thousand epitaphs that survive, mostly from Rome, commemorating slaves and ex-slaves who worked in the imperial household and the wider administration. These give us a hint of the internal hierarchies within the slave community: a 'private secretary grade one', for example, outranking a 'private secretary grade two', just as a *manager* of the tasters' outranked a plain 'taster'. They also offer a panorama of the micro-specialisms and services on which the life of the emperor and his family depended, which were simultaneously a display of imperial status (to have a dedicated slave for every tiny job was a mark of power and privilege) and possibly also an inconvenient constraint. There were no doubt conventions almost as cumbersome as those of elite court etiquette, and almost as tricky to get right, which distinguished the work of the ex-slave who supervised the wardrobe that Trajan wore 'to the theatre' from that of the supervisor of his 'private outfits'; or the work of the 'topiarist' from the ordinary 'gardener'.

The men and women who worked in the household of Livia, in the early palace compound on the Palatine, are particularly well known, largely because a communal tomb used by the empress's staff has preserved dozens of their memorials. It is not always absolutely clear what their jobs entailed. But we learn of her 'handbag carrier' (unless the Latin title, *capsarius*, actually means the 'man in charge of the linen chest'); an impressive variety of slave and ex-slave medics, including an 'eye doctor', a 'medical supervisor' and a pair of midwives (presumably for the staff as much as for Livia herself); and a whole range of domestics, from 'silver stewards', 'hairdressers' and 'footmen' to a 'carpenter', the 'supervisor of her purple garments' (or maybe the 'supervisor of her dyeing works'), 'menders and darners', 'furniture polishers' and 'window cleaners' (or perhaps, in another translation, 'mirror makers'). There is even an ex-slave by the name of Prosopas who died aged nine (he must have been given his freedom unusually early) and is described on his epitaph as a *delicium* – a 'sweetie' or, in a more technical sense, a member of one of those troupes of naked children flaunted (or exploited or cherished – or all three) by some ladies in the imperial family. Prosopas did not live to be anything more than a sweetie.

As well as these varieties of domestic service, slaves and ex-slaves holding more senior administrative jobs are recorded in Rome and

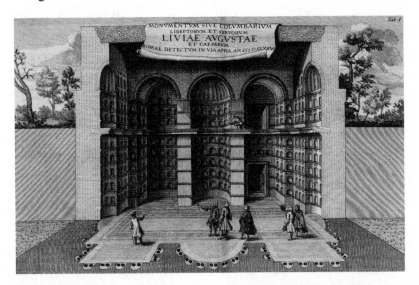

46. An eighteenth-century reconstruction of the communal tomb of Livia's household, with four of the small plaques that identified their cremation urns: Anteros, a polisher (*colorator*); Aucta, a dresser (*ornatrix*); Pasicrates, a retired accountant, 'no longer working' (*tabular(ius) immun(is)*); and another 'no longer working' (*imm(unis)*).

beyond. The father of Claudius Etruscus was head of the emperor's finance division and would have had a large enslaved staff working beneath him. Many others are known to have worked in the other sections into which the palace management was divided: the 'petitions department' (*a libellis*), the 'Latin secretariat' and the 'Greek secretariat' (*ab epistulis Latinis* and *Graecis*), the 'entertainment section' (*a voluptatibus*), the 'library division' (*a bibliothecis*), and more. Further afield, we find slaves reporting to the emperor from jobs in other imperial properties or in the administration of the provinces more widely. One notable character from the first century CE was a slave of Tiberius, Musicus Scurranus, described on his tombstone as a 'finance officer' handling the emperor's funds in Gaul. He died in Rome – perhaps on a short visit, or perhaps after leaving his financial post – where his own slaves (that is, the slaves of a slave, or 'underslaves') erected his memorial. There were *sixteen* of them in all, including a business agent, three secretaries, two cooks, a doctor, a wardrobe supervisor, two silver stewards and a woman of unspecified duties, but probably his partner. It is another powerful reminder that the emperor's slaves did not form a single homogeneous category. Some would have appeared less unequal than others.

Occasionally the epitaphs list a short sequence of jobs done by the man or woman commemorated and allow us to construct at least a skeletal biography, even for those near the bottom of the pecking order. One 'taster' went on to be 'dining room supervisor', then to work as a finance officer in departments overseeing the games, the water supply, and finally the emperor's military expenditure, gaining his freedom somewhere en route. Further down the hierarchy, we learn from the few words on his memorial plaque that the Coetus Herodianus, who may well have come to Rome as a 'human present' to the emperor from King Herod (pp. 104–5), went from being a food taster in the palace to an estate manager in one of imperial pleasure gardens (*horti*) on the edge of the city. Whether this was a promotion that Coetus

47. The epitaph of Musicus Scurranus starts with his name: 'Musicus, the slave of Tiberius Caesar Augustus, Scurranus.' It ends with a list in three columns of his own slaves who erected the memorial. Clearly legible are the two cooks: 'Tiasus cocus' (the T and the I are run together) and 'Firmus cocus'. The woman, who was probably his partner, is 'Secunda' (bottom right).

had desired or was just another episode in a lifetime of being packed up and sent on we can only guess. But there is a hint of the fragility of slave aspirations in one of the fables of Phaedrus (who, assuming he was an ex-slave himself, should have known). It is the story of a slave doorman at one of Tiberius's country residences, who, in the hope of gaining his freedom, tried to ingratiate himself with the emperor as he took a stroll round the garden by ostentatiously nipping around the hedges and sprinkling water on the path in front of him to dampen the dust. Tiberius was not taken in, and simply quipped 'Sorry mate, getting your freedom from me costs more than that'. Phaedrus tells the tale as a lesson in the futility of flattery. It's also a lesson about the powerlessness of the slave.

The translations and terminology I have used – 'finance division', 'entertainment section', 'petitions department' – tend to give the impression that this specialised workforce was close to a modern 'civil service'. There were a few similarities: the many years, for example, that some of these senior officials served in their posts gave an administrative continuity from one emperor to the next. But there is almost no sign of the rules, rational organisation or principles of promotion that define a bureaucracy in our sense. Another moral of Phaedrus's fable is that the advancement of the slave depended on nothing more systematic than the emperor's whim. In some ways, the imperial household was less a new style of administration, more a traditional Roman private household writ very large. The richest members of the Roman elite regularly employed hundreds of slaves in their city residences, sometimes in very specialised roles, and they had for centuries used their ex-slaves as agents in politics and business. The emperor was following in that tradition. Yet, as often with the emperor's status, honours and institutions, his domestic organisation was a mix of the old with something new, exclusive and distinctively imperial. There is no clearer sign of that than cases brought during the reign of Nero against two of the emperor Augustus's direct descendants, believed by some to be rivals for the throne. Among the accusations was that they each had ex-slaves in their household with the same responsibilities and called by the same titles as those in the palace: the man in charge of the 'finance division' (*a rationibus*), the 'petitions department' (*a libellis*) and the 'secretariat' (*ab epistulis*). The point was that those titles, and the structures of management that lay behind them (even if they had roots in the Republic), could now be taken to signal the power of the emperor alone.

Pride and prejudice

The most extravagant fulminations from elite Roman writers were directed at the ex-slaves in charge of those named departments in the imperial palace, or at the ones who took the role of the emperor's chief 'private secretary' (*cubicularius* is usually translated rather quaintly as 'chamberlain', but 'private secretary' captures better the duties of the man 'who oversaw what the emperor did in his *cubiculum*'. Up to a point, any lowly member of the emperor's staff was vulnerable to nasty mutterings about the undue influence with their master that came simply by virtue of proximity. Epictetus, for example, a freedman himself, told the cautionary tale of an owner who had sold off a slave cobbler 'who was useless at his job'. The man was bought up by the imperial household to be the emperor's cobbler, and from then on – 'useless' though he had been – his former master had to kow-tow to him. 'How is it that a person instantly becomes wise, when Caesar puts him in charge of his chamber pot?', as Epictetus's wry question summed up the story. But the most vivid descriptions are those of a handful among the slaves and freedmen in the palace who occupied much more senior positions than chamber-pot attendant.

The father of Claudius Etruscus, the head of the finance division, was lucky to be the subject of Statius's eulogy. Most of these characters – who might, in other circumstances, have been praised for exactly the kind of virtues that Statius picked out – are viciously attacked or scornfully derided in the surviving accounts, for their 'inappropriate' influence in private and public. Marcus Antonius Pallas, an ex-slave of the emperor Claudius's mother, and a predecessor of the father of Claudius Etruscus in the post of *a rationibus*, is the most famous case. It was he – so it was said – who persuaded Claudius to choose Agrippina, Nero's mother, as his fourth wife (other advisers had other ideas). And he was openly credited with having devised the solution, formally adopted by the senate, to one of those tricky, and characteristically Roman, problems of legal status: namely, how to treat freeborn women who cohabited with slaves (in his judgement, it depended on whether the slave's master had approved or not). For all this Pallas was richly rewarded. By a combination of official generosity and, perhaps, private graft, he amassed a fortune (some of his property holdings in Egypt are actually mentioned on land-registration records discovered on papyri there). Even more offensive to traditional Roman prejudices, he was given, despite his slave birth, the honorary rank of a praetor, second only to that of a consul in the hierarchy of senatorial office-holding. Half a century after Pallas's death, Pliny described in a letter how he had come across his tomb just outside Rome, with an epitaph boasting that the senate itself had voted him this praetorian status. Even if Pallas had later been sacked by Nero, the distinctions awarded to this 'piece of crap', this 'scumbag', were 'farcical', Pliny lamented. He didn't know whether to laugh or cry.

Pallas was not the only ex-slave of the emperor to be criticised in this way. Helico, the private secretary of Caligula, was another. He bathed, ate and played ball with the emperor, and, to the irritation of Philo, had taken the side of the Greeks against the Jews in the Alexandrian disputes. So too was Cleander, Commodus's private secretary and the semi-official head of his imperial guard at the end of the second century CE, who was rumoured to have sold consulships to the highest bidder. Some of the dirt also stuck to members of the traditional elite who put up with these people, or appeared to encourage them. Pliny may have been disappointed that the senate honoured Pallas. But that was nothing compared with the behaviour of the same obsequious senator who kept the shoe of Claudius's wife, Messalina, down the folds of his toga (p. 179). He was also pilloried for displaying golden statuettes of Pallas and another ex-slave of the emperor in a religious shrine at home. So, why did these prominent freedmen provoke such fulminations?

Part of the problem was the practical double bind in which the emperor found himself. He needed staff to carry out the administrative tasks that running the empire demanded. The senatorial elite were happy enough to govern a province, or command a legion in the old way; but paper-pushing in the palace, at the emperor's beck and call, was quite different. Besides, allowing the elite to establish themselves behind the scenes in the back rooms of power must have seemed an all too obvious way of providing an inside track for rivals to the throne. Ex-slaves offered a traditional and convenient solution, within a hierarchy of service and obedience. (It is significant that among the virtues that Pliny saw celebrated on Pallas's tombstone were 'his duty and loyalty to his masters', which were not the virtues paraded by your average senator.) Yet the inevitable consequence was to give a few ex-slaves a power of sorts over those of far higher social status. Some emperors tried to mitigate the social tension by turning instead to the ranks of freeborn equestrians, just below the senate, particularly to fill the positions in charge of the administrative divisions in the palace. So it was that the equestrian Suetonius, for example, came to serve as 'patronage secretary', 'chief librarian' and 'head of the secretariat' under Trajan and Hadrian. The offices of *a studiis, a bibliothecis* and *ab epistulis* are all recorded in his surviving CV, inscribed on stone and once probably placed underneath his statue. A century earlier the poet Horace, likewise of equestrian rank (though also the son of an ex-slave), had been offered – and had refused – a job as secretary to Augustus. But there was never a time when ex-slaves did *not* hold some of the major 'service positions' in the imperial court.

The controversies that these servants of the emperor provoked were more than just a matter of snobbery. It is true that in Rome, the practice of freeing slaves in large numbers went hand in hand with a nasty streak of prejudice against those who were freed in that way. Petronius's condescending portrayal, in his novel the *Satyricon*, of the nouveau riche freedman Trimalchio, with regiments of his own slaves and a fondness for vulgar banquets, is just one very clear example. But there was more at stake here. These attacks on senior imperial freedmen are a mark of one of the pressure points of the topsy-turvy world of one-man rule, and of the elite anxiety that (in their view) the 'natural' order of society had been upturned by autocracy. One big question was: who at court was the slave of whom? Had the freeborn elite been turned into slaves of (ex-)slaves? That was exactly Tacitus's

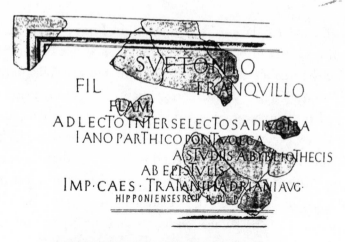

FIL

SVETONIO

TRANQVILLO

FLAM

ADLECTOINTERSELECTOSADIVCIA

IANO PARTHICO PONT VOLGA

ASTVDIIS ABYBLIOTHECIS

AB EPISTVLIS

IMP·CAES·TRAIANI HADRIANI AVG·

HIPPONIENSESRECH

48. Fragments of an inscription recording the career of Suetonius were discovered at the site of Hippo Regius, modern Annaba in Algeria, in 1950. Probably placed originally under a statue of the biographer, it may well indicate that he had some particular connection with the town, whether as a notable visitor or benefactor, or through his family. The reconstruction above indicates in bold the surviving pieces, and tries to fill in the gaps; underneath are a few of those fragments that do survive. At first sight it is hard to see how it is possible to reconstruct so much on the basis of so little, but inscriptions of this type, listing one office or employment after the next, are very formulaic and it is often not hard to guess what was in the missing bits. Here there are likely references to legal appointments and part-time priesthoods (FLAM(EN), for example, is a common priestly title). But most striking are the almost fully preserved references to his service in the palace administration. It was already known, from the *Imperial History*, that he had served as *ab epistulis*. This inscription makes clear that he had also been *a bibliothecis* (here spelled *bybliothecis*), 'imperial librarian', and *a studiis*, which I suspect was some form of 'patronage secretary' (but could indicate a research job).

point when he described the extravagant journey, 'with its huge carriage train', of one of Nero's ex-slaves, who had been sent in the early 60s CE to inspect the state of affairs in Britain after the rebellion of Boudicca. The enemy thought it a joke: 'for them the fire of freedom still blazed, they had not yet come across the power of freedmen, and they were amazed that a Roman general and his army that had finished off such a great war should obey the class of slaves.' For Tacitus, here and elsewhere, it was one of the paradoxes of empire that old-fashioned Roman virtues, including the love of liberty, now existed only among the barbarians.

But there were implications for the emperor himself too, and questions about where he fitted into the calibration of slavery and freedom. Statius had wrestled with this in his eulogy of the father of Claudius Etruscus, as he wondered how to fit his ex-slave honorand into the social hierarchy of the whole cosmos. He suggests that everyone in the world obeys the emperor, while the emperor himself obeys the gods. But an alternative thought was that some emperors might actually be under the thumb of their own slaves and ex-slaves. Pliny, in his *Speech of Praise*, looking back to Trajan's predecessors (and with a glancing warning for Trajan too), summed up that idea snappily: 'Most emperors, though the masters of their citizen subjects, were the slaves of their ex-slaves ... the chief sign of a *powerless* emperor being *powerful* freedmen.' Indeed, that notion was axiomatic in characterising Roman rulers. In reality every single emperor depended on their ex-slave staff. A few years later, as one of his letters shows, Pliny himself was hanging around in the province he governed, waiting for instructions from an ex-slave of Trajan. But one automatic definition of a 'bad' emperor – whatever the truth lying behind it – was that he was *dominated* by his freedmen. It was not merely that the palace was a slave society. Slavery provided a way of understanding, debating or critiquing the power of the emperor.

In bed with the emperor

Slaves were also among those who shared, or were *forced* to share, the emperor's bed. The most notorious of all the imperial lovers was Hadrian's Antinous, the young slave who drowned in the river Nile, when still only in his late teens. The problem here was not that, in partnering Antinous, the emperor was being unfaithful to his wife (most elite Romans would have thought sexual fidelity on the part of a married man, emperor or not, was slightly weird). Nor was the same-sex relationship in itself seen as difficult (for a man to be the active sexual partner of a younger man of lower social status was generally fine in Roman terms). The problem was Hadrian's uncontrolled – as some Romans saw it, almost effeminate – grief at Antinous's death. For he established the young man as a god, had whole towns founded in his honour (Antinoopolis, 'Antinousville') and flooded the world with his statues, far beyond the commemorations at Tivoli. I do mean flooded: more portrait sculptures survive of Antinous than of any member of the imperial 'family' ever, apart from Augustus and Hadrian himself. This was another hint of how an emperor could appear to be enslaved by a slave.

The sex life of monarchs is, however, always tricky historical ground. In real life, it might have been dull, ordinary and unsatisfying (who knows?). But there is a long tradition, stretching back to ancient Rome and beyond, of assuming that the erotic escapades of rulers are far more flamboyant than those of most of their subjects (monarchs have sex on a grander scale than the rest of us, with more glamorous partners) and that the character of a ruler is reflected in what he gets up to in bed (transgressive monarchs have transgressive sex). At the same time, the stories that those *outside* the palace walls tell of the erotic world *inside*, are also partly projections of wider anxieties or discontents, or vicarious imaginings. Not unlike modern celebrity gossip, the debates and fantasies about a ruler's sex life – which so often straddles the fragile boundary between the acceptable and unacceptable, the believable and unbelievable – highlight the problematic areas of sexual morality and of gender roles more generally. The result is that palaces are imagined to be full of paramours of all types – men and boys, women and eunuchs – extending far beyond the marriage bed.

That was certainly the case at Rome. Hadrian was not unique. There was hardly a single Roman emperor over the first 250 or so years of one-man rule who was not associated with rumours of larger-than-life sexual activity, excess or transgression. Sometimes it was a question of the incomparable beauty of those chosen to be the emperor's partner, out of reach of any ordinary citizen. In the second century, for example, the mistress of Lucius Verus, Panthea ('All-divine'), was described in a couple of contemporary essays – part eulogistic, part satiric – as a composite of the greatest beauties of Greek art and literature. The shape of her head was compared to that of the famous statue of Aphrodite from Knidos (p. 170), her nose to that of a statue of Athena by Phidias, the master sculptor of the Parthenon, and so on. It is as if the emperor's lover was almost beyond human imagining, and could only be described in terms of the greatest known works of art (though some modern critics have suspected a more subversive anti-imperialist agenda here: as if the mistress of a Roman emperor was pointedly described in terms of the masterpieces of conquered and looted Greece, dissected, chopped up and put together again).

Other stories focus on what are, to us, less palatable sides of excess. Augustus, for example, was said to have been particularly keen on deflowering virgins, whom – so the ancient gossip went – his wife Livia groomed for him, and presumably had brought to the palace. Trajan, by contrast, despite the wholesome image conveyed by Pliny, was reputedly unable to keep his hands off young boys (in our terms, a predator). The fourth-century emperor Julian was well aware of that allegation. For, in his skit on his predecessors, in which the emperors come face to face with the Roman gods, the divine Jupiter is warned to keep a careful eye on his own boyfriend, the young Ganymede, when Trajan is around – just in case Trajan tries to steal him. But in some of these stories we can detect even deeper points. We have already seen that the claims about Elagabalus's gender reassignment might have been as much anxious reflections on the mutability of gender as attacks on the emperor's dystopian, 'unnatural' world. Something similar applies to the stories of Nero's young slave Sporus, who was supposedly such a lookalike of the emperor's dead wife that he had the boy castrated and married him. These were certainly told as vivid illustrations of Nero's perversity. But they also gestured to bigger debates about marriage itself. Was the emperor flagrantly flouting the rules, or was he radically challenging the old boundaries? These issues must in some way underlie a confusing poem by Statius, in which he both glorified a eunuch 'favourite' of Domitian (who went by the decidedly creepy name of Earinus, or 'Springtime') and also praised the emperor for legally outlawing castration. But what *exactly* was he trying to say?

Whatever the truth about these imperial lovers, they were even closer to the emperor, and so potentially even more influential, than his personal barber or his chamber-pot attendant. Antonia Caenis, the ex-slave who was Vespasian's long-term mistress, is just one who is said to have profited from that proximity. She allegedly became one of the Roman super-rich by selling all kinds of public offices, from provincial governorships to priesthoods, and by using pillow talk to fix imperial decisions, at a price. But, influential as Caenis and others like her may have been, the most persistent ancient stories about the use and abuse of power in the emperor's innermost circle did not focus on the paramours, the pretty boys or eunuchs. The spotlight fell on the legitimate wives, mothers, sisters and daughters of the emperor. Their alleged poisonings and plotting, incest, adultery, murders and treason have claimed more attention than the tales of perverted passion, castration and unmanly devotion.

Wives and mothers

The steely, sadistic Livia, the dissolute Messalina, third wife of Claudius, and the commanding Julia Domna, wife of Septimius Severus, are three of the most famous, or infamous, residents of the imperial palace. No woman in Rome ever had any formal, executive power in the state, unless you count a handful of venerable priestesses. There was not even an official role as 'empress' or 'consort' of the emperor (the closest that some of the wives and mothers came to that, almost thirty of them between Livia and Julia Mamaea, was being granted the title 'Augusta', the feminine form of 'Augustus'). But writers, ancient and modern, investigating palace life, have often fixated on the emperor's female relations. They have been outraged at their political and dynastic influence. They have deplored (or drooled over) their brazen adulteries, their lechery, or – to give it a slightly softer focus – their life in the Roman fast lane.

It was almost an ancient cliché that the court was dominated by women trying to exercise control. Sometimes this came down to secretly pulling the strings of succession. Livia was the classic case of the murderous manipulator, someone who was rumoured to have systematically eliminated all those who stood in the way of her son Tiberius reaching the throne, and, according to Cassius Dio, was openly said to have made him emperor. But Livia was only the first of many. Agrippina, Messalina's successor as wife of Claudius, is said to have done the same for her son Nero (fig. 84); Trajan's widow, Plotina, was supposed, less murderously, to have contrived some clever amateur dramatics to smooth the succession of Hadrian; and 'mummy's boy' Alexander Severus was said to be literally that – owing his throne to his mother Julia Mamaea.

At other times the stories turned to their wicked or ingenious grabs for power more generally, either behind the scenes or dangerously centre stage. Rumours of incest captured the influence of some mothers over their emperor sons (Agrippina over Nero, Julia Domna over Caracalla). Almost as shocking in a world where women had always been excluded from an official political role were the ways in which some of them insinuated themselves into front-line politics. Agrippina was rumoured to have listened in to meetings of the senate, entirely off-limits for women, shielded by a thick curtain to keep her out of sight; and she apparently sometimes took her place, or tried to, in welcoming parties for official delegations. (Tacitus has the story of how one of Nero's canny advisers found a way of deflecting her from actually mounting the dais next to the emperor.) A century or so later, Julia Domna was said to have taken control of Caracalla's business correspondence, which would probably have been more offensive to elite Roman proprieties than having a (male) ex-slave in charge.

This went hand in hand with other, more lurid, allegations against them: larger-than-life stories of sex with very wrong people, in very wrong places. The women of the palace included some of the most notorious sexual transgressors in the whole history of Rome, who still play their part as libertines, adulteresses and nymphomaniacs in modern art, film and fiction. Augustus's daughter Julia reputedly had maximum fun for maximum offence by sleeping with her lovers on the main 'speakers' platform', or *rostra*, in the Forum itself, the old political heart of the city of Rome. True or not, the rumour must have conjured an uncomfortable image of the relationship between the old political order and the new (where the orators of old once addressed the people, the emperor's daughter now fucks ...). A few decades later, Messalina was said to have slept her way around the capital city. According to one story included in the encyclopaedia of Pliny the Elder, an even more ponderous moraliser than his nephew, she even beat a notorious prostitute in a competition to see who could have sex with the most men in a single day. Faustina, wife of Marcus Aurelius, apparently carried on the tradition. One of a pair of imperial wives and mothers (the daughter of another Faustina who had been married to

49. A coin with the head of 'Faustina Augusta', the wife of Marcus Aurelius. On the reverse, the figure of the goddess Juno Lucina, who was supposed to protect women in childbirth (accompanied appropriately enough by three children). There is no trace of the lurid gossip about Faustina here.

Antoninus Pius), her reputation for sex with rough trade was almost a match for Messalina's. One story even had it that Commodus – a keen follower of gladiatorial games, and nothing like his philosophical father – was actually the biological son of one of her gladiator lovers. But there were alternative versions. An even stranger and more sensational account claimed that she was smeared in the blood of a dead gladiator and then impregnated by the emperor himself, after she had confessed to him her passion for one of these fighters. According to an ancient scientific theory, the blood alone was enough to give Commodus his well-known 'gladiatorial characteristics'.

How many of these stories are true – or *how* true they are – is a matter of debate. They are inevitably hard to check out. The only independent sign of Julia Domna's direct influence on Caracalla's affairs, for example, is a letter from her to the city of Ephesus, still preserved in a version inscribed on stone there, in which she appears to promise to put a good word in for the Ephesians with 'her sweetest son': a very long way from proof of her hands-on management of his correspondence. And whatever Faustina got up to, it did not stop Marcus Aurelius from making an elaborate display of grief after her death and granting her spectacular posthumous honours (including renaming the town where she died Faustinopolis, 'Faustinaville'). In any case, the headline themes offer a very partial view of these women's lives. The other side of their story hardly ever makes it into the accounts of ancient writers (and not so often into modern ones either). But the fact is that, like almost all elite Roman women, and almost all princesses in traditional royal houses anywhere, their basic role was to be pawns in a dynastic game. They were married off, with little or no say in the matter, at what is to us a frighteningly young age in order to tie up loose branches in the family tree. The same Julia who was supposed to have partied on the *rostra* had been married at fourteen to her cousin Marcellus, in order to mark him out as heir to the throne (she was widowed by sixteen and quickly remarried twice in other dynastic initiatives). A century or so later, to shore up the succession planning, the notorious Faustina had been betrothed (though not yet married) to Marcus Aurelius, who was more than twenty years her senior, when she was aged just eight – while young Lucilla, one of Faustina's fourteen children, was married aged fourteen to her father's co-emperor Lucius Verus, presumably to cement the partnership deal.

Maybe we would get a different perspective if we had any extended account from the pen of these imperial woman. But though we know that some of them did write memoirs, these have not survived (the autobiography of Nero's mother Agrippina counting, for me, as one of the great losses of all classical literature). The result is that it is now almost impossible to know for sure where to draw the line between the reality of these women's lives and the suspicious fantasies of male writers, who have always used the stereotype of the scheming woman to explain decisions made behind closed doors by emperors and kings, presidents and prime ministers. 'Blame the wife' is still a convenient fallback explanation for the idiosyncratic goings-on in the corridors of power, as Nancy Reagan, Cherie Blair, Carrie Johnson and others could attest.

Women and power?

Nevertheless, despite those uncertainties, it is absolutely clear that the role and prominence of women in the imperial court was different from anything seen before at Rome, and the stories told about them, even if they are not all true, point to some important anxieties and conflicts in the world of the emperor and his court.

For a start, although they had no formal power, the women of the emperor's family were more *visible* than any women in Rome had ever been. The female members of the Republican aristocracy had traditionally had greater freedoms than the elite women of (for example) classical Athens: economically, socially and in legal rights. But they had no public honours or titles and there were only a handful of statues of them (usually semi-mythical figures from the past) decorating the city. That completely changed for the leading women of the court, who were publicly celebrated as part of the imperial family, and as guarantors of the continuance of the dynasty. *Their* heads too began to decorate the coinage. *Their* statues were placed next to the men whose images in marble and bronze had once dominated the city (pp. 343–52). *Their* names were plastered over buildings, from temples to shady colonnades, erected under their auspices (even if we cannot be sure how much practical involvement they had in the finance or the design). And they were given a variety of privileges and honours usually associated with men: prime seats at the games; for some, the use of a *lictor*, an attendant-cum-bodyguard who normally accompanied male officials of the state; and any number of different honorific titles beyond 'Augusta', almost matching the flamboyant epithets ('Lord of Land and Sea' and the like) sometimes applied to emperors themselves. Downmarket sex life or not, Marcus Aurelius's wife Faustina was dubbed in high-flown, austere military style, 'Mother of the Army Camps' (*Mater Castrorum* in Latin); and Cassius Dio claimed that on her death some admirers actually called Livia 'Mother of her Country', on the model of the imperial title 'Father of his Country'. Autocracy, in other words, had opened up a visible space for a few women in the civic and symbolic landscape of Rome, which was now no longer male-only. This was one of the biggest revolutions brought about by one-man rule at Rome.

To some extent the women of the imperial family really were more influential than any women in Rome had been before. Again, it was partly the power of proximity that gave them a potential sway over the ruler of the Roman world. In 121 CE Trajan's widow Plotina wrote (successfully) to Hadrian, asking him to change the rules for appointing the head of one of the philosophical academies in Athens, to allow those who were not Roman citizens to take the job – an intervention recorded in a copy of her letter that the academy had inscribed on stone and put on display. And on one occasion, early in the reign of Augustus, we know that – much as Julia Domna later promised the Ephesians – Livia tried to put in a good word with her husband on behalf of the Greek city of Samos, which was seeking tax-free status. 'My wife is very active on your behalf', Augustus wrote to the Samians, in another letter published on stone. But here there was a twist. For, in the same letter, he explicitly stated that he was nevertheless *refusing* the Samian request. It was a public refusal that nicely recognised Livia's concern for one of her favourite cities, but also asserted Augustus's own unswayable independence.

This careful balancing act is found in other documents that came directly from the emperor himself. Behind the interpretations and reconstructions of historians, ancient and modern, the emperors' actual words hint at a tricky ambivalence about the power of imperial women. One of the most intriguing of these documents is part of what is almost certainly the funeral address given by the emperor Hadrian in 119 CE for his mother-in-law, Matidia, who was also the niece of Trajan. (In this case the stone on which the text of the speech was inscribed does not survive, but luckily several manuscript copies of it made in the sixteenth century do.) Hadrian praises her devotion to Trajan, her long and chaste widowhood, her beauty, her qualities as a mother, her helpfulness and her good temper, before saying 'she was of such great restraint that she never asked anything of me, and she did not ask for many things that I would have preferred to have been asked for ... She preferred to *rejoice* in my position than to *make use* of it.' Most of Hadrian's remarks play to the traditional virtues of a Roman lady: a loyal, beautiful, maternal helpmeet. But the cumbersome sentences about how she didn't ask him for things (favours, presumably), when he would actually have preferred that she did, treads the same tightrope as Augustus's letter to Samos. It both parades the potential power of his mother-in-law, while insisting that she did not exploit it.

A similar approach was taken by the senate in the reign of Tiberius in 20 CE, when they were judging the case of a man on trial for treason and for the murder of the imperial prince Germanicus. His wife was jointly charged with him, and the elderly Livia was said to have intervened on her behalf, as a friend. The historian Tacitus, writing a century later, gives a highly coloured account of the whole incident. But the actual judgement of the senate on the charges is also preserved, verbatim, in several copies, carefully inscribed on plaques of bronze, mostly discovered in illegal excavations in Spain in the late 1980s (the main fragments of the text first appeared on the antiquities market). Tacitus refers straightforwardly to opposition to Livia's involvement here, as another case of her behind-the-scenes power. The senate's record, by contrast, publicly acknowledges her role, but they also palpably squirm in justifying it. They explain that, in exonerating the defendant's wife, they have taken into account Livia's representations, but note that she did not often try to use her influence ('although she justly and deservedly ought to have the most influence in what she asks from the senate, she uses that power very sparingly'). Time and again, we find both a recognition of the potential (or actual) influence of the women of the palace, and an attempt to play it down, or evade its awkwardness.

But what lay behind the stories of the sexual transgression of so many of these women? They were presumably driven partly by ancient and modern fantasies of sex in high places and partly by some of the women actually rejecting the sexual constraints under which they were expected to live (fantasy and reality sometimes do overlap). But the various rumours surrounding Faustina and her gladiator reveal specific dynastic anxieties. For the prospect of women's adultery opened up – in Rome as in almost every premodern society – the destabilising possibility that the 'son of the father' was not really the 'son of the father', so threatening the established order, the patriarchal line and legitimate succession. The elaborate flight of fancy about smearing Faustina in the blood of a gladiator offers more than a curious insight into Roman science. It shows just how far Roman spin doctors or storytellers were prepared to go to defend the paternity of the ruler. Adoption was one thing; the succession of a man who was the product of his mother's adultery was quite another.

But, implausible stories aside, adultery in the imperial family was seen as part and parcel of treason. There was hardly ever a plot inside the palace in which some imperial wife or princess was not alleged to have been in bed with someone she shouldn't have. In the reign of Tiberius, the plans of Sejanus – an increasingly sinister head of the imperial guard – to overthrow the emperor and seize power himself went hand in hand with his adultery with Tiberius's niece. A couple of decades later, it was Messalina's intrigues with one of her more aristocratic lovers that led to her death on Claudius's orders, after one of his ex-slaves persuaded him that they were about to stage a coup. In his terror at hearing the news Claudius is supposed to have repeatedly muttered, 'Am I still emperor? Am I still emperor?'

For within the ruling house, the female relatives of the emperor both helped to guarantee succession and simultaneously threatened to disrupt it. Adultery, and the disloyalty that came with it, was always waiting to happen. Augustus's daughter Julia was no doubt pointing to these anxieties, and forestalling them, when – according to a small anthology of her jokes assembled, or concocted, four hundred years later – she quipped that she only took lovers when she was already pregnant by her husband: 'I never take a passenger on board except when the hold is already full.'

In one sense then, as with the fears about the prominence of ex-slaves, what underlies these stories was not so much concerns about the women themselves as concerns about the emperor, whose power was always potentially undermined by their sex, sexuality and scheming.

The emperor in flesh and blood

The image of Roman emperors that has come down to us is a complicated and multilayered construction: a glorious combination of hard historical evidence, spin, political invention and reinvention, fantasies of power, and the projection of Roman (and some modern) anxieties. It makes the 'real' emperor hard to pin down. We have already seen, in the case of Elagabalus for example, how the reported idiosyncrasies of an eccentric ruler derived partly from an attempt to capture the corruption of autocracy itself. Likewise, while stories of the emperor at dinner sometimes reflect the direct experience of elaborate imperial banquets or Trajan's simple suppers, they were also speculative answers to the kind of questions we still ask about how power intersects with consumption. Can we imagine what the ruler of the empire eats? Is his food like ours, only a little more lavish – or is it of an entirely different order of complexity and expense? What would *we* consume if we were as rich and powerful as an emperor? What does his diet (or what we imagine it to be) say about him and his power? Or, to take it in a different direction, whom would *we* choose as our lovers if we could have anyone, anywhere, anyhow? Put simply, one of the most revealing ways to enter the thought-world of the Romans – their shared fears, prejudices, hopes, assumptions and aspirations – is to think harder about how they constructed the figure of the emperor. How did they represent, or even *invent*, their rulers?

Yet it is also impossible not to be curious about emperors beyond the spin and the stereotypes. Can we get a view of those real-life human beings, in all their ordinary human variety and frailty, who sat at the heart of the palace, as they hosted the dinners, greeted the senators at the *salutatio*, or just chatted to their slave barbers in the morning while they were shaved? And what was it like to be the ruler himself within a court culture of deference, deceit and dystopia? It is easy to understand how flattery humiliates the flatterers, even when it is spoken with knowing irony. We put ourselves more readily in the position of the underdog than of the autocrat. But the flattered are victims too. How did it feel to be the one person who knew that no one could ever be trusted to tell them the truth?

This curiosity about the personality of individual rulers, and about the view from the throne, launched some of the classics of twentieth-century fiction: Robert Graves's *I, Claudius*, with its donnish, doddery but shrewd Claudius, or Marguerite Yourcenar's *Memoirs of Hadrian*, with its almost dreamily mystical emperor of borderline pacifist tendencies, more akin to the ideas of the mid twentieth century than to those of the mid second. In something of the same spirit, one distinguished historian a couple of decades ago wrote a clever, albeit quirky, essay in which he imagined the dead Septimius Severus reflecting from beyond the grave on his life as emperor ('One real trouble about being emperor is the feeling that you are trapped – trapped by other

1. On an appropriately grand scale (the painting is more than 2 metres across), Alma-Tadema captures the scene of the deadly generosity of the emperor Elagabalus (or 'Heliogabalus') – as his guests suffocate under an extravagant shower of rose petals. The emperor himself, dressed in a golden robe, watches from the raised dais.

2. *The Death of Seneca.* This huge painting (more than 4 metres across), now in the Prado, by the nineteenth-century Spanish artist, Manuel Domínguez Sánchez, imagines the moment when the philosopher has finally expired in his bath, surrounded by his grieving friends.

3. Septimius Severus with his wife, Julia Domna, and young children
Caracalla and Geta (whose face has been rubbed out) – a rare surviving
example, originally from Egypt, of the paintings that were once common.
The portrait may accurately reflect the dark skin colour of the emperor;
or it may simply follow the ancient painting convention of using dark
tones to represent the skin of adult males. See pp. 357–8, 363.

4. One of the most stunning Roman wall-paintings to have survived, originally in a dining area of an out-of-town villa belonging to Livia, now in the Palazzo Massimo Museum in Rome. It brings a carefully contrived, utopian world of nature – flowers, fruit trees and birds – inside the house.

5. A turquoise cameo, under 4 centimetres wide, depicting Livia holding probably a bust of her son Tiberius (a sign of her care and ambition for him). Others have identified it as a bust of her husband Augustus.

6. Hundreds of people queued up in 1932 to see Caligula's barges as they had been uncovered, on the orders of Mussolini, at the bottom of Lake Nemi. Although a few sections of them survive, they were largely destroyed during World War II; it remains debated whether Allied or German forces were mainly responsible.

7. A nineteenth-century copy of a wall-painting from the 'House of the
Ancient Hunt' in Pompeii. At the top hang nets full of fruit. This kind
of contrivance would have allowed diners to have been showered with
falling dainties – and bulkier food – sometimes on an imperial scale.

8. A room, painted with festoons of pine, from the house on the Palatine usually shown off to visitors as the 'House of Augustus'. Exquisite as the decoration is, this was almost certainly not where the emperor Augustus lived.

9. A reconstruction of one of the large display rooms of the Palatine palace. The richly coloured marble does accurately reflect one aspect of the original appearance. But no clutter, and only a few tiny people ...?

10. One of the most famous works of art from Hadrian's Villa is this centrepiece of a large floor mosaic, showing four doves around a birdbath. It is made up of thousands of tiny pieces of stone (tesserae), which allowed the intricate details to be depicted.

11. A classic image of Roman dining from the 'House of the Chaste Lovers' at Pompeii. Men and women recline together – while the party-goer at the back is already needing some help to stand up straight.

12. A thoroughly modern, and very determined, Messalina: the nineteenth-century vision of the Danish painter Peder Severin Krøyer.

13. A bronze head of Augustus, from a full-length statue that once stood in Roman Egypt. It was severed by raiders from outside the empire to the south, and buried as a trophy under the steps of a temple in Meroe, in modern Sudan – where it was found by archaeologists in 1910 (pp. 363–4).

14. Emperors' military victories could be more hyped than real. On this gold coin issued under Trajan, the titles of the emperor are shown around his head and around the design on the reverse. But the message is in the phrase *Parthia capta* ('Parthia defeated'), with a trophy of victory and two captives underneath. In fact, the 'victory' lasted only months.

15. & 16. Statue of Augustus found at the villa of his wife Livia (pl. 4). On the left, the sculpture as it now is. The emperor wears an elaborate breastplate celebrating his recovery of the military standards lost by Crassus in 53 BCE (p. 31). At his foot, helping the statue stand up, is a small cupid – also a reminder of Augustus's family's claimed descent from the goddess Venus. On the right, an attempt to reconstruct the original colours of the piece.

17. The most extravagant imperial cameo of all, 'The Great Cameo of France' (now in the Bibliothèque Nationale in Paris). Over 30 centimetres in length and made in the first century CE, it shows Augustus in the upper level, as if in heaven; Tiberius and Livia are probably the central figures in the middle level; in the lower level are conquered barbarians.

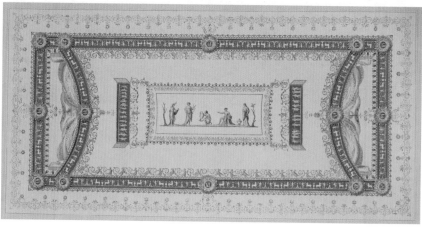

18. & 19. Above, a delicate ceiling painting from Nero's dining suite on the Palatine. Below, an eighteenth-century watercolour (by Agostino Brunias) inspired by the Neronian decoration.

20. A glimpse of the luxury of the imperial *horti*. This strip of gilded bronze, with inset gems, would have decorated the walls or prized pieces of furniture.

21. Augustus as pharaoh, on the right, making offerings to the Egyptian deities, Hathor and Horus – from the temple of Isis at Dendur in Egypt, commissioned by the emperor and displaying several images of him in Egyptian guise. Now reassembled in the Metropolitan Museum, New York, a light show evokes the original colours.

22. A second-century CE mosaic from Lyon showing a race in the Circus
Maximus. On the left a crash; in the foreground two chariots are in a close
race (the riders wearing the colours of the reds and the whites). In the centre
is the *spina* or *eripus*, on which stands an obelisk and devices for counting the
laps completed. The mosaic is quite heavily, but fairly accurately, restored.

23. A portrait of a young man from an Egyptian mummy of the third century CE. Paintings like this, inserted into mummies of the Roman period and preserved because of the hot, dry conditions, now give us the best view of the otherwise lost tradition of Roman panel painting. Paintings of emperors must once have been everywhere.

24. One of the gilded bronze peacocks – sometimes seen as a symbol of immortality – that once decorated the mausoleum of Hadrian. It now perches on stone steps in the Vatican Museums.

people's expectations, flattery, ambitions and lies', and so on). But, outside fiction or semi-fiction, how close can we get to these men and to their perspective on life in the palace and beyond?

In one particular respect we can get almost unbelievably close, to the most intimate recesses of their bodies. Although the emperors in question have been dead for close on two millennia, we still possess some of the diagnoses made, and the medication prescribed, by the man who served as doctor to Marcus Aurelius, Commodus and Septimius Severus. This was Aelius Galenus (now usually known as Galen), a Roman citizen born in 129 CE in Pergamum in what is now Turkey. The son of an architect, he studied philosophy and medicine, and held the post of doctor to the gladiators in his home town before going to live in Rome in the 160s. There he became a high-profile physician and scientist, giving lectures, conducting public dissections of animals, writing books and research papers, and treating a range of patients, including, occasionally, the residents of the imperial palace.

Galen is one of the best-kept secrets of classical literature. His surviving writing in the original Greek fills over twenty volumes, and about a third more has been preserved in early translations into Arabic, Syriac, Hebrew and Latin: a legacy of the medical interests of later Jewish, Christian and Islamic scholars, who copied and studied his work through the Middle Ages and beyond. It accounts for around 10 per cent of all the ancient Greek literature to have come down to us, many times the quantity of the much more famous classic texts of the fifth century BCE, from Herodotus and Thucydides to Euripides and Aristophanes. As well as plenty of scientific theorising, which is, to be honest, hard going, Galen offers any number of vivid autobiographical vignettes. He describes, for example, his own dissections and vivisections of animals in sometimes uncomfortable detail. On one occasion he dissected a large elephant to demonstrate, plausibly but incorrectly, that its heart contained a bone. The organ was extracted by staff from the palace kitchens, who may have intended to cook it up as an exotic delicacy, or may simply have been applying their skills in butchery to the service of science.

Elsewhere Galen discusses his own life in Rome, notably in a recently rediscovered essay, *On the Avoidance of Grief*, found by a PhD student in 2005 in the library of a Greek monastery, hiding in plain sight, in a previously unrecognised fifteenth-century manuscript copy. Written in 193 CE, in the immediate aftermath of disasters and political turmoil – a great fire in the city, a devastating plague across the empire, and the assassination of Commodus on the very last day of 192 – it reflects on the psychology of loss and distress (some of Galen's precious possessions and book manuscripts had been destroyed in the fire). In words that closely chime with Pliny's after the assassination of Domitian, Galen also takes care to distance himself from the recently overthrown emperor who had been his patient. Like Pliny, he claims to have been only a reluctant courtier, and even to have been in direct danger from Commodus ('I expected that I also would be packed off to a desert island, just like others who had done no wrong'). But there is nothing more surprising in the volumes of Galen's writing than his intimate descriptions of the emperors' symptoms and treatment, and the glimpse he offers into the royal medicine cabinet.

After an early success in curing young Commodus's tonsillitis, Galen was particularly proud of his treatment of Marcus Aurelius in 176 CE. The emperor seemed to be suffering from the onset of a potentially fatal fever, and had been up all night with diarrhoea. His resident household doctors prescribed rest and porridge, but it was soon decided that his condition was so serious that Galen should be summoned for a specialist opinion. After taking the imperial pulse, which the emperor had insisted on, Galen concluded somehow that it was no more than a tummy upset, brought on by heavy food, and not helped, we are meant to assume, by the porridge. The patient was delighted ('That's it!' he shouted out three times), and quickly recovered with the treatments recommended: some expensive ointment applied to the rectum (an early version of an anal suppository) and, as a cheaper alternative, wine mixed with pepper, taken by mouth.

Medicines were clearly crucial in the imperial regimen, and Galen was responsible for some of the most elaborate mixtures – notably theriac, a daily prophylactic used by Marcus Aurelius and several emperors before him to protect themselves against poison and some more innocent ailments. In the reign of Septimius Severus, Galen wrote technical treatises on this drug, itemising its sixty-four ingredients, including opium (which Marcus Aurelius suspected of causing him to nod off at awkward moments) and snake flesh (specially acquired, Galen suggests, by a dedicated palace snake-killer). In the course of his discussion, Galen also complained that Commodus, who refused a daily dose of theriac, had sold off most of the imperial supplies of another vital ingredient, Indian cinnamon, as well as a whole cinnamon tree that had been given to Marcus Aurelius as a present 'from barbarian lands'. As a result, when Septimius Severus decided to return to the theriac regime, Galen could find in the palace only very old and stale stock, dating back fifty years or so to the reigns of Trajan and Hadrian.

Galen offers a refreshingly different version of life and work in the court: from the contents of the storerooms to doctors disagreeing about the illness of their imperial patients and an emperor nodding off thanks to the side effects of his drug of choice. There could hardly be a more close-up picture of the imperial family than that painted by this learned doctor, as he prods his famous patients, takes their pulses and peers down their throats. But it is still the perspective of the observer and not of the emperor himself. For that, the key figure has always been Marcus Aurelius, many of whose intimate private letters have come down to us, as well as his surviving compendium *Jottings to Himself* (or *Meditations*).

From the emperor's point of view

An even better-kept secret than the works of Galen are the *Letters* between Marcus Cornelius Fronto – North African orator and theorist and, from 139 CE, one of the tutors of Marcus Aurelius – and his various correspondents, among them his imperial pupil. It is another surprising and serendipitous story of rediscovery. For in the early nineteenth century, the correspondence was found literally *underneath* a later text. That is to say, in a seventh-century CE monastery, an early parchment copy of Fronto's *Letters* – by then seriously out of fashion – had been washed down to remove the original writing, and recycled to be used for a copy of the minutes of a Council of the early Christian Church. But, as their rediscoverer realised, the *Letters* could still with difficulty be detected below the new text (the washing hadn't removed everything). These amounted to about half the original collection, including more than eighty letters written by Marcus Aurelius, before and after he became emperor.

They turned out to be something of a disappointment to their nineteenth-century audience. Fronto himself had presumably thought his correspondence worth circulating publicly and one major topic – consistent with his role as tutor – is the correct use of language. Pages are taken up with technical discussions of Latin usage (the difference, for example, between the word *colluere*, meaning to rinse the mouth, and *pelluere*, to scrub a floor), which no doubt reflect the content of the lessons he gave to Marcus Aurelius. And there is the occasional schoolmasterly ticking off, as when he complains that his pupil appears grumpy in public. But two other aspects of their correspondence are both intriguing and puzzling.

First is the apparent preoccupation, almost equalling Galen's, with illness and sharing symptoms. Whole sequences of letters between Fronto and Marcus Aurelius refer to little else: 'How was your night, my lord? I have been seized by a pain in my neck ...' 'I seem to have got through the night without a fever, and am eating well ... You can guess how I felt, learning of your neck pain', 'I am gripped by awful neck pain, but the pain in my foot has improved', 'News that your neck is better will certainly help my own recovery ... I have eaten more today, but still with a slightly upset stomach', and so on. It is hard to be sure whether this is a reflection of a more general concern with the body, characteristic of Roman elite culture in the mid second century CE (we can still read the six books that one contemporary intellectual orator, Aelius Aristides, devoted entirely to his own illnesses, symptoms and attempted cures), or whether it is a case of hypochondria in high places, or maybe a bit of both.

Equally striking is the highly sentimental, almost erotic, tone of some of the correspondence between tutor and imperial pupil, alongside the dry grammar lessons. Marcus Aurelius signs off one letter 'Goodbye, breath of my life. Should I not burn with love for you, when you have written to me like this?' He closes another by referring back to the famous homoerotic passions of fifth-century Athens (not to the Phaedrus who was the Roman fable writer). 'Socrates', he writes, 'did not burn with greater desire for Phaedrus than I have burned ... for the sight of you ... Goodbye, my greatest thing under heaven, my treasure.' Fronto replies in kind, 'Goodbye, Caesar, and love me the most, as you do. For my part I dote on each of the little letters of all the words you write ...' A few modern readers have taken these expressions as a sign that Marcus Aurelius and his tutor were lovers. Others have seen them more as high-flown, effusive rhetoric between close friends, not erotic partners (there are also plenty of warm references among the effusions to, for example, Fronto's wife). If so, was this kind of expression typical of how elite Romans in this imperial circle addressed each other in private, to match the kissing (p. 178), part of the standard language of the palace behind closed doors? Or were Fronto and Marcus Aurelius peculiarly arch, pretentious, almost camp, in the way they chose to communicate?

Those puzzles are only a taster for the puzzles raised by the *Jottings to Himself*.

Several Roman rulers are known to have written their memoirs, starting – on the cusp of autocracy at Rome – with the self-serving, politically self-justificatory accounts by Julius Caesar of his campaigns in Gaul and in the later civil war. Unlike Caesar's, most have not survived. We have no trace of the more personal autobiography of Augustus, which he wrote separately from the unadorned *What I Did* designed to stand outside his tomb. And part of the literary conceit behind the novels of Robert Graves and Marguerite Yourcenar is that they claim to reconstruct the lost memoirs of Claudius and Hadrian. The only intimate first-person account to survive from the pen of an emperor, before the outpourings of Julian in the fourth century CE (from clever satire to self-indulgent mysticism) are the *Jottings to Himself* or *Meditations* of Marcus Aurelius.

This book is now a modern bestseller, famously found on the bedside table of President Bill Clinton: the single 'book (other than the bible) that had most influenced him', according to one source. Translated from the original Greek into a slim volume of just over a hundred pages, it combines philosophical reflections, self-help advice ('It is mad to pursue the impossible', 'Do not let the future upset you') and a sprinkling of his favourite quotations culled from Greek literature with the now almost exotic authority of an ancient Roman emperor. Its origins are murkier than you might think. We have no idea exactly when or why the emperor chose to write down his fairly random thoughts on life and morals. We do not know who then chose to edit, order and publicly circulate them, or what the original title of the book was – even supposing it had one (the various modern names were invented later). And its philosophical acumen is disputed. Some modern scholars rank these *Jottings* as high-quality ethical reflections, deeply informed by the Stoic school of philosophy. Others – and I confess I am one – see them as little more than a collection of philosophical platitudes, one of those books now more often bought than read. To be honest, such homilies as 'Withdraw into yourself: the nature of the rational directing mind is to be satisfied with acting rightly and the peace that comes with it' do not seem to me to offer much to Bill Clinton or any other readers. But, leaving those doubts aside, does the book get us closer to the real, rather than fictional, view from the throne?

In some ways, it can hardly fail to, even though, alongside the philosophy, Marcus Aurelius's direct observations on life as an emperor make up no more than four or five pages of the whole. At the very beginning, for example, he lists those men (plus his mother) from whom he has learned most, and what particular qualities they demonstrated and taught. Fronto would surely have been disappointed if he had known how short his own entry was (summarised as teaching an awareness of the role of envy, capriciousness and hypocrisy in the working of one-man rule, and how true-blue aristocrats can lack human affection). By far the longest entry, more or less equal to that devoted to the lessons taught by the gods, went to his predecessor and adoptive father Antoninus Pius. In several paragraphs some of his outstanding virtues are listed: from his disdain for empty honours and his capacity for hard work, to his considerate treatment of his friends (not making them attend on him when he was abroad, for example), his tolerance of criticism and his simple lifestyle. Elsewhere Marcus Aurelius condemns flattery and the overblown pomp and ceremony of the court. 'See that you don't become "*Caesarified*"', he instructs himself using an ingenious linguistic coinage in Greek, and in one parade of modesty he defines himself simply as 'a man, of mature years, a statesman, a Roman and a ruler', ready to die when the moment comes. Among his anthology of favourite quotations are those that must have had a particular resonance for an emperor: 'It is the lot of a monarch to do good but to have a bad reputation', is one of his chosen snippets from classic Greek poetry.

There *is* something special about reading these, occasionally confessional, observations from the pen of an emperor himself, imagining him nodding to lines of Greek verse on the unenviable position of the autocrat. But at the same time, there is something disappointing – and surprising – that Marcus Aurelius's analysis of the emperor's role is so *unsurprising*. He says almost nothing on good imperial conduct that you could not find in Pliny or many other elite Roman writers: from the importance of being 'one of us' to a commitment to moderation and appropriate (not excessive) generosity, combined with an aversion to flattery. And, even in a work of such intimate privacy, there is no reference to problems of succession or of threats to his rule, and no more than a few words – of fulsome praise – about his reputedly disloyal wife Faustina ('so obedient, loving and unaffected'). The only mention of sex is a puzzling remark about how 'I did not touch Benedicta or Theodotus', probably slaves in the imperial household.

Maybe this means that the emperors (such as Marcus Aurelius) and members of the elite (such as Pliny) shared a very similar view about what a good emperor was. Maybe it also hints that Faustina's adulteries were the product of later spin, spread to damn her son Commodus – or at least that her husband knew nothing about them. But it is more likely, I suspect, that even the apparently intimate reflections of Marcus Aurelius are still actually obscuring as much as revealing the emperor as he really was. Even when we read the words from his own pen, he is still hidden from us. To put that another way, in this chapter we have made our way through the people of the imperial palace, from the slaves and the servants to the lovers and wives, but when we come as close as we can get to the emperor (even through the eyes of his doctor), he remains tantalisingly just out of reach. It is impossible to be sure exactly who he is.

That is one point of another fable told by the Roman writer Phaedrus, who knew a good deal about the emperor and his image from his position as a slave in the imperial court. It is a story about an imaginary land of the apes, which is visited by a liar and a truth teller. The chief ape claims to the visitors that he is the emperor, surrounded by his courtiers. The liar visitor agrees with him and is given rewards for his fibs. The truth teller, by contrast, replies that this 'emperor' is really an ape, and is torn apart limb from limb for his truthful answer. There are many morals here. It is, of course, a version of the modern fairy tale 'The Emperor's New Clothes' (who will dare tell the emperor that he is naked?). It reflects too on the benefits and dangers of flattery or frankness in an imperial court, and on the deception that lies at the heart of power. But the fable also points to the uncertainty about who the emperor actually *was*. In the Roman imagination apes were the greatest actors of the animal kingdom. So, was the emperor just an actor? And what was the difference between a man (or an ape) who was *pretending* to be the emperor and the real emperor? For even the pretend emperor could do you harm – just like the real one, as Phaedrus surely knew.

Over the next chapters, we will take some different routes to get closer to the emperor of Rome. We will look at him as he operated (and, just as important, was *imagined* to operate) in different contexts, at work and at play, inside Rome and outside, from answering his letters to fighting his enemies or joining the gods, from watching the games to his deathbed speeches. But first to the emperor with his paperwork.

6

ON THE JOB

Take a letter

Ten years after Pliny had been consul – and after the warm vote of
thanks he had offered to the emperor Trajan for giving him that
honour – he was appointed, by Trajan again, to be governor of the
province of Pontus-Bithynia, on the Black Sea coast of modern Turkey
(a territory carved out of two pre-Roman kingdoms, hence its hybrid
name). For most senators, 'employment' in government was sporadic,
and Pliny had held no full-time post since his consulship. We find him
instead pleading in the public courts, attending the senate, advising the
emperor on tricky points of law, and between 104 and 106 CE acting
as 'superintendent of the bed and banks of the Tiber and of the city
drains' – an administrative role, overseeing flood defences and sewers,
more strategic than hands-on, and probably no more than part-time.
All that changed around 110, when for a couple of years (the exact dates
are unknown) he was based 1,500 miles away from Rome, governing a
Greek-speaking province in the eastern part of the empire: a job that
was certainly hands-on – and a full-time headache.

Trajan seems to have registered Pontus-Bithynia as a 'problem'. For
he gave Pliny specific instructions to look into what was going wrong:
from local government corruption to potentially dangerous political
associations. How Pliny handled this we know in considerable detail

because more than a hundred business letters exchanged between the emperor and his 'man on the spot' have been preserved, as an appendix to the collection of Pliny's more literary correspondence. Originally written on papyrus or scratched into waxed tablets, they reveal not only some issues that might cross a Roman governor's desk in this part of the empire – collapsing aqueducts, rules on burials, troublesome philosophers – but also the kind of information that reached the emperor himself. At the same time, we can see how he responded to the queries and requests from the other side of 'his' world. These letters take us right into the imperial in-tray.

Sometimes it is a question of the emperor just giving a cautious blessing to Pliny's suggestions. Should the people of the city of Prusa be allowed to rebuild their public baths, the governor asks. Yes, replies the emperor, *if* they can do it without raising new taxes. And what about that new sect of Christians? Should he punish them, Pliny asks ('their obstinacy and dogged intransigence' certainly deserve it). Yes, says Trajan, punish them, but don't actively seek out the culprits or accept the word of anonymous informers; no poison-pen letters, please (pp. 403–4). Sometimes we find the emperor pouring cold water onto Pliny's more ambitious, or hare-brained, schemes. His plans to improve the transport infrastructure in the province, by building a canal to connect a lake to the sea, ring alarm bells with the practical Trajan – who points out that the end result might simply be to drain the lake of all its water. But alarm bells also ring when Pliny shares his apparently sensible idea of forming a local fire brigade. Absolutely not, comes the reply, with a dash of chilling imperial realpolitik, or anxiety. 'This is exactly the kind of organisation,' Trajan insists, 'that has caused disturbances in the province. Whatever name we give them, they soon become political pressure groups.' So he suggests instead making buckets and firefighting equipment more easily available. On other occasions there is a hint of impatience on the emperor's part. 'I think you could decide this for yourself' is a repeated refrain, in answer to the governor's more trivial worries. And when, more than once, Pliny begs for an architect or surveyor to be sent out from Rome to the province (to assess some dilapidated structure or to check that public building works had been completed according to the contract), Trajan's usual reply is a slightly exasperated: 'You can surely find one in your province, can't you. There must be plenty there.'

Of course, these exchanges may not have been exactly as they seem. Not all of the emperor's letters can actually have been written by the man himself. Like modern monarchs, presidents and prime ministers, Roman rulers must have signed off, or nodded through, any number of routine communications written on their behalf by the secretariat. 'I was glad to hear from your letter, my dear Pliny, with how much devotion and joy the troops and the provincials, under your lead, celebrated the anniversary of my accession', as one letter runs, is an obvious example of that: a standard one-line acknowledgement dispatched by an office junior. And the slow speed of delivery meant that the answers to some of Pliny's queries would have come too late to be of much practical use. In the fantasy of the Greek intellectual and hypochondriac, Aelius Aristides, letters from the emperor 'arrived as soon as they were written, as if carried by winged messengers'. In reality, letters between Rome and Pliny's province, carried by a man on a horse, took about two months each way. Unless he could afford to wait a minimum of four months for an answer, Pliny must sometimes have 'decided for himself', just as the emperor urged him. Micro-management from the centre was in part an illusion.

This correspondence remains, however, a marvellously vivid picture of a deferential governor constantly referring queries up to central command (or perhaps just trying to cover his back, hoping that when the reply eventually came it would justify what he had by then already done), and of an emperor who appears by turn to enjoy the (illusion of) micro-management *and* to wash his hands of it, while telling Pliny just to get on with the job. It is also a hint of the scale of the administration and of the size of the mailbag that poured into the palace.

Pliny was, so far as we know, the only governor to have circulated a selection of this business correspondence for wider consumption, in what has become Book 10 of his letter collection. He presumably thought it was a good way to display his own devotion to duty, and to show off the bonhomie between himself and the emperor ('my dear Pliny', as Trajan usually writes), albeit at the cost of displaying the occasional imperial ticking off. But we should probably imagine that the governors of the forty provinces of the empire, even those who did not circulate their correspondence, were doing much the same as Pliny and *all* regularly writing back to HQ in Rome. At a rough calculation – *if* Pliny wrote with typical frequency and *if* he selected for circulation, at a guess, a quarter of the letters originally written – that would have meant more than twelve letters every single day landing on the emperor from provincial governors alone, each reporting in and expecting a response from the man at the top ('like a chorus waiting for its trainer', as Aelius Aristides put it, more realistically this time). And that is before you factor in other senior officials, army commanders, and so on, who were in communication with the emperor too.

Despite all the practical difficulties, and the lengthy delays, this was *government by correspondence*. Fronto neatly summed it up when he told Marcus Aurelius that one of the main duties of an emperor was to 'send letters all over the world'.

This chapter takes its cue from the exchanges between Trajan and Pliny, to dig deeper into the idea of the emperor as letter-writer, decision-maker and administrator. It is largely concerned with the emperor upright at his desk, rather than reclining at dinner, and it asks what kind of work running the Roman world entailed, and how the image of the omnipotent ruler fitted the reality of palace administration. How hands-on were emperors in the day-to-day business of government? What kind of problems reached them, and from whom?

Did they ever set out radically to change things, or did they just try to keep the show on the road, dealing with crises as they occurred? How was it all paid for? In the course of this, we shall spotlight some precious documents from the front line of Roman power – technical administrative accounts of decisions made and rulings given – that take us straight back to the emperor's 'office' (this is another group of texts only rarely allowed out of the seminar room). We shall dip into the dry prose of some ancient legal handbooks for the human stories they contain. And we shall find out what ordinary people in the empire expected of their ruler, when and why they turned to him. The emperor at work offers a rare chance to catch sight of the fears, anxieties and grumbles of the people in the Roman street.

The buck stops here

The basic rule of the government of the empire was that the buck stopped with the emperor himself. He was deluged with requests, for advice, approval and action, not only from the likes of Pliny, but from local communities and individual men and women all over the Roman world. No grudge, grievance, problem or law case was in theory too trivial to send in his direction. Wherever he was, in Rome or on the move, he might find himself surrounded by people wanting something from him – whether a leg up on the military career ladder, the return of a lost inheritance, or the reversal of some land-grab by the neighbouring town. One of the reasons reported for the large casualty figures in an earthquake that rocked the town of Antioch (modern Antakya in Turkey) in 115 CE was that Trajan was staying there, using it as the HQ for an eastern war, and the place was full of people with their lawsuits and begging letters.

It is easy now to feel sympathy for Philo, traipsing around after Caligula, and trying to get the emperor to concentrate on the disputes in Alexandria. But maybe we should spare half a thought for Caligula too, who just wanted a few minutes to inspect one of his properties, instead of being pestered by warring factions from a city more than a 1,000 miles away, intent on thrashing out a dispute in which he had almost zero interest. Nor was he the only emperor irritated by those who tried to claim his attention. Philostratus, a Greek writer and intellectual of the third century CE, and a friend of Julia Domna, told of an encounter between Antoninus Pius and a man who had come on a delegation from Seleucia (another town in modern Turkey). When the man sensed that the emperor was not listening, he is supposed to have shouted, 'Pay attention to me, Caesar!' Caesar's sharp reply was: 'I *am* paying attention, and I know you, the guy who's always doing his hair, cleaning his teeth, filing his nails, and reeking of perfume.' We are not told the outcome of the delegation, but it is not hard to guess.

Dozens, or even hundreds, of people every day wanted the emperor to pay attention to *them*. The delegations and embassies, with their winning speeches at the ready, were just one part of it, as were the letters that arrived from Roman officials around the empire, and from those communities or private individuals who had enough money and confidence to dispatch a carrier to take their request to wherever the emperor happened to be. People could be quite determined to track him down, as we know from an inscription recording a man from Ephesus in modern Turkey who caught up with Septimius Severus and Caracalla in Britain. There were also the little pieces of papyrus (*libelli* in Latin) that were pressed into his hands, when he presided over public 'greetings' at the palace, or as he was carried through the streets, or showed up in some provincial town. This was how ordinary people usually approached him. Each *libellus* contained a request of some sort, and a brief imperial response was written underneath and then pinned up on a public noticeboard for the hopeful petitioner to inspect, before getting a witnessed copy and taking it home. Usually this involved a few days' hanging around, anxiously showing up until the decision was posted. Just occasionally a hint of the likely response came straight away. In a fictional version of one such encounter, written by Philostratus again, Vespasian is pictured receiving one of these requests and immediately reading it aloud to the assembled company. To the embarrassment of the petitioner, it was a blatant plea for cash for himself and his friends. The implication is that a firm 'no' was on its way.

There was also a long string of formal legal decisions for the emperor to make. He was not, of course, the only person to play the part of judge in the Roman world. His role was bolted onto the legal role of other officials and juries that went back to the Republic. But he acted as the equivalent of the court of appeal for the empire as a whole, as well as trying more than his fair share of regular cases, whether in the Roman Forum and other city locations, on his travels through the empire, or in his palaces (the room decorated with his star sign was where Septimius Severus liked to hold trials). How some relatively ordinary people managed to get the ruler himself to act as *their* judge is a mystery. It was probably a combination of persistence, and of knowing someone who knew someone who knew someone in the palace. And some emperors were no doubt keener than others to take on the legal side of the job. Claudius was reputed to be particularly keen, but even he sometimes lost enthusiasm and fell asleep mid-trial so that the advocates were forced to speak louder to wake him up. Or that was the story. Claudius's habit of dropping off at inconvenient points was actually something of a standing joke. When he did it in the middle of dinner, his nephew Caligula used to have his resident pranksters – the 'little shits' (p. 102) – wake him up with a whip.

Some of the responses that emperors gave to the requests that came in are still preserved, verbatim, on stone, on sheets of bronze or on papyrus across the Roman empire, and more are being discovered in excavations all the time. Others are included in Roman legal handbooks, for the simple reason that the word of the emperors effectively *was* the law and their answers to tricky problems became legal reference points. One handbook, for example, included the reply of the joint emperors Marcus Aurelius and Lucius Verus to a query about a particularly poignant case raised by a governor of the province of Africa. What should he do, he had asked, about a desperate slave who had gone so far as falsely to confess to the crime of murder, simply in order to escape the clutches of his owner? The emperors' solution was: sell the slave, compensate the owner – but do *not* send the slave back to him. The judgement presumably became a precedent for the future.

Exactly how big a slice of the emperor's time all this took is impossible to know. It was a symbol of Vespasian's notorious over-commitment to duty that he was reported to have been receiving delegations on his deathbed. And we have no clue which is more typical: the four or five *libelli* a day that, according to one fragment of papyrus, Septimius Severus and Caracalla received on a visit to Egypt between 199 and 200 CE; or the six hundred a day that, according to another papyrus, the governor of Egypt – lower down in the pecking order – received a few years later. But whichever is closer to the norm, the impression we sometimes get of the emperor as devoted agony uncle or advice columnist to the empire cannot really be quite that simple. For a start, the emperors' replies were often perfunctory. Although Commodus was specifically criticised for giving exactly the same response to large numbers of petitions, the evidence we have suggests that such standard replies were fairly typical. Besides, a frequent answer to a petition from a community outside Italy was to send it straight back, with instructions to take it to the governor of the relevant Roman province.

A perfect example of both these tendencies is found in one long inscription discovered in what is now Bulgaria, giving details of a petition by a group of local villagers to the emperor Gordian III in 238 CE, followed by the reply (the whole copied down, it says, from the imperial response posted in Rome 'in the portico of the Baths of Trajan', presumably a convenient public noticeboard). The petitioners had a heart-wrenching story of how their village – a tiny place by the name of Skaptopara, the home of some nice thermal baths and close to a popular market – had been repeatedly trashed by Roman soldiers and officials passing through, demanding free food, drink, billeting and entertainment. It was so dreadful that they were thinking, they said, of 'leaving our ancestral homes because of the violence done to us … and so we beg you, unconquerable emperor … to order that everyone sticks to his own route and does not leave the other villages and come to us and compel us to offer provisions at our own expense,

50. A glimpse of the 'paperwork' of the Roman empire. This is the start of the list of cases heard by Septimius Severus and Caracalla in Egypt (though Caracalla, not yet a teenager, could hardly have played a major role). Below the heading, the document states that it is a copy of the responses posted up in the gymnasium. The three lines of cramped writing near the top add in the formal names and titles of the emperors, obviously mistakenly omitted from the first version. See further, p. 232.

and to order that we should not have to provide accommodation to those who are not entitled'. After more than 160 lines of text in Greek laying out the villagers' case, Gordian's answer in just four lines written in Latin was that they should go back and ask the governor of their province to sort it out. No easy solution was forthcoming from the palace. The best the petitioners will have achieved is that, armed with this imperial response, their problem was fast-tracked with the local administration. Possibly that had always been their aim in any case.

Who wrote what?

Whether the replies were perfunctory or not (and not all were), the emperor had a lot of help in dealing with the deluge of requests. There was legal advice available from an unofficial roster of experts, such as Pliny or those parodies of courtiers who turned up to adjudicate on Domitian's turbot (there is no need to imagine Marcus Aurelius and Lucius Verus struggling with 'the case of the false confession' on their own). And there were also those key divisions of the palace staff – the Latin secretariat, the Greek secretariat and the petitions department. Another of Statius's poems praises the head of the Latin secretariat under Domitian, a 'father-of-Claudius-Etruscus' type, who is pictured at the control centre of a web of communications 'with the most demanding job in the palace'. The poet jokes that he processes even more messages than the god Mercury himself – the divine messenger whose winged sandals ensured speedy delivery. But the remit of these departments must have extended beyond the practical aspects of 'processing' to such jobs as taking dictation (the word 'checked' written at the end of some responses probably suggests that), working up finished drafts after a simple imperial 'Tell him no', and more. We have already seen a few replies from 'Trajan' to his man in Pontus-Bithynia that would have needed no input at all from the emperor himself, and were very likely composed entirely by the secretariat. The added extra in the story of the Skaptoparans is that Gordian was just thirteen years old when they sent their petition. He may well never have even read of their plight, let alone had anything to do with composing 'his' reply.

It is absolutely certain that no emperor answered every begging letter himself. One head of the Greek secretariat under Septimius Severus, for example, was credited by a learned admirer with being the best letter-writer in the world, excelling not only in clarity, and stylistic tricks, but also, like an actor or good ghostwriter, in capturing the imperial persona in the letters he wrote on the ruler's behalf. Greek letters might have been a special case. Even a functionally bilingual emperor might have needed help with the rhetorical niceties of Greek. But it is impossible to imagine that the other leading legal or literary figures who sometimes headed these divisions, Suetonius among them for a while, would have spent their days as merely clerks and copyists. What can never be certain is exactly who wrote what, or how *many* of the imperial pronouncements were ghosted by the staff.

Practices must have changed all the time, depending among other things on whether the emperor concerned was diligent or lazy, a control freak or a delegator, at home or on military campaign, an inexperienced teenager or a long-serving elder statesman. There is, in any case, always a fuzzy boundary between ghostwriting, editing, drafting or polishing. But just as important as who really *did* write the letters was who was *thought* to write them. And, for most people, that was the emperor.

The emperor's new pen

In the Roman imagination the ruler was always a pen-pusher as much as a libertine. Just like Fronto in his advice to Marcus Aurelius about 'sending letters all over the world', when Romans pictured the emperor, they did not only see him at dinner, or commanding his troops, or misbehaving on a grand scale, they also saw him dealing with his papers, his casework and his correspondence. That side is captured in memorable vignettes of Julius Caesar, whether working on his letters and petitions at the races (a trick later tried by Marcus Aurelius) or ostentatiously multitasking on his military campaigns, by dictating to two secretaries simultaneously as he rode on horseback. It is also captured in the story of Hadrian who – when asked to adjudicate whether a baby born eleven months after the death of its 'father' could be considered legitimate – went off to do his own research in the medical textbooks. He came up with the answer 'yes', which was bizarrely wrong even by ancient scientific standards.

Reading was part of the imperial image too. How the emperor read, and responded to, the letters he received was a good diagnostic of his character. Caligula – not an obvious candidate for devotion to paperwork – supposedly became visibly cross while scanning a letter from the governor of Judaea that gave him some advice that he did not want to hear (namely, to think twice before placing a statue of himself in the Temple in Jerusalem). Augustus reportedly sacked another governor for making a crass spelling error in a dispatch that the emperor must have seen with his own eyes (how else would he have spotted the mistake?). It was a sign of his pedantry, but also of a touch of hypocrisy, since he was said to be an erratic speller himself. More honourably, Marcus Aurelius was supposed to have wept as he read a letter that described the damage to the city of Smyrna (Izmir) caused by an earthquake: 'when he came to the passage "the west winds blow through her like a desert" he shed tears on the page' and promptly promised funds to restore the place.

It is perhaps no surprise that the humble stylus, or Roman metal pen, was one of the emperor's trademark accessories. He was always imagined as having one to hand. It was with his stylus that Julius Caesar tried to defend himself against the daggers of his assassins.

This was Domitian's weapon of choice in his nasty pastime of skewering flies. And, according to Galen in a short compilation of cruel 'pen injuries', it was with his stylus that Hadrian, in a fit of temper, stabbed the eye of a slave. He was later shamed when, in remorse, he asked the slave what gift he would like in compensation – 'my eye back', was the simple reply. For better or worse, pens and emperors went together.

And the assumption, of course, was that – unless they were dictating – emperors actually wrote with those pens too. Even if a few in the inner circle knew better, generally the words that appeared *in the name of* the emperor were taken to be the words *of*, and *written by*, the emperor. It wasn't his secretaries who were criticised for the identikit replies, it was Commodus himself.

That is one reason why the responses of the emperor were so commonly inscribed on stone or bronze in cities across the empire and put on display. Even if only a minority could actually read them (20 per cent is one common modern guess for rates of literacy among men in the empire), it was a way of putting the emperor himself on display. It is also one reason why any public hint of a gap between the emperor's words (whether written or oral) and the emperor's own authorship could be used as a weapon against him, almost as if it challenged his right to rule. Young Nero, for example, was denigrated as the first emperor to need – in Tacitus's clever phrase – 'borrowed eloquence', when he delivered a funeral eulogy for his stepfather Claudius that had actually been composed by his tutor Seneca. And the emperor Julian enjoyed a snide joke about Trajan along the same lines: he was so lazy that he had his friend Lucius Licinius Sura write his speeches for him (a rather different view from the picture of a super-conscientious Trajan that we find in Pliny). It was another important fiction of imperial culture – and another version of where the buck stopped – that whenever you received a reply from an emperor you took it for granted that it was the man himself who was writing to you. The emperor *was* what 'the emperor' *wrote* or *said*.

From the bottom up

The inscriptions recording the decisions of the emperor in answer to the petitions of individuals or, more often, of local communities, present an image of a benevolent and conscientious ruler. The words of Domitian, for example, posted on a sheet of bronze in the small Italian town of Falerio, show him coming down in favour of the Falerians in their long-running land dispute with the neighbouring town of Firmum (the emperor, or someone on his staff, had dug out a previous adjudication by Augustus decades earlier, which seemed to settle the case). Another long text, on display in a small community in North Africa, records Commodus's response in support of a group of tenant farmers who had appealed to him after being abused by a local Roman official and his partner in crime (not only had the rent been increased, but a posse of soldiers had been sent in to beat them up). In some places whole archives were inscribed for public display. At Aphrodisias, for example, a city in what is now Turkey, named after the goddess Aphrodite, one wall at the entrance to the theatre was covered with documents carved into the stone: letters from emperors, the senate and other leading Romans, including a positive reply from Hadrian to an embassy of Aphrodisians asking to be excused from some (otherwise unknown) tax on nails.

It is very easy to get the impression from all this that the empire was filled with satisfied customers, people whose disputes had been settled, cases resolved or petitions granted by (or in the name of) the emperor. There were certainly some of those and they made a lot of noise. But the evidence is overwhelmingly skewed in favour of the successful. Those whose pleas were rejected or roughly handled would not have chosen to parade their failures in writing. The people of Firmum did not choose to inscribe Domitian's decision when it went in favour of the Falerians. The only reason that we know of the unsuccessful attempt of Livia to intervene on behalf of the people of

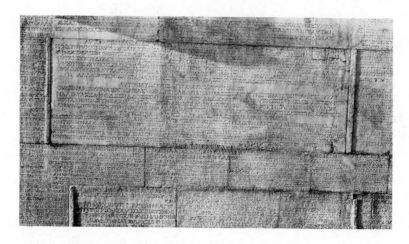

51. Part of the so-called 'Archive Wall' at Aphrodisias. It amounted to a public display of the town's relationship with the authorities in Rome, largely in the form of copies of letters from the emperor inscribed in stone.

Samos is because a copy of Augustus's letter was displayed, no doubt gleefully, by their rivals, the Aphrodisians. And the simple fact that the Skaptoparans publicised so fully their petition and its response is one thing that suggests that 'fast-tracking' with the local authorities had been the limits of their ambitions all along.

Besides, most people with problems in the Roman empire would not have got as far as failure at this level anyway. For the majority of inhabitants of the Roman world, whatever their plight, the prospect of a direct approach to the emperor was always more myth than reality. It was hard enough, as Philo found, for the well-connected, well-resourced and very determined to present their case to an elusive ruler. And the anxieties that even the educated might have in trying to win the emperor over are reflected in surviving ancient textbooks, which give detailed advice on how to do it. What should you say, for example, if you want to get him to send relief to a city that has been struck by a natural disaster? Answer: praise his compassion, say that the gods sent him to earth to help those in distress, vividly describe the devastation of the town and conjure up the idea of the whole population in tears begging for his mercy. But this kind of sophistication was well out of reach of most ordinary individuals or communities, not to mention all the practical difficulties that would get in their way.

It might have been relatively easy to take advantage of the emperor passing through your local area, and many did so (hence the casualty figures at Antioch). But appealing to the emperor in Rome from a distant province was quite another matter. It was sometimes actively discouraged by the local authorities, who preferred to keep things 'in house' (that, at least, is the implication of a ruling by Alexander Severus, quoted in a legal handbook, that governors should *not* try to prevent people forwarding their cases to the emperor). It also took a great deal of time and money, maybe a few months' journey there and back, and it needed confidence and knowledge of how things worked in the capital even to press a simple *libellus* into the emperor's hand. Where would you do it? How would you get access? Where, even, was the front door to the palace? On one occasion, at a public 'greeting', Augustus was said to have bantered with a man who was hesitating to present him with a petition (one minute holding his hand out, the next drawing it back): 'you look like you're trying to give a penny to an elephant'. It is quoted by more than one ancient writer as a great example of the emperor's sense of humour. It also captures the terror on the part of the petitioner unfamiliar with procedures.

I strongly suspect that many of the apparently ordinary cases presented to the emperor in Rome by apparently ordinary people were not quite so ordinary as they look. Sometimes there may have been more at stake than immediately meets the eye (that is my hunch with the case of the accidental homicide by chamber pot in the town of Knidos that was referred to Augustus). Sometimes it is clear that those bringing their requests were not entirely outsiders, but had their paths eased by useful connections in or near the circles of the emperor. There is a little giveaway of that in the petition of the Skaptoparans. How on earth did this remote village manage to make its voice heard in the capital? It was thanks to a villager resident in Rome itself. As the inscription clearly stated in its preamble, the petition was presented by a man who came from Skaptopara and owned property there, but was at the time serving in the imperial guard.

But even if they might be more 'special' than they seem, some of the cases brought to the emperor, as well as to lower-ranking Roman officials, bring into view the kind of problems faced by those inhabitants of the empire who are usually hidden from history. Through the perspective of the man at the top we can glimpse the difficulties and desperation of those at the other end of the hierarchy. Sometimes they are curious and (for a modern reader, though hardly for those concerned) engagingly colourful, from the cow killed in enemy action (p. 11) to clashes over going bird-hunting on a neighbour's property. More often they come down to much more routine problems of taxation, inheritance, illness, debts, and so on. In one group of thirteen responses given by Septimius Severus and Caracalla in Egypt in 200 CE, two concerned loans, three inheritances, two taxation, one guardianship of orphans, and one the question of whether illness was a sufficient reason for escaping legal obligations (the other responses, such as 'follow the decision given' give no clue about what the original question was). But if there was one particular issue that over the centuries caused the most vociferous popular complaint, and repeatedly called for action (or at least well-meaning protestations) from the emperor, it was the official transport 'system'. In a Roman world governed by correspondence, the mail service was one of the biggest hot spots of controversy.

Pliny breaks the rules

Essentially this was one of the problems of trying to run the infrastructure of a vast empire on a skeleton staff. Leaving aside the army, no other empire in the history of the world has operated with so few official boots on the ground (the Chinese empire had proportionately twenty times more senior administrators than did Rome). So, from the reign of Augustus, official transport and communication was largely outsourced, whether that was getting messages and men from one part of the empire to another, or prisoners, cash or wild beasts for the emperor's shows. If you were a Roman armed with the right permit, you were allowed simply to requisition animals, carts, lodging and hospitality from the communities through which your journey passed. The potential abuses are obvious: forged permits, non-payment of any fees due, demands for service far in excess of what was allowed, and generally abusive behaviour.

For many communities in the empire, this was the day-to-day sharp end of imperial exploitation. It's not hard to imagine what a visit from some tough, heavy-drinking couriers would be like if they showed up in *your* town, and it's one of the things that formed part of the Skaptoparans' complaint. For hundreds of years, provincials protested and emperors tried to respond. In 129 CE, for example, Hadrian claimed – his words preserved in an inscription that turned up mysteriously in the hands of a collector in Turkey in the 1990s – that he had seen for himself the poor treatment of the local people, and he (re)imposed a whole series of regulations to alleviate the problem. No wagon was to be given to anyone without a permit, all food for humans and animals was to be paid for, no local guides were to be demanded unless the roads were invisible because of snow, and so on. A few decades earlier, Nerva had actually abolished such requisitioning within Italy itself, and that abolition was celebrated on a coin minted at the time. It shows two mules happily grazing and behind them an upturned cart, no longer needed for official transportation.

This saga of 'requisitioned transport' (*vehiculatio*, more succinctly, in Latin) captures one version of the power of the emperors. They certainly appear to have listened to the pleas of their subjects and to have responded. But to judge from the repeated interventions on exactly the same topic right up to the fifth century CE, they never did enough to solve the problem. Anyway, they were happy to turn a blind eye when it suited their interests. At the very end of the book of correspondence between Pliny and Trajan, the governor writes that he had given an official permit to his wife, who wanted to visit her family in Italy after the death of her grandfather on a purely private visit that did not fall within the rules for permits at all. He later asks the emperor for special permission, backdated. 'Of course, my dear Pliny' is the reply. It is more than slightly unnerving that after over a hundred letters, apparently going out of their way to be punctiliously correct, the last one in the collection should show Trajan blithely giving the nod to Pliny breaking the rules on travel permits. So much for the emperors' claims to want to eradicate the abuse.

52. A bronze coin issued under Nerva, with a design celebrating the abolition of the system of requisitioned transport in Italy. Behind the two happily grazing mules, are the poles and harness from their cart, and the slogan written around the scene makes it explicit: '*vehiculatio* abandoned in Italy'.

Taking the initiative

You might well imagine from the size of the imperial mailbag that the emperor's job (whether he did it himself or had it done in his name) consisted almost entirely in responding to requests that poured in from the outside. And that is precisely what some modern historians have argued. They see the emperor as essentially *re*active rather than active: far from the grand image of an all-controlling autocrat, the ruler of the Roman world was actually more in the business of replying to letters, papering over the cracks, having his ear bent, and making sure that he appeared constantly available to everyone, great and small. There is something in that view. All governments are partly reactive (a lot of legislation originates in a complaint), and the image of the omnipotent emperor snapping his fingers and changing the world is more misleading than seeing him tied to his stylus or dictation. Equally misleading is the idea that emperors or their advisers devised *policy* as such, in the modern governmental sense of long-term strategic planning. That is probably true even for Augustus who, as we saw in chapter 1, brought about a more 'joined-up' programme of changes than any later ruler when he established one-man rule at Rome. To start with at least, he was almost certainly concerned as much with his own short-term survival as with devising a detailed template for centuries of autocracy. He was an improviser who became a strategist largely in retrospect.

But Augustus's successors on the throne did more than just wait for the mail. In Fronto's advice to Marcus Aurelius on the duties of an emperor, as well as sending letters his list included 'putting the pressure on kings of foreign peoples' (to which we shall return in chapter 8), 'to argue in the senate for what is in the public interest', and 'to correct unjust law'. Emperors are associated with all kinds of initiative, on matters large and small (even down to the menus in Roman cafés), 'in the public interest'.

Sometimes this was a question of troubleshooting, as in a revealing story about a junior Roman official, and whistle-blower, in the province of Britain in the early 60s CE. He wrote to the emperor to complain that, in the aftermath of the rebellion of Boudicca, the provincial governor had treated far too savagely the rebels who had surrendered. It was one of those many thousands of letters sent to the emperor from a distant province, but it is what happened next, and the series of decisions taken, that count here. Nero, the emperor at the time, responded by sending one of his ex-slaves, Polyclitus, to investigate what was going on and to see if he could mend the rift between governor and finance officer: he could not. The upshot was that as soon as there was a decent opportunity to get rid of the governor (after a minor, face-losing, naval accident), Nero replaced him with someone much more conciliatory, who calmed things down.

This is all recounted with a very negative spin by Tacitus. In his view, the junior official should not have told tales on the governor in the first place. Far from being a useful negotiator, Polyclitus was a figure of terror to the Romans in Britain and a figure of fun to the enemy, who thought it a joke to give such a responsibility to an ex-slave (pp. 191–3). And the conciliatory successor was merely lazy, 'covering up his slothful inactivity under the honourable banner of peace' (I am sure that Tacitus would expect us to spot that the successor's name, 'Turpilianus', means something like 'shameful'). But underneath Tacitus's hostility, it is easy enough to discern some effective action, and a well-judged appointment, on the part of the emperor or his advisers, even if it was, sadly, too late for the rebels. No doubt not all appointments were so well-judged, and there were plenty of hostile rumours about why some provincial governors were 'really' chosen (the future emperor Otho being sent to govern one of the Spanish provinces after Nero had taken up with his wife, or, even more fantastically, Caracalla sending those he did not like to provinces where the climate was uncomfortably hot or cold). In general, patronage, personal favour

53. The whistle-blower after Boudicca's rebellion died in Britain,
for parts of his large tombstone (more than 2 metres across) were
discovered in London in the nineteenth century, re-used in some
late Roman defences of the town. Tacitus gives his name as 'Julius
Classicianus'. This memorial preserves its fuller form in the third line
'Julius Alpinus Classicianus' – a name suggesting that his origins lay in
Gaul. Maybe for that reason he had some sympathy with the Britons.

and back-scratching were as influential as competence in appointments and promotions. But in the British case, from the Roman point
of view at least, the system had worked.

At other times, it is hard not to suspect that the force of emperors' rulings – from bans on castration to prohibiting nasty lampoons
against leading men and women or clamping down on mixed bathing
– were more symbolic than practical. That is very likely the case with
the café menus: the series of emperors' regulations from the first
century CE stipulating what could or could not be served in the bars
and fast-food outlets (*popinae*) of the city of Rome. Tiberius, according to Suetonius, 'went so far as to forbid pastries'. Cassius Dio states
that Claudius banned the sale of both 'boiled meat' and, even more
puzzlingly, 'hot water' (perhaps because, in the Roman regime of

alcohol consumption, water was the key ingredient to mix with wine), and that Nero banned anything boiled at all except 'vegetables and pea-soup'. Finally, according to Dio again, Vespasian clamped down on everything except beans, which must have made for a very dull café culture if the regulations were followed.

Almost certainly they were not, or only very haphazardly. There *are* a couple of vague references to prosecutions of miscreant pub land-lords, but in a city of a million inhabitants without a police service (the nearest to that was a squad of nightwatchmen-cum-firefighters), such rules can never have been strictly or systematically enforced, or even seriously meant to be. The function of legislation, then as now, can be to showcase values as much as to punish malefactors. The main point here, I suspect, was not to round up offenders but to display the emperor's micro-management of the Roman world and his commit-ment to frugality – at least (on the usual double standard) frugality for the ordinary people who hung out in *popinae*, not for the rich.

Something similar probably lay behind Augustus's ruling that no man could enter the Forum unless he was wearing a toga (the most formal style of Roman dress, which was no more the everyday wear of most citizens than a dinner jacket or tuxedo is today). The emperor was said to have made this the responsibility of some junior senatorial officials (*aediles*) to enforce. But were there really bouncers, checking the dress code, on the entrances to the Forum? I doubt it. This was really a much more general message about 'smartening up' and 'old-fashioned standards'.

Claudius on his soap box

Occasionally, however, we do find emperors driving major changes with real practical effect, and we can even see how those changes were justified. One example – which started with a petition in 48 CE from 'the leading men in Gaul' but developed into a major controversy – was the proposal backed by the emperor Claudius to allow men from 'hairy Gaul', the part of France on the northern side of the Alps, to hold political office in Rome and become members of the senate. The account of this, given by Tacitus, represents objections being made to the emperor by opponents of the proposal (did not Italy have enough men of its own to fill the senate, and weren't the people of Gaul the traditional enemies of the Romans anyway?), followed by a speech by Claudius himself, which swung the vote in the Gauls' favour (as a speech by the emperor was almost bound to do). But even if it was a pushover, it was a big step in the gradual extension of Roman political privileges through the empire.

What makes this decision especially interesting, though, is that what appears to be a verbatim text of Claudius's speech was carefully inscribed on a sheet of bronze and proudly put on display in the Gallic town of Lyon (Lugdunum), where a large part of it was rediscovered in the sixteenth century (fig. 2). There is an underlying logic to Claudius's arguments as we can still read them here: it had always been Rome's custom, he insisted, to incorporate outsiders, and ever since the conquest by Julius Caesar, the Gauls had been unwaveringly loyal. But the details of this rambling speech are a nasty surprise for anyone looking for persuasive rhetoric from the emperor.

More than half of the surviving text is taken up by Claudius giving an abstruse, muddled and not entirely relevant history lesson to the senate in order to illustrate Rome's tradition of welcoming foreigners. Going back more than half a millennium to the sixth century BCE, for example, he had this to say about the semi-mythical 'Etruscan' king of Rome, Servius Tullius (and I am tidying his words up slightly in this translation):

Servius Tullius, if we follow our own writers, was born of a war captive, Ocresia, or if we follow Etruscan writers, he was once a most loyal comrade of Caelius Vivenna and partner in every one of his adventures. After he left Etruria, driven out by changes of fortune, with all the remnants of Caelius's army, he seized the Caelian Hill which was his name for it, calling it after his leader Caelius. After he had changed his own name (for his name in Etruscan was Mastarna) he was called just like I've said and he ruled the kingdom with enormous benefit to the state . . .

So it goes on, and worse. At one point he tells a rather feeble in-joke: 'we don't regret already having men in the senate from Lugdunum', presumably a reference to the fact that he himself had been born in the town, when his father was serving there as provincial governor. At another, after a further ramble, he stops to remind himself to get to the point: 'Now's the time, Claudius, to tell the senators where your speech is heading' (though some modern critics have wondered whether this might actually have been an interjection from a member of the audience, who couldn't take any more of it, creeping into the text by mistake). There was no 'borrowed eloquence' here; it might have been better if there had been. Presumably, though, the inscription was more a symbol of the emperor's support for their cause than something that many burghers of Lyon would actually have stopped to read.

There is no reason to suppose that this was a typical speech from the mouth of an emperor. If we were to believe the modern – and, in part, ancient – stereotype of Claudius (slow, elderly, not quite with it, though a keen scholar who had written a book on Etruscan history), we might expect this kind of thing from him. Nonetheless, there are elements in other surviving speeches from other emperors and their families that are not so far away from what we read on the tablet from Lyon, whether the speech of the young prince Germanicus, who arrived in Alexandria and confessed to a bit of homesickness, or the wooden congratulations given by Hadrian to troops in North Africa, after he had watched their training exercises ('You have cut a trench

through hard coarse gravel and have made it even by smoothing it';
p. 320). These are all reminders that the words of the emperor might
sometimes have been more homespun than we imagine.

The citizenship revolution

Frustratingly, there are no words at all, homespun or not, that help to
explain what lay behind the single most radical reform ever introduced
by a Roman emperor. In 212 CE, the emperor Caracalla at a stroke gave
full Roman citizenship – with the status and the legal rights, from
inheritance to contracts, that came with it – to all inhabitants of the
Roman empire who were not enslaved, probably more than 30 million
of them. This was not part of the kind of revolutionary programme of
change introduced by Augustus but, as just one piece of legislation,
it had more impact than any of the individual initiatives of the first
emperor. From now on, every free person in the empire shared the
same basic rights. The legal difference between (citizen) rulers and
(non-citizen) ruled was abolished overnight, making them, at a fundamental level, equal. It is true that, over the course of the third century,
new distinctions between the 'more honourable' and 'more humble'
citizens – *honestiores* and *humiliores* – made some more equal than
others. But, all the same, this was the biggest grant of citizenship in the
history of Rome, and very likely in the history of the world.

The precise details of the legislation and, even more, what drove
it (beyond the tradition of 'incorporation' to which Claudius had
appealed 150 years earlier) is impossible to discover. One scrap of a
roughly contemporary papyrus appears to quote from Caracalla's
edict ('I therefore give everyone in the Roman world Roman citizenship'), and there are a couple of brief references to it, in Cassius
Dio and in a legal handbook. But we have only speculation – a little
ancient and a lot modern – about what the arguments around it were.

Was he emulating the myth of Alexander the Great who, or so some imagined, cherished a fantasy of world citizenship? Was he bidding for popularity after the bloody break-up with his brother Geta? Was it even the work of Caracalla himself? Writers a few centuries later could not imagine that such a positive reform was enacted by such a reputed 'monster' and ascribed it instead to Antoninus Pius or Marcus Aurelius. Or was it all a financial wheeze? Dio, followed by Edward Gibbon, claimed that the honour was a cover for making the provincial populations liable to taxes that fell only on citizens, in particular taxes on inheritances and on the value of slaves when they were freed.

This is one of the biggest 'black holes' in all of Roman history. Perhaps more than anything, we're missing any clue about how the emperor presented it to the people of Italy and of the empire more widely. How was the word spread? How did its beneficiaries get to find out about their new status? I rather doubt that Caracalla treated everyone to a history lesson in the style of Claudius, but who knows?

The bottom line

It is extremely unlikely that Caracalla's reform was driven by financial concerns, even if that is the only more-or-less contemporary explanation for it on offer. There is conflicting evidence for how hard up the imperial administration was at this period. Coins were being minted with a smaller and smaller proportion of pure precious metal (such debasement is usually a good indication of economic trouble in Rome), but several ancient writers observe that the imperial coffers were in a healthier state on the death of Septimius Severus, Caracalla's father, than they had ever been before. Even if the emperor was strapped for cash, to give full Roman citizenship to more than 30 million inhabitants of the empire, including the poorest, in order to make them liable for a few taxes, would have been a sledgehammer to crack a nut. There were other ways of raising funds. It does, however, prompt questions about the emperor and money.

The Roman empire was a sprawling and puzzling economic 'system' (and certainly not a *system* in the modern economic sense). It was, in part, highly connected, almost proto-global. There was a rudimentary common currency across the Roman world, with universally recognisable and recognised denominations in gold, silver and bronze. There were also some commodities, especially pottery, that spread across the Roman world from Scotland to the Sahara in an early example of mass production (you can see the same shiny red Roman pots piled up on museum shelves in Algeria and on Hadrian's Wall, on the Scottish border). And there are some powerful hints at the scale of industrial output and of the long-distance transport networks. The small hill that you can still climb in Rome, known as 'Broken Pot Mountain' (Monte Testaccio), is actually the remains of an ancient rubbish dump, made up of the broken fragments of more than 53 million huge jars, or *amphorae*, of olive oil (some 60 litres each), imported to Rome from Spain between the second and third centuries CE. Even that is overshadowed by recent scientific analysis of deep bores into the Greenland ice cap, which show traces of the pollution produced by Roman mining operations, many of them in Spain, that were not equalled until the industrial revolution.

Yet the majority of the inhabitants of the empire remained small-scale subsistence farmers and most of the production was still local or domestic. There were very few technological innovations to underpin any industrial 'progress', not much more than the occasional water mill. There were even fewer financial institutions, of banking and credit, and almost no economic theories. The Romans did not even have a word for 'the economy', they certainly would not have known what 'growth' was, and how they stored wealth is a mystery (except in the ancient equivalent of 'under the bed'). Financial planning for the future was basic at best. One ancient analysis of the pros and cons

54. 'Broken Pot Mountain' means exactly what it says. As
you see here, the short climb to the top of the hill involves
tramping over millions of pieces of broken *amphorae*.

of the Roman occupation of Britain is about the most sophisticated
we get. Would the military expenditure required for the conquest and
retention of the new province be recouped in tax revenue, asked the
Greek writer Strabo, who produced a geography-cum-anthropology of
the Roman world in the reign of Augustus or Tiberius. His answer was
'no'. But this was still little more than a basic profit and loss calculation.

   To put it another way, the main priority of the palace administration was simply to ensure that they had (or could mint) enough
money to pay for all the state expenditure. That was, above all, for the
army, which used about 50 per cent of the annual income, but there
is a whole list of other major outlays: staff salaries; the distribution of
a free allowance of grain (and later of olive oil) to as many as 200,000
citizens in Rome itself; construction work sometimes on a grand scale
(whole new harbours, or massive drainage projects, which put Pliny's
little canal in the shade); and the shows, spectacles and display that

were part and parcel of Roman urban culture. The income to fund all this came from various sources, ranging from the imperially owned precious metal mines to outright extortion. But the mainstay was a mosaic of different taxes, developed as was convenient and raised in different ways all over the Roman world: customs dues, road tolls, poll taxes, port and property taxes. A lot of it was levied in cash, but some came 'in kind' (such as part of the grain from Egypt, which went to the distributions in the capital). Across the Roman world some were new, distinctively Roman, demands (taxes on the sale of slaves or gladiators, or on freeing slaves), but in some provinces Roman taxes were simply adapted from whatever the pre-Roman system had been.

If the books did not balance, apart from raising tax rates (which happened occasionally), there was only one *institutional* remedy. That was to reduce the weight or the pure metal content of the coinage. The fact that for 150 years of one-man rule, up to the second half of the second century, silver coins lost only 20 per cent of their value, and gold coins much less, suggests that for that period the books did balance, crises were generally temporary, and that the tales of megalomaniac overspending by various emperors bringing the empire close to bankruptcy were exaggerated. Going into the third century, despite the reported state of Septimius Severus's coffers, and whatever the cause (increasing military activity, major pandemics, and so forth), things may well have been very different, though as an explanation for Caracalla's decision it is hardly adequate (or convincing).

The richest man in the world

The figure of the emperor himself hovers over all ancient discussions of imperial finances. Some of this comes down to individual, sometimes idiosyncratic, pieces of reform. Vespasian's tax on urine, for example, a key ingredient in the laundry and tanning industries, is still just about remembered in the old-fashioned French word for urinal, *vespasienne* (how the tax was actually levied, if it ever was, we have no clue). Domitian's temporary ruling that no more vines should be planted in Italy and that half of those in the provinces should be uprooted is still a matter of debate among historians. Was it a serious attempt to revive grain cultivation, a move to protect the Italian wine industry, or something closer to a 'back to basics' campaign? More generally, conventional stereotypes in Roman literature present 'bad' emperors as spendthrift, mean or grasping (or some ingenious combination of the three), while 'good' emperors are prudently generous.

The parade of financial responsibility and moderation was part of the imperial image. It was, for example, to Tiberius's credit that he refused to fleece the provincial populations. 'A good shepherd shears his flock, he doesn't skin them alive', he is supposed to have said in reply to some governors who wanted to raise taxes in their provinces. There was obviously self-interest in moderation, and Tiberius was certainly not suggesting that the flock should not be sheared at all. But he lived up to his slogan – putting his money where his mouth was – when he remitted most taxes for five years to a group of cities in what is now Turkey, after they had been damaged by an earthquake. Meanwhile Pertinax was only one of a series of Roman emperors who is reported to have contrasted his own probity with the extravagance of the preceding regime by publicly selling off some of his predecessor's luxuries. Commodus's bling went under the hammer, and the profits were channelled into a bonus for the soldiers. The *Imperial History* gives an implausible list of the sale items, including phallic cups and carriages with adjustable seats, designed to avoid the sun or catch the breeze – more likely a fantasy of imperial excess than an accurate inventory.

These stereotypes, however, tend to underplay the huge importance of money and wealth at the heart of imperial power and of the relationship between rulers and subjects. The force of the army, the control of the political process, and the delicate balancing act with the rest of the elite certainly underpinned the emperor's rule. So too did the simple fact that the emperor was by far the richest man and the largest landowner in the Roman world. His wealth was enhanced by some increasingly constructive fudging between what were technically 'state' funds and his own personal wealth. It was enhanced too by the steady accumulation of property thanks to gifts, inheritance and confiscations, and by the fact that whenever a new family came to the throne, their private riches and landholdings were incorporated into the emperor's portfolio. The office of emperor gobbled up the property of all those who had held it. Leaving aside the palaces and other imperial residences, across the empire were tracts of land and commercial properties, including mines and marble quarries, that were owned by (or had 'fallen into the hands of') the ruler and his immediate relatives.

In Egypt, for example, where documents on papyrus can help track landowning more accurately than in most places, we know of countless holdings of the emperor's family, including a huge commercial papyrus marsh, owned by Livia, jointly with the family of her grandson Germanicus, and land in numerous villages owned by Nero's tutor, Seneca, which was later in the hands of the emperor Titus. In some regions in the province, ancient land surveys show that half of it was imperial property. Egypt may have been a special case, but not *that* special. And there are hundreds of references – whether in inscriptions or casually dropped by ancient writers – to imperial estates all over the Roman world. The tenant farmers who were having such a hard time that they appealed to Commodus were actually tenants of the emperor (which may have helped them to put their case). Also in North Africa, Nero seems to have confiscated large stretches of land, some of which still bore his name ('Nero's Farm') more than a century later, and remained part of the imperial portfolio. There were plenty of industrial properties too. The stamps on the bricks produced there show that Marcus Aurelius's mother and sister were the proprietors of extensive clay pits near Rome itself.

So the emperor did not just *rule* the Roman world, he and his family *owned* quite a lot of it – and the revenues from these properties, in rent and in agricultural or industrial products, were a major source of imperial income. They also gave the emperor and his 'team' a different kind of presence across the empire. Some of the imperial staff – the administrators, the slaves and ex-slaves – ran the palace operations in Italy. But they were only part of it. Each one of these far-flung properties must also have been managed by a substantial number of the emperor's employees and dependants. They represented another imperial foothold in the vast territory of the empire.

Cash flow

There was also a more active side to imperial wealth. The emperor's cash – both getting it and spending it – was an indispensable player in his relationships with his subjects, especially in Italy. This went beyond the usual 'virtue' of generosity, often associated with monarchs and monarchies. As Augustus himself suggested when he gave this aspect such prominence in *What I Did*, it was partly the *job* of the emperor to give his people cash, not merely shows, spectacles, food and public amenities. Caligula took this too far, so most elite Roman observers imply, when he went onto the roof of a building in the Forum and threw coins down to the people below (powerful Romans, as we saw with the shower of presents at Domitian's picnic in the Colosseum, loved to scatter their largesse from above). But in some ways Caligula's gesture was only a flamboyant exaggeration of the norm, brilliantly capturing the basic message that the relationship between emperor and people could be summed up in the gift of money. Rulers in their lifetimes were always handing it over – to impoverished senators, to beggars or hopeful poets. Often, after their deaths, yet more was given in their wills (Augustus bequeathed from his own fortune the equivalent of the annual tax income of a wealthy Roman province to be divided among the people of Rome). They even had specialist staff (*dispensatores*) part of whose job was to hand the cash out.

Cash was best, as one anecdote about Augustus sharply illustrates. The story was that the emperor had been well entertained by a slave choir, but instead of giving them money at the end of the performance he gave them each a ration of grain. Sometime later, Augustus asked for the same choir again. 'Sorry Caesar,' their owner replied, 'they are busy at the mill, grinding what you gave them last time.' Whatever the interests of the owner (we can only speculate how much of the flour or money the slave singers saw), the point of this story is both that Augustus was willing to take criticism and to underline that emperors were *supposed* to hand over hard cash. In the story of Vespasian humiliating the petitioner who had asked for money, the man in a way got the request right. What was wrong was how he had usurped the power of the emperor by seizing the initiative in directly asking for it.

Unsurprisingly, emperors *took* cash too. One of the anguished complaints against imperial rule was that rich Romans in their own wills were often expected or forced (or sometimes chose) to leave a substantial proportion of their wealth to the emperor. It was extremely lucrative for the imperial purse (Tiberius may not have been the only one to have had a dedicated 'inheritance secretary', *a hereditatibus*), and there must have been a whole spectrum of intimidation, compulsion and sometimes goodwill involved. At one end is the accusation against 'bad' emperors that they not only insisted in being written into wills but actively hastened the deaths of those from whom they knew they would inherit. At the other are Pliny's congratulations to Trajan in his *Speech of Praise* for taking bequests only from those who were truly his friends – though his claim that this might actually have been a more profitable course of action for the emperor shows just how blurred the boundary between goodwill and self-interest could be. 'It may be more productive and fruitful,' he explained, 'not only for an emperor's reputation as well as his funds, if men *choose* to make him their heir, rather than be forced to.' But, however much pressure, or worse, was imposed, imperial power lay at the bottom of this: the power of the emperor to control the wealth of the elite, even after their death.

And that gives another significance to the head of the emperor on Roman coins. This innovation by Julius Caesar not only had the effect of making the emperor's image omnipresent, jangling in the purses of his subjects across the empire – it also made a very strong statement that the emperor's power rested partly in money.

Tough at the top?

It is impossible to know if Roman emperors (or some Roman emperors) worked hard. After all, 'hard work' means different things in different cultures. Leaving aside the show of diligence on his death-bed, we cannot now easily decode the details of Vespasian's regular daily routine as Suetonius describes it. Up before dawn, he read his letters and dispatches, then greeted his friends and colleagues, at the same time as he put on his own shoes and cloak (the biographer's point is that he was not dressed by a slave). After he had dealt with business, he took a walk and a rest, had sex, then a bath and dinner. There are simply too many vague 'thens' to be able to pinpoint what he was doing when. Much the same is true of Cassius Dio's later description of Septimius Severus's schedule. Another predawn riser, he would take a morning walk while he discussed the interests of the empire. Legal cases followed, then a horse ride, some gym and a bath. After lunch, it was a nap, more business, more discussion, another bath, and so on. These are the most explicit timetables for an imperial day that we have. But even if we were to decide that this pair, or any of the others, did count as 'hard workers', it would not necessarily be to their credit. Some of the world's most brutal dictators have been, in our terms, 'workaholics'.

The point is that the relationship between the emperor and his 'office job' remains tantalisingly elusive. We cannot know the exact connection between the man himself and the letters sent in his name, but that is only one element in a whole range of uncertainties and puzzles. The shorthands I have used – 'office', 'desk' – conceal the fact that we have no idea where and how the emperor got down to his correspondence (maybe just as likely reclining as sitting). We have little idea where, or how, any arguments for one course of action over another were thrashed out between the emperor and his staff or advisers. Tacitus darkly presents the discussions about whom Claudius should marry after the execution of his wife Messalina as a battle between three of the emperor's powerful ex-slaves – but that is part and parcel of Tacitus's view of Claudius's impotence in the face of their influence. And we have almost as little clue how emperors were trained for the tasks they would face. We know that Seneca addressed an essay, *On Mercy*, to the young Nero, and that (among a wider group of philosophers and intellectuals) Fronto gave Marcus Aurelius lessons in rhetoric, which was useful enough in a world that put such store on writing and speech making. But it is then a matter of guesswork where, if anywhere, these men picked up the more practical knowledge about how the palace, or the empire, worked (my own guess – and no more than that – is that it was from men like the father of Claudius Etruscus). Not that the emperor was the only one to be thrown in at the deep end in this way. So far as we know, when Pliny was sent to sort out the affairs of Pontus-Bithynia, the last time he had even been abroad was almost thirty years earlier, on military service in Syria.

But what is absolutely certain is how central to the life and image of the emperor all that paperwork was: the letters, the replies, the judge-ments, the regular bulletins back and forth from the provinces, and so on. We too, when we picture him, should always make sure to see him with his trademark pen in hand – and also with his piles of cash, hoarded, extorted, thrown from the rooftops and branded with his own head.

7

TIME OFF?

Games people play

The emperor Commodus was said to have been a passionate amateur gladiator and wild beast hunter, so passionate that some suspected his enthusiasm ran in his veins, inherited from the fighter rumoured to have been his mother's lover and his own natural father. In 192 CE, just a few weeks before he was killed by his trainer in a palace coup, he hosted fourteen days of bloody shows in the Colosseum, in which he himself was one of the star performers. According to Cassius Dio, who was an eyewitness, the emperor opened the murderous proceedings on the first day by killing one hundred bears. It was more a tribute to his accuracy of aim than to his bravery, for – rather than risk too close an encounter with the animals – he speared them with javelins from the safety of gangways specially constructed above the 'arena' (so called from the *harena*, or sand, which covered it). On the mornings of the following days, he did get down onto the arena floor itself, but only to dispatch less dangerous animals, or savage beasts that had already been imprisoned in nets: a wretched tiger, a hippopotamus and an elephant, among others. In the afternoons, the emperor would provide the warm-up act, again risk-free (or 'child's play' in Dio's words). Armed with a wooden sword, he fought a display bout against a professional gladiator who had only a stick for a weapon. Once he

55. & 56. Two images of Commodus. On the left, he is impersonated by Joaquin Phoenix, fighting in the arena, in Ridley Scott's *Gladiator*. On the right, in an ancient portrait sculpture, he appears in the guise of Hercules, club in hand, lion skin on head, and holding the Golden Apples of the Hesperides, the fruits of one of the hero's labours (pp. 369 and 387).

had won, as he always did, Commodus went back up to his imperial box to watch the 'real' fights for the rest of the day.

It was during these celebrations that the emperor cut off the head of an ostrich and came over to Dio and the other senators, who were sitting in the front row, and waved it at them with a menacing grin (pp. 51–2). The historian's claim that his impulse was to laugh reflected no doubt some show of senatorial resistance or disdain at the time, but in general his sneering account of the whole fourteen days of 'antics' is typical of the war of words so often waged *after* emperors had fallen from favour, been deposed and were dead. Whatever Dio's spin, it is clear that Commodus was assumed to be practised in the arts of the arena. This was one of the memorable themes of the movie *Gladiator*, which reconstructed gladiatorial combat more accurately, and vividly, than most modern attempts on film (which come down to slightly sanitised swashbuckling duels). But there was plenty of ancient talk too about Commodus fighting as a gladiator, for real, in private (sometimes killing his opponents, occasionally just slicing off their nose or ear), about the thousands of other animals he had slaughtered, including rhinoceroses and a giraffe, and about his having a private lodging in the gladiatorial barracks. There were even fantastical rumours that – had he not been assassinated – he would have soon put to death both the consuls and taken over their office himself, appearing as consul in the costume of a gladiator. And Commodus was not the only emperor with a reputation for enjoying such fights, beyond the limits of spectator sport. Hadrian was another, as was Caligula, who was said to have killed a professional gladiator who was armed only with a dummy sword when the emperor himself was equipped with a real dagger (one message of that tale was that you could never trust an emperor to play by the rules).

Roman writers often speculated on how their emperors spent their 'leisure', or their 'time off', as we would put it. In some ways those are misleading phrases to apply to the world of any autocrat, ancient or modern. In the life of a monarch, the division between work and leisure is always blurred. Whatever the emperor did, in any context – in bed or on the battlefield, in the senate or on the sports field – necessarily reflected, as we saw in the case of his dinner parties, on the character of his rule. Yet there was a difference between the pen-pushing, the speaking in the senate or the judging of legal cases and what he chose to do when he was free from official duties. Roman terms do not exactly match our own here, but there was still a significant contrast between *otium* – normally translated as 'leisure', but more accurately 'what you did when you were in control of your own time' – and its opposite '*negotium*', 'work', or 'what you had to do when you were *not* in control of it'.

The various insights we have into the emperor's *otium* range from the predictable to the curious, dark or revealing. Emperors were regularly praised for taking the study of literature and oratory seriously, for writing poetry, playing music (in private), for wholesome exercise in the form of boxing, wrestling, running and swimming, and for painting (it is hard now to imagine these men as gentlemanly watercolourists, but that – or something similar – was a skill attributed to Hadrian, Marcus Aurelius and Alexander Severus). Some were said to have had more idiosyncratic hobbies. As well as asking his dinner guests tricky questions based on his recent reading, Tiberius pursued an obsessive and out-of-proportion interest in the arcane byways of mythology, on which he used to quiz the experts ('What was the name of Hecuba's mother?'). Titus apparently had a sideline in imitating other people's handwriting, raising the spectre of the emperor as forger. The pastimes of others exposed even worse sides, whether that was the solitary fly-torturing practised by Domitian or the night-time brawls of the likes of Nero, Lucius Verus and Commodus, who – in the way of some later kings and princes – reputedly went out on the town after dark, in disguise, looking for low-life, and spoiling for a fight. Claudius not only had a weakness for the gaming board, as many other emperors did, but was so keen on gambling that he wrote a book about it. The uncomfortable question just under the surface here was how far autocracy itself was a gamble. That is what Julius Caesar had already hinted when, as he crossed the river Rubicon in 49 BCE and started the civil war that led to one-man rule, he famously declared *alea iacta est*, 'The dice have been thrown up in the air'. Empire as board game?

But the ancient spotlight most often fell on various forms of popular entertainment, from gladiatorial combat to chariot-racing and theatrical shows, where the role of the emperors was some shifting combination of enthusiastic fan, generous host and occasional performer. There is a tendency now to lump all these entertainments together, often under the banner of Juvenal's catchy but specious shorthand 'bread and circuses' – satirically summing up the bribes and distractions offered to the idle Roman rabble under the rule of the emperors (and providing a classical slogan used by those opposed to state services, benefits and food allowances ever after). But the entertainments were actually very different in character one from another, with significantly different audiences and different historical, religious and cultural traditions. And they provoked different debates about how the emperor should, or should not, behave when he was at 'leisure' or in front of the crowds. Some of those debates can appear at first sight to be not much more than the moral outrage of conservative ancient commentators ('how could the emperor demean himself, and us, by becoming an *actor*'). A closer look reveals that the apparently stereotypical complaints about the emperor strutting on stage were actually some of the sharpest analyses of the problems of Roman one-man rule to have survived.

The best seat in the house

The emperor's regular place in the Colosseum – when he wasn't balancing on gangways shooting bears – was the imperial box, in the middle of one of the long sides of the oval arena. From here, he watched a programme of shows that sometimes lasted for days on end, regularly featuring the slaughter of animals (or animals goaded to kill each other), the execution of criminals in various forms of sadistic punishment (eventually this would become 'Christians to the lions' and worse), and fights between gladiators, sometimes to the death. His was the best and most spacious seat in the house, though it does not survive well enough for us to know quite how luxurious it was. From there he not only watched the spectacles in the arena below, but had a clear view of much of the rest of the audience: 50,000 or so, arranged in strict rank order, with male citizens dressed for the occasion by law in their formal togas (and here, unlike with Augustus's

57. It is hard from the surviving remains to imagine the emperor in his place in the Colosseum. There were boxes in the centre of each of the long sides of the oval, and he would presumably have occupied the one (barely visible on the left of this picture), on the Palatine side of the building. Underneath the arena floor (partially reconstructed here) was the machinery for lifting humans and animals from the basement directly into public view.

rules for the Forum, it was a dress code that could be enforced: no toga, no entry).

There was no chance in the Colosseum of paying for better seats (admission was probably free anyway). You sat where your formal status in the Roman hierarchy put you, in what was effectively a microcosm of the social order. The basic system was that the senators were in the front rows, with a ringside view (even if occasionally a bit too close to the action for comfort), the elite 'equestrians' were just behind them, and so it went on, with people getting increasingly squashed and distant from the action, until at the very top – more than 50 metres from the arena – you reached the poorest, the women and the slaves. The only women, apart from those in the imperial family, to get a good view of the slaughter, were the Vestal Virgins, elite priestesses who had places assigned somewhere near the front. Far from being an uncontrolled crowd baying for blood, as they are often imagined, the people of the amphitheatre were aggressively *ordered* and

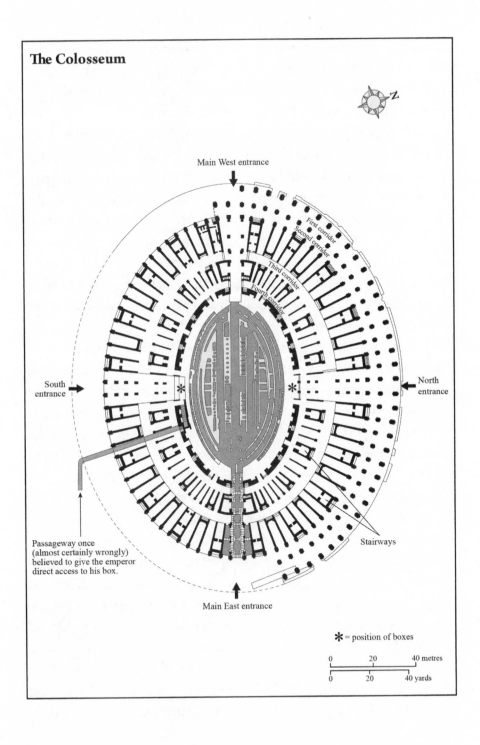

The Colosseum

Main West entrance

First corridor

Second corridor

Third corridor

Fourth corridor

South entrance

North entrance

Passageway once (almost certainly wrongly) believed to give the emperor direct access to his box.

Stairways

Main East entrance

✱ = position of boxes

| 0 | 20 | 40 metres |
| 0 | 20 | 40 yards |

dressed in their formal best. No movie has ever captured this. They were rather more like the modern audience at an opera than a mad mob – and they gave the man who looked out from the imperial box a snapshot of 'his' people, largely his *men*, on parade.

In the city of Rome itself public shows of this type came to be associated almost exclusively with the emperor. The origins of gladiatorial fighting had been small-scale and private, starting out, it seems, as part of the ritual of aristocratic funerals in the third century BCE, with the occasional bout provided as an after-dinner diversion by rich hosts. Across the empire, along with animal hunts, it spread as the characteristic form of global Roman 'entertainment', usually sponsored by local bigwigs, with private enterprise gladiatorial troupes and training camps. But, in the capital, it became one of the ruler's signature spectacles, and on a vast scale.

In the early days, the shows took place in a variety of pop-up locations. Julius Caesar presented wild beast hunts in the Forum and Augustus sometimes adapted the redundant voting hall for gladiatorial fights. The first permanent purpose-built *amphitheatre* in the city was part of Augustus's programme of new building, sponsored by one of his right-hand men ('*amphi*theatre', because unlike in a plain 'theatre' the seating went *all around*, completely enclosing the central arena). A century later Vespasian and Titus, father and son together, made an even bigger splash when they ploughed the spoils from their war against the Jews into building the Colosseum, strategically siting it, as a place of pleasure for the people, in what had been the semi-private parkland of Nero's Golden House. Meanwhile the gladiators were increasingly owned and trained out of the emperor's purse, the animals acquired and transported by his men, the shows produced and funded by him alone, or sometimes – if on a more modest scale – by those authorised by him. Emperor after emperor boasted of the spectacle and slaughter they had laid on: 10,000 gladiators displayed in the course of his reign (Augustus); 5,000 animals killed in a single day

(Titus); 11,000 animals massacred over 123 days (Trajan); and much more. Cassius Dio cautiously warned his readers against taking some of these exaggerated figures literally, but the boastful exaggeration was part of the point.

It was no doubt hard for an emperor to get the balance quite right, between being too keen and not keen enough on these spectacles. A few emperors did query the distasteful violence of the proceedings. Nero was one of the least enthusiastic about the amphitheatre, and is reported to have presided over one occasion on which no one, 'not even a criminal', was put to death. (Nero cannot have much enjoyed it when in one fatal display on another occasion a flying acrobat crashed to the ground and spattered him with blood.) Marcus Aurelius likewise was reputed to be averse to the violence, and claimed rather loftily in his *Jottings to Himself* that he found these shows 'boring', because they were always the same: slaughter and more slaughter, presumably. Indeed, when the tax on the sale of gladiators was abolished throughout the empire during his reign, in 177 CE, part of the justification was that the imperial treasury 'should not be contaminated with the splashing of human blood'. But it is hard not to suspect that his objections were more theoretical than practical. At least no such moral qualms, or grinding boredom, stopped him putting on his own gladiatorial shows, not all bloodless, I should imagine.

The violence of these shows *was* ghastly. Whether we try to explain them, as modern historians have, in terms of crowd psychology, perverted Roman militarism, or a shared ritual exploration of death, the end result was terrible. To point out that they actually took place much less frequently than we tend to imagine (the really mammoth shows were many years apart) does not do much to mitigate the horror. Nor does the fact that the casualty figures must in reality have been lower than is often assumed. Whatever the imperial boasting, it would have taken more than even an emperor's resources to bring many hippos or giraffes to Rome, and trained gladiators were too valuable to 'squander' in regular fights to the death. But even if the cruelty itself now defies explanation, we can detect a chilling logic to what happened in the arena. These occasions did not merely parade the micro-hierarchies within Roman society, they also marked an even more fundamental division: between the *us* of the audience and the *them* of those who fought, suffered or died in the arena.

For it was the excluded, the condemned, the abominated and the 'foreign' who performed here – those who were, by definition, not (fully) Roman. Gladiators were often enslaved, or they were convicted criminals who had been sentenced to fight as punishment. Even when they were free volunteers, they lost some of their citizen rights and privileges when they signed up. And, of course, the rarest, most notorious of the animals on display evoked the foreign and dangerous extremities of the natural world, which it was Rome's destiny (as many of the audience would have seen it) to conquer or tame. Whatever personal visceral pleasure the spectators may, or may not, have taken in the violence, the performances were also metaphors for the exercise of Roman power. Simply by sitting in their formal Roman dress and watching the show, the audience was experiencing the dominance of Rome and the Romans, and parading their part in it.

There was a similar point in the capital punishment sometimes carried out in the gaps in the programme between the gladiator fights and the animal hunts (the later martyrdom of Christians in the arena was a part of this). Many cultures throughout history have used the public execution of those who flout society's most fundamental rules as a powerful way of reinforcing those rules. The ghastly gallows' scenes in England only a few centuries ago, which turned the death of petty criminals into voyeuristic spectacle, is just one example of that. But in the Roman amphitheatre there was an even more horrible twist. For some of these executions were staged as re-enactments of famous deaths from myth and legend. We read, for example, of a man being set on fire, to mimic Hercules being burned alive on his funeral pyre. It is possible that the 'acrobat' who spattered Nero with his blood was one of these unfortunate victims, playing the part of the mythical Icarus, who flew too close to the sun. The condemned men were not just put to death, they gruesomely became 'the stars of their own destruction'.

These 'fatal charades' certainly featured at the inauguration of the Colosseum in 80 CE, under the eye of the emperor Titus (Vespasian did not live to see the opening), the whole occasion being commemorated by Marcus Valerius Martialis in a slim volume of verse. 'Martial', as he is now known, not only enthusiastically proclaimed Nero's parkland restored to public use. Among the inaugural displays, he celebrated the re-enactment of a legendary Roman hero burning off his own hand, an imitation of the mauling to death of Icarus's father Daedalus, and of the killing of a famous anti-hero of local folklore, the bandit Laureolus, torn apart by a wild bear. Capturing this last scene, Martial wrote of the victim in the arena (a murderer, thief or arsonist, he wondered: who exactly knew?) 'offering his raw entrails to the Scottish bear, / his mangled limbs still alive but dripping with blood, / and in his whole body there was no body left'. It is hard to know now which is the more distasteful: the sadistic violence itself, or the aestheticisation of it in Martial's celebratory verse. The 'body [with] no body left' is a phrase of which I fear the poet would have been proud.

Overseeing all this was the emperor. He was the impresario and the crucial choreographer, even if the actual work must have been done by hundreds of palace slaves (on which side of the barrier did they feel *they* belonged?). It was he who paid for it and he whose ultimate power was on show, as the final arbiter of whether the defeated gladiator should live or die. But more than that, in the 'fatal charades' he not only presided over the humiliation and degradation of the offenders. He was almost staking a claim to bring myth and legend literally to life – or death – in the world of the arena, staking a claim to make them *true*. As Martial observed in the last line of his poem on Laureolus, 'what had been (just) a story, became a (real) punishment'.

So why on earth did the emperor Commodus leave his box and join the world of the abject and abominated on, or very close to, the arena floor?

Stage fright

Part of the answer is that there were always two sides to the image of the gladiator. On the one hand, gladiators were officially despised, marginalised, deprived of their rights and the victims of state violence. On the other, they caught the Roman cultural imagination. The figure of the arena fighter was sometimes used by Roman writers as a symbol of bravery in the face of death, as a metaphor for the moral struggles of the philosopher and as a symbol of male sexual prowess (in Latin *gladiator* meant literally 'fighter with a *gladius*' – and *gladius* meant both 'sword' and, colloquially, 'penis'). Commodus's mother, Faustina, was not the only elite Roman lady to be accused of an affair with a gladiator. It was almost a cliché. Earlier in the second century, for example, in an uncomfortably misogynistic satire on women, or more specifically on the disadvantages of marriage, Juvenal targeted the pampered wife of a senator, who had left her home, abandoned her husband and children, and run away to Egypt – with a gladiator. 'He had a great lump on his nose, and nasty pus oozing out of his eye, but the important thing is that *he was a gladiator*'. Another Roman version of rough trade.

Most of this was probably more imagination than reality. I strongly suspect that the idea of their wives running off with gladiators had more to do with the nightmare fantasies of elite men than with much actual infidelity on the part of the women (and, in a way, that might be Juvenal's point). But, all the same, the image of the gladiator was exciting enough for the Roman senate to go to the lengths of expressly, and repeatedly, prohibiting the upper classes from appearing in the arena. Part of the original wording of one such decree from 19 CE survives, inscribed on a bronze plaque found in central Italy in the 1970s. This was a series of minutely detailed regulations forbidding senators and equestrians and their descendants from both fighting as gladiators and appearing on stage. There were even regulations preventing them from taking on supporting roles, 'in a subordinate capacity', in the arena (no one was going to get round these rules, in other words, by claiming that they were only 'helping' the gladiators). And when Roman writers mention the gladiatorial enthusiasm of various emperors, they are often concerned to show how they managed to stay, just, within acceptable limits. Augustus, for example, did put equestrians to fight as gladiators, but Suetonius stresses that this was *before* that had been officially banned. Other emperors fought in person themselves, but only in private, or as some element in a youthful training-cum-fitness regime, and so on. What was different about Commodus was not his enthusiasm. It was that, in the careful balancing act between acceptable and unacceptable, he crossed the line. Even in his case, Septimius Severus later accused the senate of hypocrisy in their disapproval of Commodus's performance in the arena: 'Do none of *you* fight as a gladiator', he is supposed to have asked. 'If you don't', he went on, 'how and why was it that some of you bought up his shields and those golden helmets of his?' – referring to the sale of Commodus's gladiatorial kit with his other effects after his assassination.

There was, however, more to it than that. For the logic of the arena and its ordered hierarchies was not just a way of keeping the people in general in their place. It kept the emperor in his place too, and provided a framework against which he could be judged. Like many highly regulated systems, this was a world of rule-*breaking*, real or imaginary, as well as rule-*keeping*. When emperors were accused of awful transgressions in the amphitheatre they were not (merely) being accused of random acts of capricious cruelty. The bigger point was that these subversions appeared to turn the logic of the place on its head. They were another way of capturing a vision of a world turned upside down under a transgressive emperor. Nothing and no one were where they should be. That was the implication of the emperor swapping his imperial box for the arena floor, to appear as one of the lowliest performers; or – as Nero was rumoured to have done – asking or compelling senators to move from their assigned seats in the front row and become fighters.

The gossip, or fantasy, that Commodus planned to take potshots at the ranks of spectators with his bow and arrow, as if he was Hercules on one of his labours, killing the man-eating Stymphalian birds, was an even more complicated example of this. Here it was the emperor himself, rather than a condemned criminal, who was to re-enact the myth, while at the same time the role of the audience and the victims/ performers were to be dangerously reversed. Those who should have been safe in their seats *watching* the slaughter were instead threatened with the arrows of death. There was even a bizarre rumour that in private Nero had overturned the hierarchies even more dramatically. Dressing up in an animal skin, he was said to have 'played a kind of game', in which he attacked the genitals of people tied to stakes. Here it was almost as if the emperor had literally become the wild beast.

But the biggest question for the emperor in the arena was: who was the real star of the show, who was the focus of the audience's attention? In formal terms, it ought to have been himself. But inevitably, for most of the time, the eyes of the spectators were not on the man in the imperial box. They were on the gladiators and wild-beast hunters in their potentially deathly combat. At every spectacle, the emperor was almost certain to be upstaged by the fighters who held the gaze of the whole audience. Caligula is said to have explicitly complained about that when one gladiator was given especially rapturous applause. 'How is it', he shouted, 'that the people who rule the world give more honour to a gladiator than to my own noble presence?' But the story was that he had got up from his seat so quickly in order to make this intervention that he had trodden on the hem of his toga and tumbled down the steps of his box. The emperor's dilemma was whether to play his due part, and so allow himself to be upstaged; or to reclaim the spotlight by getting down into the arena (or even just by loudly objecting), and so break the rules *and* appear foolish.

It is hard to have much sympathy for Commodus (Roman writers do their best to make sure that we don't). But we should perhaps flip Dio's account for a moment and reflect on what it would have felt like to be on your own in the middle of the amphitheatre, out of place, pathetically waving an ostrich head at the ranks of senators who were all munching on their laurel leaves and barely concealing the fact that they were laughing at you. The Colosseum could be lonely for the man at the top.

A day at the races

Far less lonely was the Circus Maximus or, literally, 'the biggest Circus', a long racetrack that occupied the valley at the foot of the Palatine Hill and which under the emperors was the main venue in the city for chariot- and horse-racing (though, especially before the permanent amphitheatres were built, it sometimes doubled as a venue for gladiators and animal hunts). It was so close to the imperial palace that a connecting passage was opened, probably under Trajan, giving direct private access to the Circus for the emperor and his staff. And on one occasion when people began to pour in at midnight, to claim their seats in advance of the next day's events, they kept Caligula awake with their noise. He sent men in to clear them out, but in the crush to leave – so it was said – many of them were killed. Much the same story is told of Elagabalus almost two centuries later, but with a classic fantasy twist. He is said to have sent in not soldiers but snakes 'and many people were injured by the fangs or just in their flight'.

The Circus Maximus was abandoned in the sixth century CE and has all but disappeared. It was gradually encroached upon by the modern city, including a large nineteenth-century gasworks right on top of it, until the site was cleared and turned into a park in the 1930s as part of Mussolini's archaeological projects. The outlines of the seating were at that point faked up with mounds of earth to give an idea of what had once been there (the floor of the track is actually buried almost 10 metres beneath the modern surface). It now makes for a rather dreary visit. Only very limited excavations have been carried out and if you want to get any idea of what it originally looked like, a series of ancient images on mosaic floors are the best guide (pl. 22), combined with some of the works of art that once stood on the central reservation (a surprising gallery of treasures), and were dug up by Renaissance popes to be redisplayed elsewhere. The Colosseum, by contrast, dominates the modern imagination, for obvious reasons. Much of it still survives, unmissable in the middle of a vast traffic island in central Rome. It is

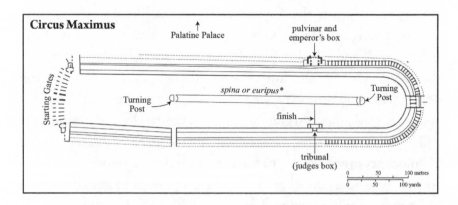

Though this hardly comes across from the ground plan, the central reservation of the Circus was one of its most resonant areas. Known as the *spina* (literally 'backbone') or *euripus* (from the Greek for a narrow channel of water), it was the site for impressive antiquities and works of art.

58. A view of the Circus Maximus looking across to the Palatine
palace, showing how closely connected the two were. At bottom right
is the turning point between the two lanes of the course; the starting
gates are at the other end. The tower, near the turn, is medieval.

a place of pilgrimage in memory of the Christians who were martyred
there (largely after the period I am covering in this book), the biggest
tourist attraction in Italy (complete with its fake gladiators outside,
offering photo opportunities at a price), and it has been copied and
recopied to make millions of modern miniature souvenirs to decorate
shelves, mantelpieces and fridges almost everywhere.

But in the ancient world the Circus stole the show. It was far bigger
than the Colosseum. Its arena – twelve times the size of the Colosseum's – allowed for a dozen chariots, driven by four or more horses, to
race up and down the 500 metres of track, on either side of the central
reservation, known as the *spina* or *euripus*. Compared with the 50,000
spectators in the Colosseum, it could fit somewhere between 150,000
and 250,000 spectators – the upper end of that range giving it more
than twice the capacity of the largest football stadium anywhere now.
And it was much more frequently used than the Colosseum. According to a calendar of the mid fourth century CE (although the numbers

59. The obelisk that is now in the Piazza del Popolo in Rome once stood in the central reservation of the Circus Maximus. Quarried and carved in Egypt, towards the end of the second millennium BCE, it was brought to Rome on the orders of the emperor Augustus.

had grown over time), the races filled sixty-four days of the year, and regular gladiatorial combat just ten.

The races had a longer history too. Chariot- and horse-racing were originally part of the city's traditional religious festivals and – whatever secular image they now have (more like mass sport than mass worship) – they always kept a close connection with the gods. Augustus, for example, noted in his *What I Did* that he had built in the Circus a new viewing platform or shrine (*pulvinar* is the technical Latin term), where images of the gods were placed, as if to watch the show. And according to Roman myth it was here, during a religious celebration on the site of the future Circus soon after the city was founded, that the earliest Romans had tricked their neighbours the Sabines, and carried off their daughters to be Roman wives (the so-called 'Rape of the Sabine Women'). The first permanent Circus building was said to have been constructed on the same spot a couple of centuries later, half a millennium before there was any permanent amphitheatre in the city.

Religion did not make the races solemn affairs. Far from it. This was not the ordered world of the Colosseum. For a start, there was less audience segregation. Although senators and equestrians did have reserved seats in the front rows, and Augustus ruled that here too togas should be worn, men and women sat and watched together. The Roman poet Ovid even joked, in his spoof poem on the *Art of Dating,* that the Circus was a great place for a pick-up: 'Sit next to the girl, no one's stopping you / rub up side by side, as close as you can', he advises, after a cheesy (or tasteless) nod to the Rape of the Sabine Women, to give a historical background to the erotic aspect of the location. Some ancient descriptions, admittedly often from disapproving intellectuals, suggest that here the crowds really could go wild, as the contestants negotiated the dangerously tight corners at each end and fought it out for the lead, over a course of usually seven laps around the central reservation. Pliny is relatively low-key in his disdain: 'thousands of grown men behaving like children'. The Christian writer Tertullian, a century later, was much more ghoulish about the spectators at the races than those in the amphitheatre. He saw their frenzy, blind passion, madness, shrieking and cursing as the work of the devil, while pointing to the extra element of betting, which did not, so far as we know, feature at gladiatorial contests. And the excitement was enormously intensified by four rival fan bases, the ancient equivalent of supporters' clubs, backing the teams of riders from rival stables, with their different-coloured tunics and perhaps different-coloured chariots too: the 'Blues' and the 'Greens', the 'Reds' and the 'Whites' (Domitian tried to add two more, the 'Golds' and the 'Purples', but they didn't catch on). Pliny again offers deadpan, if not supercilious, puzzlement: why on earth all this fuss about a *colour*?

High stakes

For the emperor, engagement with the races involved a familiar kind of balancing act. Although much more private money went into chariot-racing and the infrastructure of the stables than into the shows in the

Colosseum, emperors were careful to be seen as generous sponsors, paying for extra races, boosting the prize money for the winning teams, enlarging and improving the Circus itself and patching it up when damaged (Antoninus Pius, for example, made some speedy repairs after a pillar, supporting some of the upper seating, gave way during a race and killed, according to the *Imperial History*, 1,112 people). Rulers were praised for treating the occasion seriously. It was a bad idea to use the time in the Circus to catch up with correspondence, a good idea for the emperor to politely excuse himself, as Augustus did, if he could not attend. Where he sat mattered. Despite the disdain that he expressed elsewhere for the proceedings on the racetrack, in his *Speech of Praise* Pliny congratulated Trajan for watching 'on the same level' as the people, in their midst, on the public seats. It was not the emperors' regular place, though. It seems that they usually sat alongside the divine statues in the *pulvinar*, which somehow doubled as the imperial box – so, the reverse of democratic, and not on the same level as ordinary mortals at all. And, of course, imperial enthusiasm for chariot-racing had to be judiciously calibrated. Several emperors are reported to have aped the professional charioteers, who despite the substantial prize money they might win and their popular fan base, were almost as socially déclassé as gladiators. But by and large they kept their performances to more private racetracks in the city, or to those on foreign soil (Caracalla is said to have raced in Germany, or in Mesopotamia, modern Iraq, Nero openly competed in races in Greece). Even Commodus, according to Cassius Dio, drove chariots in public only in the dark, on moonless nights, so he would not be seen.

Chariot-racing, however, raised other dilemmas for, and about, the emperor. How could he fit into the rivalries of the fan groups? Did his presence skew the competition? Did it spoil the fun, if the most powerful man in town was backing one side? Most emperors were fans of the Greens, Vitellius and Caracalla, in backing the Blues, being the only two who made any other choice. (Vitellius, before he became emperor, even won a military command thanks to the influence of another Blues fan at court, or so it was rumoured.) And there are plenty of stories of emperors letting their favouritism turn vicious. It was, for example, when the crowd applauded one of the rival teams too enthusiastically that Caligula is supposed to have turned threateningly on them and snarled, 'I wish the Roman people had only one neck' (hinting that he would have liked to have decapitated them all at a stroke). Vitellius was said to have had some innocent supporters killed, after they had bad-mouthed the Blues. But being a fan could rebound on the emperor and his image in other ways. It was an ancient commonplace that passion for their racing teams could lead even ordinary people to ridiculous extremes. Pliny's uncle, in his encyclopaedia, records the death of a fan who threw himself on the funeral pyre of his favourite charioteer of the Reds. Galen intriguingly refers to supporters (or possibly trainers) sniffing the dung of their favourite horses, to gauge if these would-be winners were being fed correctly. The enthusiasms of emperors followed this pattern, albeit on a grander scale, and showed just how dangerous (or ludicrous) it might be to have a ruler whose mind was on the races.

Caligula's passion for his favourite racehorse – 'Incitatus' ('Full Speed') – goes far beyond the stories of inviting the animal to dinner or threatening to make him consul. It was part and parcel of the emperor's over-the-top fandom for the chariot races more generally. Caligula was supposed to have doted on Incitatus so excessively that he sent soldiers to the stables on the night before a race to make sure that no one disturbed the horse's sleep, as well as giving him a marble stall, an ivory manger, purple blankets (the imperial colour) and a whole range of other luxuries, including a house, furniture and his own slaves. Caligula was not the only one said to have gone to such lengths. Lucius Verus had his favourite horse, 'Volucer' ('Flyer'), brought to him at the palace, covered in another of those purple blankets and fed on raisins and nuts instead of barley. He even commissioned a miniature golden statue of the animal, which he carried around with him, and in the end gave him a special tomb. Commodus was similarly besotted with a horse called Pertinax (something like 'True Grit'), on one occasion having his hooves painted golden for a parade in the Circus, and outdoing the others in putting not a coloured blanket but a golden hide on its back. The message was that emperors, as fans, didn't know where to stop.

But it was the number of spectators, and the dramatic encounter between the ruler and his people, that gave the races in the Circus Maximus an extra frisson. There were no formal institutions in Rome that allowed the citizens as a group, rather than as individuals or small delegations, to put their views to the emperor. So any major gathering at which he was present offered the people at large a chance to object, protest, beg or demand, in short to be *noticed* by him. That could sometimes happen in the Colosseum (where Hadrian once took a risk by responding to some popular demand through a herald rather than addressing the people himself). Sometimes, as we shall see, it could happen in the smaller theatres in the city. But by far the biggest and most significant meeting place of ruler and ruled was the Circus Maximus, where close to a quarter of the total population of the city could be present, with the emperor in their sights and within earshot. More than anywhere else, it was here that he was exposed to the mass of those he governed. A day 'off' at the races could also be a day of politics for the emperor – and the crowds.

The Jewish historian Josephus saw the logic of this very clearly. It was around the racetrack, he explained, that the Romans could tell the emperor what they wanted, and it was in his interests to give in to their demands. How often this happened we have no idea. But my guess is that, when it did, emperors would mostly have given the crowd what they asked for. For there was little room to negotiate an honourable refusal or compromise in front of hundreds of thousands of angry or pressing people, who thought they had safety in numbers. What tends to attract comment from Roman writers are the occasions when emperors made *dis*honourable refusals, and when, from the other side, the numbers were not as safe as they might have seemed. Josephus's remarks, for example, were prompted by the demands made at the Circus in 41 CE that Caligula lower taxes. He said 'no' by sending in soldiers to arrest and kill the leading protesters (the rest soon quietened, though it is hard to imagine that they concentrated very hard on the races after that). It was a brutal and heavy-handed form of crowd control, but perhaps his only practical option in the circumstances, apart from saying 'yes'.

The idea that the Circus Maximus was *the* place to gain concessions from the emperor spills over into protests that happened there even when the emperor himself was not present. In the civil wars of 193 CE, when Didius Julianus came briefly to the throne – the man for whom Cassius Dio had 'moulded his face' (p. 77) – crowds of people spent twenty-four hours in the empty Circus demonstrating against him, though eventually they got so hungry that they went home. Rather like Trafalgar Square in London, it was a convenient open space, but also one strongly associated with the voice of the people.

There was a grimmer outcome to a protest that happened while the races were actually being held in 190 CE, under Commodus. It was in the middle of a famine that was (wrongly) blamed on the ex-slave Cleander, who was the emperor's private secretary and credited with enormous influence at court. In an elaborately staged demonstration, immediately after the seventh race in the day's programme, a group of children rushed onto the track led by a 'scary' woman (later taken to be a goddess) and chanting slogans against Cleander, which the rest of the crowd took up and repeated. As Commodus was not on hand, a huge number of protesters went off to find him at one of his suburban estates, the Villa of the Quintilii, to demand Cleander's death. Dio, who tells this story, claims that it was cowardice that led Commodus to concede, and to allow the man's head to be paraded around the city on a pole. But it is another reminder of how little room for manoeuvre the emperor often had. In Josephus's terms, it was generally in his interests to give in.

The high stakes of these encounters make it unsurprising that the Circus races could also mark the beginning of the end for some emperors. The attack launched by Caligula on the crowd was supposed to have been one of the factors that spurred his assassin to take action. But dark premonitions of death could lurk even in the emperors' successes on the track. In the end, Commodus might have regretted his enthusiasm for Pertinax, his favourite horse. The animal was greeted by its other supporters in the Circus with warm shouts. 'It's Pertinax, it's Pertinax', they cried. But it was of course an omen of what was to come, for the name of the man declared emperor immediately after Commodus's assassination was also called Pertinax. And even at the time, the shouts of 'It's Pertinax' were said to have been greeted by some mutterings of 'If only!' True or not (and, like all such omens, this is probably a later concoction, invented or adjusted retrospectively to fit the circumstances) the story captures the dangers, as well as the pleasures, of the races for the ruler.

Acting up

Romans in general were actually as keen on drama of all sorts as they were on the bloody spectacles or racing chariots for which they are now best known. But the theatre could be another risky place for the emperor. By the end of the reign of Augustus, there were three permanent, open-air theatre buildings in the city, and any number of temporary or pop-up locations, where you could see different styles of performance: from farce to tragedy and revivals of classic Greek drama, from stand-up and slapstick to recitals, spoken or sung. Some, like the Circus races, were attached to official religious festivals, others were more private enterprise. The theatres were far smaller in capacity than the other entertainment buildings. The largest of the three was the so-called 'Theatre of Marcellus', started by Julius Caesar and completed by Augustus, in memory of one of those potential heirs who didn't live long enough. It now houses some very upmarket apartments, after its remains were converted into a palatial residence in the sixteenth century. Even this theatre would have seated at most 20,000 people in the audience, and probably a couple of thousand fewer. But, to offset the smaller capacity, theatrical performances were much more frequent than other shows, with the same fourth-century calendar that marked sixty-four days for circus races marking 101 days for drama.

The same strict principles of segregation were supposed to operate in the theatres as in the Colosseum: men and women kept separate, the audience in semi-circular banks of seats facing the stage, in rank order, the senators given places at the very edge of the performance space itself. Where the emperor himself regularly sat is not so clear

60. The exterior of the Theatre of Marcellus, with the Renaissance additions above. The three columns in the foreground belong to a temple of Apollo, also built in the reign of Augustus.

(partly because in none of the city's theatres does the seating area survive). But he was certainly visible to the audience and so a target once again for their demands. It was in a theatre that Tiberius was forced by audience protests to give back the antique Greek statue he had taken for his own house from outside a set of public baths. And Augustus suffered a dose of full-view humiliation at the opening of the Theatre of Marcellus. On that occasion, he must have been with the senators around the performance space because he was using a portable *sella curulis*, an elaborate folding chair that was as close to a physical 'throne' as the Romans usually got. Embarrassingly for the emperor, the joints of this chair gave way. It completely collapsed and he fell flat on his back in front of the assembled people.

What was distinctive about these theatrical performances, though, was the way that satirical critique of the emperor was scripted into the shows or was improvised by daring actors, and enjoyed by the audience. Part of the freedom (or licence, *licentia*) of the theatre meant the freedom to jest about those in power, even to their face. One of the best and most damning 'jokes' came from a performer by the name of Datus in a musical during the reign of Nero. Rumours were then current that the emperor had not only been complicit in the murder by poison of his adoptive father, the emperor Claudius, but that he had also attempted to drown his mother by sending her off from Baiae in a collapsible boat, which disintegrated on the open sea. (She actually survived by swimming to the shore – Nero hadn't reckoned on mum being a swimmer – and he was then supposed to have sent a hit squad to finish her off.) One of the songs Datus had to sing included the line 'farewell father, farewell mother'. He delivered these words with added hand actions, first pretending to drink (poison), and then pretending to swim. A hundred years later Marcus Aurelius had to put up with a couple of actors on stage making a feeble pun on the name of one of the supposed lovers of his wife Faustina. One character in the play asked the other what the name of *his* wife's lover was: 'Tullus

Tullus Tullus' was the reply. 'I don't get it', responded the first man. 'I've told you three times', came the follow-up, 'it's "Tullus"'. The predictable, groan-making joke here was that the name of Faustina's lover was 'Tertullus', or, literally, 'Three times (*ter*) Tullus'.

The question for the emperor was how best to react to jibes like this. It was easy to get it wrong. Caligula is reported to have had a writer burned alive for introducing a double entendre (against the emperor, presumably) into one of his lines. Marcus Aurelius, however, did not apparently win much praise for patiently sitting through the jibes on the name of Tertullus without punishing the culprits. It looked as if he was allowing himself to be walked over, by the comedians as well as by his wife. On this score, it was Nero who performed the imperial balancing act best, showing that he could take a joke, but was not a pushover. He did not put him to death, but merely sent Datus into exile for his cheeky poisoning and swimming impressions.

But Nero was also at the centre of big controversies connected with the stage: namely, how to align his role as emperor with his personal passion for acting and performing. Actors, like gladiators and charioteers, were socially despised but at the same time glamorous and sexy celebrities. Claudius, for example, is supposed to have put up with repeated heckling in the theatre about why the famous actor Mnester was not performing – when it was widely believed that Mnester was having fun in the palace with Messalina, Claudius's then wife. And, as with the fighters in the arena, there were enough members of the Roman elite who fancied trying their hand on stage that it was thought worthwhile banning them from doing so. It was Nero, however, who was believed to have broken these rules most flagrantly, and was remembered for centuries as the 'actor-emperor'.

It all started in private, but gradually, according to the usual story, Nero went public, first in Naples, where ominously the theatre collapsed directly after he had appeared, and later in Rome itself, acting in recitals (not as member of a regular cast, but as a solo performer with a small backing troupe), singing, and playing the lyre. There are any number of colourful and curious anecdotes about his performances and theatrical ambitions. He took on some extravagant roles, playing both men and women, 'Canace in Childbirth' being one of the most notorious (the part of a Greek mythological 'heroine' who gave birth to her brother's baby, then killed herself). But he had a whole repertoire of themes about mythical kings and tyrants, including the 'Blinding of Oedipus' and 'Orestes the Mother-Killer'. He was reputed to keep tight control of the audience. No one was allowed to leave the theatre while he was performing (it was said that some people even pretended to be dead in order to make their escape, and women actually gave birth at their seats for want of an exit route). The future emperor Vespasian was even banished from Nero's circle because he was caught napping during one of his recitals. And Nero's interest in theatre repeatedly appeared to trump his interest in government. When he was preparing a task force to fight an uprising in Gaul at the end of his reign, his first priority was arranging the wagons to transport his stage equipment. Most famously of all, he turned the great fire of Rome into a performance opportunity, watching from a safe distance and singing to his lyre on the theme of the destruction of the city of Troy, the original 'fiddling while Rome burns'.

Some of this is straightforward exaggeration. If Vespasian *was* distanced from the emperor's circle the exclusion did not last long, for he was very soon appointed to a major command in the Jewish War. Whatever Nero did during the great fire, it is fairly well established that the relief programme he sponsored after it (including opening his own grounds to the homeless) was unusually effective. Even hostile ancient critics conceded that. Anyway, some of these performances were probably rather popular. (It's all too easy for ancient and modern writers to give a dark impression by injecting, here and elsewhere, a hint of compulsion, suggesting that 'many people were *compelled* to attend' when they might well have been there of their own free will.)

But, skewed or exaggerated or not, these stories of Nero's theatricals are much more than outrage about an emperor's bad behaviour or tyrannical tendencies. In exploring the implications of the emperor as actor, Roman writers were cleverly turning the spotlight onto the problems and discontents of one-man rule.

As we saw in the fantasy dystopian world of Elagabalus, one of the most destabilising questions of Roman autocracy was how you could recognise what was true, or how, in the world of the emperor, you could ever know whether to believe what you saw and heard. The fact and fiction of the stage put a particular spin on that. For a start, in some of the stories of Nero's performances, the business of 'pretending to be someone you are not' fell not on the actor, but on the audience. They might have to act dead in order to escape, or (unless they were Vespasian) pretend they were enjoying it. It was as if, when the emperor was an actor, everyone else was forced to be an actor/dissembler too.

But there was also the question of the difficult, shifting boundary between, on the one hand, Nero the emperor and, on the other, the stage parts he played. Some of his most famous roles had clear resonances with his own life. The 'Blinding of Oedipus' (on discovering, according to the myth, that he had married his mother) surely chimed with allegations that Nero had himself committed incest with his own mother, Agrippina. And, not so very different from Datus's joke, 'Orestes the Mother-Killer' recalled the reports that he had later killed her. Those resonances were amplified by his stage costume. Following ancient tradition, he wore a mask to perform, but in his case it was said that the mask was not the usual, highly stylised creation that actors regularly wore, but was sometimes made with his own recognisable features. When he played women, it had the features of his female partner at the time. In other words, he took the part of the most famous Mother Killer of mythology while wearing a mask that mimicked his own face. So how *did* you tell the difference between the real emperor and the stage character? Was the emperor always acting?

To put it another way, as Philostratus, the Greek intellectual, mused one hundred and fifty years later, what separated an actor who played a tyrant on stage and then wanted to become a tyrant in real life from a tyrant in real life, such as Nero, who wanted to play a tyrant on stage?

These questions of pretence and dissembling are captured most vividly in the story of one of those 'time-off' occasions when Nero went out at night, in disguise, searching out seedy bars, low-life, brawling and worse (Suetonius claims that some of his victims got dunked in the sewers). On this particular evening, the fun went horribly wrong for an innocent, and otherwise unknown, senator by the name of Julius Montanus. He was out with his wife when Nero, in his wig and careful camouflage, made a rough pass at her in the street. Montanus responded by beating the emperor up and leaving him with a black eye. Dio, in his version of the story, points out that all would have been well if Montanus had then just kept quiet. But many people in Rome were well aware of what Nero was getting up to after dark, and the unfortunate senator, who had recognised the emperor, wrote to apologise. That was a big mistake. When he read the letter, the emperor simply said: 'So he knew he was hitting Nero.' Hearing of that reaction, Montanus killed himself, no doubt fearing worse to come. In the logic of the story, his crime was spotting the real emperor through the acting.

Hunting for boys

When Commodus shot the animals from gangways across the Colosseum, he was only *pretending* to be a hunter. But in the Roman repertoire of recreation there was another side to killing animals. Far from the amphitheatre, some emperors, notably Trajan and Hadrian, made hunting in the wild, on horseback or on foot, their trademark pastime, which was on at least one occasion immortalised in sculpture in the city of Rome, in scenes of the emperor triumphant over a lion, a boar and a bear. Yet despite all the associations of the chase with bravery, masculinity and glamour, and without a large and possibly confrontational audience, this particular imperial pleasure too carried reputational risks.

Hunting had an ambivalent image at Rome. One school of thought condemned what it regarded as the 'Eastern' tyrannical practice of keeping animals penned up in special enclosures or game parks, to be sitting targets for the huntsman (not so very different from Commodus's animal victims), while approving of the skill and risk of 'real' hunting, for 'real men'. Others wondered whether hunting, even in the wild, was good training for military combat or merely a playful

61. Relief panels of Hadrian hunting, re-used from an earlier monument, were incorporated into the Arch of Constantine, completed in 315 CE. Here Hadrian and his party are shown hunting a boar. The face of Hadrian (the main figure on horseback) has been recut to resemble that of Constantine, but Antinous is recognisable in the background (second from left).

distraction from it. Others thought that, if you were just killing for fun anyway, why would you bother to go into the wild. You might as well just watch in the arena, 'and keep your legs whole instead of getting them scratched to bits as you jog through the woods'. There were very different styles of hunting too. Pliny was predictably at the bookish end of the spectrum, taking his writing materials with him when out chasing boars, just in case a thought should occur to him that was too good to forget.

Even if hunting was largely practised away from the public eye, those different styles could say a lot about the character and qualities of different emperors. On one occasion the young Marcus Aurelius, who was also rather bookish, explains in a letter to Fronto how he came back from the chase, not actually having seen what they had caught, took off his hunting gear and devoted himself to two hours' reading of classic Roman speeches (no doubt exactly what his tutor wanted to hear). Augustus was apparently not a hunting man in the 'big game' sense at all, preferring an afternoon's quiet angling. And the contrast between Domitian and Trajan in how each hunted gave Pliny, in his *Speech of Praise*, another way of exposing their vices and virtues.

Trajan's recreation, according to Pliny, was to go out alone on foot, climb lofty mountains, and chase beasts from their lairs, or drive them out of the low-lying ground and protect farmers from the damage they did. It was almost as if he was doing in his spare time what he did in his day job: defending Rome against its enemies and protecting its citizens. Domitian, by contrast, was one of those whose amusement was to kill animals that were more or less in captivity anyway, in a game park at his Alban estate. Suetonius describes him, pointlessly and nastily (even if with a sharp aim), shooting two arrows into the heads of his victims to make it look as if they had a pair of horns. One Greek intellectual, another Dio, nicknamed 'the Golden Mouth' (*Chrysostom*), puts it even more clearly. Some emperors, of whom he disapproved, whimpered and wailed on the stage in their spare time (he had Nero in mind here), or they went to no effort at all to bag game that was penned up in their private parks. Good emperors, such as Trajan, showed their mettle in the kind of activities that made them stronger, braver and more ready for the fight.

Pliny's line was that the emperor was revealed most clearly in what he chose to do in the time he had for himself. But his loud defence of Trajan's hunting may suggest that not everyone thought Trajan had got it right. Certainly, we can detect all kinds of debates and anxieties about the passion for hunting of his successor, Hadrian.

Hadrian left the traces of his hunting across the Roman world, not only on those sculptures in Rome itself. He founded a city, in what is now Turkey, with the name of 'Hadrian's Hunts' (Hadrianoutherae) because of a successful hunting expedition there, and he appeared on the city's coinage in hunting costume. After killing a bear in Greece, he dedicated 'the best parts of it' to Eros, the god of love. In an uncomfortably sentimental dedication inscribed on stone, which still survives, he asks the god to breathe on him the grace of his mother Aphrodite. A few years later in 130 CE, in Egypt, he went hunting with his boyfriend Antinous, an occasion elaborately commemorated in Greek verse by an Egyptian poet of the time, Pankrates, who has been remembered only because he was lucky enough to have the emperor notice and enjoy this tribute. Four lines survive, quoted in a vast literary miscellany compiled a few decades later, but over thirty more lines, almost certainly from the same poem, have been discovered on scraps of Egyptian papyrus.

These verses build up the chase of Hadrian and Antinous into an epic encounter, against a lion that had been ravaging huge tracts of the North African countryside. Hadrian strikes first, with his bronze spear, but only wounds the animal who is left raging, foaming at the mouth, gnashing his teeth and pawing the ground so violently that the cloud of dust raised obscures the sunlight. Hadrian's near miss was intentional, for he wanted to discover how straight Antinous could throw (the over-the-top, epic language, more reminiscent of Homer than of a description of a hunt in the here and now, even gives the 'lovely' young man divine parentage: 'the son of the god Hermes', he is called). Which of the two men in the end killed the lion we do not know, for that section of the poem is lost. But in a surviving romantic touch, combined with some pretence of abstruse learning, we read that it was the lion's blood, dripping to the ground, that gave the distinctive red colour to the Egyptian red lotus flower. That, of course, is not the only romantic touch in the poem. Following a long-standing ancient theme that saw the hunt not just as a symbol of martial prowess and endurance but as a metaphor for erotic pursuit (as it still is, in the phrase 'on the hunt'), Pankrates hints that Hadrian's target is as much the lovely Antinous as it is the fierce lion.

What ancient readers thought about the emperor being 'on the hunt', in that sense, we can only guess. But there is evidence that Hadrian's passion for the chase itself was seen by some to go too far. The *Imperial History*, for example, suggests that it was too much even for Trajan, who is supposed to have recalled him to Rome from Spain, when he was a young man, to keep him away from the hunting opportunities there. And too much, for me, is the poem that Hadrian composed to be inscribed on the gravestone of his favourite hunting horse, Borysthenes, the ancient name for the Dnieper river, from where, presumably, the horse came.

There was a long-standing tradition in Greece and Rome of leaders honouring their mounts, the classic example being Alexander the Great and his war horse Bucephalus, whom he buried with full honours on his eastern campaigns. Caligula and the other racehorse-mad emperors looked slightly bathetic in comparison, getting so worked up about an animal that they did not ride themselves and that only galloped up and down the track of the Circus Maximus. Hadrian with his hunting horse was a bit closer to Alexander. But this poem of sixteen short lines, known from a copy taken from the gravestone itself in the seventeenth century (it has since been lost), is a dreadful piece of sentimental doggerel from the imperial pen – unless, of course, he contracted the writing out to one of his staff. It celebrates, to capture the flavour of the Latin, 'Caesar's steed ... who flies along with speed', even including a tribute to the animal's spit, 'spraying from his lips ... to his tail at the very tips'. Borysthenes, the poem concludes, has finally been laid to rest, 'his limbs unharmed from toil ... lying here beneath the soil'. As verses go, these are not unlike those in a modern greetings card.

But whether we see this literary effort on the emperor's part as embarrassingly dreadful or, more generously, as a touching, albeit naive, expression of affection for the animal, it is an important reminder of how fragile the boundary is, even now, between the reputations of the 'good' and 'bad' emperors, between those who got away with it and those who didn't. If this poem had been composed by Caligula about his Incitatus, by Lucius Verus who gave a splendid burial to his favourite racer Volucer, or by Commodus about his Pertinax (the four-legged version), ancient and modern writers would probably treat it as a sign of the emperor's madness in his private passions. Just look at how Hadrian honoured *his horse*. As it is, we tend to regard it, at worst, as some clumsily bad poetry by an emperor who got things, here as elsewhere (think of all those statues of Antinous), wildly out of proportion, as only emperors could – whether that was on the hunting field, on stage, at the races or in the Colosseum.

But for Hadrian, hunting was one part of his experiences abroad that were to do with more than equine interests. That Egyptian hunt with (and of) Antinous took place on a much longer foreign expedition, which had – as we shall now see – some tragic casualties and some quite other aims in view.

8

EMPERORS ABROAD

A singing statue

Within a couple of months of their great lion hunt in 130 CE, Hadrian and Antinous set sail up the river Nile, on what seems to have been mostly a sightseeing trip. They were travelling in a flotilla of boats, with a large party that also included the emperor's wife Sabina and her poet friend Julia Balbilla, who was both a Roman citizen and an Eastern princess. It was partly the ancient jet set at play, partly a military-style transport operation.

The mysterious drowning of Antinous in the river, two weeks or so into the trip, must have blighted the holiday atmosphere. But they pressed on upstream, nevertheless, to one of the most famous sights in the whole of Egypt: a pair of statues 18 metres tall, set on the banks of the Nile just outside ancient Thebes (modern Luxor), which attract busloads of visitors even now, and which probably look much the same today as they did then.

They were originally made as images of Pharaoh Amenhotep III, who had ruled Egypt 1,500 years before the time of Hadrian, but they had at some point been re-identified as the hero Memnon (a mythical Ethiopian king, said to have fought in the Trojan War), and the one on the right was believed to have possessed miraculous powers. First thing in the morning it sometimes produced what appeared to be a

62. The Colossi of Memnon, outside Luxor in Egypt, still
attract tourists, almost two millennia after Hadrian's sightseeing
trip. It was the statue on the right-hand side that 'sang'.

spontaneous whistling sound. Whether this was caused by a serendipitous crack in the stone opening up in the heat of the sun, or – as
at least one sceptical ancient writer wondered – by some local con
artist, it was regularly claimed to be the voice of Memnon, singing to
his divine mother, the goddess Dawn.

We can be absolutely certain that Hadrian's party came here in
mid-November 130 CE, because Sabina had a line of Greek carved
into the statue's left leg to say that she, 'wife of emperor Hadrian', had
heard the voice of Memnon. Balbilla – better remembered today for
the eye-catching monument on Philopappos Hill in Athens, which
she erected to commemorate her brother Gaius Julius Philopappos –
composed four Greek poems on her experiences there, also inscribed
on the same leg. This was not an isolated act of vandalism by a couple

63. Julia Balbilla's memorial to her brother, Philopappos, in Athens. She commemorated him as a combination of Eastern royalty, Roman citizen and consul (which he was under Trajan, a few years after Pliny).

of entitled royals. It was something of a local custom. More than a hundred such carvings, commissioned by ancient tourists (we can't imagine that they actually did the chiselling themselves), are still preserved on this statue. And it was not just here. Another Roman lady, very likely also a member of Hadrian's party, had some Latin poetry, lamenting the death of *her* brother, carved into the Great Pyramid, suggesting that the pyramids, 400 miles downstream, outside modern Cairo, were on this imperial itinerary too.

Balbilla's poetry, which, like Sabina's one-liner, is still clearly legible, reveals that the visit was not a total success. On the first day, the statue failed to make a sound. But she managed to put on a brave face, by claiming that it was playing 'hard to get' in order to entice 'the lovely Sabina to come back again'. There was better news on the following days, when 'frightened by the power of mighty Hadrian', Memnon performed both for him and for the ladies. The story offers a curious ancient glimpse of a surprisingly modern touristic experience (though I should warn you that the statue has not made a sound, faked or genuine, for many centuries).

These poems give no hint of the other people in the imperial party. It is almost as if the trio of the emperor, Sabina and Balbilla were there on their own, when – to count friends, courtiers, staff, bodyguards and other hangers-on – the entourage probably numbered in the hundreds. Imperial visits, such as this, offered a great opportunity for the local communities through which they passed. Ordinary people

64. The left foot of the singing Colossus. One of Balbilla's poems is inscribed to the left of the crack, seen here at a 90 degree angle.

had the rare chance to ask for favours face to face and to press their petitions into the emperor's hands, and on this occasion the Egyptians were given a whole new town (whether they wanted it or not), founded by Hadrian to commemorate Antinous at the place where he drowned: Antinoopolis ('Antinousville'), it was to be called. But the opportunity of access to the emperor came at a price. For the burden, trouble and huge expense of catering for the imperial visitors – feeding them, providing hospitality, lodging and transport – would have fallen largely on the locals. It went far beyond the inconvenience that came with the regular travel permits.

Thanks to some scraps of papyrus and messages scrawled on broken pieces of pottery (the ancient equivalent of sticky notes), we can see some of the preparations in Egypt for the arrival of Hadrian, which started months in advance and were on an enormous scale. One particularly revealing document is a memorandum, from the end of 129 CE, between two local officials, noting the supplies that had been put in store for 'the impending visit of the emperor'. The papyrus is badly damaged, but we can still see the vast quantities that these two officials alone were dealing with: 372 suckling pigs, 2,000 sheep (or 200, as a more modest restoration of the text would suggest), 6,000 kilos of barley, 90 kilos of unripe olives, 3,000 bundles of hay, and so on. It is hard to be certain about the implications of this. These men might have been overestimating the length of the emperor's stay or the number in his retinue, or just playing it very safe. But this is not the list of provisions for a small group of VIPs, families and friends. This is almost a whole court on tour in its empire.

And it raises some big questions. How often did emperors travel around like this? Where did they go? How was it all organised? And what drew them outside Italy, from sightseeing and cultural tourism to military expeditions, both successful and disastrous, and giving pep talks to the troops on distant army bases?

Hadrian on the move

Hadrian was the imperial traveller beyond all others. Whatever was driving him – curiosity, itchy feet, a desire to engage with the empire – he got everywhere. This visit to Egypt was not a quick hop across the sea for a vacation. It was just one small part of the second of two long tours he made around the empire, which kept him away from Italy for years on end. The first began in 121 CE and took him to Germany, Gaul, Britain (where 'his' Wall was being built) and Spain, before he turned round to make the 2,500-mile journey to Syria, at the opposite end of the Mediterranean, moving on to what is now Turkey and Greece. He was finally back at home by the summer of 125, as the

Hadrian's travels, 121–134CE

An emperor on the move. The details of where exactly he stopped and when are hazy, but this map gives a good idea of the extent of Hadrian's travels during his reign.

inscribed copy of one of his letters, signed off then from his estate at Tivoli, shows (p. 161). The second tour started in 128 CE, and he had already been to North Africa, Greece, modern Turkey, Jerusalem and Gaza by the time he travelled up the Nile in 130 . He was again in Italy by the summer of 134 (as another inscribed letter, signed off from Rome, proves), but not before he had made return visits to Greece, Turkey and perhaps Judaea. When we think of Hadrian, we should think of him *on the move*, as much as presiding over his empire from palaces in Rome or Tivoli. All the way from Britannia to Syria, it must have been a slow, cumbersome and often uncomfortable 'progress', on horseback, in wagons or by boat. The result was that there was hardly a single province of the Roman empire that he had not visited.

All kinds of puzzles remain about these journeys. Their exact route is harder to plot than most confident modern maps of them, my own included, imply. There are a few fixed points where we can be fairly certain of his presence (because it is mentioned in his biography or in a surviving inscription), but working out how he got between them is often not much more than a game of joining the dots. We can only guess how the business of running the empire was coordinated years on end between a travelling court and the rest of the administration. Where, for example, did men like Pliny send their letters? How could you have effective 'government by correspondence' if you didn't know the emperor's address? Besides, we have very little idea of precisely who the members of this travelling court were, from Sabina (who shared some of her husband's journeys, but not all) to more lowly staff and soldiers. A teenager by the name of Lucius Marius Vitalis is one of the very few of the back-up team that we can plausibly pin down. His tombstone, put up by his mother, records that, in his keenness to learn some art and culture (or so he told his mum), he had joined the imperial guard and left Rome with Hadrian, never to return. He had died on the journey, the stone records, aged just seventeen years and fifty-five days.

It is clear that there was more to all this than sightseeing, even if some of that was in the mix. There was a military purpose behind some of Hadrian's chosen destinations, such as his visit to the northern province of Britain, and very likely also to the front line of the war against the Jews, who rebelled in the 130s CE. Sometimes we find him taking an active interest (or meddling) in the politics of provincial towns, and rubbing shoulders with their rich and powerful (and it was probably on one of these journeys that he first rubbed shoulders with the slave Antinous). Sometimes, perhaps, he was keen to project his image in front of a different backdrop, rather as modern politicians carefully curate their photo opportunities. But crucially, he was in the business of leaving his mark, in marble, brick and concrete, in different parts of the Roman world. In a way these journeys were the mirror image of his project at Tivoli, where he constructed his own private estate almost as a miniature replica of the empire. When he was on the move, he literally built 'Hadrian' into the Roman world.

Almost everywhere he went, he commissioned new buildings and sponsored rebuilds: theatres and amphitheatres, temples, bridges, aqueducts, gymnasia, port installations and whole new towns. He was not by any means the only emperor to found cities from scratch, but to do that in order to mark the place where his lover had died (Antinoopolis), or where he himself had had a particularly successful hunting trip (Hadrianoutherae), made a very distinctive and personal statement. There were small-scale, occasionally quirky, interventions too. Not even run-down tombs escaped his notice. In Egypt, he is reported to have spruced up the tomb of Pompey, Julius Caesar's enemy, and re-inscribed it with commemorative verses that he himself had composed. (The monument was well enough known for Septimius Severus to pay it a visit a few decades later.) And we know of half a dozen others elsewhere that got similar treatment. He paid for the restoration of the tomb of Alcibiades, the charismatic and maverick Athenian politician of the fifth century BCE (and a close associate of the philosopher Socrates), who was also honoured with a new statue, and he renovated the memorials believed to mark the burial place of Hector and Ajax, mythical fighters in the Trojan War. These were in a way just minor building works, but the bigger message was that the history, culture, heroes and myth of all the Roman empire came under Hadrian's benevolent protection, and control.

It is, however, in the story of Hadrian and Athens that we can see his relations with one particular community in his empire under a magnifying lens. Athens was no typical city. It was the most famous cultural, artistic and intellectual centre of the Mediterranean world, though at the beginning of the second century CE rather down on its luck and living off its past glories, and it was the place where Hadrian spent longer during his reign than anywhere else apart from Rome and Tivoli, as the guest of some of its rich residents. It is the extreme case of his patronage outside Italy. For acting as both emperor and as Athenian citizen – an honour the Athenians had granted him before he came to the throne, with a canny eye to the future – he set about launching a revival of the city's fortunes. He established a raft of new religious festivals and put his name (how much hands-on work is another question) to a wide range of civic reforms, from tax cuts and an overhaul of local finances to reorganising the olive oil trade and tinkering with the rules on Athenian citizenship. But most ostentatiously, he sponsored building projects that changed the face of the city more radically than any individual had ever done before, including the famous Pericles of the fifth century BCE, who had been responsible for such landmark monuments as the Parthenon on the Acropolis. Even now there is more of Hadrian left in the surviving monuments of Athens than of Pericles.

You can still visit the remains of his temple to the god 'Olympian Zeus', the biggest in the whole of Greece (roughly twice the Parthenon's floor area), which had been started in the sixth century BCE, left unfinished for almost 650 years, and finally completed by

65. The remains of the Temple of Olympian Zeus, started centuries earlier and finished by Hadrian. Its glorious state did not last very long, it was attacked during an invasion of Greece only a century or so after Hadrian, and was never fully restored.

Hadrian with a tremendous fanfare and an opening ceremony featuring a gushing, and long, speech from one of his favourite Greek intellectuals. The emperor had commissioned all kinds of luxuries and curiosities to adorn it, including a colossal gold and ivory statue of the god and a snake specially brought from India, a symbol, presumably, of Rome's global power and influence. Four larger-than-life statues of himself stood at the entrance (perhaps making a pointed link between emperor and god), and many more smaller ones filled the precinct around the building. No less lavish, and even larger, was his new library and arts centre, which – according to one slightly starstruck ancient writer – was originally decorated with gilded ceilings, ornamental pools and a hundred columns of multicoloured marble

66. One of Hadrian's apparently more modest monuments in Athens,
celebrating both the old city and Hadrian's 'new' development.
On one side of the arch, the inscription reads 'This is Athens, the
ancient city of Theseus', on the other side (in this view) 'This is
the city of Hadrian, not of Theseus'. But who takes precedence,
Hadrian or Theseus, the mythical king and founder of the place?

(its now rather bare remains don't quite capture it). And there were
many other projects too, from the practical to the showy, from a river
bridge and an aqueduct to baths, a gymnasium and more.

In return for this sponsorship and prestige, the Athenians granted
Hadrian a whole range of civic honours. They adjusted one of their
systems of dating, to make it start from the moment he came to the city
('fifteen years after the first visit of Hadrian', as they now sometimes
marked the year) and they rebranded local customs and institutions
with his name ('Hadrianis'). The usual assumption is that this shows
how grateful the Athenians were for the emperor's interest. Many no
doubt *were* grateful. It is hard not to suspect, though, that a few were

more ambivalent. Partly, this generosity came at a cost. The emperor certainly poured some of his own cash into these projects, but he also made sure (somewhere on the spectrum between encouragement and compulsion) that the local bigwigs dug deep into their pockets too. And, for those who had to house and entertain him and all his hangers-on, an imperial visit might well have seemed a mixed blessing. There was a whiff of 'takeover' as much as 'benefaction' about it all too. Public inscriptions claimed that Hadrian had replaced, or at least upstaged, the legendary founder of the city, King Theseus, and his portrait was even displayed in one of the most sacred spaces of Athens, inside the Parthenon. It was a fine line between the emperor enhancing the city and exploiting its traditions and cultural fame to enhance himself.

Emperors behaving badly?

Hadrian pushed the idea of the 'travelling emperor' to its limits, in terms of distances covered, time taken and impact made. But in some ways his journeys can be seen as a more extreme and more elaborate version of what most emperors did in some form or another. It is true that there were a few 'stay-at-home' types. Antoninus Pius is a good example of that, never once leaving Italy during his reign. And anyway 'stay-at-home' must have meant something different when emperors increasingly came from outside Italy (where was 'home'?). The majority of Roman rulers, though, whether before or after they came to the throne, made some trips 'abroad' for purposes very like Hadrian's, including fact-finding, getting on kissing terms with influential locals, visiting the troops on the front line and recreational tourism.

But there was often a reputational risk, and an emperor's keenness to get away could be interpreted in different ways. Tiberius, for example, was commonly assumed to be sulking, or escaping his wife, when he moved to Rhodes for several years during the reign of Augustus. But more than any other, Nero's visit to Greece, over sixteen months between 66 and 67 CE, was ridiculed, by Roman writers, as a series of embarrassing antics, megalomaniac schemes and pointless power play: an object lesson in how *not* to be an emperor abroad. Nero was so keen, it was said, to compete in all the major Greek festivals (the Olympic Games and others), that they were rescheduled to fit in with his stay and then rigged so that he won every event he entered, whether artistic or sporting. On one notorious occasion he took home the prize, despite actually falling out of the chariot he was driving and not finishing the course. No better, it was claimed, was his supposedly madcap, and soon abandoned, project to dig a canal right through the narrow isthmus of Corinth. According to one hostile essay written in the second century CE, he inaugurated this work himself, first singing a song to some gods of the sea, then ceremonially striking the ground three times with a golden mattock. Suetonius adds the detail that he himself carried off the first basketful of earth on his shoulders.

No better either was the self-advertising display of his own generosity, when during the same visit he granted 'freedom' – including freedom from taxation – to the Roman province of Achaea, which covered the southern part of modern Greece. In what must have been an elaborate ceremony staged during the Isthmian Games (at Corinth again), the emperor himself proclaimed the new liberty of Greece. The text of the speech he gave on the occasion, in Greek, still survives, inscribed on a stone that was later reused, and preserved, as a building block in a medieval church. Indeed, the words do now seem embarrassingly hyperbolic: 'It is a completely unexpected gift that I am giving you, gentlemen of Greece, except there is nothing that cannot be hoped for from my munificence. I am delighted to be giving you such a great favour that you never even thought to ask for it ... Other leaders have freed cities, only Nero has freed a whole province.'

There probably were aspects of this trip that crossed the line between what was acceptable and what wasn't. In particular, Nero took part in public competitions where other Roman rulers were happy merely to watch from the audience. Apart from anything else, this presented the locals with the tricky problem of how to award the prizes when the ruler of their world was one of the competitors. If the stories about the rigging of the contests are true, their straightforward, understandable, though ultimately absurd, solution was simply to let him win everything. But, in many ways, Nero's trip was probably far less ridiculous and out of the ordinary than the outraged accounts suggest, all written years after and partly with the intention of making him look simultaneously foolish and tyrannical.

For a start, despite the emperor's own boast that he was the first 'leader' to free a whole province, over 250 years earlier, in 196 BCE, a Republican general had done just that – proclaiming the freedom of Greece on the very spot where Nero made his own proclamation (that can hardly have been a coincidence). He was the first *emperor* to do so, for sure, but not, in broader terms, the first *Roman leader*. Besides, his plans to construct what we now call the 'Corinth Canal' through the isthmus, which was finally completed in 1893, were not necessarily as crazy as they have been painted. Such a safe short cut for shipping was a practical measure that others, Julius Caesar included, had explored before – and history has proved Nero right. But as Pliny discovered when he shared with Trajan his own project for a canal in Pontus-Bithynia, ambitious engineering work in the Roman world always risked being dismissed as ill-considered folly – or, in the emperor's case, megalomania.

Almost everything depends on how these visits were written up, by whom and with what axe to grind. Again, as with the poem in memory of the horse, it does not take much imagination to see how Hadrian's flamboyant gestures could easily have been treated with the kind of hostility shown to Nero's. What would have been said if Nero had decorated the entrance of a temple with four larger-than-life statues

of himself, and displayed an Indian snake inside? It would hardly have
been star-struck wonderment. Nor is it hard to see how Nero's Greek
schemes could have been presented (as indeed they sometimes were)
as benefaction rather than mad profligacy.

I strongly suspect that in broad terms Nero's visit to Greece was not
so very different from, for example, the visit to Egypt a few decades
earlier of the imperial prince Germanicus. In Tacitus's view, Germanicus was really on a heritage tour. But he also made a splash in
Alexandria. He reduced the price of grain, staged public walkabouts
without bodyguards and, in the same speech as he confessed to be
missing his granny, he warmly praised the splendour of the city –
which was enhanced, he was careful to add, 'by the generosity of my
grandfather Augustus'. Only then did he set out up the Nile to visit
the attractions, from the pyramids to ancient Thebes (where he had
a special history lesson, and the hieroglyphs translated for him, by an
elderly priest), and, of course, to the famous singing statue. In this case,
according to Tacitus, it was the emperor Tiberius who was hostile to
the visit. Germanicus had gone to Egypt without his permission, and
there was a suspicion that he might be making trouble or currying
favour. The city of Rome was so dependent on Egyptian wheat that
Augustus had devised the rule that all high-ranking Romans needed
the emperor's explicit approval simply to visit the province – just in
case, presumably, they were tempted to make their own bid for power,
by blocking the transport and starving the capital into submission.

The reaction of the locals to such imperial visits is another matter. As
with Hadrian, there is plenty of evidence for an enthusiastic welcome
given to emperors on their travels. One grateful Greek response to
Nero's proclamation of freedom for the province is preserved on the
same stone as the emperor's own words – and it is equally hyperbolic.
Nero is greeted as a 'new sun shining on the Greeks ... the one and
only greatest Greek-loving emperor of all in history'. And, according to the papyrus that preserves the speech given by Germanicus

in Alexandria, the poor man at times could hardly get a word in, as the crowds kept interrupting with cheers and wishes of 'Good luck'. Whether these reactions were sincere or not – and, of course, what the locals said in public might not have been what they felt – we get the impression that some of these encounters between emperor or prince and communities abroad would have seemed like 'feel-good' occasions on both sides.

But it is not only cynical modern historians who suspect that not everyone, in every city, would have been keen to host an imperial visit. We can occasionally find clear hints of discontent. It may have been partly the lingering hostilities of the civil war between Octavian and Mark Antony (in which Athens had been on Antony's side) that caused friction when the recently renamed 'Augustus' was in Greece over the winter of 22–21 BCE. A statue of the goddess Athena on the Acropolis is supposed to have miraculously swivelled on its base to face Rome and proceeded to spit blood in Rome's direction. August- us himself, probably wisely, decided that he would give Athens itself a miss and stay on the nearby island of Aegina instead. Likewise, we are presumably witnessing negative spin against Augustus in the story of his encounter with the remains of Alexander the Great. It was said that, when he was in Egypt, he had Alexander's body brought out of the shrine where it was kept, but that, in his eagerness to touch it, he had actually managed to break off the corpse's nose (it had presum- ably been embalmed). The point was that, while some Roman rulers restored and improved the burial places of earlier 'heroes', others trashed them. Visiting emperors were not always welcome.

Supply and survival

Royal visits have often been a terrible imposition for the visited. In Elizabethan England there were people who dreaded the arrival of the

Queen and her court, for the cost of the entertainment could mean bankruptcy (one anxious minor aristocrat in 1600 even wrote to her right-hand man, begging that she did not come). No doubt, as in Athens, there were men of means in many Roman provinces who both relished and feared the idea of the emperor and his entourage showing up to stay, literally eating them out of house and home. But the biggest downside of a royal visit was the imposition and expense that fell on ordinary people, wherever the court touched down.

Almost no Roman writer bothered to notice this. Cassius Dio does refer to the burdens on the elite, when Caracalla demanded that new racecourses and amphitheatres be built in the places he was visiting, and the claims that Elagabalus travelled around with a convoy of 600 wagons (implausibly said to be full of prostitutes) gives a hint of the scale of imperial journeys in the Roman imagination. But it is from the papyri of Roman Egypt, straight from the filing cabinets of local officials, that we can begin to see what it was like on the ground. The preparations for the imminent arrival of Hadrian, with those 372 pigs and all the rest, are only one example of the burdens that fell on the locals. Other documents look forward to a visit by Alexander Severus and his mother in the 230s (we do not know if it actually took place), and insist that all requisitioning of supplies should be done in a legal and transparent manner, with the precise demands posted up publicly in larger towns. One papyrus, from further down the administrative ladder on the same projected visit, contains a report from a village official to say that he has forty pigs ready for the imperial party, giving their total weight as 2,000 Roman pounds, so averaging roughly 17.5 kilos each. Either they were very young animals or (as archaeological evidence indicates) ancient pigs were considerably smaller than their modern European domestic counterparts, which regularly weigh in at over 300 kilos.

But the most vivid evidence for what went on behind the scenes when an imperial visit was on the horizon is found in a large dossier of papyri from the Egyptian town of Panopolis, about 370 miles south of Alexandria. In this case, it was a later emperor, Diocletian, on the throne from 284 to 305 CE, who was expected. Among a wealth of other official documents dealing with local government appointments, delayed accounts and the like, the dossier takes us into the in-tray of one particular regional official, as he struggled to put all the arrangements for the emperor's arrival in place, sending a whole series of anxious (or bad-tempered) letters to those above and below him in the administration.

Reading between the lines, it looks like the unfortunate man (whose name we do not know, only his title, *strategos* in Greek, a 'regional administrator') was at the end of his tether. He was trying to put pressure on his subordinates to get a move on. 'In preparation for the fortunately upcoming visit of the emperor ... I have told you once, I have told you twice to appoint as quickly as possible overseers and receivers for the supplies for the distinguished military force who will be coming into the town', he wrote to a certain Aurelius Plutogenes, a local council leader who was obviously dragging his feet. And a couple of weeks later he contacted the man again, this time worrying about a bakery that needed to be got ready to feed the hungry soldiers. 'This is now a pressing requirement. I ask you urgently to appoint in the customary way a manager who with all due fairness will see to the repair of the bakery, and provide for the bakers who are going to work there.' At the same time he was writing to his boss, putting the blame firmly on Plutogenes for any delays. 'I asked him to appoint collectors, distributors and receivers of grain separately, to make the collection and distribution go smoothly. But he used a different system, to disrupt and undermine the military supply chain.' It was even worse, he explained, with the refurbished ships that were needed for the occasion. When asked to appoint a surveyor to start these renovations, Plutogenes 'had the nerve to turn round and reply that his town didn't need to be bothered with this'. We should probably imagine that a 'fortunately upcoming visit of the emperor' (a phrase often repeated in the dossier) would in almost every case have tried the patience and frayed the nerves of those tasked to organise and supply it.

Emperors at war

It was warfare more than anything else – sightseeing, wanderlust, fact-finding or public relations – that took emperors outside Italy. One of their formal titles, *imperator* (from which our word 'emperor' derives) literally means 'military commander'. And images of rulers in battle guise were found everywhere in Rome and across the Roman world: from the columns of Trajan and Marcus Aurelius that blazoned a narrative of their successful military campaigns, often spotlighting the figure of the emperor himself, to any number of marble statues of the ruler kitted out in elaborate armour; or that famous ancient bronze image of Marcus Aurelius on horseback, which for centuries was the centrepiece of the Renaissance piazza on the Capitoline Hill (fig. 44). He may now seem peaceable enough, but you read the message rather differently when you realise that there was originally a figure of a barbarian under the horse's raised hoof, being trampled to death. That is certainly how those on the other side saw him. In a strange collection of Jewish and Christian texts composed from the second century BCE on – part prophecies, part attacks on Roman power – the Roman emperor is repeatedly imagined as a man who kills his enemies. His trademark is 'man-destroying war'.

According to Roman logic, a good emperor was by definition a good general. One of the easiest ways of undermining the ruler's status was to ridicule his abilities in the field. A classic example is the story of Caligula on campaign in 40 CE, on what was probably an abortive invasion of Britain. On the shores of the English Channel, looking out towards the as yet unconquered island, he drew up his battle lines and,

67. Hadrian kitted out for warfare, symbolically at least. He is wearing an oak wreath (or 'civic crown'), an honour given to those Romans who had saved the lives of fellow citizens in battle.

trumpets blaring, ordered his soldiers not to press ahead to military glory but instead to collect seashells on the beach. The story might or might not be true. It might be the result of a wilful, or inadvertent, mis-understanding (some ingenious modern scholars have suggested that there has been a confusion of Latin terminology and the emperor had really ordered them to pick up their *boats* or their *huts* not shells). But whatever lies behind it, the anecdote was told and retold for obvious reasons: to show up Caligula as a ruler who turned bravery into bathos,

68. A moment in the Dacian Wars from Trajan's column. The
emperor in the centre addresses the troops in front of him,
while behind him Roman soldiers wade through a river.

and who embarrassed his troops by forcing them to undertake a trivial
– almost effeminate – task. Caligula was a parody of a general.

The military role of the emperor was not, however, quite so simple
as that makes it seem. For here too, the Roman ruler was faced with
a delicate balancing act. The first two centuries CE were not an age of
major expansion. The empire, in the sense of overseas conquered territory, had largely been formed hundreds of years earlier, between the
third and first centuries BCE, long before one-man rule. The last really
large tracts of land – including Egypt – had been added to it early in the
reign of Augustus. Then, after a catastrophic defeat in the Teutoburg
Forest near Osnabrück in modern Germany in 9 CE, which perhaps
left as many as 20,000 Roman soldiers dead (casualty estimates for
ancient battles are rarely much more than 'perhaps'), Augustus is supposed to have decided on no further imperial expansion. He even left
explicit written advice for Tiberius, his heir, that 'the empire should be

restricted to its existing boundaries'. After a humiliating wake-up call, he presumably judged that military resources were already spread too thinly and were almost too expensive to sustain. The simple message from one of the founding fathers of Roman autocracy was that future emperors would be ill-advised to increase the empire's size.

This still left Augustus's successors some opportunities to shine. He was hardly advocating pacifism. There was always glory to be won by resisting threats from outside the empire. The Column of Marcus Aurelius celebrates one such campaign of resistance, against pressure from tribes beyond the river Danube. Kudos might come too from quashing insurrection and rebellion within Roman territory. Hadrian, for example, could claim credit for brutally – or 'resolutely' as he would have put it – suppressing the Jewish revolt of the 130s CE. In any case,

69. The scenes on the column of Marcus Aurelius often appear more brutal than those on the earlier column of Trajan. Here the Romans attack a German village (with its distinctive huts), while a woman and child attempt to escape.

70. A stereotype of a Roman victory in a relief sculpture from Ephesus, showing a defeated 'barbarian' – in standard 'barbarian' trousers – slumped over his horse. Fragments of Roman soldiers can be seen behind.

the 'boundaries' of the empire were never the simple lines that appear on modern maps. They were much more fluid, with Roman imperial power and control extending in practice far beyond the limits of the official provinces, often across frontier *zones* rather than linear *frontiers*. Despite appearances, even Hadrian's Wall in England does not mark the edge of Roman territory and influence, which went much further north (the Wall itself was more a boastful assertion of Rome's dominance over the landscape than a boundary marker). So, it would have been possible to adhere to Augustus's advice in the broad sense, while still enjoying the prestige of turning what had been a zone of influence into a formal province within the empire, or of bringing new territory into Rome's practical but indirect control. There were plenty of foreign kings who were prepared, if pushed, to be Roman puppets.

All the same, there was an underlying clash between the risk-averse position of more or less adhering to the territorial *status quo* and the traditional view that glory came from military expansion – and the enduring popular fantasy that Rome's destiny was to have an 'empire without limit' (to quote the words that Virgil puts into the mouth of the god Jupiter in his epic *Aeneid*). There was a clash, in other words, between the image of the emperor as commander-in-chief of legions that were effectively a police force on guard duty, and the image of the emperor as heroic general, in the traditional Roman mould that went back to the Republic, leading his troops into battle in a project of ever-greater expansion. How was it possible to be a 'great' Roman without also being a 'great' conqueror? The idea that an emperor should extend the empire was never quite off the table.

Statues of the emperor in battle dress played a part in papering over these cracks. They did not merely *commemorate* his role as military leader, they were also a *substitute* for it – all those heavy-armoured cuirasses and military 'skirts' in marble helping to disguise the fact that the emperor did not often put them on in real life. Likewise, at Ephesus, in modern Turkey, a series of spectacular sculptures depicting Roman victories over some rather stereotypical 'barbarians', put up under Antoninus Pius in the mid second century CE, was no doubt partly designed to make up for the fact that no such wars were being fought at the time. Stereotypes are exactly what these barbarians were. But we also find, throughout the first two centuries CE, a series of campaigns that did relatively little to alter the overall extent of the Roman empire, and certainly not for long, but did provide the emperor with a victory to exaggerate as well as celebrate. These were the military 'vanity projects', with all the loss of life, on both sides, that such 'vanity' inevitably involved.

Victory!

It is now next to impossible to reconstruct the processes by which any emperor decided to embark on military action. There was no war department in the palace secretariat, as there were departments for accounts or petitions, for example. And despite the dreams of some analysts in modern military academies (who have always wanted to theorise Roman 'success'), there is little sign of military *policy* for the medium or long term, still less of a 'grand strategy' of empire. The closest we get to that, and it is not very close, are those reported words of Augustus, advising that the empire be 'restricted to its existing boundaries'.

Most day-to-day military operations empire-wide were reactive. Like so many of the other decisions in the imperial administration, decisions involving the army were taken largely by provincial governors, or by commanders of units in the field, in response to trouble as and when it arose, or in pursuit of very local initiatives. Little of this can have been done with direct reference to the emperor himself. No doubt many letters were sent back to the palace, in much the same way as Pliny reported to Trajan and asked his advice. But army commanders could not usually have afforded to wait, possibly for months, for whatever orders might come in reply. In so far as the emperor and his advisers (whoever they were) had any kind of hands-on control, it was for the most part indirect: by issuing a few general instructions, by ratifying, or not, what their subordinate commanders had chosen to do after the event, by authorising the movement of soldiers from one part of the empire to another, and by hiring and firing the men on the ground. Nero replacing the governor of Britain who was making matters worse after the revolt of Boudicca is a perfect example of that.

The exceptions to the general pattern come in a sporadic series of high-profile, apparently pre-planned campaigns, where the emperor was directly involved, at or near the front line. These were campaigns that were partly at least designed to serve his public image, or were written up afterwards with that in mind. Two of the most revealing cases of this, with very different outcomes, were Claudius's conquest of Britain, which began in 43 CE, and Trajan's campaigns in the east, as far as the Persian Gulf, which ended at his death in 117.

Claudius had come to the throne after the assassination of Caligula in 41 CE and, whatever fluke, or wheeling and dealing behind the scenes, led to his selection, he was an unexpected and unlikely choice. According to the usual picture, he was the elderly uncle whom everyone assumed had been passed over in any succession planning. Suetonius even quotes from a series of letters from Augustus to Livia, written when Claudius was still young (where he found them, we do not know), in which the emperor regretted what a problem the boy was. Could he ever hold public office, Augustus wondered. Should he be kept out of the imperial box at the races? What *were* they to do with him? Against this background, one way for the new emperor to stake his claim to being up to the job was to embrace the old traditions of military heroics and *make a conquest*. Britain was a particularly tempting target. It posed no threat whatsoever to the security of the empire, although some specious excuse for invasion was dreamed up. But in the Roman imagination, it was a remote place of mystery, glamour and danger, lying on the other side of the 'Ocean' (a name which sounds more fearsome than our 'English Channel'). It was the final frontier, at the edge of the world, populated by strange people who dyed their skin blue, consumed milk and meat rather than bread and wheat, and dressed in animal hides. The Britons had also already foiled the invasion attempts of both Julius Caesar in the 50s BCE and probably Caligula (at the time of the 'seashells incident'). So, the new emperor had a great chance to shine – by outdoing his predecessors.

The advance troops were sent out under the overall command of a high-ranking senator and ex-consul, Aulus Plautius. It must have been a complicated logistical exercise, from transport and food supplies to equipment, encampments, communications and getting the timing right. There were all kinds of delays because, according to Cassius Dio, the soldiers were at first reluctant to venture beyond the limits of the known world, and the ex-slave from the palace administration sent out by Claudius to give them a pep talk did not go down well. Altogether it was a force of some 20,000 men in four legions, one of them commanded by the future emperor Vespasian, long before his own imperial ambitions had emerged (making him, unless you count Julius Caesar, the first Roman emperor ever to have set foot in Britain).

Claudius himself came out from Rome later, in time for the final stages of the initial take-over. Different accounts circulated of his role in the campaign. Dio presumably recorded the official – and maybe widely believed – version, when he wrote that Plautius got into difficulties and eventually had to summon the emperor to help him out, and that it was only on the arrival of Claudius that the clinching battle was won and the tribes surrendered. Most other writers, ancient and modern, have cast Plautius as the sole architect of Roman success, with Claudius showing up at the very end just to claim the victory as his, accompanied by a posse of (probably useless, but awe-inspiring) elephants. The emperor then went straight back to Rome where, among other honours, he was given the extra name 'Britannicus', and gave it also to his baby son. It was a traditional humiliation, going back centuries, that peoples conquered by Rome should see themselves paraded in the names and titles of their conquerors, 'Africanus', 'Asiaticus', 'Germanicus', and so on. There was even a dark joke that, after he had killed his brother Geta, the emperor Caracalla should be called 'Geticus'.

Despite the victory celebrations, from the Roman point of view Britain proved to be a terrible drain on resources. The pessimistic economic assessment by the geographer Strabo that conquering the place was likely to be more costly than it was worth had been right. Anyway, what 'conquering' really meant is unclear. For the majority of Britons in the countryside, life did not change very much, even if there was a new superstructure of towns, villas and, as Tacitus cynically observed, Latin and togas. Yet, at enormous cost in men and money, and facing persistent guerrilla warfare if not open revolt, they did manage to hold onto parts of the island – they never controlled it all – until the early fifth century CE.

It was different with some of most high-profile conquests of the emperor Trajan fifty years after Claudius, which were lost almost as soon as they were gained. Partly thanks to his surviving column, which still displays in the centre of the city of Rome hundreds of scenes of the emperor as *imperator*, Trajan is now thought of as one of the most military and expansionist of all Roman rulers. In a way, he was. He spent roughly half his time as emperor on campaign outside Italy, which makes him in one sense almost as much a 'traveller' as Hadrian, and, because of the tracts of land he formally annexed as provinces, his reign is often said to mark the moment when the empire covered its biggest area ever. But it was just a *moment*. Some of Trajan's conquests amounted to maximum boast for minimum lasting effect – military glory for its own sake.

The column itself commemorates his wars against Dacia (in today's Romania) in the first decade of the second century CE. Though it now stands in splendid isolation, this was originally just one element in his vast 'Forum' – a multipurpose complex, including markets, libraries, porticoes, a triumphal arch and any number of sculptures of bound and captive Dacians – erected to celebrate Trajan's victory and the creation of the new Roman province of Dacia apparently in the old traditions of imperial expansion. This Forum has been an extremely effective advertisement over the centuries for the emperor's military prowess. But – as it was no doubt designed to do – it has obscured as much as it celebrates. You would never have guessed from this bombastic building, still on the 'must-see' list of attractions for visiting dignitaries to Rome 250 years later, that Trajan was essentially doing little more in Dacia than continuing Domitian's earlier operations; that the new province had been carved out of territory that was already more or less in Roman control anyway (after a puppet king had refused to play the puppet any longer); and that the celebratory Forum lasted much longer than the province whose creation it celebrated, which was abandoned by the Romans in the third century.

Trajan's conquests in the east that began in 113 CE, and his victories over the Parthians in what is now Iraq, are an even more extreme, and puzzling, case of hyperbole, and of the clash between the image making of the emperor and military reality on the ground. There has been a long debate, starting in the ancient world itself, on what lay behind these campaigns. Cassius Dio thought Trajan was driven by nothing more than lust for glory. Others have been more generous, pointing to some of the same problems as in Dacia that needed sorting out: ill-defined zones of Roman control and wobbly puppet rulers (though Dio judged all that to be merely a pretext). There was also powerful political capital to be gained out of a victory over the Parthian empire, Rome's only serious rival power in the east until you reached China. It had been an enemy, on and off, since Crassus had been defeated and decapitated in 53 BCE, and any victory by Trajan would be a notable public relations coup. But whatever the causes, and whatever the many disputed details of date and route, the outline of events is clear enough.

With a fighting force that some modern historians have estimated at 80,000 (enough to make the invasion of Britain look like a mere skirmish), Trajan and his generals embarked on a hit-and-run campaign at the eastern edges of the empire, through the territory of ancient Mesopotamia, capturing the Parthian capital of Ctesiphon (just south of modern Baghdad) in 116 CE, and creating three completely new Roman provinces before ending up on the shores of the

Persian Gulf. Honours predictably followed. The emperor was given the extra name 'Parthicus' and his successes were proudly blazoned on coins (pl. 14). He himself compared his victories to those of Alexander the Great, as Roman generals loved to do – while regretting that he was no longer young enough to follow in Alexander's footsteps as far as India ('empire without limit'?). But while he was on a pilgrimage to the place in Babylon where his hero had died in 323 BCE, which had evidently become a tourist attraction, everything was already unravelling, as it often has for Western powers (or meddlers) in that part of the world. The supposedly conquered territories were in revolt – it had been, after all, just hit-and-run – and Trajan himself was seriously ill. He died on the way back to Rome, accompanied by Plotina, who – if you believe the stories – fixed the handover of power. One of the first acts of Hadrian, as his successor, was simply to abandon the new provinces. They had been part of the Roman empire for less than two years.

This image of Trajan as an emperor who was a victim of his own hyperbole makes an awkward contrast with Pliny's down-to-earth vision of the same man, with his lack of pretension, careful attention to detail and his simple suppers.

One of the lads

The emperors' parade of their commitment to warfare was not merely part of an attempt to gain, or grab, military glory for themselves. It was also designed to put them on the same side as their soldiers. Roman power and security were ultimately built on force, overt or concealed, and it was an absolute priority for the emperor to keep the loyal support of the troops – who by the second century CE numbered closer to half a million than a quarter of a million empire-wide. The emperor's nightmare was that the force of the army would be turned against him. That is one reason why enormous amounts of money continued to be invested in generous pay and retirement benefits, with occasional cash handouts as an added extra. But loyalty also depended on hearts and minds and, to win those effectively, the emperor needed to present himself as 'a fellow soldier' or a 'comrade' (*commilitio*). It was another balancing act that Pliny picked up in his *Speech of Praise* when he congratulated Trajan for acting like a *commilitio* while at the same time being an *imperator*. Or as Dio 'the Golden Mouth' put it, also addressing Trajan: if a ruler doesn't get to know those who face danger in order to protect his empire, he's like a shepherd who doesn't know those who help him guard the sheep – and that is liable to let the wild beasts in.

There were various ways for an emperor to be 'a fellow soldier'. It certainly did not mean him actually joining in the fighting, hand-to-hand, even on those occasions when he was technically leading the army. It is now almost impossible to recreate the experience of an ancient battle (probably much smaller-scale and messier than the grandiose ancient accounts suggest, with more men dying days later from infected wounds than struck down on the field itself). But whatever the public image, emperors themselves did not plough into battle, any more than the famous generals of the Republic had. Augustus, for example, was famously pictured by Virgil at the naval Battle of Actium in 31 BCE standing heroically 'high on the stern' of his ship, commanding his troops from the midst of the fray, when actually, as other accounts make clear, his friend Marcus Agrippa was in practical control and Augustus (Octavian, as he then was) watched from a small boat on the sidelines, not standing high on any stern at all. And the stories of the bravery of Titus at the siege of Jerusalem in the late 60s CE – dodging the hostile arrows, killing twelve of the enemy (with, as Suetonius has it, a perfect shot each time), standing firm against pressure from the other side – are, significantly, from the period long before he came to the throne. In this respect, at least, the military scenes on Trajan's column are more accurate. They show the emperor in a commanding role – addressing the troops, conducting religious rituals, receiving prisoners – but not fighting, not leading the charge, and not always in battle armour.

It was much more a question of being seen as 'one of the lads'. Whatever the truth behind the story of the soldiers and the shells, Caligula was certainly helped by having been brought up as a child on army bases with his father Germanicus, where he was dressed as a miniature soldier as a kind of army mascot. Even the name 'Caligula', by which we now generally know him, went back to that time. Meaning literally 'Little Boots', it refers to the tiny army boots he used to wear ('Bootikins' probably gets the flavour of the Latin, and helps explain why Caligula himself did not much like the name). But in general, when emperors were with their troops, they had to be seen to *help out* and *muck in*. Again, they had to be 'one of us', though in a different way from being 'one of us' with the Roman elite.

Roman writers had a fairly standard, repetitive checklist of what was expected of an emperor in this context. He should know the soldiers' names and look after them when they were sick (Trajan gets full marks on one occasion in the Dacian war for cutting up his clothes to make bandages). He should go bareheaded and use the same style of accommodation as the ordinary soldiers. He should not get special rations. In a striking inversion of the hierarchy of eating in the palace, emperors were supposed to eat exactly the same camp food as the others. Hadrian, for example, mucked in with cheese, bacon and cheap wine. Septimius Severus set an example to the others by being the first to drink dirty water when nothing else was available. Caracalla, who gets a better press in this respect than in most things, is supposed to have gone even further, volunteering to carry the weighty legionary standards himself (despite being rather small), not to mention digging ditches, eating off plain wooden platters, grinding his own grain rations and baking coarse bread in the ashes of the fire.

But beyond these, perhaps over-generous, anecdotes, the only *direct* sight we have of the relations between an emperor and ordinary soldiers takes us back again to Hadrian in the continent of Africa, not on active campaign but on an inspection of a long-term army base. It was during his second grand tour, in 128 CE, some months before his great lion hunt with Antinous, that he visited the fort at Lambaesis in what is now Algeria, just over 100 miles north of the Sahara. There he reviewed several military units as they did their manoeuvres, and gave them an oral report on their performance. We know this because the words of that report were later inscribed on stone and put on display in the parade ground of the fort, where several blocks and many fragments were rediscovered by archaeologists in the nineteenth century. I was perhaps a little unfair when I referred (pp. 240–41) to Hadrian's style on this occasion as 'wooden'. Much of it does now read like that: 'You did everything by the book. You filled the training ground with your manoeuvres, you threw your spears not inelegantly, although they were stiff and short, some of you hurled your lances expertly ...' Even where the emperor offers a personal opinion, it is very much in the same tone: 'I do not like counter movements, nor did Trajan whom I follow as my model. A cavalryman should ride out from his cover ...' But maybe 'wooden' is part of the point. This is not the emperor 'mucking in' in the sense of sharing the ham and cheese, but he is speaking the language of the soldiers *to* the soldiers, following the rules of the training manual as they had learned them, with only minimal personal spin (the appeal to Trajan as his model suggests that, whatever the fragility of Trajan's victories, he went down well with the troops). Here we find Hadrian, the emperor and *imperator*, with his soldiers, playing it, as he says, 'by the book'.

Trouble with triumphs

It is easy to ridicule Claudius for claiming a victory while taking at most a symbolic part in the fighting. But those claims were formally correct. Whatever role the emperors played on the ground, whether they were even present at the front line at all, they were always officially the commander-in-chief, and, in that sense, all military victories were theirs. And that is why it was, technically, correct that they should monopolise the ancient ceremony of 'triumph', which went back – so the Romans believed – to the very origin of their city and the reign of King Romulus.

The triumph was traditionally an honour granted by the senate only to the most successful Roman commanders-in-chief – or, to see it from the other side, to those who had presided over the bloodiest massacres (one rule apparently said that 5,000 of the enemy had to have been killed before a triumph could be awarded). It involved an elaborate procession through the city, cheering crowds, and all kinds of fun (the poet Ovid thought it as good a place to pick up a woman – 'conquest' in another sense – as the races). The general stood in a special ceremonial chariot dressed in the costume of the god Jupiter. His prisoners and his booty were paraded in front of him, as well as placards giving details of his victories (it was in one of his triumphs that Julius Caesar displayed the famous slogan *Veni, vidi, vici*; 'I came, I saw, I conquered'). The soldiers cheered, sometimes singing bawdy songs, as they followed behind their commander, no doubt not entirely sober. It was an occasion that put the distant parts of the empire on display in the capital itself. Looted gold, silver and precious artwork was only part of it. Sometimes even trees that grew in those distant locations, as well as models and paintings of captured foreign cities, were on parade. For many of the aristocracy in the Republic, it was the height of their ambitions. It allowed a general to be a god for the day.

This changed during the reign of Augustus. From then on, no 'ordinary' generals were ever granted a triumph. The honour was restricted to emperors (as the official commanders-in-chief) and their direct heirs only. In some practical respects, for some of them, that was a mixed blessing. It was actually a rather uncomfortable ceremony: standing up for hours in a chariot, with no springs or suspension, trundling over the cobbled streets of the city. The notoriously plain-speaking Vespasian is supposed to have hobbled down from the chariot, after his triumph in 71 CE to celebrate victory in the Jewish War, with the words, 'That'll teach me to want a triumph at my age'. Septimius Severus is said to have actually turned the honour down on the grounds of his arthritis. But the new restriction hammered home the point that, whoever actually did the fighting, all military success belonged to the emperor (figs. 3 and 12).

It was impossible, however, to conceal the problems that lurked under the surface of the new-style ceremony. In part, it drew attention to the incongruity of the role of the emperor and – for some, no doubt – the emasculation of the old elite. Did those who watched the elaborate triumphal procession of Claudius in 43 CE, even including a cameo appearance of his wife Messalina in a smaller vehicle, believe the official version that the emperor had militarily saved the day? Did they accept that, whatever part he played on the ground, Claudius was the proper recipient of the honour? Or was it a flagrant sign that Aulus Plautius, who was actually responsible for the victory, had been squeezed out? But it also raised bigger questions about what a triumph was for and, once again, about the fakery and deception that hovered over the rule of the emperors.

When Nero returned from his trip to Greece in 67 CE, he held a 'triumph-like' ceremony in Rome to celebrate all the prizes he had won. It was said that he processed in the very same chariot that Augustus had used in the triumphs that celebrated his military victories. His substitute soldiers walking behind the chariot were a group of his cheerleaders, and the placards at the front detailed not battles won but his athletic and artistic victories. Instead of ending up at the Temple of Jupiter Optimus Maximus (Jupiter Best and Greatest) on the Capitoline Hill, as the regular triumph did, Nero made for the Temple of Apollo, an appropriately 'arty' god, known for his lyre-playing. Was this a constructive attempt to redefine the very notion of what kind of 'victory' a triumph might celebrate, beyond the merely military? Or was it an attempt to subvert, or mock, the whole idea, and ideology, of the traditional ceremony – as much a parody as Caligula's conversion of his soldiers into seashell collectors?

In other cases, even within the traditional military definition of the triumph, pointed questions were raised about how you could ever trust what you saw in the emperor's procession or believe in the victories that were being celebrated. Two of the funniest, and barbed, stories are told about Caligula and Domitian, both of whom celebrated, or planned to celebrate, triumphs to mark victories over the Germans, which had been massively exaggerated or had not really happened at all. (We might suspect that another way to gain military

71. A bronze coin issued by Nero. Part of the emperor's official titles are around the edge. In the centre is the figure of the god Apollo, the lyre player – or, perhaps, of Nero taking the role of Apollo.

glory, in the face of Augustus's advice, was simply to invent your victories, as Caracalla was alleged to have done with some trumped-up heroics against, yet again, the Parthians, more than a century later.) But how do you have a procession of prisoners if none had actually been taken? Caligula's answer, according to Suetonius, was to dress up some Gauls as Germans, dye their hair red, teach them a bit of the German language and give them German names. Domitian's solution was similar, though with an added extra. To take the place of the non-existent booty, he used some treasures from the palace stores. The message was that, where the emperor was concerned, even in the triumph, you could never quite believe your eyes. As you stood watching the procession, could you ever entirely banish the suspicion that it might all be counterfeit?

By far the strangest occasion, however, was the triumph that was held to celebrate the victories of Trajan in Mesopotamia sometime in 117–18 CE. It is easy to see the major problem this presented for Hadrian. How was he to mark the successful campaigns of his predecessor, who was already dead? The answer was that a model of the dead emperor was made, probably out of wax, and that was processed in a chariot around the city. And all of this was to celebrate some conquests that were all about superficial glory, and that, by the time of the triumph, were already in the process of being given up. Sometimes it is hard to understand how the Romans kept a straight face.

9

FACE TO FACE

At close quarters

He was notably handsome ... he had clear bright eyes ... though in old age he did not see well through the left one. His teeth had gaps, were small and pock-marked. His hair was slightly curly and yellowish. His eyebrows met. His ears were medium-sized. His nose stuck out at the top, bent in at the bottom. His complexion was between swarthy and pale. He was short in stature ... but this was concealed by the good proportion and symmetry of his figure so that his shortness was not noticeable except by comparison, if someone taller was standing next to him. It is said that his body was covered in spots and he had birthmarks over his chest and abdomen ...

That is part of Suetonius's description of the appearance of the emperor Augustus, one of a series of pen portraits in his imperial biographies that – even if not quite so intimate as the reports of some of their medical details – focus on the face, the body and the blemishes of Roman rulers. Caligula, he wrote, was 'tall, and very pale, with an ill-proportioned figure and extremely spindly neck and legs, his eyes and temples hollow ... his hair thin, and entirely bald on top'. Galba, Nero's immediate and very short-term successor, was 'completely bald, with blue eyes and a hooked nose' and had a nasty hernia that he could hardly hold in with a bandage. Otho, who briefly followed

Galba, wore a wig to disguise *his* thinning locks, so well fitting that no one suspected that it was not his real hair. Vespasian's expression made it look as if he was straining to relieve himself ('I'll tell you a joke when you've finished your shit', as a sharp talker once said to him). Domitian had a pot belly, thin legs and hardly any hair. He even wrote a book *On Care of the Hair*, including sections on how to come to terms with baldness. Sadly, it does not survive.

All this suggests that the appearance of Roman rulers was well known and well recorded. What is more, ancient writers give the impression that quite ordinary people often saw the emperor at close quarters, when across the empire they pressed their begging letters into his hand, bumped into him during his night-time antics in the streets of Rome, or in even more day-to-day situations. One story about Hadrian from the *Imperial History* imagines him mixing in with the average visitors to the public baths, all naked together. While he was there, he spotted a veteran soldier, whom he had known in the army, rubbing his back against the marble wall, and he asked why on earth the man was doing it. 'Because I don't own a slave to rub me down', was the reply. So the emperor gave him some slaves, plus money for their upkeep. Sometime later he was in the baths again, and he saw a whole group of old men all rubbing their backs on the marble. There was no gift this time. He told them that they should rub each other down.

The story is told specifically to illustrate the emperor's care for his subjects, combined with his down-to-earth, jocular common sense: he is generous; he does not fall for an obvious trick; nor does he punish the culprits with anything more than some wry wit at their expense. But there is more to it than that. It offers another instance of the callous parcelling up of 'humans-as-gifts', while also showing that Hadrian has the practical awareness that slaves cost money to house, clothe and feed. It gestures again to the role of the emperor as 'one of the lads' (he remembers the man from army days). But it also puts him right in the middle of the ordinary people, in the baths – where, according to the *Imperial History* 'he *often* bathed with everyone else'.

The idea that the emperor would get up close to his subjects was fundamental to his reputation, hence all the anecdotes and bon mots on that theme – most neatly summed up by the story of the ordinary woman who supposedly told Hadrian to his face to 'stop being emperor', if he didn't have time to listen to her. In general, there was a huge fanfare around his *accessibility*. But the reality could not possibly have matched the ideology. In practice, only a tiny proportion of the 60 million or so inhabitants of Italy and the empire could ever have seen the emperor in the flesh. We can only guess how often Hadrian visited the public baths, but I doubt that it was more than a few staged occasions, probably with some hefty bodyguards in attendance. And, although he was by far the most travelled emperor of them all, he would never have come within miles of the overwhelming majority of the empire's population. Even when Roman rulers showed up at the Circus Maximus, sitting in their prominent box, or maybe facing demonstrations from the crowd, they would have been visible to most of the audience only as tiny dots, one among hundreds of thousands of other spectators – too far away to spot any bald patches or gap teeth.

Images of power

Most of the empire's inhabitants would have seen the emperor in their dreams more often than in real life. I mean that literally. In a handbook on the meaning of dreams, written around 200 CE – one of those surprising technical treatises to survive from the ancient world, often overlooked among the 'classic' greats of poetry and philosophy – various case studies focus on dreaming about emperors. It could be a very bad sign (you are going to die), but some interpretations are more hopeful. We read of a man who dreamed that he had kicked 'the emperor' (no specific name is mentioned, just a generic 'emperor'). This meant, according to the handbook's author Artemidorus, that he was going to find, and tread on, a gold coin with the emperor's head. There is also the case of a man who dreamed that he was given two teeth from 'the emperor's' mouth. Whatever Freud would have made of it, for Artemidorus, it was another good sign. The interpretation offered is that in a single day he would win two legal cases that he was pleading.

But millions more people would never have known or recognised the emperor from his appearance in the flesh or in their sleep, only from the images of him and his family that once flooded the Roman empire. They came in every size and material, prominent statues decorating porticoes, public squares, courtrooms and temples, as well as smaller-scale versions in private homes across the empire. They could be found on the coinage, in marble, bronze, silver and very occasionally golden sculptures, in painted portraits, expensive cameos, pricey earrings, even in super-sized statues 30 or more metres tall. They were everywhere. Above all – leaving out of the count the literally millions of coins, precious miniatures and small pieces of bric-a-brac – many thousands of life-size portrait sculptures of them still survive, now lining museum walls around the world, and forming our own image of Roman rulers. After two millennia we still look these emperors in the eye, face to face.

There is not a single statue among them that looks remotely like any of the descriptions given by Suetonius. So, which is 'accurate', in the sense of offering a reliable guide to what any of these Roman rulers actually looked like? Frustratingly perhaps, my best guess is that neither are accurate in that way. The pen portraits tend to convince us rather too easily, because of their vivid individuality. But how far Suetonius could reliably have known about Augustus's teeth, or spots, is a big question. There is also a suspicious tendency in his biographies for the 'good' emperors to have fewer physical blemishes than the 'bad'

72. Tiberius to Alexander Severus. First row: Tiberius, Caligula,
Claudius, Nero. Second row: Vespasian, Titus, Domitian, Nerva.
Third row: Trajan, Hadrian, Antoninus Pius, Marcus Aurelius.
Fourth row: Lucius Verus, Commodus, Septimius Severus,
Caracalla. Fifth row: Elagabalus, Alexander Severus.

ones. The portraits in marble and bronze – or, for that matter, on coins – tell a quite different story. We may spot in them occasional touches of personal individuality. But those are few. If Domitian's thinning locks were so famous that he actually wrote a book on the subject, you would never guess that from his surviving portraits, in which he appears to have an ample head of hair (fig. 7). Instead, these are carefully constructed images of power, devised to represent *the emperor* as much as any individual man on the throne, and sometimes, as we

73. A statue of the English King George I, in the full kit of a Roman emperor; a sculpture by Michael Rysbrack, 1739.

shall see, literally to stand in for him. They were meant to spread the imperial face around the whole of the Roman world, like never before.

These official images of Roman emperors can seem rather bland and stale, one head or lookalike body after another, the stereotype of a decidedly unexciting version of classicism. Many people now walk quickly past them. But the apparent blandness is partly a consequence of the emperors' success in establishing this visual language of power, which outlived the Roman empire itself by many centuries, and to which we are still the heirs. There has scarcely been a dictator or dynast in the history of the West who has not occasionally borrowed – to trumpet his own position – the images that the Roman emperors invented for themselves. We tend to take them for granted. But to those who watched these images appearing in public places and in their purses at the end of the first century BCE, they would have seemed revolutionary. Far from a dreary stereotype, this would have been 'the shock of the new'.

The sculptural revolution

This imperial revolution in image making – and image spreading – goes back ultimately to Julius Caesar, at the very start of one-man rule. He was not only the first living Roman to have his head displayed on coins minted in the city, and so to break with the old Republican tradition that allowed only gods, mythical heroes and the long dead onto the coinage. But according to Cassius Dio, there were also grandiose plans to place his statue throughout the cities of the empire and in every temple in Rome. Even if Dio, writing over two hundred years later, was exaggerating, it does look as if there was a novel scheme – backed, if not devised, by the man himself – to make Caesar visible throughout the Roman world. More than twenty pedestals have indeed survived, from modern Turkey to ancient Gaul, with inscriptions to show that

74. This is currently the favourite candidate for an authentic portrait of Julius Caesar, sculpted in his lifetime. It was discovered in 2007 in the river Rhône, near Arles in France, to a great fanfare. The only evidence for its identification is its supposed similarity to Caesar's portraits on coins (fig. 9).

they once held a statue of him, erected during his lifetime. But he was assassinated before any such plans could be completed, and no contemporary portrait sculpture of him has ever been conclusively identified. There have been any number of optimistic claims, pin-pointing this statue or that as the authentic face of Julius Caesar (even some of the most hard-headed archaeologists seem to want to gaze into the eyes of the dictator). It is actually only the tiny face on some coins of 44 BCE that we can be absolutely sure is meant to be him.

It was his successor who, over a reign of forty-five years, had a chance to put Caesar's plans into practice. In Italy and right across the Roman world, around two hundred sculpted heads, busts or full-length statues have been discovered, now more or less firmly identified as Augustus. They are almost never found with names attached (they have long been separated from the pedestals that probably did identify them) and it is not always certain whether a sculpture is intended to represent Augustus himself, or one of his heirs, or some local bigwig aping the imperial 'look'. But after a couple of centuries of painstaking archaeological work – comparing the various portraits both to the tiny images on coins, which *are* named, and to each other – the disputed pieces are now relatively few.

What is particularly striking is that sculptures of the emperor that were once on display in different parts of the empire, hundreds or thousands of miles apart, often reveal minute similarities in design, even down to the precise layout of the locks of the hair. That itself is a strong clue to how they were produced. Many must actually have been made locally, in different parts of the world, as they were carved in the local stone. But – in order to end up being *so* similar to each other – it

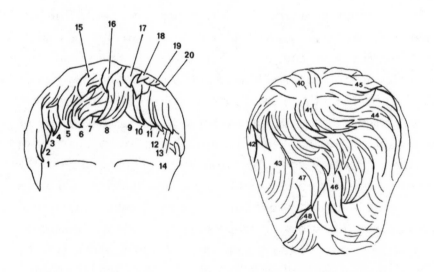

75. Portraits going back to the same model have often been identified by a detailed comparison of the arrangement of the locks of hair. This is a diagram of the 'lock-scheme' of the statue of Augustus found at Livia's villa (pl. 15).

is all but certain that they were based on models, in wax, clay or plaster, sent out from the centre as 'the official image' of Augustus. There is no other plausible way to explain it. But how exactly that process was organised is a puzzle. It is one of those cases where the working of the palace administration, despite the rich information we have on other parts of it, is completely obscure. We cannot begin to see who was directing this operation, who was making what we might call the 'propaganda' decisions, still less who was making the models or the sculptures themselves. Even though they were part of one of the most significant moments of artistic change in the history of the world, we cannot name a single sculptor of any of the marble and bronze portraits of Augustus that have survived. This was nothing like the world of the prominent artist and patron-monarch – of Holbein and Henry VIII, or of Titian and Philip II of Spain. It is much more anonymous, much more behind closed doors.

Nor can we be sure what proportion of the original number of portraits those two hundred or so surviving pieces were. The best (admittedly very wide) guess, that by the time of Augustus's death in 14 CE between 25,000 and 50,000 such images of him were on display, gives some idea of the scale. Wherever in the empire you lived – never mind his image on the coins in your pocket – you would have been brought face to face with Augustus, life-size in marble, bronze or even silver, in your local town. This is where it is hard not to think of a modern dictator, peering down from every billboard. In much the same way, even before printing and posters, Augustus was unavoidable.

But the revolution was not just in quantity. Augustus, or whoever was advising him, also inaugurated an entirely new *style* of Roman portraiture, to match some of his more strictly political changes. The elite of the Republic had tended to adopt a 'warts and all' idiom in portraiture: haggard, wrinkled and elderly. Whether this was an accurate representation of them or not (and we have no way of checking), it traded on the power of seniority and authority. Augustus changed

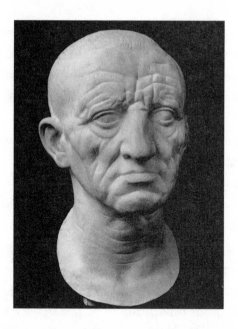

76. The wrinkles, sunken cheeks and craggy features of this portrait are characteristic of the style of the early first century BCE. It was, no doubt, as much a 'rhetoric of power' as the later youthful and 'classicising' images of emperors (we do not need to assume that these were actually taken from life). But one of the most striking aspects of the portraits of Augustus is that they were *not like this*.

all that. His own image looked back to the idealising traditions of fifth-century BCE Greek sculpture. In his full-length statues, he was portrayed with an ideal classical body, in a limited number of poses (standing in a toga or in armour, or occasionally on horseback). His head was an equally ideal and youthful creation, which remained so over the more than four decades of his reign. He looked the same in his sculptures when he was aged thirty as he did when he was seventy. There is often something of that age gap in portraits of power. Queen Elizabeth II, for example, did not get older on the coinage with the same speed as she did in real life. But in Augustus's case, the disjunction is unusually glaring.

There was, in other words, hardly a trace of conventional 'realism' here. It is quite possible that Augustus never 'sat' for his portrait as modern monarchs do, and as a few ancient rulers did too (Alexander the Great, for one, had his own favourite portrait artist). It is also quite possible that his statues would have been a badly misleading guide to recognising the man in the flesh. This was, instead, a style of *political realism* that captured the emperor's new deal in Rome, his break with the past, and that almost impossible combination of being both *princeps* ('leader') and 'one of us'. No Roman had ever been represented like this before – and no emperor ever actually looked like this.

The image of Augustus, with its roots in what Julius Caesar had started, provided the pattern for portraits of Roman emperors for centuries after. In every reign except perhaps the very shortest (and even short-reigning emperors could be quick off the mark), we can detect the same process of the replication of their statues. Even though there are rather more contested identities in later periods, we can still count one hundred and fifty or so surviving busts and full-length figures of Hadrian, the second highest total for anyone after Augustus, and perhaps as many as one hundred of his boyfriend Antinous, who ranks third. Many of these were part of a campaign from the centre to spread the image of the ruler across the empire, or, in the case of Antinous, the consequence of Hadrian's personal desire to commemorate his lover. Others were very likely the result of local initiatives, by communities keen to show their loyalty, and to display the emperor in *their* town. But even in those cases, some kind of authorised design was involved. The community presumably asked permission to put up the statue, and received the official model in return. Or that was what was supposed to happen. A friend of Hadrian once wrote to the emperor to warn him that a statue at Trapezus (modern Trabzon on the Black Sea) did not 'look like him' and that a replacement should be sent out. I suspect he meant that it did not look like the official image, not that it did not resemble the man himself. The implication was that Trapezus had 'gone it alone', with an unofficial design of their own.

There were also aspects of the style established under Augustus that never changed between the end of the first century BCE and the beginning of the third century CE. In free-standing sculpture, the form of the emperor's body is always more or less identical. All rulers are depicted with the same perfectly proportioned figure, in the same limited range of costume and poses, whether in a toga or battle dress, or occasionally nude or half-nude, like the mythical heroes or divine figures of classical Greek art. Unlike the images of the corpulent Henry VIII of England, or the increasingly plump Queen Victoria, there is no gesture towards individuality or distinguishing features, and certainly no pot bellies.

77. & 78. Two of the standard templates for representing the emperor's body: on the left, a perfectly (almost) nude Lucius Verus; on the right, a toga-clad Tiberius. For the military alternative, see fig. 67.

There is, it is true, a wider range of poses on sculpted relief panels, as when we see Trajan in the company of his soldiers or Hadrian at the hunt, but the dress and underlying figure type hardly deviate. There are also some slight shifts over time: more battle dress and fewer togas in the second century CE than in the first. But essentially what is on display is the body of '*the* emperor', not of any individual ruler. This is partly what makes them seem at first glance so much one and the same. It *is* the same body – with just a different head.

Augustus's principle of agelessness was more or less unbroken too. Emperors do not get obviously older in their portraits. Except in a few cases where we may have images of emperors as children, though these are hard to pin down, Roman rulers remained forever at the age they were represented when they came to the throne, or indeed younger. Even the elderly Nerva, who was sixty-five when he succeeded Domitian in 96 CE, has barely a wrinkle. It is almost the inverse of Oscar Wilde's *Picture of Dorian Gray*, his story of a portrait that visibly ages while its subject stays forever young. Roman emperors, by contrast, physically aged, while the portraits remained impossibly youthful.

Yet in some details of the faces themselves, and, intriguingly, of their facial hair, there is a rather more complicated and changing story. It raises the question of how we tell one emperor's statue from another, and in some cases whether we are even meant to.

Identity parade

The emperors' portraits were not about individuals in the way we would now expect. No matter how carefully we examine them, they tell us nothing about the particular ruler's character, or even what the sculptor was trying to say about him as a person. There are no hints of villainy, perversion or of any kind of virtue beyond the political. As often, though, taking the emperors together rather than individually can be much more revealing. The line-up on page 329 shows at a glance the heads of all but the shortest reigning emperors between Tiberius (who came to the throne in 14 CE) and Alexander Severus (assassinated in 235). What do the visual similarities and differences between them tell us?

Most importantly they take us back to some of the issues surrounding succession and the transmission of power from one ruler to the next. Even the thumbnail images make it clear that one way to establish the chosen heir as the one-and-only legitimate successor was to make him *look* like the man he was to succeed. And one useful tactic for a new emperor, in asserting his claim to the throne, was to be represented as the spitting image of his predecessor, as if in a seamless transition of power from one lookalike to another. There was room for

79. Mistaken identities? This portrait in the British Museum reflects the typical features of Julio-Claudian emperors and heirs, but exactly which one is anybody's guess.

the odd touch of individuality, to be sure, and the paint that was originally applied to many of these portraits probably contributed to that. But as a general principle, emperors were made to imitate the man who gave them the right to rule. Those in the first century CE who based their position on their close links to Augustus – whether by adoption, in the case of Tiberius, or through descent from Augustus's natural daughter, in the case of Caligula – copied his features in their public portraits. Later in the second century CE, the run of adopted emperors who followed Hadrian all look much like their adopted father and predecessor. It hardly comes as a surprise, for example, that the public image of Septimius Severus was modelled on that of Marcus Aurelius, to whom, by one of those imperial sleights of hand, Septimius had retrospectively invented his own adoption.

This is another factor that helps explain the 'one-emperor-looks-much-like-another' reaction that many people have. The truth is that they often do look very similar. It is only a few experts who can now distinguish (or think they can distinguish) some of the portraits of those adoptive emperors in the second century CE. And even experts disagree on some notorious cases. One marble head, now in the British Museum, has been named variously as Augustus, Caligula and two of Augustus's chosen heirs who died young, Gaius and Lucius Caesar. Another in the Vatican has been put down as Augustus, Caligula, Nero and the same young Gaius Caesar. Perhaps that was part of the point, and – despite the best efforts of archaeologists to tell one from another – the intention all along was to blur the images of the founding father and his successors and potential successors. 'Indistinguishability' could be a useful weapon.

Or sometimes precisely the reverse. One of the basic tools for distancing an emperor from the legacy of his predecessor, after an assassination, for example, or civil war, was to construct an image of him that looked completely different. A textbook case of this was the official image of Vespasian, who came to power in 69 CE, as the final

80. Vespasian paraded his traditional, old-fashioned Italian
stock. This portrait, from the second half of the first century CE,
echoes the earlier Republican style, suggesting a return to the
values of the past – in contrast to the excesses of Nero.

victor in the conflicts that followed the fall of Nero. In almost every
respect Vespasian made a point of setting himself apart from Nero,
and of exploiting (and partly, no doubt, creating) the stereotype of
his predecessor as a luxury-loving, megalomaniac spendthrift. The
construction of the Colosseum, as a place of public entertainment,
on the site of the Golden House, Nero's private pleasure palace, was
only one example of that. Significantly, Vespasian's portraits, wrinkled
and definitely a bit thinning on top, revert almost to the 'warts and
all' style of the old Republic. This is one imperial image in which it is
easy to imagine that we are being given a hint of Vespasian's character as a down-to-earth kind of bloke. But whatever he actually looked
like, whatever the lavatorial jokes about his appearance, there is no
reason to suppose these images are realistic. Their 'down-to-earthness'

is more part of their political message than any character insight. 'The new man in charge is nothing like Nero,' they tell you. 'He is an upholder of traditional, no-nonsense, old-fashioned values.'

There is, however, an even more obvious change in this line-up of imperial faces. In 117 CE, at the accession of Hadrian, and after one hundred and fifty years of emperors and their heirs being represented clean-shaven, they start to be portrayed with full, sometimes luxuriant, beards (often exquisitely rendered in what must count as a flamboyant triumph of sculptural technique, almost for its own sake). Even the teenaged Elagabalus and Alexander Severus are sometimes shown with more whiskers than their youth would have suggested.

On the logic just laid out, we might have expected Hadrian's portraits to have closely followed those of Trajan, his adoptive father – especially in what had been an uncomfortably awkward succession. So, why the sudden change? There is no sign that this simply reflected a wider shift in fashion for elite men. Was it, then, a rare case of an aspect of the emperor's personal appearance featuring in his portraits – and then catching on? That is what the author of the *Imperial History* seems to imply when he rather desperately claims that Hadrian adopted a beard to cover up his spots. Or was something bigger at stake in creating this new face of power? Some modern historians have suggested that, decades before Marcus Aurelius became known for his philosophical interests, Hadrian was already parading an image of 'emperor as philosopher' or 'emperor as lover of Greece', with a 'Greek-style' beard. Maybe. But it has proved hard to identify any distinctively Greek prototype on which he was drawing, not to mention the difficulty of aligning the supposedly 'philosophically inspired' heads with all the heavily armed and cuirassed imperial bodies on which they so often sat. In the end, this change remains another of those mysteries of imperial art and culture. But it is, at least, a useful guide for those wanting help in distinguishing one adult emperor's head from another. If he is clean-shaven, you can be confident that he belongs somewhere between the start of one-man rule and the emperor Trajan. If he has a beard, he is either Hadrian himself, or one of his successors over the next hundred years or so. Even well into the fourth century CE, most sported facial hair – although on these later ones it was usually less bushy.

What about the women?

The portraits of the women in the imperial family were even more revolutionary than those of the men. This was not just because they too were produced in very large numbers, even if not on quite the same scale as the emperors themselves (some ninety surviving sculptural portraits of Livia, for example, compared with the two hundred or so of her husband Augustus). More to the point, this was the first time that any portraits of women had been regularly and publicly displayed in Italy (though there were some earlier examples in the Eastern Mediterranean). If you had walked around the city of Rome in the 50s BCE, you would hardly have seen the image of a woman who was not a goddess or mythical heroine. A hundred years later you could not have avoided seeing statues of the emperor's female relatives. The visual world had been transformed.

The line-up on page 344 shows some of the most prominent women in the imperial family between Livia, the wife of Augustus, and Julia Domna, the wife of Septimius Severus. Once again, for the puzzled museum visitor, hair – on the head this time – is a key pointer to the date, and so to the identity, of the statues. The relatively undemonstrative styles of the women in the court of Augustus and his immediate successors were replaced towards the end of the first century CE by elaborate topknots, of curls upon curls. This was a clear marker of aristocratic privilege (no one could have done any manual labour with such a pile on their heads) and – assuming the portraits reflected the real-life hairstyles of these women rather than being mere sculptural

81. Empress of Rome. Top row: Livia, wife of Augustus and mother of Tiberius; Agrippina the Younger, wife of Claudius and mother of Nero. Middle row: Domitia Longa, wife of Domitian; Plotina, wife of Trajan. Bottom row: Faustina the Younger, wife of Marcus Aurelius and mother of Commodus; Julia Domna, wife of Septimius Severus and mother of Caracalla and Geta.

bravura – the whole coiffure must have been enhanced by some ancient equivalent of hair extensions. A century later, after rather more modest styles in the first part of the second century, portraits of Julia Domna regularly depicted her wearing a wig. This was not intended as disguise, or to be mistaken for her own hair. In fact, some of the sculptures positively draw attention to its artificiality by showing wisps of 'natural' hair (in marble) escaping from beneath it. It was as if, now, the very artistry of false hair could be a sign of status.

But hairstyle alone does not make an empress. Predictably perhaps, it has proved harder to attach a name to these portraits than to those of the men. The similarities between some of the statues found in different parts of the Roman world suggest that they too depended on models sent out from the centre. There was also an element of 'succession politics' in how they were represented. Just as Septimius Severus was carefully likened to Marcus Aurelius in his portraits, so too the images of his wife Julia Domna were sometimes made to match those of Marcus Aurelius's wife, Faustina. Occasionally, the features of the women of the family even seem to have been modelled on those of the relevant emperor, as if to underline the point that their public status depended on his. But the fact that there are fewer of them to compare and contrast, fewer images on coins, and nothing in Suetonius (who didn't bother to describe the women), means that the identifications are far less certain. There is a good chance that some of those portrayed with a lavish topknot, currently assumed to be a female relative of a late first-century CE emperor, whether Titus or Domitian (take your pick), should really be labelled 'Unknown Roman Woman', with the same fashionable hairstyle.

This problem of identification is vividly illustrated by three ladies in marble, excavated at the small Roman town of Veleia in north Italy. The inscribed pedestals on which the statues once stood were found nearby, making it clear that they represented Livia, Agrippina the Elder (the mother of Caligula) and her daughter Agrippina the

82. A line-up of almost identikit images of Livia, Agrippina the Elder and the Younger from a group of thirteen statues of emperors and their families, discovered in Veleia, in northern Italy in the eighteenth century.

Younger (the wife of Claudius and mother of Nero). But even with that clue, it is impossible to work out which is which. They look more or less identical. Maybe the message was that one imperial wife or mother was much like another. Whatever the gossip about women's malevolent scheming or subversive sexuality, and the dark portrayal of some of them in ancient literature, in public sculpture at least they are largely presented as a line-up of dutiful mothers, wives and daughters, each playing the same role, adopting much the same stance and dress. It is almost as if their official image was designed not only as a symbol

83. A slightly larger than life-size statue of Messalina, as perfect mother, made in Rome in the middle of the first century CE. The design was pointedly based on a Greek sculpture of the early fourth century BCE, by Cephisodotus, showing the goddess of Peace cradling her son 'Wealth'.

of the women's part in the survival of the dynasty, but directly to counteract some of the scurrilous stories. One notable statue, depicting almost certainly Messalina, the allegedly adulterous, sex-crazed wife of the emperor Claudius, shows her cradling her son Britannicus in her arms, in a pose based on an earlier Greek statue of the benign goddess of Peace. 'No trouble here', was the message.

It is only very occasionally that we find an image of an imperial woman that appears – at least at first sight – to break the generic mould and to challenge the usual safe domestic stereotypes. One of

84. One of the panels from probably the most important discovery of
Roman sculpture of the last hundred years – once decorating a precinct in
honour of the Roman emperors at Aphrodisias in modern Turkey (fig. 51).
Agrippina crowns her son Nero, who came to the throne in 54 CE (within
a few years, he would have her put to death). Here the new emperor has
taken off his military helmet (it sits at his feet) to allow the crowning.

the boldest of these is another version of Agrippina the Younger, on a
large sculpted panel found at the ancient town of Aphrodisias in what
is now Turkey. Here it is not so much a question of how she looks, but
what she is depicted doing. For she is shown in the act of crowning
her son Nero with a laurel wreath, as if she were actually investing him
with imperial power.

The panel came to light among the remains of a temple and attached
portico, erected by some local Aphrodisian grandees in the middle of
the first century CE to celebrate the Roman emperors, and was rediscovered by archaeologists in excavations between 1979 and 1984. The

building complex was covered with dozens of sculpted panels and other free-standing figures. Where exactly the local designers found their inspiration for this ambitious sculptural project, and how much input there was from central Roman models, we cannot be sure. But the sixty or so sculptures that survive more or less complete – some still linked with their inscribed titles, making the identification of the characters certain – count as one of the largest and most important discoveries of Roman art in the twentieth century. There are some monumental personifications of the peoples and places of the Roman world, from the Dacians to Crete, and a veritable anthology of recognisable, and not so recognisable, themes from Greco-Roman myth, including the Roman founding hero Aeneas rescuing his father from

85. Among the sculptures of Aphrodisias is the earliest representation of Britannia, as a victim of the emperor Claudius. The province, portrayed as a vulnerable woman, is trampled (or worse) by the victorious emperor (pp. 313–14).

Troy; the god Zeus, in the form of a swan, assaulting the Spartan princess, Leda; and a trio of anonymous, naked heroes mysteriously patting a dog. Also prominent is a series of scenes featuring emperors and their families, drawn from the history, and symbols, of one-man rule at Rome.

Among these is one panel with Augustus standing victorious over a bound captive, not far from a scantily clad Claudius 'heroically' defeating Britannia, and Nero slaughtering the kingdom of Armenia, in the form of an almost completely naked woman. Armenia was another of those 'signature conquests' or 'vanity projects', which on this occasion, despite the 'hands-on' image of the sculpted panel, delivered

86. A smaller panel than the crowning scene from Aphrodisias (fig. 84) – this is less than a metre square. But the basic idea is the same: Caracalla's mother, Julia Domna, in the guise of the goddess of Victory crowns her son (a military trophy stands next to him, with two captives crouching underneath). Now in the National Museum of Warsaw, it probably originally came from Syria.

military glory to the emperor without any direct involvement whatsoever, on his part, in the campaign. The 'coronation scene', in which Agrippina literally crowns her son, is no closer to reality than that. No such ceremony ever took place in real life. Roman emperors were not literally crowned. Symbolically, however, this image seems to repeat, in unabashed visual terms, the claim made by some Roman writers that Nero owed his elevation to the machinations of his mother. It is echoed in a few other works of art. In one cameo, for example, Agrippina again crowns her son. And in another sculpted panel, a century and a half later, Julia Domna does the same for Caracalla.

It is very tempting to see these images as a rare experiment in representing a more active version of women's authority within the imperial family and in the processes of succession. Do we, for once, have a daring parade of female political power and agency that runs counter to the usual visual stereotypes? I would like to think so, but I am not so sure.

It makes a huge difference that in each of these images the empresses are shown with the attributes of goddesses: Agrippina both at Aphrodisias and on the cameo is depicted holding the trademark cornucopia ('horn of plenty') of the goddess Tyche, or 'Good Fortune' (though the figure may also evoke the goddess Ceres, the protector of crops and produce); Julia Domna is shown in the guise of the goddess Victory. It was not unusual for imperial figures, especially but not only the women, to be depicted with the symbols of divinity. In part, this clothed them with an aura of sanctity, distinguishing them from ordinary mortals, and it fitted with a wider pattern of presenting the role of the emperor in divine terms (as we shall explore in the next chapter). But it was often much trickier than it seems. In the case of one over-life-size statue of the emperor Claudius, half-clad as Jupiter, and including the god's eagle nuzzling at his knee, it came at the cost of making the emperor look, frankly, a bit silly. In the case of Agrippina and Julia Domna, the divine attributes fudge the question of where – in the hybrid of empress and goddess – the real power lies. From one perspective, at least, the goddess not only overshadows the empress but actively obscures any idea of her authority. This was not a real woman (with some attributes of a goddess) crowning her son, so much as a goddess (with some attributes of a real woman) validating the emperor's right to rule. The divine image was not *boosting* the power of the empress. It was *burying* it.

87. A statue 2.5 metres tall, from the town of Lanuvium near Rome, showing the emperor Claudius as Jupiter. The symbol of the god, the eagle, is at his feet. He may originally have held a thunderbolt in his right hand (the libation bowl is an incorrect modern restoration). His oak wreath straddles the boundary between divine and human: oak is a tree associated with Jupiter, but the oak crown was awarded to soldiers for bravery in battle.

Variations on a theme

The standard modern image of Roman emperors and their families is defined by all those – once revolutionary, now taken for granted – life-size bronze or marble statues, and by countless imperial heads on coins from all over the empire. They were crucial in defining the image of the emperor in antiquity too, and summing up in visual form the politics of one-man rule. But they were not the whole story. Across the Roman world, images of emperors did not just stand in public squares and porticoes. They decorated people's homes, filled their crockery cupboards, and adorned their clothing and their jewellery, at different prices to suit almost any pocket. In modern studies, these have rarely had the same share of attention as the grand imperial sculptures. To be honest, only a handful have much artistic quality, and many of them now remain out of sight in museum stores and basements. But if we bring them back into the picture, we get a more varied and colourful impression of *how* the emperor might be seen (and imagined) in the Roman world, *where* and *at what scale.*

At the top of the range – and some of these certainly do count as masterpieces – were exquisite and expensive cameos and gems, shamelessly parading the imperial family in miniature, from whole dynastic groups to key individuals (pls. 5 and 17). Many of these must have been commissioned by and for the emperor himself (who else would have had the money?). They were no doubt intended to decorate imperial residences, to grace palace banqueting tables, or to be presented as gifts to special friends or influential foreign delegations. A little way down the pecking order, pricey silver vessels displayed the ruler in the homes of the elite in Italy (fig. 12). But perhaps more immediately appealing to us are some of the humbler objects, like those pastry moulds that put the emperor straight into the mouths of his subjects (fig. 3).

Tiny portraits of rulers and their relations were used to decorate

88. A selection of cheap decorations featuring Roman emperors: on the left, a finger ring incorporating a coin of Caracalla; below, a glass medallion, with the face of (probably) Tiberius, and two younger members of the imperial family to either side; and on the right, the centre of a ceramic bowl, showing Augustus with a ceremonial, priestly staff.

cheap pottery lamps, soldiers' armour, mirrors and sundials, and were stamped onto ordinary furniture. As well as the Septimius Severus-branded earrings (fig. 4), Antoninus Pius's wife Faustina (the mother of the Faustina who was married to Marcus Aurelius) features on a tiny gold plaque, once the prize possession of an inhabitant of Roman Colchester in southern Britain, while the 'heads' of imperial coins – Domitian, Trajan, Caracalla, Alexander Severus and many more – were regularly inserted, as the centrepiece, into unassuming finger rings. The imperial family even put in an appearance on the gaming table: the head of Augustus's wife Livia, among others, provided the design for cheap gambling tokens, used in ancient board games.

In modern terms, this was a world not only of official 'image management', but of the emperor's face on the ancient equivalent of fridge magnets, mass-produced mugs and tote bags, making him part of the domestic, day-to-day routine. Unlike some royal souvenirs now, these images cannot possibly have been spread from the centre, with a uniform design, as many, or most, of the public portraits in bronze or marble were. The imperial administration had neither the manpower nor the will to control how the emperor appeared in ordinary homes. They can only have been the result of local initiative, produced by small-scale businessmen with an eye to a profitable trade (people must actually have wanted to buy these things), and indirectly based – second- or third-hand, copies of copies of copies – on the central model. That is, after all, how we can still recognise them. There were almost certainly more of them around than we can spot today, because, like the 'portrait' that Hadrian's friend saw in Trapezus, they were more or less completely independent of the official types. Wherever you were, there was nothing in the end to stop you inventing the image of the emperor for yourself.

That is exactly what we can see happening in Roman Egypt, not in private homes but in the decoration of public temples. Egypt was the Roman province with the longest history of all, attracting Hadrian and other emperors as heritage tourists on their trips up the Nile. But who would have guessed that plate 21 shows one of only a handful of large-scale portraits of the emperor Augustus to be found anywhere in the Roman world that are explicitly identified as such. Carved on the façades of Egyptian temples of Augustan date, these show the emperor as an ancient pharaoh making offerings to local Egyptian gods. His name – without which we would never recognise him – is inscribed variously as 'Caesar', 'Emperor' or 'Pharaoh' in hieroglyphs alongside. Some later emperors were represented in Egypt in the same way, including Claudius, Nero, Trajan and Caracalla.

There is no reason to suppose that emperors ever actually dressed up in pharaonic costume. These carvings could have been an attempt by Roman rulers to conscript for themselves the power of the pharaoh. More likely they were an attempt by Egyptians to recreate an image of the Roman emperor on their own traditional terms. Whatever the explanation, it shows just how flexible the image of the emperor could be. If the majority of the inhabitants of the empire would have imagined their ruler in battle dress or a toga, there were also some who would have pictured him naked to the waist, wearing the traditional 'double crown' of Upper and Lower Egypt and an Egyptian kilt or shendyt.

The variety of emperors in art extends even further if we take into account those images that have been lost. I do not mean random losses, but whole categories of images that have disappeared because of the fragility (or reusability) of the material in which they were made. Breakable glass would be an obvious example of that. Likewise, the relatively small number of bronze statues, compared to marble, is mostly a consequence of how easy it was to melt down the metal and turn it into something else. The famous bronze of Marcus Aurelius on horseback, which has been continuously on public display in Rome since it was made in the 170s CE, was probably saved because it was wrongly identified in the Middle Ages (fig. 44). It was thought then to be the emperor Constantine, of the early fourth century CE, the first officially Christian Roman ruler – a serendipitous misidentification that probably frightened off Christian scrap-metal merchants and recyclers. But in the whole of the history of ancient art the rich tradition of portable painting is the biggest loss. Painting was as distinguished and prominent an art form as sculpture in the Roman world. But you would never guess that from the small amount that survives. It is the portraits of emperors painted on wood and linen that constitute the most misleading gap in our record.

These were once everywhere. In the 140s CE, for example, Fronto wrote to his then pupil, Marcus Aurelius, to say that he saw Marcus's paintings (though it could be his painted statues) all over the city, 'in booths and shops, in colonnades, entrance-ways and in windows'. They were very badly done, he joked rather snobbishly, by artists with no talent, but nevertheless he always gave a little kiss when he saw them (or, to follow another version of the uncertain Latin here, and adding to the patronising tone, 'they always make me giggle'). At the upper end of the market, Pliny's uncle mentions in his encyclopaedia a painting that must have been commissioned by the emperor himself: an oversized portrait, 35 metres tall, of Nero on linen, displayed in one of the imperial *horti*, on the edges of Rome. There are also plenty of references to paintings of the imperial family being carried in religious processions and displayed on military standards, or lodged in temples. And they were used to transmit some pointed imperial messages. So, for example, before he arrived in Rome after his succession, Elagabalus is supposed to have sent ahead a large painting of himself, in his full eastern priestly regalia, to hang prominently in the senate house and get the senators accustomed to his unusual costume. There must once have been as many emperors in paint as in marble.

Only one single example has survived (pl. 3). It is a small circular wooden panel about 30 centimetres across, carrying the recognisable portraits of Septimius Severus, his wife Julia Domna (spot the hairstyle) and their son Caracalla, as well as an obliterated image of a figure who was presumably his younger brother, Geta. Now in Berlin, the panel has a complicated history. It must have been preserved in the dry climatic conditions of Egypt. But how or where exactly it was discovered – before it turned up on the antiquities market in the twentieth century – is a mystery. It seems to have been cut down from a larger painting, which *may* have come from an Egyptian temple, *may* be mentioned in a surviving inventory on papyrus of temple possessions, and *may* have been commissioned locally to mark a visit to Egypt by the imperial family around 200 CE.

Whatever the story (and the '*mays*' are crucial), most historians have tended, somewhat perversely, to be more interested in the face that has been removed than in the three portraits that remain. What we still see is much more luscious than most statues, with lavish golden wreaths on the men, and what look like pearls in Julia Domna's jewellery – and in contrast to the ever-youthful appearance of the sculpture, there are traces of grey hair on the emperor himself (though this kind of feature might originally have been painted onto marble portraits). But with just a single example it is hard to draw many conclusions, even on the quality of the artwork. One art historian has recently called this painting 'relatively crude', another has hyped it, less plausibly, as a 'masterpiece' of 'exceptional quality'.

Gigantic size could destroy an image too. Hard as they are to picture now, enormous statues of Roman rulers and their family members, sometimes ten or fifteen times life-size, were once a common feature of cities across the empire – and they are another major loss. These giant works of art have been a victim of their own construction techniques. It would have been almost impossible to sculpt anything truly colossal entirely out of marble and, even if you could, it would have been far too heavy to stand up. Michelangelo's *David*, at just over 5 metres tall, a minnow in Roman terms, approaches the limit of what is feasible in solid stone, at least for a free-standing figure (seated ones are easier). In the face of this, one Roman solution was to use an engineered frame construction: a wooden or brick skeleton built to the desired size to form the body, then 'clothed' with thin sheets of metal, and perhaps replaceable fabric, and only the extremities carved in stone and then attached to the frame. These extremities are all that now survive, the remains of their faces, or fragments of feet and hands that sometimes look little more than great lumps of stone, giving hardly any idea of how impressive or intimidating the original might have appeared.

The other solution was to use hollow-cast bronze, which was lighter and more flexible, and was the material of choice for the most celebrated of these statues. This is how the most famous Roman colossus of all was constructed, the gilded bronze statue of the nude Nero that originally stood in the vestibule of his Golden House, and – if it really did reach over 35 metres – was roughly three quarters of the height of Trajan's column. But statues of this type were invariably melted down later and recycled, and so have left even less behind than the engineered versions. To get any sense of the impact of these enormous creations, we rely on what Roman writers tell us.

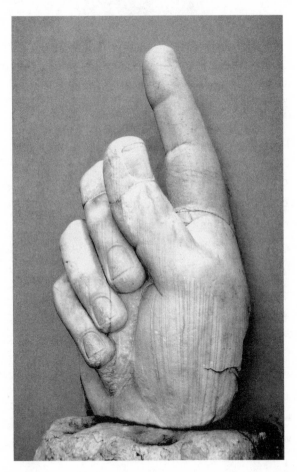

89. A many-times life-size hand of the emperor Constantine, of the early fourth century CE. One of the surviving marble extremities of a statue of the emperor (we also have the feet and head), constructed on a wood and brick frame, originally depicted seated, at a height of more than 12 metres.

90. A tiny amethyst gem, of the late first century or early second century CE, bravely trying to depict the colossal statue of Nero. It is just possible to make out here that the nude emperor was shown wearing a crown, and his right arm was supported by (as we know from other sources) a rudder.

The poet Statius is one vivid witness, in more than a hundred lines of verse devoted to a colossal bronze statue of Domitian on horseback that was erected in the centre of the old Roman Forum around 90 CE. The monument was officially commissioned by the senate to celebrate whatever victory over the Germans the emperor was supposed to have won (or not). To judge from the likely traces of its 'footprint' discovered in excavations, it would have stood about 18 metres high, including the pedestal. The poet is predictably hyperbolic. Domitian, he writes, shines above the temples that surround him, his head reaching into the pure clear air. In his left hand he holds a statue of the goddess Minerva, goddess of wisdom and of war ('no sweeter resting place did the goddess ever choose'), and the brazen hoof of his horse tramples underfoot an image of the river Rhine, captured and bound. The statue will stand, he predicts, 'so long as the earth and heavens' endure.

Since antiquity (and the Renaissance), reinforced concrete has dramatically changed the scale of what is possible. The tallest statue in the world now, in Gujarat, is over 180 metres high, depicting an Indian lawyer and politician, and there are dozens more (many of them images of the Buddha) that would dwarf the colossal image of Nero, let alone that of Domitian at a mere 18 metres. But that super-sized Nero still keeps its place in the top ten tallest statues of 'ordinary' human beings ever made. As Statius reminds us – far from the real-life scale of the statues we see in museums and galleries – many Romans would have had occasion to *look up*, a very long way, to images of their emperors.

Statue Wars

Statius's prediction that the colossal statue of Domitian would last for ever was drastically wrong. Within just a few years it had disappeared without trace, except for some archaeological marks of its footing under the surface of the Forum. Writing during the emperor's lifetime, Statius had already hinted – alongside the praise – at some anxieties about this intrusion into the civic space of the city. The statue had almost gobbled up the Forum with its vast mass, he conceded. The ground itself gasped because of the weight it had to sustain. And the poet's comparison of the statue with the mythical Trojan horse, the ruse used by the Greeks to capture the city of Troy, seems double-edged. Quite how far was Domitian's horse a danger to the city of Rome? Whatever the answer, it is easy to understand why such an aggressive image of an assassinated ruler would not long survive his overthrow.

Like so many aspects of one-man rule at Rome, statues involved some tricky balancing acts. Augustus might have cleverly constructed an image that combined citizenly equality with almost superhuman perfection, but visual expressions of power could easily be taken for expressions of megalomania. Statues in precious metals were one obvious example of that. These were not uncommon, but they were always risky – and many did not last long. An emperor could gain as much kudos from melting them down as from putting them up. Augustus had already seen the reputational danger of statues in silver, as a signal of excess, when he boasted in *What I Did* of destroying around eighty of them depicting himself (presumably donated by others) and using the profits to make gifts to the god Apollo. Marcus Aurelius and Lucius Verus followed the same logic when, as a surviving inscription records, they refused to allow old and battered silver statues of emperors in Ephesus to be recycled into images of themselves.

There was something of the same danger in colossal size. To represent the emperor on such a superhuman scale risked puncturing any myth that he was 'one of us'. Some got away with it. There are passing references to colossal figures of Augustus in Rome, and to a group of cities from the Eastern Mediterranean commissioning a vast statue of Tiberius in the centre of the city, in thanks for his towering generosity in providing relief after an earthquake. But the fate of Nero's 35-metre painting shows the danger. Pliny the Elder, in his brief description, calls it complete 'madness', and notes that it was soon destroyed, ominously, by a flash of lightning (a punishment, we are meant to conclude, for going too far). Between those two extremes, the story of the colossal bronze statue of Nero shows the balancing act at work.

Pliny regarded this statue much more favourably than the painted equivalent. He had seen inside the studio when the artist, Zenodorus (for once we know his name), was making it and judged it a superb work of art by a genius with immense technical skill. Yet it has become one of the symbols of Nero's excess and ostentation, perhaps more for modern historians than for the audience in ancient Rome itself, where it managed to survive for centuries. After Nero's fall, whether or not the statue had been finally completed, Vespasian is said to have commissioned a new head for it – not with the features of an emperor but of the god of the Sun (though according to Cassius Dio, some observers claimed that it was an image of Vespasian's son and successor,

Titus). In a major transportation exercise under Hadrian, involving twenty-four elephants, it was moved a short distance from its original position, to make way for the construction of a new temple. But it was still around, to be given the features of Commodus, at the end of the second century CE (with an added club to make it look like Hercules), before being turned back into the Sun again. We do not know exactly what happened to it in the end. It is last heard of in the fourth century CE, and the best guess is that it was melted down and recycled sometime in the early Middle Ages. By then, it seems to have given its name to what we call the Colosseum, near which it stood, and which preserves its memory.

In some ways, Nero's Colossus might seem to have had a lucky escape. As with the Domitian on horseback, one way of marking the death or replacement of an unpopular predecessor (or one way of branding a predecessor as unpopular) was to cancel him – in vividly material terms. The senate sometimes voted to obliterate a previous emperor's name from public inscriptions. And either spontaneously, or by a carefully directed campaign, his statues might be pulled down and discarded (a good number certainly ended up in the Tiber), and paintings of him defaced. That is what happened to Geta, Caracalla's brother and briefly co-ruler, blotted out after his murder in 211 CE, to leave the blank patch in the painted panel of Septimius Severus's family. (The idea that there are traces of shit still on the panel, which had been smeared on just to make sure that no one missed the point, is a modern academic myth.) And in numerous sculptural groups in Rome and beyond, it is still easy to spot a suspicious gap, which marks the place where Geta once was.

Statues of emperors could be targets for Rome's external enemies too. One of the most famous surviving heads of Augustus (pl. 13) has been preserved only because it was a focus of anti-Roman protest. Originally part of a series of bronze statues of the emperor put up to assert his power in Egypt, in 25 BCE, the head was severed by raiders from further south, beyond the area of Roman control, carried off as a trophy, and buried under the steps of a temple of Victory in their capital at Meroe, in what is now Sudan. There it stayed, until it was rediscovered almost two millennia later by archaeologists, who had never expected to find a Roman emperor's head in their excavations so far outside imperial territory.

What saved Nero's Colossus for so long was that series of alterations and re-identifications. The Romans were, in general, more imaginative in their 'statue wars' than we are in ours. We have just three options for an image of someone who has fallen from favour: pull it down, leave it up or put it in a museum. They, by contrast, tended to

91. Detailed analysis of a number of statues of emperors has revealed traces of how their identities were changed. Here, by reworking and trimming the hair and adding wrinkles to the brow, craftsmen have turned a Nero into a Vespasian.

see even solid statues much more as 'works in progress', pieces that were always open to adjustment, to re-carving, no doubt re-painting, or even to the fitting of new heads. The panel showing Hadrian and Antinous on their hunt has come down to us only as it was reused on the fourth-century CE Arch of Constantine, and re-carved to give what had been the face of Hadrian the 'look' of that later emperor (fig. 61). And according to Statius, there was another statue, standing not far from the colossal Domitian on horseback, which had originally represented Alexander the Great, but the head had been replaced with that of Julius Caesar. It was more than a casual alteration. It was a way of making Caesar almost literally step into the shoes of Alexander – though Statius cannot resist a little joke: 'his neck was amazed to find it bore Caesar's face'.

It was not always so dramatic, or so public, as with those major works of art. Similar, smaller-scale adjustments and re-carving were often part of the processes of imperial succession and can still be traced on dozens of surviving portraits, especially but not only in the first century CE. If you examine these pieces carefully, it is possible to detect how the particular conventions of representing one ruler have been changed into the conventions used for his successor. What was a Caligula has been turned into a Claudius, a Nero into a Vespasian, a Domitian into a Nerva. There are several possible explanations for this. Simple economy is one. Why pay for a whole new statue of a new emperor when you can more cheaply and quickly re-carve the portrait of the old (especially when the differences between them are not very great anyway)? A political desire to cancel the old regime in favour of the new is another. To recut the head of the fallen emperor with the features of his successor might be interpreted as the ultimate obliteration: Vespasian has literally replaced Nero, and so on. But it also signalled just how interchangeable emperors were. It was Marcus Aurelius's aphorism replayed in marble: 'same play, different cast'.

Emperors in the mirror

So where was the emperor himself in all this? We do not know what part he took in devising his official image, or the images of his family. Nor do we even know if he ever came face to face with any of the artists who painted or sculpted 'him' (though my guess is that Nero would have met Zenodorus). What *is* clear is that for many in the empire, especially those who would never see him in the flesh, the emperor was in a sense embodied in his statues. At the very least, there was a significant overlap between the living ruler and his image. Statues of the emperor were thought to share some of his power.

The question of where you draw the boundary between a portrait and the person portrayed – between, in the standard jargon, 'image and prototype' – is one faced in almost every culture. After all, what fuels our own arguments about which statues to take down or leave up is the fact that for us they are more than lumps of marble or metal with crafted human features. They embody some of the qualities and character of the person they represent. In Rome the boundary was much more radically blurred. That is the point made by a little vignette in Tacitus's account of the civil wars that followed the death of Nero. As the rival contenders rose and fell in a matter of months, so too did their hastily produced statues. The historian tells what happened in one military camp, after the elderly Galba had been overthrown and replaced by Otho. The jubilant soldiers must have knocked Galba's gilded statue off its pedestal and elevated in its place, not the *image* of Otho, but the living Otho himself. The real emperor temporarily occupied the pedestal on which a statue had once stood: emperor and statue were synonymous.

This blurring had practical, as well as symbolic, aspects too. Statues of emperors could act, for example, as witnesses to oaths. All you had to do was take your oath in front of one of them. They also had the power to protect those who appealed to them for help, support or asylum. Pliny (the Younger) faced that power in his province of

Pontus-Bithynia in the early second century CE, when he was dealing with the complicated case of a slave, Callidromus (a name that means, uncomfortably, given the details of the story, 'good runner'). According to Pliny's letter to Trajan on the subject, Callidromus claimed that several years earlier, as the slave of a high-ranking Roman, he had been captured by the enemy during the emperor's Dacian wars, sent as a gift – on the now familiar pattern – first to the Dacian king, then to the emperor of Parthia, before running away and ending up working for a pair of bakers in Pliny's province. Escaping once again, he now claimed protection at the emperor's statue. Pliny seems uncertain what to do, and hints that he does not entirely believe the man's account. Nevertheless, he plans to send Callidromus from the *statue* of the emperor to the *real* emperor in Rome, for adjudication.

Yet there was always a nagging question of quite how far you could push this overlap between the power of the imperial image and the power of the emperor himself. If someone insulted a statue, for example, was it really deemed to be the same as insulting the ruler? One mark of the 'bad', or paranoid, emperor is that his answer to that question was 'yes'. Tiberius was said to have made it a capital offence to undress near a statue of his predecessor Augustus, or to enter a brothel or a lavatory carrying even a coin stamped with Augustus's head. Two centuries later Caracalla is supposed to have had people put to death for urinating in places where images of emperors stood, as if they were urinating in front of the emperor himself. It is hard to believe that these stories are literally true. But they are not capricious fantasies either. They are a reminder of the high stakes there were in distinguishing (or not) the *real* emperor from stand-ins or imitations. Where was the line to be drawn?

Emperors, however, also had a much more straightforward role in relation to their images – so straightforward that it can be easy to forget. When we think of who these images were originally *for*, or simply who looked at them, we tend to think of a range of people, from the grateful

92. Just three of the portraits of Lucius Verus, with his characteristic beard and curly hair, from his villa at Acqua Traversa outside Rome. In a sense, his house became a gallery of himself.

senator cherishing a cameo he had been given as an imperial gift or the councillors of some far-flung town commissioning a statue of the new emperor, to the slave clinging for protection to the ruler's image or the crowd chucking the old emperor's portrait into the river. The one person we overlook is the man at the centre. Roman rulers and their families were not just the *subjects* of their portraits, they were also *viewers* of them. Indeed, very many of our most impressive images of emperors have been discovered on imperial property itself.

The famous Augustus, raising his arm to an imaginary audience, dressed in his battle costume (pl. 15) was found at a villa that belonged to his wife Livia, just outside Rome. The exquisitely carved, and unashamedly over-the-top, bust of Commodus, with the lion skin of Hercules on his head and a club in his hand (fig. 56), was found in an underground storeroom in the same imperial *horti* that Caligula had been redecorating a century and a half earlier. It may well have been taken off display after Commodus's death and consigned to storage, alongside a couple of surplus-to-requirement busts of Domitian. The finest collection of second-century imperial portraits has been unearthed, in excavations that began in the sixteenth century, at a villa that belonged to Lucius Verus, also in the city suburbs: sixteen in all, including no fewer than seven of Lucius Verus himself. Many of the cameos too, with their extravagant scenes of imperial power, belonged to the palace.

We can only guess what Augustus himself, with (if we believe Suetonius) his gappy, pock-marked teeth, his spots and birthmarks, would have made of that perfect image he would have seen at his wife's villa. We can only guess how any ageing emperor would have viewed his own perpetual youthfulness in his statues, cameos and coins. But such images of power always carry messages for the ruler as well as for the ruled. They are not only intended to inculcate loyalty and admiration in his subjects, successfully or not (all propaganda is partly wishful thinking). They also teach the ruler how to see, and believe in, himself *as ruler*. Millions of people across the empire learned of the emperor through his images. But their purpose was also to convince the ordinary human being on the throne, with all his human frailties and uncertainties, that he really was *emperor of Rome*.

10

'I THINK I AM BECOMING A GOD'

Stairway to heaven

One of the funniest works of Roman literature to survive – the only one ever to have made me laugh out loud – is a skit on the emperor Claudius's adventures on his way to Mount Olympus after his death. Shortly after his funeral, in 54 CE, following a fairly standard practice, the Roman senate declared that the dead emperor was now a god, complete with his own priests, official worship and a temple. This spoof, almost certainly written by Nero's tutor, the philosopher Seneca, claimed to lift the lid on what really happened during that process of 'deification', or 'becoming a god'. It went under the almost unpronounceable title *Apocolocyntosis* (which means something like '*Pumpkin*ification').

The joke is that the learned but doddery old emperor, who was said to have been finished off eventually by his wife Agrippina with some poisoned mushrooms, was not really fit to join the divine company. As he climbed up Mount Olympus, those sent to meet him found that they could not understand a word he was saying, though when Hercules arrived on the scene, the two of them swapped a few lines of Homer's poetry ('thank goodness there are some scholars in heaven'

Claudius enthused). The gods, however, decided to meet in a closed session in their senate house to decide whether they were going to allow Claudius to join their number. 'Opinions were mixed, but were coming down generally in Claudius's favour', when the emperor Augustus, who had been made a god forty years earlier, swung the vote decisively against his successor. Claudius had been such a monster, Augustus insisted (slightly nervously, as it was his first ever speech in the divine senate), that he should definitely not be allowed to become one of the gods. 'He may look as if he couldn't startle a fly, but he used to kill people as easily as a dog has a shit.'

So, despite the vote of the human senate that had given Claudius official divine status, in Seneca's skit the 'real' gods sent him packing, to be deported from Mount Olympus within three days. He was to spend eternity in the underworld with a load of other wrongdoers, and appropriately punished. The emperor who was rumoured to be completely under the control of the palace freedmen, became literally that: he was assigned forever to be the legal secretary to one of the emperor Caligula's ex-slaves.

Turning dead emperors into immortal gods, by a vote of the senate, can now seem one of the most baffling, even silliest, aspects of Roman religion and politics under one-man rule. Can they really have been serious about the instant grant of immortality, the panoply of temples, the special priests and the religious rituals that this involved? Was it all just a crude political stunt? Seneca's takedown of the deification of Claudius seems to chime with many modern views of the procedure, and with the invective of early Christian writers. For Christians, the very idea of turning a decidedly imperfect autocrat into a superhuman immortal deity was an easy target, and it became one of their trump cards against traditional Roman religion. Even an emperor thought it was worth a deathbed joke. Among his last words, Vespasian is supposed to have quipped, 'Blimey, I think I am becoming a god' (and 'Blimey' is an apt translation for the slightly archaic 'Vae' of the Latin).

But it was not as silly as it might seem at first. It made a lot more sense in the context of Roman ideas of the gods, how they were created and how they operated. And it was part of an elaborate set of rituals with its own logic. Religion was an important part of being an emperor, and of the imperial image. So too was death, from carefully staged, sometimes preposterously lavish funerals to the massive imperial tombs that still survive in the city of Rome. And it was not only Vespasian's last words that had a pointed message. Deathbed scenes could offer important lessons in how, or how not, to be an emperor.

Last rites

Emperors died in all kinds of different, and sometimes unsavoury, circumstances. The brutal assassinations have always been the most memorable, from the murder of Julius Caesar in 44 BCE to the sordid dispatch of Elagabalus in 222 CE and the fatal attack on his successor, Alexander Severus, by his own soldiers in 235 somewhere near modern Mainz, in Germany. (Caligula ambushed in an alleyway in the palace complex in 41, Domitian stabbed in his *cubiculum* in 96, Caracalla knifed while he was having a pee on campaign in the east in 217 are some of the high – or low – spots in between.) These violent ends are partly explained by the fact that death was the only recognised way for an emperor to leave the throne and be replaced by another. Apart from one bungled abdication attempt in the civil war of 69, no Roman ruler ever gave up the throne, willingly or not, until Diocletian in 305. If you wanted a change of regime, you had to kill for it. But many emperors still died in or near their beds (or couches), even if there were often dark rumours of the part that might have been played by a dose of poison. Roman writers were almost as curious about their rulers' final illnesses as about the details of the assassination plots. We read, for example, about the cold-water cures taken for a fever that caused Vespasian's fatal diarrhoea in 79, about the terrible sweats and shivering of Nerva just before he died in 98, and the overindulgence in Alpine cheese that caused Antoninus Pius's decline in 161.

Inevitably the style of the funeral varied according to the circumstances of the death and whether it was in anyone's interest to give the dead emperor a splendid send-off. Some of the victims of assassination – if they did not simply end up in the Tiber, like Elagabalus, or on an improvised pyre in the Forum, like Julius Caesar – were quickly cremated by whatever friends and staff had not yet changed sides, and then were quietly buried. In Caracalla's case, his ashes were put into an urn and delivered to his mother, Julia Domna, in Antioch (modern Antakya in Turkey) – which according to one ancient writer drove her to suicide. But, those cases apart, there was a standard, though adjustable, format for imperial funerals in Rome, first established for the funeral of Augustus in 14 CE. This was based on the distinctive funerary traditions of the old Republican elite. A eulogy of the dead man, followed by cremation, was only part of these. The corpse was put on public display in the Forum (sometimes, rather ghoulishly, propped up to make it look as if it were standing) and, most distinctive of all, there was a family procession, in which the living members wore portrait masks to impersonate the family's distinguished ancestors, as if they too were among the mourners. But, for the funerals of emperors, the ceremony was given a new imperial spin.

Augustus had died of natural causes (unless you believe the rumours of Livia poisoning him), at Nola near Naples, almost 150 miles from Rome, on 19 August 14 CE. Over the next two weeks his body was carried from town to town towards the capital. Embalming was regarded suspiciously as an Egyptian practice and only very rarely practised in Italy at the time. Hence Suetonius delicately notes that 'because of the time of year' (that is, during the intense heat of summer), it travelled by night. Even so, by the time the emperor's remains reached Rome, they must have been already seriously decomposed – and the funeral did not take place for another week or so. This is probably why, when it was eventually put on display in the Forum, the body itself remained hidden, with a wax model of the emperor placed above it for all to see.

The funeral ceremonies were presented almost as if they were a triumph. The model of the dead emperor was dressed, like the triumphing general, in the costume of the god Jupiter. Another image of Augustus in the cortège was displayed in a triumphal chariot. And the senate decreed that the route of the procession from the Forum to the place of cremation on the so-called Campus Martius (the 'Field of Mars', just over a mile to the north), should follow that taken by triumphal processions, though in the reverse direction. This was funeral as victory parade, treading a fine line between Roman citizenly tradition and blatant autocracy.

It was also a ritual that placed the emperor at the centre of the whole Roman world, and the whole sweep of Roman history. Following the pattern of the traditional funeral ceremony, there were images of his forebears, but these were not only Augustus's own direct family ancestors. Here, whether in the form of masks or busts, all 'Romans who had been distinguished in any way' (in Cassius Dio's words), were on display in the parade, right back to the founder Romulus – as were representations of 'all the nations he had acquired'. Just like in the Forum of Augustus, even an image of Pompey the Great, Julius Caesar's adversary, was on show – as if the *enemies* of one-man rule could retrospectively be conscripted into Augustus's backstory too. And the body was carried, not by family members, but by elite Romans and senatorial office-holders, while a period of mourning was imposed on all citizens, a year long for the women, though only a few days for the men. One of Augustus's honorific titles had been 'Father of his Country' (*pater patriae*). The funeral acted out the implications of that: all Roman heroes counted among his ancestors; all citizens were part of his family.

Two hundred years later, the historian Herodian described the funeral in Rome of Septimius Severus as an example of the standard pattern for such ceremonies. Not much had changed. Herodian refers to people wearing masks representing Roman generals and emperors of the past (though he describes them now as travelling in chariots, not walking on foot), to choirs singing dirges, and to the procession from the Forum to the place of cremation. But in this account the wax image played an even more prominent role. Septimius Severus had died in York, in northern England, and had been cremated there, before his ashes were brought back to Rome. There was no body whatsoever at this funeral, not even a decomposing one. The waxwork was all there was. According to Herodian, this was displayed for a week on

93. The base of Trajan's column, which formed his burial chamber. The inscription over the door boasts that the height of the column equalled that of the ground that had been removed to build the huge forum (of which the column was just one part).

a couch at the entrance to the palace, 'looking like a sick man', with the whole senate in attendance. Every day, doctors would come and pretend to examine the model emperor and agree his condition was deteriorating, until they eventually pronounced him dead and the waxwork was taken down to the Forum. A similar model, dressed in triumphal costume, was used in the official funeral celebrations of the emperor Pertinax in 193 CE, which were held three months after he had been assassinated and his dismembered body had been buried. On this occasion, a 'handsome boy' was assigned to the waxwork, 'swatting the flies off it with peacock feathers, as if it really was somebody sleeping'. These were variants on Trajan's waxwork triumph: here again we have a wax model representing a living emperor who was, in fact,

94. The mausoleum of Hadrian is still a landmark in central Rome. As the Castel Sant' Angelo, it has had a more eventful modern history. It functioned, among other things, as a prison – locking up the radical theorist Giordano Bruno, and providing the setting for part of Puccini's opera *Tosca*.

already dead – but, as an added extra, in the case of Septimius Severus the model was supposed to be dying in front of everyone's eyes, with living doctors as part of the performance, or the charade.

It is Trajan who must take the prize for the most unforgett-able tomb in the history of Rome, if not the world. We do not know whether he had planned it as his last resting place all along, or if it was the bright idea of one of the staff of his successor Hadrian. But, after his cremation, near the place he had died in modern Turkey, Trajan's ashes were interred in the small chamber at the base of his famous column, where they were later joined by the remains of his wife. The images of the emperor's achievements in Dacia spiralled above, almost as a visual version of *What I Did*, with his statue perched on the very top (the St Peter who now balances up there is a sixteenth-century replacement). No other imperial tombs were quite so idiosyncratic. The ashes of most emperors and their families ended up in one of two huge mausolea, the biggest tombs anywhere in the Roman world: the mausoleum built by Augustus, which contained the urns of twenty of Augustus's family and descendants, plus Nerva as a later insertion (fig. 13); and the mausoleum built by Hadrian, which in a series of labyrinthine internal chambers housed the remains of most of the next generations of rulers, from Hadrian himself to Septimius Severus and his family (even the much-travelled ashes of Caracalla seem to have ended up here). Later converted into a papal fortress, under a new name, Castel Sant'Angelo, this structure still dominates one of the banks of the Tiber in the modern city of Rome.

Together – ten minutes' walk from each other – these formed a pair of unmissable memorials to imperial dynasties and imperial power, both originally standing well over 40 metres high (that is, higher than Trajan's column at 38 metres), and roughly 90 metres across. To judge from what we can reconstruct of the later of these, whose details and fittings are better preserved and documented, the decoration was lavish, including a colossal statue of Hadrian himself, of which we

95. The tombstone of Agrippina the Elder to mark the resting
place of her *ossa* (bones or remains), as the first word proclaims.
Originally from the mausoleum of Augustus, it survives because
it was recycled as a grain measure in the Middle Ages.

still have the head, a flock of gilded bronze peacocks and a bronze
bull (pl. 24). One particularly luscious lid of a large porphyry coffin
(showing that some of the occupants of this mausoleum must have
been buried, not cremated) was later recycled as a baptismal font in
St Peter's Basilica.

But, displayed inside the mausolea or fixed to their façades, the
actual inscribed memorials of the individual emperors and their
family members were striking for their almost aggressive modesty –
at least, that is what those that survive, or were copied down by early

antiquarians, suggest. The epitaph of Agrippina the Elder, the reputedly formidable mother of Caligula, says nothing about her apart from her relationships to her male relatives ('daughter of ...', 'wife of ...'). The emperor Tiberius was commemorated equally briefly, with fewer than twenty words summing up his career almost entirely in terms of the old Republican-style offices that he held (priest, consul, military commander). Even the slightly longer memorial of Commodus – a victim of assassination who was nevertheless lodged with his family in the Mausoleum of Hadrian – is largely bulked out with the names of his father, grandfather, great-grandfather and so on. Leaving aside the text of his *What I Did* inscribed by the entrance doors of Augustus's mausoleum, there was no bombast here, no career detail,

96. In the vault of the Arch of Titus, the emperor is shown ascending to heaven. You still look up and catch Titus looking down on you, clinging rather perilously to the eagle's back.

almost nothing at all that did not fit Republican traditions, not even a sanitised hint of their sometimes eventful lives. The imperial epitaphs were understated and rather ordinary.

Free the eagle!

The cremation of an emperor in Rome – whether of his actual body or his waxwork – had an extra function. Not only part of the funerary ritual, it also played a key role in what Seneca was satirising in his *Apocolocyntosis*: the processes by which some Roman emperors and some of their family members formally became gods or goddesses.

It is hard now – and always was, I suspect – to pin down who exactly was responsible for the deification (*consecratio* in Latin) of any individual member of the imperial family. The wishes of the reigning emperor must have played a large part in whether his predecessor, or his dead wife or child, officially became a god or goddess. When Nero's baby daughter, Claudia, was made a goddess in 63 CE, after she had died at the age of just four months, it seems very unlikely that anyone apart from the emperor could have been behind it. All the same, deification was not simply in his gift. Only a formal vote of the senate could officially decide that a dead human had become a new god. In the case of Claudia, Tacitus accused the senate of abject sycophancy in voting to consecrate her. But, sycophancy or not, this was another side of the delicate balancing act between the senate and the emperor. If the emperor had aspirations to become a god after his death – rather than enter the shadowy, limbo underworld where most Romans thought the dead resided – those aspirations were in the hands of the senate.

What happened on the imperial pyre was important too. Herodian describes the huge multilayered structure, built around a wooden frame, with dry sticks inside to get the fire going, and paintings, ivory carvings and gold-embroidered textiles around the outside, which must also have gone up in smoke. At the last minute, an eagle (presumably glad to escape the flames beneath) was released, soaring up in the sky as if it was taking the soul of the emperor to join the gods – a scene pictured rather awkwardly (with the emperor apparently clinging to the bird's back) on the ceremonial arch of the emperor Titus, still standing at the edge of the Roman Forum.

Whether anything like that was contrived for baby Claudia we do not know, but the eagle was said to have performed at the cremation of Augustus. It gave Robert Graves in his novel *I, Claudius* an irresistible opportunity for his own satire. In imagining the scene of the emperor's funeral, he says that the grieving widow Livia had hidden an eagle in a cage at the top of the pyre, with a string attached that was to be pulled at the right moment to let the bird free. But it didn't work. So 'the officer in charge', instead of letting the poor thing burn to death, was forced to climb up the blazing pyre and open the cage by hand. But other aspects of the 'apotheosis' raised ancient and modern eyebrows too. According to Cassius Dio, among others, there were sometimes witnesses who were prepared to swear on oath that they had actually *seen* the soul ascending to heaven. It was one way to get rich. Livia was said to have paid a small fortune to the man who claimed he had witnessed the ascent of Augustus.

Whoever masterminded the deification on each occasion, the result was that between Julius Caesar and Alexander Severus – who, thanks to the efforts of his successor but one, was belatedly deified in 238 CE, three years after his assassination – a total of thirty-three members of the imperial family became gods or goddesses (*divus*, for the men, *diva*, for the women, being their new official title). These included seventeen emperors themselves (counting Julius Caesar), plus a range of wives, sisters and children, and in Trajan's case, his natural father and his niece. Some of these – what we might perhaps call the 'vanity deifications' – made hardly any impact on religious worship. Nero's divine

97. A section of the religious calendar from the army base at Dura Europos. Some of the information is still fairly clear to make out. The Roman numerals at the left edge of the papyrus are parts of the dates of the festivals. *Ob natalem* ('on account of the birthday of ...'), legible in the second, fourth, fifth lines and more, indicates ceremonies to mark the birthdays of members of the imperial family, living and dead.

daughter seems to have been forgotten almost as soon as she was made a goddess. And, although Roman writers list the divine honours given to Caligula's dead sister, *diva* Drusilla (including twenty priests, both men and women, and an annual festival dedicated to her on her birthday), there is hardly a trace of her divinity in any other evidence we have.

Some of them, however, clearly *were* treated as immortal gods, with worship continuing over decades or centuries after their death. These included Claudius, who – despite the ending of Seneca's satiric fantasy – was not actually demoted or thrown out of heaven and, like many others, had his own prominent temple in the city of Rome. (The temples of *divus* Julius (Caesar), *divus* Vespasian and *divus* Antoninus (Pius) and his wife *diva* Faustina still dominate the Roman Forum.) What is more, inscribed records give us the names of numerous priests of these emperors, while also listing occasions when that central act of ancient worship – the sacrifice of an animal – was performed for *divi* or *divae*. On his birthday, on 23 September, *divus* Augustus could expect to have an ox slaughtered in his honour. Livia (or *diva* Augusta, to use her divine name) would have received a cow – following the usual Roman religious rule that male animals were offered to male gods, and female ones to goddesses.

These forms of worship were practised a long way outside the city of Rome too. Throughout the provinces – whether on their own initiative, or with a gentle nudge from the provincial governor, or following instructions handed down from someone in the palace itself – local communities honoured the emperors, not only the dead and officially deified, but occasionally also treating the living ruler as a god. Bigwigs often competed with one another to be provincial priests of the emperors. New temples dedicated to them went up everywhere. The building at Aphrodisias, which displayed that panel of Nero and Agrippina (fig. 84), was only one of many of these, and they included the temple dedicated to Augustus, still standing in modern Ankara, on whose walls the main surviving text of his *What I Did* was found inscribed. It was following one of those nudges from the governor that in 9 BCE the eastern province of Asia, part of modern Turkey, rearranged its calendar so that the year began on Augustus's birthday, with a month called 'Caesar'. This was all part and parcel of what is now often known (though it sounds misleadingly creepy) as 'the imperial cult'.

We can see exactly what this meant for one Roman army unit stationed at the base of Dura Europos on the river Euphrates, in what is now Syria, where a surviving papyrus – discovered in excavations there in the 1930s – opens up the world of the religion of the soldiers. It is one of those bureaucratic military documents that reveal much more than they seem to do at first sight: a calendar, dating to the 220s CE, listing the religious rituals to be carried out officially by the unit, month by month throughout the year. What is especially striking is that the great majority of these rituals are focused on the emperor and the imperial family in some way. Major anniversaries in the life and reign of the current ruler, Alexander Severus (his accession to the throne, the first time he was consul, and so on) are marked with various rituals in his honour, which stopped short of the full sacrifice of animals that was offered only to those who were officially gods. His deified predecessors, however, *are* honoured with a full sacrifice, to mark their birthday or their accession. The long-forgotten 'vanity deifications' do not feature, but Septimius Severus, Caracalla, Commodus, Antoninus Pius, Faustina, Hadrian, Trajan, Claudius, Augustus and more are all given their due, right back to Julius Caesar. That is to say, almost three hundred years after his assassination, *divus* Julius, the first god in the imperial family, was still regularly receiving an ox on his birthday, from a group of soldiers at the far eastern edge of the empire. Their religious calendar was a calendar of emperors, dead and alive.

This imperial cult could sometimes rebound. Tacitus claimed that the temple of *divus* Claudius in the main town of Roman Britain partly sparked the rebellion under Boudicca, in the 60s CE during Nero's reign, because it was seen as a symbol of oppression (not to mention provoking the anger of the local British elite, who found that the 'distinction' of being a priest came at more expense than they could afford). But, in general, it was another way of putting emperors centre stage in the empire, but this time as a divine presence.

When is a god not a god?

So, was the Roman emperor really a god, or – to be more precise – did some of them (and their families) become gods after their deaths? The answer obviously depends on what we mean, or the Romans meant, by a 'god'.

From a modern perspective the imperial cult can look like a very cynical set of manoeuvres. I am not thinking so much about the trickery on the pyre. There are few religions that do not occasionally pull such tricks. Whatever illusion, or hoax, lies behind the miraculous liquefaction of the dried blood of the third-century saint Januarius three times a year in modern Naples does little to dent his reputation, still less that of the Catholic Church. So too, the ruse with the caged eagle (intended, perhaps, not to be taken literally but as a *symbol* of transformation) would not necessarily have dented the authenticity of the consecration as a whole. More problematic is the blatant political convenience that now seems to lie behind this transformation of human emperor into heavenly immortal.

As with many aspects of Roman imperial succession, whether a dead emperor was made a god depended not so much on his worthiness but on how useful his deification was to the man who came after him. For many rulers, being able to add the phrase 'son of a god' to their names was a welcome extra among their badges of power, and it was often proudly displayed from the very beginning of one-man rule. 'Augustus, son of a *divus*' (*divi filius*), referring back to his adoptive father, Julius Caesar, was an important part of the 'signature' of the first emperor. And the reason that the emperor Tiberius was not made a *divus* on his death in 37 CE was presumably because it held no particular advantage for his successor and great-nephew Caligula, who based his own right to rule, back through his father and mother, to Augustus himself. Besides, whatever sympathies we might now have with the rebellious Britons in their reactions to the intrusion of a large temple of *divus* Claudius, emperor worship in the provinces often looks as if it were encouraged, or imposed, as a useful focus of political loyalty more than anything else. There were, it is true, a few occasions on which an emperor made a show of modestly refusing a request from citizens of some provincial town that they be allowed to erect a temple in his honour. But such refusals, you might argue, were a good way of ensuring that the currency of deification was not devalued.

It is inconceivable that there was no hard-headed cynicism or political calculation on the part of emperors and their advisers in promoting the worship of the *divi* and *divae*, and in presenting imperial power in divine terms. But it was not quite as simple as that. The imperial cult makes more sense, or at least looks less manipulative or absurd, if we put it back into the context of the principles that governed Roman religion more generally. For some of those aspects of the worship of emperors that make it most difficult for us (as for ancient Jews and Christians) to take seriously fit much more comfortably into traditional Roman assumptions of what gods were and how their power worked in the world.

For a start, Roman religion generally welcomed new gods. In all its different versions – and there was never a single orthodoxy across the Roman world – it was a *polytheism*. Not only were there many gods rather than just one, but the total number of them was not fixed, or even known. New ones were recognised all the time, while others were quietly forgotten, even if not actually abolished. Roman antiquarians enjoyed digging up weird time-expired deities, who may not have had much longer public recognition than Nero's *diva* Claudia. More important, though, in the context of divine emperors, some of these gods, both old and new, were said to have originally been human beings. Hercules, for example, after his life as a mortal strongman, was only deified on his funeral pyre. Romulus, Rome's founder, was also said to have become a god after his death.

To put that another way, for Romans, the boundary between the categories of human and divine was crossable and could be blurred in significant respects. Some mortals were thought to have had gods among their direct ancestors. The family of Julius Caesar famously traced their descent back to the mythical Trojan hero Aeneas and, through him, to his mother, the goddess Venus (it's no coincidence that Caesar inaugurated a new temple in Rome to Venus *Genetrix* – the 'ancestor' of the Roman race *and* of his own family). But they were not the only ones. Suetonius claimed that the family tree of Galba, who briefly ruled after the death of Nero, made Jupiter his ancestor on his father's side and, on his mother's side – in what might have seemed a dangerously ill-omened inheritance – the divine Pasiphae, who gave birth in Crete to the monstrous half-bull, half-human Minotaur.

Even outside this world of myth, extraordinary human power and success at Rome had often been presented, and understood, in divine terms. The costume of Jupiter, which the Roman general had traditionally worn in his triumphal procession, is the clearest example of this. It is as if, at the height of his renown, he *was* a god, or on the cusp of *becoming* a god, or *looking the part* of a god – even if it was only just for a day. In the Greek world, too, divine status was permeable. Long before the Romans appeared on the scene, one of the ways in which the old city states came to terms with the dominance of the kings who controlled the Eastern Mediterranean in the aftermath of the conquests of Alexander the Great was to treat them (and worship them) more or less as gods. It was part of established religious traditions that notable humans could be redefined as divine.

Those are among the coordinates that lie behind the deification of emperors. Some elements of the imperial cult in the east almost certainly derive directly from the treatment of those earlier kings. Encouraged by the Romans or not, local communities were in a way acting towards emperors as they had acted towards the Greek monarchs who had previously ruled over them. And when the funeral ceremonies of Augustus were designed partly on the model of a triumph, with the waxwork of Augustus himself dressed in triumphal costume, the point must have been to exploit the associations of the triumphing general with the gods. Much the same is true for Commodus's appearance, in real life and in statues, in the guise of Hercules (fig. 56). Megalomania it might have been, but Hercules, as 'man-turned-god', was an absolutely appropriate template for a Roman emperor on the cusp of divinity.

The strongly political character of emperor worship was entirely traditional too. Some of the very features that make the imperial cult look so *un*-religious to us, were what made it typically *religious* in Roman eyes. For in Rome there was never a division between 'church' and 'state', and religion was not founded on personal devotion, individual faith or tenets of 'belief'. It was founded instead on the simple axiom that Rome's military and political success depended on the gods being properly worshipped. Or, to put it the other way round, if they were *not* properly worshipped, the state would be in danger. Personal piety hardly came into it.

98. A scene of sacrifice from an arch in honour of Septimius Severus put up by a group of silversmiths or moneychangers in Rome. The emperor, his head covered, as was usual when performing a sacrifice, makes a preliminary libation over an altar loaded with fruit (the actual sacrifice of the animal is depicted on the panel below). Julia Domna is at his side, and the figure of Geta, once standing to the right, has been erased (see pl. 3).

That was one of the reasons why Augustus was so insistent in his *What I Did* that he had restored eighty-two temples in the city (the message was that, after the civil war that brought him to power, he was repairing Rome's relations with the gods). It was one of the reasons why Elagabalus's rumoured replacement of Jupiter with his own Syrian god would have seemed so dangerous. And it suggests an underlying logic behind what would eventually become the persecution – or 'punishment', to give it a Roman perspective – of the Christians. There must have been a lurking fear among the authorities that wholesale Christian rejection of the traditional gods would put the state in peril. More generally, however, the axiomatic connection of politics and religion provides a context in which the links between the emperor and the gods would not seem so contrived and cynical as they almost inevitably do to us.

Another aspect of that connection was that the people who handled the state's relations with the human world also handled its relations with the world of the gods. The Vestal Virgins – the priestesses charged with keeping alight the sacred flame of the goddess Vesta in the Forum, while also remaining virgins (of course, there were all kinds of rumours and scandals) – were the one significant exception. Otherwise, all the major groups of priests in Rome were made up of senators. They had their own particular responsibilities, for dealing with signs sent from the gods, for example, or for the worship of individual deities. But they were not exclusively *religious* practitioners, not full time, and had no pastoral responsibilities for any congregation. Romans did not go to a priest for personal advice or spiritual counselling.

As a member of all those priestly 'colleges', as they were called, the emperor himself was effectively the 'head of Roman religion' and the chief priest. That is how we often still see him, depicted in sculpture on public monuments, conducting a sacrifice, displaying his piety. Alongside all the begging letters and governors' reports, the regular contents of his in-tray would have included religious matters too: requests for permission to move someone's great-uncle's coffin according to the terms of divine law, or to fill vacancies in any of the priestly groups. One other important aspect of the emperor's power was that it was through him, more than anyone else, that human relations with the gods were properly maintained. And some emperors moved relatively seamlessly at their death from that role to being gods themselves.

The impossible conundrum

Nevertheless, the harder you look at the imperial cult, the more slippery it becomes and the more puzzles, contradictions and uncertainties there are. The women and other family members are one obvious problem. A clear Roman logic lay behind the power of the emperor being understood in divine terms, but did that really extend to the wives and baby daughters (even if they did clutch cornucopias and other attributes of goddesses in their sculptures)? There were also all kinds of doubts and reservations about, for example, how far deified emperors were gods in exactly the same way that the other, 'regular' immortals were. They might all have had temples, priests and sacrifices, but we find strong hints that there was a line to be drawn between the ex-emperors and the gods proper. They were not even called by the same name. For while *divus* was the usual term for a 'promoted' emperor, *deus* was the term for a traditional god. The rules were not absolutely hard and fast (Vespasian's deathbed phrase was actually 'I think I am becoming a *deus*'). But that difference between *divus* and *deus* suggests that divine emperors were not so much gods, as *god-like*. Seneca's joke, that *divus* Augustus had never once opened his mouth in the divine senate until the would-be *divus* Claudius turned up, points in that direction too. Compared with the other residents of Mount Olympus, Augustus was of a distinctly subordinate status.

Even the apparently basic principle that emperors did not (or *should* not) become gods until after their deaths is not quite so basic as modern historians have sometimes assumed. It is true that we can detect a range of seemingly nit-picking details in religious rituals that appear to have reinforced the boundary between living and dead rulers. That is exactly what is spelled out in the military calendar from Dura Europos, in its precise specification of what was to be offered to emperors in different categories: animals might be sacrificed *to* the traditional gods '*on behalf of*' the living emperor, but sacrifices made directly '*to*' an emperor, as they were made '*to*' a god, were reserved exclusively for those who had been officially deified after their death. And it was one of the clichés of the 'bad' emperor that he insisted on being treated as a god while he was still alive. Domitian, for example,

99. Although Antoninus Pius and his wife Faustina died twenty years apart, they are shown travelling to heaven together, on the back of a strange, winged creature. This sculpture is part of the base of a column erected in the emperor's honour (now largely lost, it was undecorated and smaller than those of Trajan and Marcus Aurelius).

was ridiculed for his megalomania in wanting to be addressed as a full-blown '*deus*' (not just '*divus*').

But in practice it was rather more complicated. Customs certainly varied in different parts of the empire: to treat the living ruler as a god might have been acceptable in some traditions of the Eastern Mediterranean but not necessarily in Rome itself. There was, in any case, a very fuzzy line between a human emperor, a divine emperor and a *god-like* one. What in the end was the difference between making religious offerings, as was sometimes done, to the *genius* ('spirit') of Augustus, rather than to the living Augustus himself? And did most people, beyond a few religious experts, notice the distinction between sacrificing '*on behalf of*' the emperor rather than '*to*' him? There was an impossible conundrum here that I doubt even those experts ever managed to solve: what *was* the exact status of a god before he became a god?

Almost equally difficult and confusing is the question of how the transformation from man to god actually took place. The reticent epitaphs in the two imperial mausolea make absolutely clear that the emperors were buried as mortal human beings (that is part of the point of the reticence: these cannot be the graves of immortal gods who, by definition, did not die). But what happened next? How were people supposed to imagine what went on when the emperor joined the Olympians? That is, of course, one of the prompts for Seneca's skit on the deification of Claudius, and – to return to the pyre – it lies behind the stories, ancient and modern, about those tricks with eagles.

Some famous Roman attempts to visualise the process in sculpture expose the problem just as clearly. The image of Titus awkwardly clinging to the back of the eagle (fig. 96) is just one small version of that. On a much grander scale, two large sculpted panels survive in Rome that show the apotheosis of Hadrian's wife Sabina and of Antoninus Pius with his wife Faustina. Modern art historians tend to treat these images rather reverentially, as splendid examples of Roman sculptural technique. So, in a way, they are. But the unidentifiable hybrid figure, a human body with vast wings, which in both cases transports the imperial passengers to the heavens, looks perilously absurd. In trying to capture the scene in marble, the sculptors have perhaps succeeded in making an even more important point. They have shown just how impossible it was convincingly to envisage the processes of turning an emperor into a god.

Famous last words

When Suetonius included that phrase 'Blimey, I think I am becoming a god' among Vespasian's last words, it was to illustrate the emperor's down-to-earth attitude to the prospect of deification – not to suggest, as others might interpret it, that Vespasian was simply stating the obvious or expressing a wistful hope for immortality to come. In general, over the almost three hundred years of one-man rule, from Julius Caesar to Alexander Severus, the last words of emperors – whether on occasion accurately recorded, or more often embellished, elaborated or tendentiously invented – sum up one version of the character of the ruler, or bigger truths about imperial rule. That, of course, is precisely what they were embellished or invented to do.

Suetonius's biographies include some particularly pointed examples. In another choice line from the same deathbed, he imagines Vespasian during his final bout of the runs trying to get up and muttering 'An emperor should die on his feet'. It was an appropriate farewell from the diligent ruler, who had been dealing with his papers and receiving embassies almost right up to the end. And the biographer's long description of the last days and hours of Nero in 68 CE captures some of the brutal truth about what happened (and still happens) when a ruler loses power. Stuck in the palace, as the victory of the armies who had risen up against him became inevitable, Nero finally

100. The epitaph of Claudia Ecloge, who had a cameo role in the history of the empire. According to Suetonius, she had been Nero's wet nurse, stayed by his side till the end and arranged the burial of his ashes. The faint last line of this inscription reads *piissim(ae)* or 'the most loyal'.

realised that his authority had gone when his bodyguard had disappeared and no one came when he called – 'even the caretakers had made a dash for it', observed Suetonius, 'taking the bed clothes with them'. (The last hours in power of some modern political leaders have not been entirely dissimilar: no one listens to what they say.) The emperor made his escape with a few retainers, including his old wet nurse, to an out-of-town villa, and eventually, with some assistance, managed to kill himself. Among many desperate cries, feeble jokes, and quotations from poetry, he made his most famous final utterance: 'What an artist is dying!' It was as if to show that his overconfident inflation of his own artistic talent lasted until the very end. It was not, however, as barbed as the words that Seneca concocted for the dying Claudius in the *Apocolocyntosis*: 'Blimey, I think I've shat myself'. And just in case his readers had missed the point, he goes on, 'whether he had or not, I don't know – but he certainly made a shit of everything'.

Other emperors were said to have taken a loftier tone. Hadrian is supposed to have written a poem to his own soul just before he died, so, in the eyes of some, sealing his reputation for melancholic mysticism, and providing a fitting end to his twentieth-century fictional autobiography by Marguerite Yourcenar ('Dear little wandering, lovely soul/ the guest and companion of my body,/ into what regions will you now depart/ you pale little thing, naked and stiff/ unable to crack jokes as usual'). Antoninus Pius uttered just one final word, 'Composure', which he gave from his deathbed as the day's password for the soldiers of the imperial guard. Septimius Severus was imagined to have been more practical. According to Dio, he handed down some advice for ruling the empire to his sons, Caracalla and Geta, which – if at all correctly reported – they signally failed to follow ('Do not quarrel, pay the soldiers and take no notice of anyone else'), and, like Vespasian, asked for more work ('If there's anything to do, give it to me'). Only a few months later, as Geta, clinging to his mother, became the victim of his brother's hit squad, his last words really did state the poignantly obvious, 'Mummy, mummy, I'm being killed'.

But it is Suetonius's description of the final hours of the emperor Augustus in 14 CE that encapsulates some of the most important and difficult truths of one-man rule. In this deathbed scene, Suetonius offered an important, but perhaps surprising, lesson in the autocracy that Augustus had established, right down to the fakery.

The emperor, now seventy-five years old, had spent several days relaxing on the island of Capri, and partying on board ship around the Bay of Naples – although he was beginning to suffer from the diarrhoea that was a sign that his end was near. By the time he arrived at what had been his father's house at Nola, he was feeling much worse. On what turned out to be his final day, from his couch in the very room in which his father had died, he requested a mirror and had his hair combed and his sagging jaw straightened. He then had some friends brought in and, turning to them, asked 'if he had played his part in the comedy of life properly', adding a couple of lines of verse in Greek: 'since the play has gone down well, give us a clap/ and send us away with applause'. Their reply is not recorded. But after he had dismissed them, he asked after the health of one of his young relatives, his step-granddaughter, who was sick, before kissing his wife Livia (no trace here of the story that Livia had been doctoring his fruit with poison). Then he uttered what were supposed to be his very last words: 'Live on, remembering our marriage, Livia, and farewell.' The only sign of any confusion was when he called out that he was being carried away by forty young men, but this was actually an accurate prophecy, for forty soldiers would soon carry him out to begin that hot summer journey to Rome.

This wonderful concoction of a deathbed scene highlights many of the personal qualities you might hope to find in an emperor. Surprisingly perhaps, there was nothing here – unlike with Vespasian and Septimius Severus – about getting on with the paperwork, but it focuses instead on concern and care for his family. He refers to his enduring marriage and loyalty to his ancestral line (that's the point of him dying in the very same room as his father). There is also a sense of him being 'one of us', welcoming his friends to his deathbed, and of his desire to present a good image (that, rather than pure vanity, was the reason for the mirror and the comb). Overall, it was a calm exit from the world, in which even what might have seemed like delirium showed that the emperor knew what the future held.

But most revealing of all was the quip about 'playing his part in the comedy of life', underlined by the other theatrical allusion about 'the play going down well'. The question of faking and deception, of image and reality, has never been far away from my picture of the Roman emperor. Alongside all the paper-pushing, the power dining and the simple suppers, the succession struggles and the begging letters, we have seen Nero the wannabe actor, Trajan in his waxwork triumph, Commodus the pretend gladiator, and Elagabalus's dystopian fakeries.

Suetonius's imagination takes that right back to the very beginning of one-man rule. It tells us so much about Roman autocracy that the founding father of the imperial system was said to have summed up his career as a piece of theatre, *as an act.*

THE END OF AN ERA

Why stop here?

It was in 235 CE – just 221 years, and almost thirty emperors, after the peaceful, and carefully choreographed, death of Augustus – that Alexander Severus was murdered, together with his mother, Julia Mamaea, by some of his own soldiers on an army base in Germany (or, according to a less plausible alternative account, in Britain). He was twenty-six years old, and the cousin, adopted son and successor of Elagabalus, who had been thrown into the Tiber in a coup thirteen years earlier. Alexander fell victim to his own poor showing in war on the frontiers. Emperors' failures in conquest or defence were just as likely to be punished as their apparent successes were hyped. In this case, the emperor had scored an inglorious draw with the Persians, who were threatening Rome's territory in the east (despite a triumph being celebrated in Rome to disguise the dubious result), and he was now doing little better against German raids from the north. He was also the target of other complaints that had often been made against Roman rulers in the past: that he was miserly and under the thumb of his mother, who had gone with him on campaign.

Mother and son were almost certainly cremated in Germany, and their remains taken back to Rome, perhaps to be interred in the third-largest ancient tomb to have been found in the city. Though not as imposing a monument as the mausolea of Augustus and Hadrian, parts of this are still preserved in a public park in the suburbs. If it is Alexander's burial place (and that has been a common assumption since the Renaissance), then it is possible that the famous blue glass 'Portland Vase', now in the British Museum, but originally found in the tomb, once contained his ashes.

The truth about his reign is predictably murky. The fact that there are such divergent traditions about where he was killed is one sign of how little we actually *know*. But, whatever his failings in warfare or the issues with his mother, he was by and large written up as a 'good' emperor in the old school. The *Imperial History* treats him as one of a contrasting pair with Elagabalus: the transgressive over-turner of the natural and social order versus the honourable, citizenly emperor and 'one of us'. He respected the senate, he was a wise judge and dealt diligently with the requests and begging letters from his subjects, he sponsored building and restoration projects in the city of Rome, and he clamped down on luxurious dinner parties (no falling rose petals here, and none of his servants wore gilded uniforms). His reign – as we read of it, at least – follows the imperial 'job description' that we can infer from Augustus's *What I Did*, or Pliny's *Speech of Praise*.

With the death of Alexander, the job description began to change. That is why I have chosen to make 235 CE the end point, more or less, of *Emperor of Rome*. It is not that later emperors were 'bad' rather than 'good' in traditional terms. It is that the coordinates of *what it was to be a Roman emperor* shifted dramatically. For the next fifty years, rulers came and went rapidly, rivals seizing power from each other in quick succession, in long periods of civil war. Of the thirty or so emperors (or briefly triumphant usurpers), who claimed to rule between 235 and 285 'some were on the throne for six months, others for a year, a number for a couple of years, or at most three'. That is how the author of the *Imperial History* put it, for whom Alexander was not only a paragon but the end of an era. Many of them came from outside the

101. A changed world. A rock-cut relief sculpture of the mid third century CE, from near Persepolis in modern Iran. Two Roman emperors, Philip the Arab and Valerian I, are depicted in submission to the Persian king, Shapur.

traditional elite, had worked their way up through the army ranks, and were brought to the throne in military coups. It was often not 'one-man rule' at all. Increasingly, in different kinds of formal or informal arrangement, they shared power or effectively controlled just one part of the empire. Many were *regional* emperors only. And they repeatedly failed, or were at best questionably successful, against enemies from outside the Roman world.

These men have always been easy to caricature. Maximinus Thrax ('the Thracian'), declared emperor by the army in Germany in 235 CE immediately after the assassination of Alexander, had risen through the army, was supposedly illiterate, and three years later was murdered by his own soldiers before he had ever set foot in the city of Rome as emperor. (It is a moot point whether the claim of illiteracy is more revealing of elite Roman prejudice, social mobility at the top, or the new ruler's thuggishness.) Months before his death, one unlikely pair – an elderly senator, who was governor of the province of Africa, and his son, rather grandly entitled Gordian I and Gordian II – had already challenged Maximinus from the other side of the Roman world, and been recognised as joint emperors by the senate, at a distance. Within three weeks they were eliminated by another Roman faction in North Africa (one killed in battle, the other hanging himself), and in the process they took the prize for being the briefest-ruling Roman emperors ever. But perhaps most vivid of all is a memorable image of Valerian I (who died in Persian captivity around 262) and Philip 'the Arab' (emperor between 244 and 249). It is a rock carving in what is now Iran, showing – in a striking reversal of the usual representations of power – these two submissive Roman rulers paying homage to the victorious Persian king, Shapur.

The reality was, of course, more nuanced. Many of the changes were driven by bigger issues in the history of the empire and its neighbours: pressure on the border zones and a changing power balance between army, senate and people, as well as long-standing questions about how emperors were legitimately chosen. In a way, when the legions took succession into their own hands, they revealed that, from the very beginning, there had never really been much of a *system* behind the transmission of Roman power. And the developments certainly did not all happen immediately on the death of Alexander. Some of the conventions of imperial rule we have been tracing in earlier chapters continued in much the same way for decades, including the begging letters. The young emperor, Gordian III, who responded – admittedly briefly – to the petition of the Skaptoparans in 238 CE was none other than the grandson and nephew of Gordian I and II, who had been overthrown earlier in the year. Gordian III did not himself last long. He was killed during a campaign against the Persians, either by his own soldiers or by a Roman rival.

At the same time, some of the apparent novelties of this period were not, individually, quite as novel as they are often presented. The legions had already intervened in choosing new emperors in the civil wars that followed the death of Nero. There had been periods of joint rule over the empire before. And Marcus Aurelius in the 170s CE, was already facing the kind of pressure on the frontiers that characterised later centuries. Earlier Roman rulers were probably more adept at dressing up their military failures as successes. But the triumphant images on the monument of Shapur are, in a way, reminiscent of that looted bronze head of Augustus buried as a symbol of 'victory' against Roman power in the temple in Meroe (pp. 363–4). That said, the *combination* of all this in the mid third century was new. Someone close to the imperial court a couple of hundred years earlier would have found the world of Maximinus or the Gordians a strange and unfamiliar place.

Things changed again towards the end of the century. The reigns of Diocletian and Constantine – more than two decades each, between 285 and 337 CE – are one sure sign of that. But there was no going back to emperors in the old style. Some of the improvisations made during the decades of 'crisis' earlier in the third century were now actually formalised. Diocletian, for example, officially divided the empire into the western and eastern provinces, ruled by four emperors, a senior and junior partner in each half. And in the decades that followed, a system of shared rule in some form was the norm. What is more, the re-established authority of the emperor seems to have come at the cost of an increasing distance between ruler and ruled. There was more elaborate ceremonial to set the emperor apart from his subjects, more overt obeisance to him, and far fewer simple suppers shared with the likes of Pliny. Again, there were precedents. Statius's account of dinner with Domitian, for example, rests on wonder from afar, not on intimacy. And alongside all that friendly kissing between emperor and senators, there was plenty of bowing and scraping in earlier centuries too (a lot depends on who is telling the story). Nevertheless, by the beginning of the fourth century the myth of the emperor as 'one of us' had far less meaning than before, for anybody.

THE END OF AN ERA

Blood of the martyrs

Christianity was a crucial element in this transformation too. So far, the Christians of the Roman empire have found a rather small place in this book. That is because, for the first two centuries of the rule of the emperors, there were very few of them indeed and they very rarely claimed the attention of the Roman authorities. One reasonable estimate (inevitably something of a guess) is that there were around 7,000 Christians across the Roman world in 100 CE (or 0.01 per cent of the empire's population) rising to roughly 200,000 by 200 (or 0.35 per cent). Later Christian writers, with the benefits – or disadvantages – of hindsight, give a very different impression: of a burgeoning church combined with systematic persecution directed by the emperors. Martyrdom, which paraded the defiant bravery of even the frailest Christians in the face of cruelty and torture, certainly became one of the most powerful proofs of the faith. Yet the truth was that in the first two centuries CE most people in the Roman empire would never have met a Christian. And any violence against them was local and sporadic.

Of course, sporadic violence is as cruel and painful to its victims as systematic persecution. The emperor Nero's punishment of the Christians as scapegoats for the fire of Rome in 64 CE was recorded even by non-Christian authors in chilling terms (crucified, burned alive, or torn apart by dogs), and the Christian accounts of the death of martyrs in the amphitheatre at Lyon in the later second century, however embellished, are equally shocking. But much more common was the attitude of benign if watchful neglect shown by Trajan in his correspondence with Pliny ('don't get too worked up, don't look for trouble'), or the sarcastic joking of whoever drew the graffito parodying the crucifixion in the servants' quarters of the palace. The *Imperial History* even claims, rightly or wrongly, that in a shrine at home, alongside images of assorted divine figures (including some of his predecessors, now gods, and Abraham), Alexander Severus kept an image of Jesus.

But from his reign, up to the early fourth century CE, when Constantine became the first Roman emperor openly to embrace Christianity, there was a series of centrally sponsored persecutions, on a scale never seen before in the empire. One short-term ruler around 250 even demanded that all its inhabitants perform a sacrifice to demonstrate their loyalty to the traditional gods, and to get a certificate to prove they had done so (he didn't last long enough to see the scheme through). Behind this change lay a combination of factors. The number of Christians continued to increase. If we extrapolate the same rate of growth as in earlier centuries, there may well have been six million Christians by 300. They were much more visible. And this no doubt intersected with anxieties that some of the disasters of the period had been caused by a breakdown in Rome's relations with its traditional gods. Put simply, the new religion of Christianity, sometimes uncompromising in its outright rejection of the old religion, could be seen – at least by some – as the ultimate cause of the empire's 'crisis'.

Exactly why so many Romans, from top to bottom of the social hierarchy, then converted to Christianity, and why the Roman empire became a Christian state, are among the most debated questions, and biggest mysteries, in the whole history of Rome. What *is* clear is that the effect of the Christian revolution in culture and politics, as well as in faith, was to overturn many of the foundations on which the old order of the Roman emperor had been based. We explored, for example, in chapter 7 how the emperor fitted into the logic of the amphitheatre: the division between 'them' and us' that the gladiatorial games and wild beast hunts symbolised; the social hierarchy that those occasions underpinned; and the dangerous glamour associated with those who fought in the arena. The martyrdom of Christians in the amphitheatre – 'Christians to the lions!' – turned all that on its head. Whatever individual members of the audience made of the

102. A new-style image of the Roman emperor. A ceremonial silver dish of the late fourth century CE, showing at the centre the emperor Theodosius I, on a huge scale, with his co-rulers, on either side, all with haloes. He is channelling the power and authority of the Christian god.

spectacle, the culture of Christianity now presented those who had traditionally been the abominated victims of the arena as its heroes, triumphant in facing death for their faith, with God on their side. And, in so doing, it destroyed the logic of the old order. When gladiatorial games waned under the Christian Roman empire, it was not only because Christians thought they were cruel (though that was part of it). It was also because they no longer made sense.

So too with the image of the emperor himself. Christianity did not diminish the power of the (Christian) Roman emperor. It enhanced it. But it did so with completely new religious coordinates. When I observed that the over-life-size statue of Claudius as the god Jupiter looked a bit 'silly' (p. 351), I was partly seeing it under the influence of Christianity. The new visual language of imperial power did not deploy eagles nestling by the emperor's leg, or empresses balancing horns of plenty as if they were the goddess Good Fortune. It depended in part on seeing the emperor in the image of Jesus, and Jesus in the image of the emperor. This was not Jesus 'meek and mild'. Imperial power was validated by (and also validated) a new divine order. It was a very different *Emperor of Rome*.

Taking stock

The old-style *Emperor of Rome* who has been the focus of this book has left an enduring mark on the history and culture of the West. His statues have bequeathed a template for representing power, clad in battle dress or toga. His titles lie behind the modern language of autocracy, from emperor (*imperator*) to prince (*princeps*), Kaiser to Czar (both from *Caesar*). He is a figure who has given us an image of how to rule, as well as a warning of how not to. Roman emperors are too easy either to admire (grudgingly) for their long-lasting model of political control, or to deplore for the tyranny and cruelty, luxury and licence associated with their names. They present an extreme case of the historian's dilemma. How do we understand the Roman emperor on his own terms, and yet not lose sight of our own moral compass, and our obligation to evaluate, as well as to describe, the past? It is not enough, for example, to expose the logic of the gladiatorial games over which he presided if you do not point to their violence and cruelty. Nor is it enough merely to deplore the sadism if you do not try to understand what the underlying logic of these terrible 'games' might have been.

I have attempted to tread the tightrope between, on the one hand, giving ancient Roman emperors a 'free pardon' simply because they lived so long ago (and so cannot be judged on our terms) and, on the other, finding them guilty of the crime of simply *not being like us*. The Roman empire was a murderous world in which problems, from supposedly disloyal relatives to protesters in the Circus Maximus, were regularly solved by killing. It is very hard for us now to process that, still less explain it. I have not tried to look inside the head – or assess the character – of any individual ruler. In my view, that is not a remotely feasible project (though I have occasionally wondered how things might have looked from his perspective, sitting, for example, in his box in the Colosseum). Instead, I have explored how, and why, we have come to characterise the emperors as we do (megalomaniac Nero, down-to-earth Vespasian, and so on). I have also reflected on how the people of the Roman empire constructed an image of 'the emperor' for themselves. And I have repeatedly tried to put the ruler back into his habitat and among his closest associates. He did not rule alone, nor in a vacuum. We understand him better if we understand where he lived, how and what he ate, who took his dictation and delivered his letters, or who he slept with. That *is* a feasible project.

Across the empire, many thousands of people, enslaved and free, worked for the emperor and his court, some terribly exploited, rebellious and discontented, others happy enough, or even proud, to be doing what they were doing. It is an uncomfortable fact that, throughout history, autocracy – tyranny, dictatorship or whatever we call it – has depended on people at all levels who accept it, who adjust to it, or even find it a comfortable system under which to live. We have encountered many of them in this book, from Pliny to the father of Claudius Etruscus, or Nero's wet nurse who was still on hand to bury him after his suicide: men and women who had never known any other kind of regime. It is not violence or the secret police, it is collaboration and cooperation – knowing or naive, well-meaning or not – that keep autocracy going.

But if we are searching for a critique of one-man rule at Rome, we can find it in Roman writing. I am not thinking here mainly of the high-minded dissidents in the senate (the 'awkward squad', as I have called them), nostalgic for what they believed was the freedom of the Republic. They have had far more than their fair share of the limelight. I am thinking of all the Roman literature, even from the pen of those who were *not* open dissidents, that repeatedly presented the emperor as a fake or distorter of the truth and one-man rule itself as pretence and performance. From the dystopian world of Elagabalus with which I started (its false food, and its homicide masquerading as generosity), through the strange triumphal procession, in which a wax model of the dead Trajan celebrated 'victories' that were more like defeats, to the supposed last words of the emperor Augustus, casting himself as a comedy actor, this has been one of my recurring – and I hope eye-opening – themes. Autocracy, it suggests, upturns the 'natural' order of things and replaces reality with sham, undermining your trust in what you think you see.

I have often insisted that ancient Rome has very few direct lessons for us, in the sense that we cannot turn to it for ready-made solutions to our problems. The Romans will not, and cannot, give us the answers. But exploring their world does help us to see our own differently. While I have been writing *Emperor of Rome* over the last few years, I have thought hard about that view of autocracy as fundamentally a fake, a sham, a distorting mirror. It has helped me to understand ancient Roman political culture better – and has opened my own eyes to the politics of the modern world too.

WHAT'S IN A NAME?

From Caligula to Caracalla, Nero to Elagabalus, the names by which we now know the Roman emperors were not their official titles, or only a very abbreviated form of them. 'Caligula' or 'Bootikins' is a nickname that goes back to the army boots the emperor wore as a child (his alternative short name, which he preferred, was 'Gaius'). 'Caracalla', similarly, was taken from his favourite style of cloak or *caracalla*. 'Nero' is just one of the names he took from the emperor Claudius when he was adopted by him ('Nero' being a family name of Claudius). 'Elagabalus' is a nickname taken from the name of the god he sponsored. And there are variants too: I have chosen, for example, to use the form 'Alexander Severus', though others use 'Severus Alexander'.

These are not simply modern conventions. They were the names by which Romans often referred to their various rulers (they were shorter and snappier and more distinctive than the official titles), and which we have taken over. But they were not the names regularly used to the emperor's face. Addressing Caligula as 'Caligula' would have been a very bad idea indeed. 'Caesar' was the commonest way of speaking to the Roman ruler in person, as we saw in Pliny's *Speech of Praise*. And they are not the names found in formal documents, and on many of the inscriptions that I refer to in this book, where his official titles *were* used. These can now be hard to decode.

To take just one extreme example, **Septimius Severus** is commemorated on his triumphal arch in the Roman Forum not as plain 'Septimius Severus' as we know him, but as:

Imperator Caesar Lucius Septimius, Marci Filius, Severus Pius Pertinax Augustus, Pater Patriae, Parthico Arabico, Parthico Adiabenico ...

Imperator Caesar Lucius Septimius, son of Marcus, Severus Pius Pertinax Augustus, Father of his Country, Conqueror of the Parthians in Arabia, Conqueror of the Parthians in Adiabene ...

In addition to his birth name, Lucius Septimius Severus, this includes the standard imperial titles (Imperator Caesar Augustus), a reference to his

invented adoption by Marcus Aurelius ('son of Marcus'), the names of predecessors with whom he wanted to be associated (Pius and Pertinax), and – to
complete the mouthful – some honorific epithets.

In its simplest form, the way the emperor's name changed over his lifetime amounts to a mini biography. **Augustus** was born 'Gaius Octavius', then
formally became 'Gaius Julius Caesar' in 44 BCE when he was adopted in Caesar's will (though modern writers tend to call him 'Octavian' to distinguish
him from the dictator). From 27 BCE, he ruled as 'Imperator Caesar Augustus', setting a pattern for his successors. **Tiberius** was born 'Tiberius Claudius
Nero', became 'Tiberius Julius Caesar' after his adoption by Augustus, and
ruled officially as 'Tiberius Caesar Augustus'. **Caligula** was born 'Gaius Julius
Caesar' and ruled as 'Gaius Caesar Augustus Germanicus'. And so on.

Those variants are largely clear enough. But even specialists struggle with
the similarity of the official titles that emperors used during their reigns, from
the later first century CE on. Sometimes, as this selection of rulers shows,
it is only a single element among many in the name that distinguishes one
emperor from another (I have omitted the extra epithets):

Vespasian: Imperator Caesar Vespasianus Augustus

Titus: Imperator Titus Caesar Vespasianus Augustus

Trajan: Imperator Caesar Nerva Traianus Augustus

Hadrian: Imperator Caesar Traianus Hadrianus Augustus

Marcus Aurelius: Imperator Caesar Marcus Aurelius Antoninus Augustus

Commodus: Imperator Caesar Marcus Aurelius Commodus
Antoninus Augustus

Caracalla: Imperator Caesar Marcus Aurelius Severus Antoninus
Pius Augustus

Elagabalus: Imperator Caesar Marcus Aurelius Antoninus Pius
Felix Augustus

Alexander Severus: Imperator Caesar Marcus Aurelius Severus Alexander
Pius Felix Augustus

I am sure that Romans did not always spot the difference, any more than we do, between the official name of Commodus and that of his father Marcus Aurelius, or that of Vespasian and his son Titus. No doubt that was part of the point. Just like the similarities between the imperial portraits, and just as confusingly now, these almost identical names served to legitimate the power of one emperor on the model of his predecessors. In the case of Commodus, Caracalla or Elagabalus, whatever their reported transgressions, their official names present them almost as a composite of (good) emperors of the past.

To explore the details further, the best recent guide is the careful listing of imperial titles in Alison E. Cooley, *The Cambridge Manual of Latin Epigraphy* (Cambridge UP, 2012), 488–509.

FURTHER READING
AND PLACES TO VISIT

The bibliography on the Roman emperor, and on the lives and careers of individual emperors and their families, is vast. What follows is inevitably selective. It aims first to give some general background reading for the whole topic, and to point to convenient ways to access the ancient evidence that underlies my account. Then, chapter by chapter, I offer suggestions of books and articles that will help readers explore further the themes discussed, and contributions that I myself have found particularly useful. I have tried to identify the precise source for facts and arguments that might otherwise be hard to track down from my account through standard reference books and good search engines – and to note where there are academic controversies or important technical studies. At the end of most sections, I highlight significant archaeological sites that are open to the public, and some relevant museum collections.

General

Almost all the ancient literature to which I refer is available in modern translations. The Loeb Classical Library (Harvard UP) includes the mainstream authors, and many more, with the original Greek or Latin and a facing English translation. Reliable English translations (a more restricted selection, without the original language, but more affordable) can also be found in the Penguin Classics or the Oxford World's Classics series. Most texts are also available free online. Particularly useful sites are LacusCurtius (http://penelope.uchicago.edu/Thayer/E/Roman/Texts/home.html) and Perseus Digital Library (http://www.perseus.tufts.edu/hopper/collections). Both contain a mixture of original texts and English translations, including some from early editions of the Loeb Library. I give pointers in the sections below to any translations not included in these collections, or to especially useful versions. The translations in my main text are my own, except where I note otherwise here.

Warning: There are, confusingly, different modern systems for referencing the work of a few of the main ancient writers. This is especially the case for the later books of Cassius Dio's *Roman History* (usually referred to here as just 'Cassius Dio'), which have survived only in excerpts and summaries in later writers, and for the *Letters* of Fronto. Rather than litter this section with all kinds of alternative numbering, I have stuck to one system and, with Fronto in particular, I have also directed readers, where possible, to translations in recent anthologies. Even so, just occasionally a little perseverance may be required to locate a particular reference!

There are many accessible discussions of some of the main ancient literary accounts of imperial rule. For those new to Tacitus, Rhiannon Ash, *Tacitus* (Bristol Classical Press, 2006) is a good starting point. *Tacitus* (Oxford Readings in Classical Studies), edited by Ash (Oxford UP, 2012) is a useful collection of recent critical approaches. The foundation of modern studies of Suetonius is Andrew Wallace-Hadrill, *Suetonius: The Scholar and his Caesars* (2nd ed., Bristol Classical Press, 1998; originally published 1983), now followed by *Suetonius the Biographer: Studies in Roman Lives*, edited by Tristan Power and Roy K. Gibson (Oxford UP, 2014). Likewise, Fergus Millar, *A Study of Cassius Dio* (Oxford UP, 1964) is the basis of the modern understanding of Dio, followed by *Emperors and Political Culture in Cassius Dio's Roman History*, edited by Caillan Davenport and Christopher Mallan (Oxford UP, 2021). For the *Imperial History*, see 'Prologue' below.

I also draw on many inscriptions and papyrus documents. These can be much more difficult to find, often published in huge multi-volume compendia. The biggest of these is the *Corpus Inscriptionum Latinarum*, on-going since the nineteenth century, which has collected hundreds of thousands of inscriptions in Latin. But even its searchable online version (https://cil.bbaw.de/, in German and English) is not for the faint-hearted. And there are similar compendia for inscriptions in ancient Greek, the language in which many texts relevant to the emperor were written. A. E Cooley, *The Cambridge Manual of Latin Epigraphy* (Cambridge UP, 2012) 327–448, gives a detailed introduction to the mysteries of where, and how, Latin inscriptions have been published. Papyri can be similarly tricky, with any number of separate volumes collecting texts of papyri from different findspots and in different modern collections. *Papyri.info* (https://papyri.info/) is a massive database of these, but again it can take some effort to find what you want. *POxy: Oxyrhyncus Online* (http://www.papyrology.ox.ac.uk/POxy/) is a much more user-friendly site, featuring papyri now in Oxford (and including some of those I discuss). Happily, there are also many handier volumes, which draw together inscriptions and/or papyri on particular themes or from particular periods, often with translations. In the sections below, for my key examples, I shall where possible (it isn't always) direct readers to these.

For the general history of the period between 44 BCE and 235 CE, there are good wide-ranging, analytical surveys in Martin Goodman, *The Roman World 44 BC – AD 180* (2nd ed., Routledge, 2011), and in the first parts of Clifford Ando, *Imperial Rome, AD 193 – 284* (Edinburgh UP, 2012), David Potter, *The Roman Empire at Bay, AD 180–395* (2nd ed., Routledge, 2013) and Michael Kulikowski, *Imperial Triumph: The Roman World from Hadrian to Constantine* (Profile, 2016). More detailed are the relevant volumes (10–12) of the *Cambridge Ancient History* (Cambridge UP). I have also found helpful, and sometimes eye-opening, discussions in Christopher Kelly, *The Roman Empire: A Very Short Introduction* (Oxford UP, 2006), Greg Woolf, *Rome: An Empire's Story* (1st ed., Oxford UP, 2013; 2nd ed., 2021), and Peter Garnsey and Richard Saller, *The Roman Empire: Economy, Society and Culture* (2nd ed., Bloomsbury, 2014). Instructively, perhaps, most general histories discuss Julius Caesar in the context of the Republic, not the period of one-man rule. David Potter, *The Origin of Empire: Rome from the Republic to Hadrian, 264 BC – AD 138* (Profile, 2021) is a useful exception.

The turning point in the study of the Roman emperor was Fergus Millar, *The Emperor in the Roman World (31 BC – AD 337)* (1st ed., 1977; 2nd ed. Bristol Classical Press, 1992). Most work on the subject since has been in dialogue with Millar's vast book. Keith Hopkins's review of Millar in the *Journal of Roman Studies* 68 (1978), 178–86, is an important critical response; Olivier Hekster, *Caesar Rules: The Emperor in the Changing Roman World (c.50 BC – AD 565)* (Cambridge UP, 2023) – which appeared after I had finished my main text – is a book-length dialogue with Millar. There has been important recent work on the emperor in the context of his court and court culture. I have learned much from Andrew Wallace-Hadrill, 'The Imperial Court', in the

Cambridge Ancient History vol. 10 (2nd ed., Cambridge UP, 1996), 283–308, Aloys Winterling, *Aula Caesaris* (Oldenbourg,1999) (in German), and Jeremy Paterson, 'Friends in High Places', in *The Court and Court Society in Ancient Monarchies*, edited by A. J. S. Spawforth (Cambridge UP, 2007), 121–56. *The Roman Emperor and his Court c. 30 BC – c. AD 300*, two volumes, edited by Benjamin Kelly and Angela Hug (Cambridge UP, 2022) came out when I had more or less finished *Emperor of Rome*. The second volume is a collection of ancient texts, documents and images illustrating various historical themes of the Roman court culture discussed in the essays in volume I.

Biographies of individual emperors, or members of their families, have become something of a publishing industry over the last few decades. My own approach is very different, but I have repeatedly returned to consult some of these, including: Miriam T. Griffin, *Nero: The End of a Dynasty* (2nd ed., Routledge, 1987); Anthony R. Birley, *Hadrian: The Restless Emperor* (Routledge, 1997) and *Septimius Severus: The African Emperor* (2nd ed., Routledge, 1999); Barbara M. Levick, *Faustina I and II* (Oxford UP, 2014); and T. Corey Brennan, *Sabina Augusta: An Imperial Journey* (Oxford UP, 2018). Less traditional in style, but still focused around a single emperor or imperial family, are Danny Danziger and Nicholas Purcell, *Hadrian's Empire: When Rome Ruled the World* (Hodder and Stoughton, 2005) and Peter Stothard, *Palatine: An Alternative History of the Caesars* (Oxford UP, 2023), featuring the family of the emperor Vitellius. Tom Holland, *Dynasty* (Little, Brown, 2015) and *Pax* (Abacus, 2023), are lively, broadly biographical, histories of Rome, from the beginning of one-man rule to the mid second century CE.

My analysis of the Roman emperor has been founded on wider thought about autocrats and autocracy in different times and places (even if in the book I have kept explicit comparative examples to a minimum). No one who is interested in court culture can ignore Norbert Elias, *The Court Society* (originally written in the 1930s, first published in German in 1969, translated Blackwell, 1983). I have been influenced by later work responding to Elias, notably: a series of studies by Jeroen Duindam, including *Myths of Power: Norbert Elias and the Early Modern European Court* (Amsterdam UP, 2014) and *Dynasties: A Global History of Power* (Cambridge UP, 2015); *Hof und Theorie* (Böhlau, 2004), a collection of essays, in German and English, edited by Reinhardt Butz et al.; and the lavishly illustrated, *Princely Courts of Europe,*

1500–1700, edited by John Adamson (Weidenfeld and Nicolson, 1999). The comparison of ancient courts, including Rome, is the theme of *The Court and Court Society in Ancient Monarchies*, edited by Spawforth. The comparison between Chinese and Roman emperors, and empires, has recently been a particularly rich theme. Important contributions include *Rome and China: Comparative Perspectives on Ancient World Empires* (Oxford UP, 2009) and *State Power in Ancient China and Rome* (Oxford UP, 2015), both edited by Walter Scheidel.

The *Oxford Classical Dictionary*, edited by Simon Hornblower et al. (4th ed., Oxford UP, 2012, and progressively updated online) is a reliable first point of reference on people, places, authors and texts of the Roman world.

Prologue

The main ancient texts which detail, or invent, Elagabalus's cruel and extravagant habits are: Cassius Dio, Books 79–80; Herodian, *History*, Book 5; and his biography in the *Imperial History*. He is the subject of two worthwhile recent biographies: Martijn Icks, *The Crimes of Elagabalus: The Life and Legacy of Rome's Decadent Boy Emperor* (I. B. Tauris, 2011), especially good on the cultural 'construction' of the emperor and his reception in modern art and fiction; and Harry Sidebottom, *The Mad Emperor: Heliogabalus and the Decadence of Rome* (Oneworld, 2022), perhaps too confident that it is possible to access the truth about the reign. An excellent dissection of the biography in the *Imperial History* is performed by Gottfried Mader, 'History as Carnival, or Method and Madness in the *Vita Heliogabali*', *Classical Antiquity* 24 (2005), 131–72. Fergus Millar, *The Roman Near East, 31 BC – AD 337* (Harvard UP, 1993), 300–9, offers a clear introduction to the politics and culture of Emesa.

The puzzles of the *Imperial History* (often abbreviated to 'SHA', *Scriptores Historiae Augustae*) have been debated for well over a century. There is a clear overview by Anthony Birley in the introduction to his Penguin Classics translation, *Lives of the Later Caesars* (Penguin, 1976). More up-to-the-minute, while more technical, is an excellent essay by Michael Kulikowski, 'The *Historia Augusta*. Minimalism and the Adequacy of Evidence', in *Late Antique Studies in Memory of Alan Cameron*, edited by W. V. Harris and Anne Hunnell

Chen (Columbia Studies in the Classical Tradition, Brill, 2021), 23–40.

Most of what is mentioned in this chapter is discussed in greater detail later in the book. Specific references to the practice and malpractice of individual emperors can usually be found in the relevant *Life* of Suetonius or the *Imperial History*. Additionally note the following. Caesar's behaviour at the races is referred to in the biography of his successor, Suetonius, *Augustus* 45. The anecdote of Hadrian being stopped by a woman is told by Cassius Dio, 69, 6. The translation of Augustus's full response to 'the case of the falling chamber pot', preserved on an inscription, can be found in Robert K. Sherk, *Rome and the Greek East to the Death of Augustus* (Cambridge UP, 1984), no. 103, while the details and context of the other legal cases are discussed by Serena Connolly, *Lives behind the Laws: The World of the* Codex Hermogenianus (Indiana UP, 2010). Augustus's jokes (and some of his daughter Julia's) were collected by Macrobius (*c.*400 CE) in the second book of his *Saturnalia.* Julian's skit goes variously under the title *The Caesars, Symposium* or *Saturnalia*. The speech of Germanicus, in the original Greek and in translation, is given by James H. Oliver, *Greek Constitutions of Early Roman Emperors* (American Philosophical Society, 1989), no. 295 (though his translation misses the domestic familiarity of 'granny'). The reasonable guess of 25,000–50,000 is that of Michael Pfanner, 'Über das Herstellen von Porträts', *Jahrbuch des Deutschen Archäologischen Instituts* 104 (1989) 157–257 (esp. 178–9). This type of pastry mould is discussed by George C. Boon, 'A Roman Pastrycook's mould from Silchester', *Antiquaries' Journal* 38 (1958), 237–40. (Maria Letizia Gualandi and A. Pinelli, 'Un trionfo per due', in '*Conosco un ottimo storico dell'arte …*', edited by Maria Monica Donato and Massimo Ferretti (Edizioni della Normale, 2012), 11–20, doubt that these objects really are pastry moulds but suggest no better alternative.) The surviving earring features in Karsten Dahmen, *Untersuchungen zu Form und Funktion kleinformatiger Porträts der römischen Kaiserzeit* (Scriptorium, 2001), no. Anhang 13, 18. 'Vanity projects' is the phrase of Clifford Ando, *Imperial Rome*, 28. 'Same play, different cast' (slightly less snappy in the original Greek) is Marcus Aurelius's view at *Jottings to Himself* 10, 27, also including earlier Greek monarchs among the 'cast'. The Christian bishop is Synesius, who makes the joke in his *Letters* 148, 16, translated as *The Letters of Synesius of Cyrene*, by A. Fitzgerald (Oxford UP, 1926).

Chapter 1

Pliny's *Speech of Praise* is wonderfully illuminated by Shadi Bartsch, *Actors in the Audience: Theatricality and Doublespeak from Nero to Hadrian* (Harvard UP, 1994), 148–87, and by the essays in *Pliny's Praise: The* Panegyricus *in the Roman World*, edited by Paul Roche (Cambridge UP, 2011). The dismissal ('universal contempt') is the judgement of F. R. D. Goodyear in the *Cambridge History of Latin Literature*, edited by E. J. Kenney and W. V. Clausen (Cambridge UP, 1982), 660. Roy K. Gibson, *Man of High Empire: The Life of Pliny the Younger* (Oxford UP, 2020) is the best modern overview of Pliny's career. The idea of Pliny's *Speech of Praise* (and Augustus's *What I Did*) amounting to a job description for the role of emperor is also explored by Michael Peachin, 'Rome the Superpower: 96–235 CE', in *A Companion to the Roman Empire*, edited by David S. Potter (Blackwell, 2006), 126–52.

The story of the rise of the Roman empire, of the 'prequels to autocracy', and of the revolution brought about by Julius Caesar, is explored much more fully in my *SPQR* (Profile, 2015). Among many studies of Caesar's career and the civil war following his assassination, useful starting points include: *A Companion to Julius Caesar*, edited by Miriam Griffin (Blackwell, 2009); Greg Woolf, *Et Tu Brute: The Murder of Caesar and Political Assassination* (Profile, 2006); T. P. Wiseman, *Remembering the Roman People* (Oxford UP, 2009) (chapter 10 on the assassination); Barry Strauss, *The War that Made the Roman Empire: Antony, Cleopatra and Octavian at Actium* (Simon and Schuster, 2022); and Josiah Osgood, *Caesar's Legacy: Civil War and the Emergence of the Roman Empire* (Cambridge UP, 2006).

Even more has been written about the 'new deal' of Augustus. A reliable short introduction to his reign is Andrew Wallace-Hadrill, *Augustan Rome* (2nd ed., Bloomsbury, 2018). Several useful collections of essays explore the main themes I discuss, from different angles: *Caesar Augustus: Seven Aspects*, edited by Fergus Millar and Erich Segal (Oxford UP, 1984); *The Cambridge Companion to the Age of Augustus*, edited by Karl Galinsky (Cambridge UP, 2005); *Augustus*, edited by Jonathan Edmondson (Edinburgh UP, 2009), gathering together some of the most influential essays about the period; and *The Alternative Augustan Age*, edited by Josiah Osgood et al. (Oxford UP, 2019), challenging the modern concentration on the figure of Augustus himself.

Fergus Millar's notable series of articles on Augustan politics are reprinted in the first volume of his collected essays, *Rome, the Greek World and the East: The Roman Republic and the Augustan Revolution,* edited by Hannah M. Cotton and Guy M. Rogers (University of North Carolina Press, 2002). The crucial notion of *civilitas* (being 'one of us') is the subject of Andrew Wallace-Hadrill, '*Civilis Princeps*: Between Citizen and King', *Journal of Roman Studies* 72 (1982), 32–48.

Discussions of Cassius Dio's staged debate, between Agrippa and Maecenas (Book 52 of his *Roman History*) include: Millar, *A Study of Cassius Dio* (above, 'General'), 102–18; J. W. Rich, 'Dio on Augustus', in *History as Text: The Writing of Ancient History,* edited by Averil Cameron (Duckworth, 1989), 86–110; and Christopher Burden-Strevens, 'The Agrippa-Maecenas Debate', in *Brill's Companion to Cassius Dio,* edited by Jesper Majbom Madsen and Andrew G. Scott (Brill, 2023), 371–405. The best introduction to all aspects of *What I Did* is Alison E. Cooley, Res Gestae Divi Augusti: *Text, Translation and Commentary* (Cambridge UP, 2009). Augustus's emphasis on urban monuments is analysed by Jaś Elsner, 'Inventing imperium', in *Art and Text in Roman Culture,* edited by Elsner (Cambridge UP, 1996), 32–53. A now classic analysis of the Temple of Mars 'the Avenger', and the surrounding 'Forum of Augustus', is found in chapter 10 of Paul Zanker, *The Power of Images in the Age of Augustus* (University of Michigan Press, 1988), a book which is a wide-ranging study of the role of visual arts at the beginning of one-man rule. Zanker's essay, 'By the Emperor, for the People', in *The Emperor and Rome: Space, Representation and Ritual,* edited by Björn C. Ewald and Carlos F. Noreña (Cambridge UP, Yale Classical Studies 35, 2010) 45–87, discusses different forms of imperial 'generosity' in building. The programme of the sculptures in the Forum of Augustus is the theme of Joseph Geiger, *The First Hall of Fame: A Study of the Statues of the Forum Augustum* (Brill, 2008).

Much of the history (both ancient and modern) of one-man rule at Rome has been written in terms of the relations between emperor and senate. The senate's institutional role under the emperors is the theme of Richard J. A. Talbert, *The Senate of Imperial Rome* (Princeton UP, 1987). Sophisticated discussion of relations between emperor and senators can be found in Keith Hopkins, *Death and Renewal* (Cambridge UP, 1983), 120–200 (chapter written jointly with Graham Burton) and in Matthew Roller, *Constructing Autocracy: Aristocrats and Emperors in Julio-Claudian Rome* (Princeton UP, 2001).

Different views of how the idea of the Republic, and Republican 'liberty', was mobilised under one-man rule are offered by Alain M. Gowing, *Empire and Memory: The Representation of the Roman Republic in Imperial Culture* (Cambridge UP, 2005) and Matthew Roller, 'The Difference an Emperor Makes', *Classical Receptions Journal* 7 (2015), 11–30. S. P. Oakley, '*Res olim dissociabiles*: Emperors, Senators and Liberty', in *The Cambridge Companion to Tacitus*, edited by A. J. Woodman (Cambridge UP, 2010), 184–94, considers Tacitus's view of emperors and the senate. For joking and laughter as weapons in these political stand-offs, see Aloys Winterling, *Caligula: A Biography* (University of California Press, 2011), 64–5, and my own *Laughter in Ancient Rome* (University of California Press, 2014), 1–8 (on Commodus and the senators in the Colosseum, Cassius Dio 73, 18–21). Emily R. Wilson, *Seneca: A Life* (Penguin, 2016) is a good introduction to the life and death of Seneca. The ethos of a 'cooperator' is well captured in Gibson, *Man of High Empire* (above).

In addition to references in the relevant *Life* of Suetonius or of the *Imperial History*, note the following specific points. Pliny's account of the eruption of Vesuvius is given in two letters to Tacitus, *Letters* 6, 16 and 20; the octogenarian's accident is described in *Letters* 2, 1. Crassus's observation about who counted as rich, and the fate of his head, are reported by Plutarch, *Crassus* 2 and 33. The quip about the stars was made by Marcus Tullius Cicero, reported by Plutarch, *Julius Caesar* 59. The details of Brutus's usury are also provided by Cicero, *Letters to Atticus* 5, 21 and 6, 1. Augustus's choice of name is explained by Cassius Dio 53, 16 (in addition to Suetonius, *Augustus* 7). Macrobius, *Saturnalia* 1, 12 records the renaming of Quinctilis in 44 BCE (it is uncertain whether it was before or after Caesar's assassination) and of Sextilis in 8 BCE (also reported by Suetonius, *Augustus* 31 and Cassius Dio 55, 6), Augustus's precautionary body armour and thoughts of resigning (partly prompted by illness) are mentioned by Cassius Dio 54, 12 and 53, 30 (also by Suetonius, *Augustus* 35 and 28). What Roman soldiers actually wore is discussed in *Wearing the Cloak: Dressing the Soldier in Roman Times*, edited by Marie-Louise Nosch (Oxbow, 2012). More than you could ever need to know about the ceremony of triumph can be found in my book, *The Roman Triumph* (Harvard UP, 2007). One of the most plausible attempts to put a price on the Roman army is the short appendix to Keith Hopkins, 'Taxes and Trade in the Roman Empire (200 BC–AD 400), *Journal of Roman Studies* 70 (1980), 101–25. Tacitus describes the toothless old soldiers at *Annals* 1, 34 and the change in elections at 1, 15. The size of the voting hall is discussed by Henrik Mouritsen, *Plebs and Politics* (Cambridge UP, 2001), 27–8; Suetonius, *Augustus* 43 almost certainly refers to gladiators there (though there are questions about the exact reading of the original Latin text). Augustus's eradication of the sponsor of the fire brigade (on charges of conspiracy) is explained – from a pro-Augustan point of view – by a loyalist historian, writing under Tiberius, Velleius Paterculus, *Roman History* 2, 91. Epictetus's reference to the undercover agents is in Arrian, *Discourses of Epictetus* 4, 13 (with background in Fergus Millar, 'Epictetus and the Imperial Court', in the second volume of his collected essays, *Rome, the Greek World, and the East: Government, Society, and Culture in the Roman Empire*, edited by Hannah M. Cotton and Guy M. Rogers (University of North Carolina Press, 2004), 105–19). Tacitus, *Annals* 1, 74 describes the exchange between Tiberius and the faux-naive senator. The speech advocating the return to the Republic after Caligula's assassination (and the ring incident) is quoted in Josephus, *Jewish Antiquities* 19, 166–85, discussed and contextualised in T. P. Wiseman, *The Death of Caligula* (2nd ed., Liverpool UP, 2013).

Places to visit: There is a new museum close to the site of the Battle of Actium (and the town of Nicopolis – 'Victoryville' – founded there), near Preveza in Greece. The Roman temple in Ankara, whose walls carry the text of *What I Did*, is not currently open to visitors, but you can get a good view from the outside. In Rome, Mussolini's replica text can be seen, for free, preserved on the basement wall of the new museum housing Augustus's 'Altar of Peace', next to the Piazza Augusto Imperatore. The Temple of Mars 'the Avenger', the surrounding Forum of Augustus, and other imperial developments nearby, including Trajan's column and *its* surroundings are open to the public (though they can be seen almost as well from the main road that now cuts through them, the Via dei Fori Imperiali). A few remains of Julius Caesar's voting hall (*Saepta* in Latin) can be seen from the street directly on the east of the Pantheon.

Chapter 2

The issues of succession, and the increasingly diverse origins of Roman rulers, are as embedded in the history of one-man rule as the clashes between emperor and senate. Every modern biography of an emperor discusses succession planning, and the biographies of the key women explore their role in the process for good or ill – for example Anthony A. Barrett, *Agrippina: Mother of Nero* (Batsford, 1996) and *Livia: First Lady of Imperial Rome* (Yale UP, 2002). The dynastic mausoleum of Augustus is one focus of Penelope J. E. Davies, *Death and the Emperor* (Cambridge UP, 2000), 13–19, 49–67. The principles and problems of succession are discussed in *The Julio-Claudian Succession: Reality and Perception of the 'Augustan Model'*, edited by A. G. G. Gibson (Brill, 2013), and they are a major theme in Olivier Hekster, *Emperors and Ancestors: Roman Rulers and the Constraints of Tradition* (Oxford UP, 2015), who has a very useful discussion of Septimius Severus's fictitious adoption, 205–17. John D. Grainger, *The Roman Imperial Succession* (Pen and Sword, 2020) goes through the circumstances of each succession, chronologically. The role of omens and wonder-working at the accession of Vespasian has been the subject of much detailed discussion, including by Albert Henrichs, 'Vespasian's Visit to Alexandria', *Zeitschrift für Papyrologie und Epigraphik* 3 (1968), 51–80 and Trevor S. Luke, 'A Healing Touch for Empire: Vespasian's Wonders in Domitianic Rome', *Greece and Rome* 57 (2010), 77–106. The very different character of adoption in the Roman and modern worlds (including imperial adoptions up to the third century CE) is discussed by Hugh Lindsay, *Adoption in the Roman World* (Cambridge UP, 2009). Barbara Levick, *Claudius* (2nd ed., Routledge, 2015), 38–44, is one who shares some of my uncertainties about quite how innocent Claudius was in the coup that brought him to the throne (with further thoughts by A. G. G. Gibson, '"All Things to All Men": Claudius and the Politics of AD 41', in *The Julio-Claudian Succession*, 107–32). The circumstances of Nerva's adoption of Trajan are explained by Julian Bennett, *Trajan Optimus Princeps* (2nd ed., Routledge, 2001), 42–52.

The destruction of the previous emperor's statues and the erasure of his name are the subject of the second part of Harriet I. Flower, *The Art of Forgetting: Disgrace and Oblivion in Roman Political Culture* (University of North Carolina Press, 2006). Pliny's career under Domitian (and the different views taken by modern historians) is discussed by Christopher Whitton, 'Pliny's Progress: On a Troublesome Domitianic Career', *Chiron* 45 (2015), 1–22, and Gibson, *Man of High Empire* (above, 'Chapter 1'), 92–102, with the text and translation of the inscribed CV (now largely known only in a fifteenth-century manuscript copy), 162–6. Pliny and Tacitus are considered together by Martin Szoke 'Condemning Domitian or Un-damning Themselves? Tacitus and Pliny on the Domitianic "Reign of Terror"', *Illinois Classical Studies* 44 (2019), 430–52. The verdict that Pliny would have made a career 'under any despotic regime' is that of Karl Strobel, 'Plinius und Domitian: Der willige Helfer eines Unrechtssystems?' in *Plinius der Jüngere und seine Zeit*, edited by Luigi Castagna and Eckard Lefèvre (K. G. Saur, 2003), 303–14. Pliny, *Letters* 4, 22 describes the dinner party with Nerva. Different interpretations of the occasion are offered by William C. McDermott, 'Pliny, *Epistulae* iv 22', *Antichthon* 12 (1978), 78–82 (Nerva's naivety); Paul Roche, 'The *Panegyricus* and the monuments of Rome', in 'Pliny's Praise', edited by Roche (above, 'Chapter 1') (Nerva's failure to break with the past); and *The Roman Emperor and his Court*, edited by Kelly and Hug (above, 'General'), vol. II, no. 4.30 (tensions within Nerva's court).

Most of the specific points are easily tracked down in the relevant ancient biographies of Suetonius or of the *Imperial History*. For other references, note the following. The story of Livia and the figs is told by Cassius Dio 56, 30. There are slightly different versions of Tiberius's plans for joint rule in Cassius Dio 58, 23 and Suetonius, *Tiberius* 76. Elagabalus dressing up in Caracalla's clothes and the quip about 'finding a father' are both mentioned by Cassius Dio 79, 30 and 77, 9. Gibbon's famous quote comes from chapter 3 of the first volume of his *History of the Decline and Fall of the Roman Empire* (first published 1776), echoing Niccolò Machiavelli, in his *Discorsi sopra la prima deca di Tito Livio* (first published, posthumously, in 1531; in English, *Discourses on Livy*). Various examples of foul or canny play when power changed hands are reported by Tacitus, *Annals* 1, 5 (Livia's news management), *Annals* 6, 50 (smothering of Tiberius), and Cassius Dio 66, 71 (denial of rumours of foul play at the death of Vespasian). Dio describes 'moulding his face' at 74, 13. The travelling philosopher quelling the mutiny was Dio Chrysostom ('Golden Mouth'), and the incident is described by Philostratus in his third-century CE *Lives of the Sophists* 488.

Places to visit: At the time of writing, the mausoleum of Augustus in Rome, at the centre of the Piazza Augusto Imperatore, is closed to visitors, but reopening is promised. The surviving piece of Pliny's inscribed CV can still be seen in Milan, set into the forecourt wall of the church of Sant'Ambrogio (Piazza Sant'Ambrogio).

Chapter 3

Domitian's 'black dinner' is imagined by Cassius Dio 67, 9; the dinner party as a rehearsal for a funeral is referred to by Seneca, *Moral Letters* 12, 8. The connection of dining and death is a theme in Catharine Edwards, *Death in Ancient Rome* (Yale UP, 2007), 161–78. Roman dining in general has been the subject of much recent study. A good introductory overview is Katherine M. B. Dunbabin and William J. Slater, 'Roman Dining' in *The Oxford Handbook of Social Relations in the Roman World*, edited by Michael Peachin (Oxford UP, 2011), 438–66. Dunbabin's *The Roman Banquet: Images of Conviviality* (Cambridge UP, 2003) focuses on visual representations. John H. D'Arms explores the spectacular aspects of feasting in 'Performing Culture: Roman Spectacle and the Banquets of the Powerful', in *The Art of Ancient Spectacle*, edited by Bettina Bergmann and Christine Kondoleon (National Gallery of Art/Yale UP, 1999), 300–19, and the relationship between the reality of dining and the imagination in 'The Culinary Reality of Roman Upper-Class *Convivia*: Integrating Texts and Images', *Comparative Studies in Society and History* 46 (2004), 428–50. Examples of elaborate dining outside the imperial family include the graded dining rooms of the first-century BCE grandee, Lucullus (Plutarch, *Lucullus* 41) and Pliny's water dining room (Pliny, *Letters* 5, 6). Emperors at dinner are the particular theme of Justin Goddard, 'The Tyrant at Table', in *Reflections of Nero*, edited by Jaś Elsner and Jamie Masters (Duckworth, 1994), 67–82, Susanna Morton Braund, 'The Solitary Feast: A Contradiction in Terms?', *Bulletin of the Institute of Classical Studies* 41 (1996), 37–52, and John F. Donahue, *The Roman Community at Table During the Principate* (University of Michigan Press, 2017), 66–78. Verena Schulz, *Deconstructing Imperial Representation: Tacitus, Cassius Dio, and Suetonius on Nero and Domitian* (Brill, 2019), 11–32, engages with several examples of the emperor's dinners that I discuss in this chapter.

The latest claimed location for Nero's revolving dining room (Suetonius, *Nero* 31) is briefly discussed (in French, but with ample plans and photographs) by Francoise Villedieu in the online periodical *Neronia Electronica* 1 (2011): http://www.sien-neron.fr/wp-content/uploads/2011/11/Neronia-Electronica-F.1.pdf. A succinct account of the dining room of the so-called 'Baths of Livia' can be found in Thorsten Opper, *Nero: The Man behind the Myth* (British Museum Press, 2021), 219–22; and more fully in Italian, in *Aureo Filo: La Prima Reggia de Nerone sul Palatino*, edited by Stefano Borghini et al. (Electa, 2019) (p. 13 mentions the role of the Duke of Beaufort, the fate of whose marbles in general is explored by Lucy Abel Smith, 'The Duke of Beaufort's Marble Room', *Burlington Magazine* 138, no. 1114 (January 1996), 25–30). Statius's poem is *Silvae* 4, 2 (*Silvae* means literally 'woods' or 'forests', perhaps for us 'natural verses', or almost 'a garland of flowers'). It is discussed by Carole Newlands, *Statius' Silvae and the Poetics of Empire* (Cambridge UP, 2002), 260–83, by K. M. Coleman, *Statius Silvae IV* (Oxford UP, 1988), 8–13, 82–101 (a more technical linguistic study), and by Martha Malamud, 'A Spectacular Feast: *Silvae* 4. 2', *Arethusa* 40 (2007), 223–44. The architecture of the dining room that was very likely the location of Domitian's dinner, or of part of it, is reconstructed by Sheila Gibson et al., 'The Triclinium of the Domus Flavia: A New Reconstruction', *Papers of the British School at Rome* 62 (1994), 67–100. Other dining sites are discussed by Deborah N. Carlson, 'Caligula's Floating Palaces', *Archaeology* 55 (2002) (the pleasure barges), and (on Hadrian's villa) by Eugenia Salza Prina Ricotti, 'The Importance of Water in Roman Garden Triclinia', in *Ancient Roman Villa Gardens*, edited by Elisabeth Blair MacDougall (Dumbarton Oaks, 1987), esp. 174–81, William L. MacDonald and John A. Pinto, *Hadrian's Villa and Its Legacy* (Yale UP, 1995), 102–16, and *The Roman Emperor and his Court*, edited by Kelly and Hug (above, *General*), vol. II, no. 2.21. Caligula's 'nest' is described by Pliny, *Natural History* 12, 10, Nero's floating restaurant (where the public were crushed in the melee) by Cassius Dio 62, 15 (and rather differently by Tacitus, *Annals* 15, 37). Statius's poem on the picnic in the Colosseum is *Silvae* 1, 6, discussed by Martha Malamud, 'That's Entertainment! Dining with Domitian in Statius' *Silvae*', *Ramus* 30 (2001), 23–45, and Newlands, *Statius' Silvae*, 227–59. *Petronius: A Handbook*, edited by Jonathan Prag and Ian Repath (Blackwell, 2009) offers a useful introduction to Trimalchio's dinner party and its literary context. The extravagance of

Roman dining as represented in literature (including the 'Shield of Minerva') is subtly dissected by Emily Gowers, *The Loaded Table: Representations of Food in Roman Literature* (Oxford UP, 1996). Trimalchio's pea-sheller features at Petronius, *Satyricon* 28.

The comics and entertainers at imperial dinner parties are discussed in my *Laughter in Ancient Rome* (above, 'Chapter 1'), 142–5. The profession of the cook, in the palace and elsewhere, is the subject of M.-A. Le Guennec, 'Être cuisinier dans l'Occident romain antique', *Archeologia Classica* 70 (2019), 295–327. The individual tombstones can be hard to track down and their main discussions are often not in English. They are all listed and briefly discussed by Konrad Vössing, *Mensa Regia* (K. G. Saur, 2004), 509–29 (in German). The text of Primitivus's memorial is published in *Corpus Inscriptionum Latinarum* (above, 'General') VI, 7458 and 8750; that of Herodianus in the same *Corpus* VI, 9005. Zosimus and the food tasters are discussed by Leonhard Schumacher, 'Der Grabstein des Ti Claudius Zosimus', *Epigraphische Studien* 11 (1976), 131–41. Plutarch's glimpse into the kitchens at Alexandria is found in his *Antony* 28. Brian K. Harvey, *Roman Lives: Ancient Roman Life as Illustrated by Latin Inscriptions* (Focus, 2004), nos. 74 and 76, gives texts and translations of two other epitaphs of the imperial kitchen staff.

One version of the power relations of the dining room is illustrated by the arrangements at Antoninus Pius's villa at Anagni, briefly discussed by Elizabeth Fentress et al., 'Wine, Slaves and the Emperor at Villa Magna', *Expedition* 53 (2011), 13–20 (available online: https://www.penn.museum/documents/publications/expedition/PDFs/53-2/fentress.pdf) and in more detail by Fentress and Marco Maiuro, 'Villa Magna near Anagni: The Emperor, his Winery and the Wine of Signia', *Journal of Roman Archaeology* 24 (2011), 333–69. Emlyn Dodd et al., 'The spectacle of production: a Roman imperial winery at the Villa of the Quintilli, Rome', *Antiquity* 97 (2023), 436–53 discuss a similar dining arrangement. Suetonius, *Augustus* 74 notes the social barriers at the emperor's dinners. The display of deformity (including the hunchbacks on the platter) is the theme of Lisa Trentin, 'Deformity in the Roman Imperial Court', *Greece and Rome* 58 (2011), 195–208. The story of Vedius Pollio is told by Seneca, *On Anger* 3, 40 and Cassius Dio 54, 23; that of the death of Britannicus by Tacitus, *Annals* 13, 15–17. I discuss the abuse of laughter, including several of the stories referred to here, in my *Laughter in Ancient Rome* (above,

'Chapter 1'), 129–35. The dining rooms at Sperlonga, Baiae and elsewhere are the subject of Sorcha Carey, 'A Tradition of Adventures in the Imperial Grotto', *Greece and Rome* 49 (2002), 44–61 and Michael Squire. 'Giant Questions: Dining with Polyphemus at Sperlonga and Baiae', *Apollo* 158, no. 497 (2003), 29–37. Tacitus tells the story of the collapsing cave (*Annals* 4, 59) and of the last night of Agrippina (*Annals* 14, 4–9); Lawrence Keppie is one who would tie the dining room at Baiae to the site of her last meal, in '"Guess who's coming to dinner?": The Murder of Nero's Mother in its Topographical Setting', *Greece and Rome* 58 (2011), 33–47.

On other specific points of the use and abuse of dining, apart from the references easily found in the relevant ancient biographies, note the following. Hadrian's napkins are referred to in the *Imperial History* biography of *Alexander Severus* 3. The pickpockets taking advantage of those watching the king's dinner at Versailles are noted in *Visitors to Versailles: From Louis XIV to the French Revolution*, edited by Daniëlle Kisluk-Grosheide and Bertrand Rondot (Metropolitan Museum of Art, Exhibition Catalogue, 2018), 21–2. Cicero's account of hosting Caesar is in his *Letters to Atticus* 13, 52. Herod's dinner time lobbying is described by Josephus, *Jewish Antiquities* 18, 289–97. Cassius Dio 57, 11 refers to Tiberius's welcoming routine (the goodbyes are in Suetonius, *Tiberius* 72). Claudius's good humour is mentioned by Plutarch, *Galba* 12, as well as by Suetonius, *Claudius* 32; dinner time adulteries by Seneca in his essay *On the Firmness of the Wise Man* 18, and also by Suetonius, *Caligula* 36 (similarly in *Augustus* 69).

Places to visit: The remains of the main imperial dining room on the Palatine in Rome is open to the public (at the time of writing the 'Baths of Livia' are again closed but they should open up in due course – and some of the decoration is on show in the nearby Palatine Museum). The painting from 'Livia's Garden Room', which was used for dining, is now displayed in the Palazzo Massimo Museum, near Rome's central station. In Italy, you can explore several luxury eating areas in Hadrian's villa at Tivoli, as well as at the grotto at Sperlonga (with attached museum) and a reconstruction of Claudius's water dining area in the Archaeological Museum of the Phlegraean Fields (at Baia). What is left of Caligula's barges is in the Roman Ship Museum at Nemi (though some of their more splendid fittings are in the Palazzo Massimo Museum). There are many more modest, but still impressive, dining rooms to be seen in the houses at Pompeii and Herculaneum. Among the inscriptions, you can see one of the memorials to Zosimus on display in the Uffizi Gallery in Florence, the other is in Germany in the State Museum (Landesmuseum) in Mainz.

Chapter 4

Philo's description of his encounter with Caligula is in his *On the Embassy to Gaius* (*Legatio*) 349–67. The occasion (and the background to the Alexandrian dispute) is discussed by Erich S. Gruen, *Diaspora: Jews amidst Greeks and Romans* (Harvard UP, 2002), 54–83. Panayiotis Christoforou teases out Philo's views on 'emperorship' in this text in '"An Indication of Truly Imperial Manners": The Roman Emperor in Philo's Legatio ad Gaium', *Historia* 70 (2021), 83–115. A useful introduction to Roman gardens of all types including the imperial *horti* is Katharine T. von Stackelberg, *The Roman Garden: Space, Sense and Society* (Routledge, 2009), with discussion of Caligula and the *horti Lamiani*, 134–40. Kim J. Hartswick, *The Gardens of Sallust: A Changing Landscape* (University of Texas Press, 2004) gives an excellent idea of the artwork that decorated such *horti*. Amanda Claridge, *Rome: An Oxford Archaeological Guide* (2nd ed., Oxford UP, 2010), 330–33, offers a clear discussion of the 'Auditorium of Maecenas', as well as being a reliable guide to all the imperial residences in the city of Rome.

The history (and pre-history) of the Augustan Palatine and the imperial residences is the theme of T. P. Wiseman, *The House of Augustus: A Historical Detective Story* (Princeton UP, 2019), with further details in 'Access for Augustus: "The House of Livia" and the Palatine passages', *Journal of Roman Studies* 112 (2022), 57–77. In my view, despite many other theories, Wiseman has conclusively shown that what is now known as the 'The House of Augustus' and 'House of Livia' cannot possibly be what they are called. Cicero's claim about seeing (and being seen by) the city from his Palatine house is from his speech, *On his House* 100. Josephus's description of the murder of Caligula and its context on the Palatine is from his *Jewish Antiquities* 19, 1–273, translated by Wiseman in *Death of Caligula* (above, 'Chapter 1'). The description of the layout of the early palace is at 117 (I have here used Wiseman's translation). He takes the history of the Palatine up to the third century CE in 'The Palatine, from Evander to Elagabalus', *Journal of Roman Studies* 103 (2013), 234–68.

The Neronian developments on the Palatine are discussed in *Aureo Filo* (above, 'Chapter 3'). The main ancient discussions of the Golden House are Suetonius, *Nero* 31 (including the quip about 'living like a human being', with verses quoted at 39), Tacitus, *Annals* 15, 42 and Cassius Dio 64, 4 (Vitellius's sneer). There are good discussions of what remains and how it should be reconstructed (with reference to further technical archaeological studies) in Opper, *Nero* (above, 'Chapter 3'), 228–41, with earlier Palatine buildings, 216–28; Edward Champlin, *Nero* (Harvard UP, 2003), 178–209 and Anthony A. Barrett, *Rome is Burning: Nero and the Fire that Ended a Dynasty* (Princeton UP, 2020), 175–222. The architectural innovation is the subject of Larry F. Ball, *The Domus Aurea and the Roman Architectural Revolution* (Cambridge UP, 2003). Maren Elisabeth Schwab and Anthony Grafton, *The Art of Discovery: Digging into the Past in Renaissance Europe* (Princeton UP, 2022), 190–225, is an excellent recent discussion of the encounters between Renaissance artists and the Golden House. The poet Martial, in his *On the Spectacles* 2, refers to Rome being restored to itself.

Martial, *Epigrams* 8, 36 hypes the splendour of the new developments, comparing them to the pyramids. The complexities of the main Palatine palace are clearly introduced by Jens Pflug and Ulrike Wulf-Rheidt in *The Roman Emperor and his Court*, edited by Kelly and Hug (above, 'General'), vol. I, 204–38, with further material by Paul Zanker, 'Domitian's Palace on the Palatine and the Imperial Image', in *Representations of Empire: Rome and the Mediterranean World*, edited by Alan Bowman et al. (*Proceedings of the British Academy* 114, Oxford UP, 2002), 105–30 (including the observation that the circuitous route at the *salutatio* showed off the palace's splendour) and Wulf-Rheidt, 'The Palace of the Roman Emperors on the Palatine in Rome', in *The Emperor's House: Palaces from Augustus to the Age of Absolutism*, edited by Michael Featherstone et al. (Walter de Gruyter, 2015), 3–18. The context of the remains of the palace among the earlier building is illustrated by Maria Antonietta Tomei, *The Palatine* (Electa, 1998). The complexity of the Japanese palace is described by Duindam, *Dynasties* (above, 'General'), 185. The idea of a stadium garden is evoked in Pliny, *Letters* 5, 6. Many of the events in the history of the Palatine palace, and its particular features, are referred to in the relevant ancient biographies. But note also the following. Cassius Dio 68, 5 mentions Plotina speaking from the steps; and Aulus Gellius, *Attic Nights* 4, 1 and 20, 1 recalls the intellectual chat while waiting for the emperor's *salutatio*. The extent of the fire of 192 is discussed by Cassius Dio 73, 24. Herodian describes the division of the palace between Caracalla and Geta (*History* 4, 1) and the murder (*History* 4, 4).

In his *Natural History*, Pliny the Elder discusses various works of art in the Palatine and other palaces: for example, the Laocoon (36, 37), Tiberius's painting (35, 69) and the sculpture whose return to the public was demanded (34, 61–62). Augustus's goat is the subject of a poem in the *Greek Anthology* 9, 224 (available in the Loeb Classical Library and elsewhere). Josephus, *Jewish War* 7, 162 refers to particular treasures from the Temple ending up in the palace. The culture of cameos is discussed by R. R. R. Smith, 'Maiestas Serena: Roman Court Cameos and Early Imperial Poetry and Panegyric', *Journal of Roman Studies* 111 (2021), 75–152. The 'world's first paleontological museum' are the words of Adrienne Mayor, *The First Fossil Hunters* (revised ed., Princeton UP, 2011), 143 (with more general discussion of imperial and other collections 142–54). Augustus's relic of the 'Calydonian Boar' and the 'keepers of the wonders' are mentioned by Pausanias, *Description of Greece* 8, 46. Phlegon, *Book of Marvels* 34 tells the story of the centaur; translation and discussion by William Hansen, *Phlegon of Tralles' Book of Marvels* (University of Exeter Press, 1996). Steven Rutledge, *Ancient Rome as a Museum: Power, Identity, and the Culture of Collecting* (Oxford UP, 2012) explores the relationship between collecting and power at Rome. The graffito of the crucifixion is briefly discussed by Mary Beard et al., *Religions of Rome* (Cambridge UP, 1998), vol. II, no. 2.10b; all the graffiti are published (with the archaeological context) in Heikki Solin and Marja Itkonen-Kaila, *Graffiti del Palatino, I Paedogogium* (Finnish Institute in Rome, 1966) (in Italian). There is further recent exploration of the building, the meaning of the satire and the presence of Christians in the emperor's household in Felicity Harley-McGowan, 'The Alexamenos Graffito', in *The Reception of Jesus in the First Three Centuries*, edited by Chris Keith et al. (T&T Clark, 2019), Vol. 3, 105–40; Peter Keegan, 'Reading the "Pages" of the *Domus Caesaris*' in *Roman Slavery and Roman Material Culture*, edited by Michele George (University of Toronto Press, 2013), 69–98; and Michael Flexsenhar III, *Christians in Caesars Household:*

The Emperor's Slaves in the Makings of Christianity (Penn State UP, 2019).

Out of town imperial villas are reviewed by Michele George in *The Roman Emperor and his Court*, edited by Kelly and Hug (above, 'General'), vol. I, 239–66. Studies of individual properties include: *Villa Magna: An Imperial Estate and its Legacies*, edited by Elisabeth Fentress et al. (British School at Rome, Oxbow Books, 2017); Federico Di Matteo, *Villa di Nerone a Subiaco* (L'Erma di Bretschneider, 2005); Clemens Krause, *Villa Jovis: Die Residenz des Tiberius auf Capri* (Philipp von Zabern, 2003); *La villa dei Quintili*, edited by Andreina Ricci (Lithos, 1998); R. Paris, *Via Appia: La villa dei Quintili* (Electa, 2000); and Robin Darwall-Smith, 'Albanum and the Villas of Domitian', *Pallas* 40 (1994), 145–65. Marcus Aurelius's lifestyle in the country is evoked in a letter to his tutor, Fronto, *Letters to Marcus* 4, 6, also included in Caillan Davenport and Jennifer Manley, *Fronto: Selected Letters* (Bloomsbury, 2014) no. 6; the visit to Trajan's villa is described in Pliny, *Letters* 6, 31. The document from the Alban villa (concerning the dispute between Falerio and Firmum, p. 229) is translated in Robert K. Sherk, *The Roman Empire from Augustus to Hadrian* (Cambridge UP, 1988), no. 96; the letter from Tibur is reprinted in Greek by Oliver, *Greek Constitutions* (above, 'Prologue'), no. 74 *bis* (too fragmentary to translate).

The best overall account of Hadrian's villa in English, including the engagement of later artists, is MacDonald and Pinto, *Hadrian's Villa* (above, 'Chapter 3'); with, more briefly, Thorsten Opper, *Hadrian: Empire and Conflict* (British Museum Press, 2008), 130–65. In Italian, the work of Eugenia Salza Prina Ricotti has been particularly influential, including *Villa Adriana: Il sogno di un imperatore* (L'Erma di Bretschneider, 2001). The aesthetics of its sculptural display is explored by Thea Ravasi, 'Displaying Sculpture in Rome', in *A Companion to Ancient Aesthetics*, edited by Pierre Destrée and Penelope Murray (Blackwell, 2015), 248–60. In 'The Antinoeion of Hadrian's Villa: Interpretation and Architectural Reconstruction', *American Journal of Archaeology* 111 (2007), 83–104, Zaccaria Mari and Sergio Sgalambro present the new discoveries on site and argue (not entirely convincingly) that they are the tomb of Antinous. Some excavations of the gardens are discussed in Wilhelmina F. Jashemski and Salza Prina Ricotti, 'Preliminary Excavations in the Gardens of Hadrian's Villa' *American Journal of Archaeology* 96 (1992), 579–97. The underground tunnels are the subject of Marina De Franceschini,

'Villa Adriana (Tivoli, Rome). Subterranean Corridors', *Archeologia Sotterranea* 2012 (online journal: www.sotterraneidiroma.it/rivista-online). Gemma C. M. Jansen, 'Social Distinctions and Issues of Privacy in the Toilets of Hadrian's Villa', *Journal of Roman Archaeology* 16 (2003), 137–52, is a clever analysis of the lavatories. The one literary text that has been used to identify the different areas is the *Imperial History, Hadrian* 26.

Places to visit: The main residences of the emperor in Rome are open to visitors, from the Palatine itself (though not currently the Neronian levels) to the Golden House. For a view of the *horti*, the 'Auditorium of Maecenas' is open (prebooking usually required), as is the new museum of the *horti Lamiani* ('Museo Ninfeo'). Much of the luxury material from the imperial 'gardens' is on display in the Capitoline Museums (and a substantial amount of sculpture is in the Ny Carlsberg Museum in Copenhagen). The graffito of the crucifixion is usually on display in the Palatine Museum. Outside Rome, as well as the dining rooms (above, 'Chapter 3'), Hadrian's villa at Tivoli is an easy visit (though the site is very large), but you can also explore Nero's villa at Anzio, the villa of the Quintilii just outside the city (between Rome and Ciampino airport), Trajan's villa at Arcinazzo Romano and parts of Nero's villa at Subiaco. Some sections of the villa of Domitian can be seen in the gardens of Castel Gandolfo (there are various tour options through the Vatican Museums). The remains of Tiberius's villa are one of the highlights of modern Capri.

Chapter 5

The poem on the father of Claudius Etruscus is Statius, *Silvae* 3, 3; his career in the palace is discussed by P. R. C. Weaver, 'The Father of Claudius Etruscus: Statius, *Silvae* 3, 3', *Classical Quarterly* 15 (1965), 145–54. Recent studies of Roman court culture are noted above, under 'Prologue'. In addition to references to the idiosyncrasies of the court easily found in the relevant ancient biographies (or in Marcus Aurelius, *Jottings to Himself*), note the following. The troupes of children are referred to in Cassius Dio 48, 44. The presence of the young Titus at the death of Britannicus is recorded by Suetonius, *Titus* 2. The comparison between senior courtiers and children is implied in Arrian,

Discourses of Epictetus 4, 7. Tacitus, *Annals* 15, 23 tells of Thrasea Paetus's exclusion, and one of Plutarch's essays (*On Talkativeness* 11) recounts the story of the suicide of Fulvius. The ban on kissing because of the herpes outbreak is reconstructed from Pliny, *Natural History* 26, 3 and Suetonius, *Tiberius* 34. Seneca, *On Benefits* 2, 12 mentions the kissing of Caligula's feet. The flattery practised by the elder Vitellius is described in Suetonius's biography of his son, *Vitellius* 2. The satire on the turbot is Juvenal, *Satires* 4, well introduced by Christopher S. van den Berg, 'Imperial Satire and Rhetoric', in *A Companion to Persius and Juvenal*, edited by Susanna Braund and Josiah Osgood (Blackwell, 2012), esp. 279–81, with the now classic analysis by Gowers, *The Loaded Table* (above, 'Chapter 3'), 202–11. The meaning of 'selling smoke' is dissected by Jerzy Linderski, '*Fumum vendere* and *fumo necare*', *Glotta* 65 (1987), 137–46.

The imperial slave, and ex-slave, household is the subject of P. R. C Weaver, *Familia Caesaris: A Social Study of the Emperor's Freedmen and Slaves* (Cambridge UP, 1972), Rose MacLean, *Freed Slaves and Roman Imperial Culture: Social Integration and the Transformation of Values* (Cambridge UP, 2018), 104–30 (focused on ex-slaves), and a very useful essay by Jonathan Edmondson in *The Roman Emperor and his Court*, edited by Kelly and Hug (above, 'General'), vol. I, 168–203. The graffiti of the slaves on the Palatine are discussed in Solin and Itkonen-Kaila, *Graffiti del Palatino* (above, 'Chapter 4'). The doctor of Titus features in Alison E. Cooley and M. G. L. Cooley, *Pompeii and Herculaneum: A Sourcebook* (2nd ed., Routledge, 2014), 110; Garrett G. Fagan, 'Bathing for Health with Celsus and Pliny the Elder', *Classical Quarterly* 56 (2006), 190–207 (on 204) is, uncharacteristically, one of the killjoys. Susan Treggiari discusses Livia's staff in 'Jobs in the Household of Livia', *Papers of the British School at Rome* 43 (1975), 48–77. Musicus Scurranus is briefly discussed by Keith Bradley, *Slavery and Society at Rome* (Cambridge UP, 1994), 2–3; the epitaph is translated in Harvey, *Roman Lives* (above, 'Chapter 3'), no. 68 (along with a selection of other texts on imperial slaves, including the keeper of Trajan's 'private outfits', no. 77). The inscription detailing the career of the taster is translated in Harvey, *Roman Lives* no. 74, and in *The Roman Emperor and his Court*, edited by Kelly and Hug, vol. II, no. 5.11; the epitaph of Coetus Herodianus is referred to above, 'Chapter 3'. Phaedrus, *Fables* 2, 5 tells the story of Tiberius and the slave, discussed by John Henderson, *Telling Tales on Caesar: Roman Stories from Phaedrus* (Oxford UP, 2001), 9–31. In *Annals*

15, 35 and 16, 8, Tacitus refers to cases against those who had 'imperial style' secretariats.

The idea of the powerful freedman is interrogated by Henrik Mouritsen, *The Freedman in the Roman World* (Cambridge UP, 2011), 66–119, and by P. R. C. Weaver, 'Social Mobility in the Early Roman Empire: The Evidence of the Imperial Freedmen and Slaves', in *Studies in Ancient Society*, edited by M. I. Finley (Routledge, 1974), 121–40. Epictetus's story of the cobbler can be found at Arrian, *Discourses of Epictetus* 1, 19. The career of Pallas is discussed by MacLean, *Freed Slaves*, 107–11, and the reaction of Pliny by James McNamara, 'Pliny, Tacitus and the Monuments of Pallas', *Classical Quarterly* 71 (2021), 308–29 (whose translation of the letter I have drawn on). His landholdings are documented in a papyrus now in London (*P.Lond* II, 195 recto): https://www.bl.uk/manuscripts/FullDisplay.aspx?ref=Papyrus_195(A-B). The statuette of Pallas in the shrine is mentioned by Suetonius, *Vitellius* 2. Philo attacks Helico at several points in *On the Embassy to Gaius*, 168–206; the 'case against' Cleander is summed up by A. R. Birley in the *Cambridge Ancient History* vol. 11 (2nd ed. Cambridge UP, 2000), 189–90. Horace's rejection of the job of Augustus's secretary is mentioned in Suetonius, *Horace* (a parallel series of literary lives). For the portrayal of Trimalchio, see above, 'Chapter 3'. Tacitus's description of the mission of Nero's freedman (Polyclitus) is at *Annals* 14, 39. Pliny, *Letters* 10, 63 and 67 show him waiting on the imperial freedman.

The representations of (and fantasies about) the erotic life of emperors are well discussed by Caroline Vout, *Power and Eroticism in Imperial Rome* (Cambridge UP, 2007) (including discussions of Antinous, Sporus, Earinus and Panthea), with Anise K. Strong, *Prostitutes and Matrons in the Roman World* (Cambridge UP, 2016), 80–96. As well as passages on sexual exploits and partners in the relevant ancient biographies, note the following. Julian's joke about Trajan is told at *The Caesars* 311c, Statius's poem on Earinus is *Silvae* 3, 4, the wealth of Caenis is mentioned by Cassius Dio, *Roman History* 65, 14 (her tombstone is illustrated in *The Roman Emperor and his Court*, edited by Kelly and Hug, vol. II, no. 3.50, above, 'General').

The role of the emperor's wives and female relations is an important part of almost every modern discussion of court politics and imperial history, and biographies of empresses have become a minor industry (some of my favourites are cited above, under 'General'). A clear recent introduction to imperial women across the first three centuries of one-man rule is Mary T. Boatwright, *Imperial Women of Rome: Power, Gender, Context* (Oxford UP, 2021). Particularly notable studies that are not strictly biographical are (on Livia) Nicholas Purcell, 'Livia and the Womanhood of Rome', *Proceedings of the Cambridge Philological Society* 32 (1986), 78–105, and (on Agrippina the Younger) Judith Ginsburg, *Representing Agrippina: Constructions of Female Power in the Early Roman Empire* (Oxford UP, 2006). For specific references, in addition to those that can be easily tracked down in Suetonius or the *Imperial History*, note the following. The open claim that Livia was responsible for Tiberius's succession is reported by Cassius Dio 57, 3. Tacitus, *Annals* 13, 5 explains that Seneca nudged Nero to leave the dais himself, to meet Agrippina. Cassius Dio 78, 18 mentions Julia Domna taking charge of Caracalla's correspondence. Julia's sex on the rostra is deplored by, among others, Seneca, *On Benefits* 6, 32, and Messalina's competition with the prostitute by Pliny, *Natural History* 10, 172. Levick, *Faustina I and II* (above, 'General'), 79–80, unpicks the story of Faustina and the gladiator, and the theories behind it. Cassius Dio 58, 2 notes that some called Livia 'Mother of her Country' (a slightly different version is given by Tacitus, *Annals* 1, 14). Plotina's letter to Hadrian is fully discussed (with translation) by Riet van Bremen, 'Plotina to all her Friends: The Letter(s) of the Empress Plotina to the Epicureans in Athens', *Chiron* 35 (2005), 499–532; the intervention of Livia on behalf of the Samians, by Joyce Reynolds, *Aphrodisias and Rome* (Society for the Promotion of Roman Studies, 1982), no. 13 (104–6); Hadrian's speech on Matidia is discussed (with translation) by Christopher P. Jones, 'A Speech of the Emperor Hadrian', *Classical Quarterly* 54 (2004), 266–73 (Jones suggests the speech was delivered at her formal deification, not her funeral). Tacitus refers to the disapproval of Livia's influence at *Annals* 3, 17. The inscription is the subject of Alison E. Cooley, *The Senatus Consultum de Pisone Patre: Text, Translation. and Commentary* (Cambridge UP, 2023). Suetonius, *Claudius* 36 is perhaps less colourful than the favourite modern version I have used (literally, he did 'nothing but ask if his throne was safe'). Julia's quip about adultery is quoted by Macrobius, *Saturnalia* 2, 5. Translations of some of the inscriptions I have cited, or parts of them, are included in *The Roman Emperor and his Court*, edited by Kelly and Hug (above, 'General'), vol. II, no. 3.27 (Livia and the Samians), 3.29 (Livia influencing the trial), 3.32 (Plotina and the Ephesians), 3.34 (Julia Domna and the Ephesians).

The quirky essay in the voice of Septimius Severus is by Keith Hopkins, 'How to be a Roman Emperor: An Autobiography', in *Sociological Studies in Roman History*, edited by Christopher Kelly (Cambridge UP, 2018), 534–48. *The Cambridge Companion to Galen*, edited by R. J. Hankinson (Cambridge UP, 2008) and Susan P. Mattern, *The Prince of Medicine: Galen in the Roman Empire* (Oxford UP, 2013) are good introductions to Galen and his work. Claire Bubb, *Dissection in Classical Antiquity* (Cambridge UP, 2022) is a good guide to Galen's place in the history of dissection (quoting material that is not available in standard translations). *On the Avoidance of Grief*, found by Antoine Pietrobelli, has been translated in *Galen: Psychological Writings*, edited by P. N. Singer (Cambridge UP, 2013), and is fully discussed in *Galen's Treatise* Peri Alupias (De indolentia) *in Context: A Tale of Resilience*, edited by Caroline Petit (Brill, 2019), a collection that includes Matthew Nicholls's essay on Galen's views of Commodus, 245–62. Translations and discussions of Galen's imperial consultations can be found in Mattern, *The Prince of Medicine*, 200–1 (Commodus's tonsils), 205–7 (Marcus Aurelius and the porridge), and 207–12 (theriac).

The rediscovery of Fronto and his relationships with the imperial family are clearly introduced by Davenport and Manley, *Fronto* (above, 'Chapter 4'), who translate a useful selection of letters: for example, nos. 20 and 21 (illness), 24 (grumpiness), 26 (illness) = *Letters to Marcus* 5, 55; 5, 23; 4, 12; 5, 25, according to the most recent standard numbering. The preoccupation with illness in the correspondence is the theme of Annelise Freisenbruch, 'Back to Fronto: Doctor and Patient in his Correspondence with an Emperor', in *Ancient Letters: Classical and Late Antique Epistolography*, edited by Ruth Morello and A. D. Morrison (Oxford UP, 2007), 235–56. My brief quotations on sickness are drawn from *Letters to Marcus* 5, 27–30. Aelius Aristides's illnesses are described in his *Sacred Tales*. The erotic dimension of the letters is emphasised by Amy Richlin, *Marcus Aurelius in Love: The Letters of Marcus and Fronto* (Chicago UP, 2006), including a further selection of letters. I have quoted from Richlin's nos. 1, 3, 9 (*Letters to Marcus* 3, 9; additional letters 7; *Letters to Marcus* 3, 3).

Most translations of Marcus Aurelius's *Jottings* go under the title *Meditations* (which I have avoided as it sounds rather too profound or mystical). All my references can easily be found there. A good introduction to different aspects of the text, as well as the emperor's biography, is *A Companion to Marcus Aurelius*, edited by Marcel van Ackeren (Blackwell, 2012). The story of the apes is Phaedrus, *Fables* 4, 13 (with Henderson, *Telling Tales on Caesar*, 177–80).

Chapter 6

Pliny's post in Pontus-Bithynia is well discussed by Gibson, *Man of High Empire*, 190–237. His correspondence with Trajan is analysed by Greg Woolf, 'Pliny/Trajan and the Poetics of Empire', *Classical Philology* 110 (2015), 132–51 and Myles Lavan, 'Pliny *Epistles* 10 and Imperial Correspondence', in *Roman Literature under Nerva, Trajan and Hadrian: Literary Interactions, AD 96–138*, edited by Alice König and Christopher Whitton (Cambridge UP, 2018), 280–301. The language of the exchanges is the subject of Kathleen M. Coleman, 'Bureaucratic Language in the Correspondence between Pliny and Trajan', *Transactions of the American Philological Association* 142 (2012), 189–238. The role of the secretariat in writing 'Trajan's' letters is discussed by A. N. Sherwin-White, 'Trajan's Replies to Pliny: Authorship and Necessity', *Journal of Roman Studies* 52 (1962), 114–25. Book 10 of Pliny's *Letters* is easy to navigate, but for some of the themes I have mentioned see: 10, 17b–18 and 39–40 (architects and surveyors); 10, 23–4 (baths at Prusa); 10, 33–4 (fire brigades); 10, 41–2 and 61–62 (the lake); 10, 53 (standard 'one-liner'); 96–7 (Christians). Aelius Aristides's hype on the emperor's letters is in his *Roman Oration* 33, and the 'chorus waiting for its trainer' is in *Roman Oration* 32 (I follow the translation of J. H. Oliver, in 'The Ruling Power', *Transactions of the American Philosophical Society* 43 (1953), 871–1003). 'Government by correspondence' is taken from the title of Fergus Millar's article, 'Trajan, Government by Correspondence', in the second volume of *Rome, the Greek World and the East*, edited by Cotton and Rogers (above, 'Chapter 1'), 23–46. Fronto stresses the role of letters in imperial rule in *To Marcus Aurelius, On Eloquence* 2.7.

The role of the emperor in legal decisions or responding to requests is one theme of imperial biographies. Apart from those passages in the relevant *Life*, note the following. The crowds at Antioch are mentioned by Cassius Dio 68, 24, Antoninus's reply to the man from Seleucia by Philostratus, *Lives of the*

Sophists 2, 5. The inscription recording the embassy from Ephesus to Britain is briefly discussed (for other reasons) by A. J. Graham, 'The Division of Britain', *Journal of Roman Studies* 56 (1966), 92–107 (esp. 100–1). Vespasian receiving the request for cash is a vignette in Philostratus, *Life of Apollonius of Tyana* 5, 38. The case of the false confession is summarised in *The Digest of Justinian* 48, 18, 27 (translated by Alan Watson, University of Pennsylvania Press). The most convenient version of the responses given by Septimius Severus and Caracalla (not yet a teenager at that point) is in William Linn Westermann and A. Arthur Schiller, *Apokrimata: Decisions of Septimius Severus on Legal Matters* (Columbia UP, 1954), though there have been later additions and improvements to the text. The papyrus suggesting a possibly untypical 600 petitions per day to the governor (*PYale* 1, 61) is briefly discussed by William V. Harris, *Ancient Literacy* (Harvard UP, 1989), 215. The inscription from Skaptopara no longer survives. A version with translation is given by Connolly, *Lives behind the Laws* (above, 'Prologue'), 167–73. Statius's poem addressed to the *ab epistulis* is *Silvae* 5, 1. The brilliant ghostwriter is praised by Philostratus, *Lives of the Sophists* 2, 24. Plutarch, *Julius Caesar* 17 records Caesar's multitasking, and Aulus Gellius, *Attic Nights* 3, 16 Hadrian's obstetric researches. Caligula reading is described by Philo, *On the Embassy to Gaius* 254–60, Marcus Aurelius crying by Philostratus, *The Lives of the Sophists* 2, 9. The relevant passage of Galen (*Diseases of the Mind* 4), is translated by Thomas Wiedemann, *Greek and Roman Slavery* (Routledge, 1981), no. 198. 'Borrowed eloquence' is Tacitus's phrase at *Annals* 13, 3. Julian's joke about Trajan is at *The Caesars* 327.

The record of the dispute between Falerio and Firmum ('signed off' from Domitian's Alban villa) is translated in Sherk, *The Roman Empire from Augustus to Hadrian* (above, 'Chapter 4'), no. 96. The response of Commodus to the tenant farmers is translated by Dennis Kehoe, *The Economics of Agriculture on Roman Imperial Estates in North Africa* (Vandenhoeck & Ruprecht, 1988) 67–8 (and reproduced online, with further discussion: https://www.judaism-and-rome.org/coloni-north-africa-complain-mistreatment-roman-officials-cil-viii-10570). The documents on the 'Archive Wall' at Aphrodisias are translated and discussed in Reynolds, *Aphrodisias and Rome* (above, 'Chapter 5'); the nail tax, no. 15. How to address the emperor is explained by Menander Rhetor, *Treatise* 2, 12. Alexander Severus's insistence that people should not be discouraged from appealing to the emperor is recorded in a papyrus discussed and translated by Oliver, *Greek Constitutions of Early Roman Emperors* (above, 'General'), no. 276. The quip about giving a penny to an elephant is quoted by Macrobius, *Saturnalia* 2, 4, as well as Suetonius, *Augustus* 53. The problem of bird-hunting is the subject of an imperial ruling, quoted in *The Digest of Justinian* 8, 3, 16. The thirteen responses by Septimius Severus and Caracalla are discussed by Westermann and Schiller, *Apokrimata*. The problems of re-quisitioned transport are well surveyed by Stephen Mitchell, 'Requisitioned Transport in the Roman Empire', *Journal of Roman Studies* 66 (1976), 106–31; Hadrian's regulations of 129 CE are published by Tor Hauken and Hasan Malay, 'A New Edict of Hadrian from the Province of Asia', in *Selbstdarstellung und Kommunikation*, edited by Rudolf Haensch (C. H. Beck, 2009), 327–48 (see also, for a slightly later example, Christopher P. Jones, 'An Edict of Hadrian from Maroneia', *Chiron* 41 (2011), 313–25). Nerva's reform is documented in the coin, fig. 52. Pliny's rule-breaking is obvious in *Letters* 10, 120–21.

The model of the Roman emperor as essentially reactive was a hallmark of Millar's approach in *The Emperor in the Roman World* (above, 'General') and more succinctly in his article 'Emperors at Work', *Journal of Roman Studies* 57 (1967), 9–19. Tacitus, *Annals* 14, 38–9 describes the events in Britain and the whistle-blower. Emperors' regulations on café food are fully discussed by Annalisa Marzano, 'Food, *Popinae* and the Emperor', in *The Past as Present*, edited by Giovanni Alberto Cecconi et al. (Brepols, 2019), 435–58 (though she takes the regulations less symbolically than I do); key passages in Cassius Dio include 60, 6 (Claudius), 65, 10 (Vespasian). Other regulations (includ-ing the 'toga' ruling) can be found in the relevant biographies by Suetonius. Claudius's speech and its full background is the subject of S. J. V. Malloch, *The Tabula Lugdunensis* (Cambridge UP, 2020), though he is kinder to Claudius than I am; with a literary version by Tacitus, *Annals* 11, 23–5. I discuss Caracal-la's citizenship edict in my *SPQR* (above, 'Chapter 1'), 527–9. It is the subject of a full study by Alex Imrie, *The Antonine Constitution: An Edict for the Cara-callan Empire* (Brill, 2018), who discusses, among other aspects, the state of the imperial coffers). Myles Lavan, 'The Spread of Roman Citizenship, 14–212 CE', *Past and Present* 230 (2016) considers the impact of the edict on the total number of Roman citizens.

The economy of the Roman empire is the subject of many recent (and competing) studies. *The Cambridge Economic History of the Greco-Roman*

World, edited by Walter Scheidel et al. (Cambridge UP, 2007), provides reliable background to the topics I mention here, and more briefly Garnsey and Saller, *The Roman Empire* (above, 'General'). A non-technical account of the deep bores in Greenland and elsewhere is given by Philip Kay, *Rome's Economic Revolution* (Oxford UP, 2014), 46–9. Strabo's assessment of Britain is in his *Geography* 2, 5. Suetonius and the *Imperial History* reference many of the individual emperor's economic measures. Note also the following. As well as Suetonius (*Domitian* 7), Statius mentions the failure of the vine edict in *Silvae* 4, 3; there is a short introduction to the controversies over this in Brian W. Jones, *The Emperor Domitian* (Routledge, 1992), 77–8. The fullest account of the earthquake and Tiberius's response is Tacitus, *Annals* 2, 47. The sale of the property of Commodus is reported in the *Imperial History*, *Pertinax* 7–8. The evidence in scattered papyrus documents for emperors' estates in Egypt is collected by G. M. Parassoglou, *Imperial Estates in Roman Egypt* (Hakkert, 1978), and more briefly by Dorothy J. Crawford, 'Imperial Estates' in *Studies in Roman Property*, edited by Moses I. Finley (Cambridge UP, 1976), 35–70. 'Nero's Farm' (Saltus Neronianus) is discussed by Mariette de Vos, 'The Rural Landscape of Thugga', in *The Roman Agricultural Economy*, edited by Alan Bowman and Andrew Wilson (Oxford UP, 2013), 143–218. Levick, *Faustina I and II* (above, 'General'), 23 and 178, provides reference to the bricks of Faustina. Slightly different figures for Augustus's vast bequest are given by Suetonius, *Augustus* 101, Tacitus, *Annals* 1, 8 and Cassius Dio 56, 32. The story of the choir is told in Macrobius, *Saturnalia* 2, 28. Septimius Severus's daily schedule is summarised by Cassius Dio 77, 17. Tacitus, *Annals* 12, 1–3 recounts the debates on Claudius's marriage.

Places to visit: In Rome, visits can be booked to 'Broken Pot Mountain' (Monte Testaccio), though it is not regularly open to walk in. Many of the inscriptions I have referred to are stored in museum basements. But those normally on display include, in Lyon, the text of Claudius's speech, in the Museum of Gallo-Roman Civilisation, and in London in the British Museum, the tombstone of Gaius Julius Classicianus, the whistle-blower. The sharp-eyed will spot many imperial slaves and freedmen in the small, unlabelled epitaphs set into the walls of the old galleries in the Capitoline Museums in Rome.

Chapter 7

The full account of Commodus in the amphitheatre and of his gladiatorial obsession is in Cassius Dio 73, 17–22. The ancient biographies frequently refer to what emperors got up to in their spare time, and most of my references can be tracked down there. The positive attitude to swimming can be inferred from the fact that Suetonius criticises Caligula specifically for not being able to swim (*Caligula* 54). Although the Latin (of Suetonius *Julius Caesar* 32) is now the standard version, Caesar's phrase on crossing the Rubicon was spoken in Greek (as in Plutarch, *Pompey* 60). 'Bread and circuses' is from Juvenal, *Satire* 10, 77–81. Clear reviews of Roman spectacles and entertainments of different types can be found in *Gladiators and Caesars: The Power of Spectacle in Ancient Rome*, edited by Eckart Köhne and Cornelia Ewigleben (University of California Press, 2000); Kathleen Coleman, 'Entertaining Rome', in *Ancient Rome: The Archaeology of the Eternal City*, edited by John Coulston and Hazel Dodge (Oxbow, 2000), 210–58; David S. Potter, 'Spectacle', in *A Companion to the Roman Empire*, edited by Potter (above, 'Chapter 1'), 385–408; and Nicholas Purcell, '"Romans, play on!": City of the Games', in *The Cambridge Companion to Ancient Rome*, edited by Paul Erdkamp (Cambridge UP, 2013), 441–58. *The Roman Games: Historical Sources in Translation*, edited by Alison Futrell (Blackwell, 2006) collects ancient evidence for the amphitheatre and races. Katherine Dunbabin, *Theater and Spectacle in the Art of the Roman Empire* (Cornell UP, 2016) focuses on surviving visual images.

The Colosseum and its shows are the focus of my book, written with Keith Hopkins, *The Colosseum* (Profile, 2005), where most of the topics raised here can be followed up. But there are many other illuminating explorations of the culture of the Roman amphitheatre, including: Jerry Toner, *The Day Commodus Killed a Rhino: Understanding the Roman Games* (Johns Hopkins UP, 2014), from whom I have borrowed the comparison with the opera; Garrett G. Fagan, *The Lure of the Arena: Social Psychology and the Crowd at the Roman Games* (Cambridge UP, 2011); Jonathan Edmondson, 'Dynamic Arenas: Gladiatorial Presentations in the City of Rome' in *Roman Theater and Society*, edited by W. J. Slater (University of Michigan Press, 1996), 69–112. Katherine E. Welch, *The Roman Amphitheatre: From Its Origins to the Colosseum* (Cambridge UP, 2007), examines the architectural form of the arena. The games hosted by a particular emperor and his attitude to the arena are often mentioned in the relevant biography of Suetonius or the *Imperial History*. In addition, note the following. Augustus gives the total of gladiators displayed in *What I Did*, 22. Cassius Dio 68, 15 notes the 11,000 animals killed in Trajan's games, while at 43, 22 he warns of the exaggeration in such figures. Marcus Aurelius's dismissal of the violence as 'boring' is made in *Jottings to Himself* 6, 46 and his aversion to bloodshed is noted by Cassius Dio 72, 29. The comment (made by a senator) about 'contamination' can be found in James H. Oliver and Robert E. A. Palmer, 'Minutes of an Act of the Roman Senate', *Hesperia* 24 (1955), 320–49, esp. 340. 'Stars of their own destruction' is the apt phrase of Toner, *The Day Commodus Killed a Rhino* 10; 'fatal charades' is drawn from the title of a groundbreaking article by K. M. Coleman, 'Fatal Charades: Roman Executions Staged as Mythological Enactments', *Journal of Roman Studies* 80 (1990), 44–73. Martial's praise of the opening games in the Colosseum can be found in his short book *On the Spectacles* (the return to public use is stressed in poem 2). Juvenal's barbs on the senator's wife are in his *Satire* 6, 82–113. Legislation against the elite appearing in the arena is discussed by Barbara Levick, 'The *Senatus Consultum* from Larinum', *Journal of Roman Studies* 73 (1983), 97–115. Septimius Severus's accusations of hypocrisy are quoted in Cassius Dio 76, 8.

Chariot-racing in general is the subject of Fik Meijer, *Chariot Racing in the Roman Empire* (Johns Hopkins University Press, 2010). The archaeology and function of circuses in the empire, including the Circus Maximus, is discussed in detail by John Humphrey, *Roman Circuses: Arenas for Chariot Racing* (University of California Press, 1986). Alan Cameron, *Circus Factions: Blues and Greens at Rome and Byzantium* (Oxford UP, 1976) is a history of racing and its participants from Augustus to the Byzantine empire. The erotic side of the Circus is brilliantly evoked by John Henderson, 'A Doo-Dah-Doo-Dah-Dey at the Races: Ovid *Amores* 3. 2 and the Personal Politics of the *Circus Maximus*', *Classical Antiquity* 21 (2002), 41–65.

The connection between the palace and the Circus is briefly discussed by Wulf-Rheidt, 'The Palace of the Roman Emperors on the Palatine in Rome' (above, 'Chapter 4'), 13. The fourth-century calendar is the so-called *Chronography of 354*, discussed by Michele Renee Salzman, 'Structuring Time: Festivals, Holidays and the Calendar', in *The Cambridge Companion to Ancient*

Rome, edited by Erdkamp, 478–96. Augustus's new *pulvinar* is mentioned in *What I Did* 19, discussed by Cooley, Res Gestae Divi Augusti (above, 'Chapter 1'), 187–8. Ovid, *Art of Dating* (*Ars Amatoria*), 136–62, jokes about the potential for a pick-up in the Circus. Pliny's disapproval is registered at *Letters* 9, 6, Tertullian's at *On the Spectacles* 16. The 'equality' of Trajan in the Circus is praised by Pliny, *Speech of Praise* 51. Herodian, *History* 4, 7 and 11 refers to Caracalla racing abroad, Cassius Dio 73, 17 to Commodus driving chariots in the dark. The suicide of the fan of the Reds is reported by Pliny, *Natural History* 7, 186, the dung sniffing by Galen, *On the Method of Medicine* 7, 6 (translated in Loeb Classical Library). As well as Suetonius (*Caligula* 55), Cassius Dio 59, 14 reports the pampering of Incitatus, and 74, 4 tells of Commodus's horse Pertinax and the omen of the name. Hadrian using a herald in the Colosseum is described by Cassius Dio 69, 6. Josephus, *Jewish Antiquities* 19, 24 gets straight to the logic of the emperor's position in the face of popular demands. The protests against Didius Julianus and Cleander are described by Cassius Dio 74, 12–13 and 73, 13 (he explicitly makes the point about 'safety in numbers' at 79, 20).

A useful introduction to the range of Roman theatrical performance is Richard C. Beacham, *The Roman Theatre and its Audience* (Harvard UP, 1996). Theatre buildings are the focus of Frank Sear, *Roman Theatres: An Architectural Study* (Oxford UP, 2006). The heckling about Mnester is reported by Cassius Dio 60, 28. The problems of Nero and the stage are well introduced by Catharine Edwards, 'Beware of Imitations: Theatre and the Subversion of Imperial Identity' in *Reflections of Nero*, edited by Elsner and Masters (above, 'Chapter 3'), 83–97, Opper, *Nero* (above, 'Chapter 3'), 158–73, and they are analysed in detail by Bartsch, *Actors in the Audience* (above, 'Chapter 1'), 1–62. The collapsing theatre is reported by Tacitus, *Annals* 15, 33–4. Slightly different accounts are given of Nero 'fiddling while Rome burns' by Suetonius, *Nero* 38, Tacitus, *Annals* 15, 39 and Cassius Dio 62, 18. Nero's theatrical masks are noted by Cassius Dio 62, 9. Philostratus's musing is at his *Life of Apollonius* 5, 7. The slightly different accounts of Nero's clash with Montanus (Suetonius, *Nero* 26, Tacitus, *Annals* 13, 25, Cassius Dio 61, 9) are discussed by Bartsch, *Actors in the Audience*, 16–20.

J. K Anderson, *Hunting in the Ancient World* (University of California Press, 1985) offers an overview of hunting in Rome and Greece, with more recent observations by Steven L. Tuck, 'The Origins of Imperial Hunting

Imagery: Domitian and the Re-definition of *Virtus* under the Principate', *Greece and Rome* 52 (2005), 221–45; Eleni Manolaraki, 'Imperial and Rhetorical Hunting in Pliny's *Panegyricus*', *Illinois Classical Studies* 37 (2012), 175–98; and Matthew B. Roller, 'Dining and Hunting as Courtly Activities', in *The Roman Emperor and his Court*, edited by Kelly and Hug (above, 'General'), vol. I, 318–48, esp. 336–48. The Hadrianic hunting scenes on the Arch of Constantine are discussed by Mary Taliaferro Boatwright, *Hadrian and the City of Rome* (Princeton UP, 1987), 190–202 (who also gives reference to the 'hunting coins' from Hadrianoutherae) and by Opper, *Hadrian* (above, 'Chapter 4'), 171–3. The joke about scratching your legs can be found at Varro, *Menippean Satires* fragments 293–6 (French translation by J.-P. Cèbe in his Varron *Satires Ménippées*, vol. 8). Pliny's style of hunting is described at Pliny, *Letters* 1, 6; Fronto's at *Letters to Marcus* 4, 5 (translated by Richlin, *Marcus Aurelius in Love* (above, 'Chapter 5'), no. 38). The comparison between the hunting of Trajan and Domitian is made by Pliny, *Speech of Praise* 81–82; and between the good emperor and bad emperor by Dio Chrysostom, *Discourse* 3, 133–8. Translations of Hadrian's poem 'To Eros' are elusive. Birley, *Hadrian: The Restless Emperor* (above, 'General'), 184–5, has a partial version; a full translation (and discussion) is provided by Ewen Bowie, 'Hadrian and Greek Poetry' in *Greek Romans and Roman Greeks: Studies in Cultural Interaction*, edited by Erik Nis Ostenfeld et al. (Aarhus UP, 2002), 172–97 (esp. 180–1). The main text of Pankrates's verses comes from Athenaeus, *Deipnosophistae* (*Sophists at Dinner*) 15, 21, combined with the more than thirty lines on papyrus, *POxy* 8, 1085 (= Loeb Classical Library, *Select Papyri* 3, no. 128). The erotic implications are discussed by Vout, *Power and Eroticism* (above, 'Chapter 5'), 59–60. Hadrian's poem on Borysthenes can be found in the Loeb Classical Library, *Minor Latin Poets* vol. II, Hadrian no. 4.

Places to visit: The Colosseum is the biggest tourist attraction in Rome; it is enormously impressive from the outside, but it is hard to get a good idea of the original appearance inside. What remains of the Circus Maximus is free to wander around, as is the exterior of the Theatre of Marcellus. The excavated remains of a smaller theatre in the city, the Theatre of Balbus (Crypta Balbi), are also open to the public. The sculptures of Hadrian at the hunt are still visible on the Arch of Constantine, adjacent to the Colosseum.

Chapter 8

I discuss the singing statue in my *Civilisations* (Profile, 2018), 23–32. Strabo, *Geography* 17, 1 is sceptical about the sound. The poetry is discussed by T. Corey Brennan, 'The Poets Julia Balbilla and Damo at the Colossus of Memnon', *Classical World* 91 (1998), 215–34, and Patricia A. Rosenmeyer, *The Language of Ruins: Greek and Latin Inscriptions on the Memnon Colossus* (Oxford UP, 2018). Birley, *Hadrian: The Restless Emperor* (above, 'General'), 246, gives a translation of the poem on the Pyramid (now known only from a medieval manuscript copy). Balbilla's monument to Philopappos is discussed by Ian Worthington, *Athens after Empire: A History from Alexander the Great to the Emperor Hadrian* (Oxford UP, 2021), 299–302. The papyrus with details of the preparations for Hadrian's visit is most conveniently accessed online, with translation at https://papyri.info/ddbdp/sb;6;9617.

Good introductions to Hadrian's journeys are Elizabeth Speller, *Following Hadrian: A Second-Century Journey Through the Roman Empire* (Review, 2003) and, more briefly, Danziger and Purcell, *Hadrian's Empire* (above, 'General'), 129–38. The epitaph of Vitalis is translated in Brian Campbell, *The Roman Army, 31 BC – AD 337: A Sourcebook* (Routledge, 1994), no. 196, and by Purcell and Danziger, 163. The evidence for Hadrian's attention to tombs is collected and discussed by Mary T. Boatwright, *Hadrian and the Cities of the Roman Empire* (Princeton UP, 2000), 140–2; Septimius Severus honouring the grave of Pompey is mentioned by Cassius Dio 76, 13. Boatwright, 144–57, also provides a useful review of Hadrian's relations with Athens, the archaeology of his 'improvements', and the scattered written sources for it; likewise Worthington, *Athens after Empire* 302–31 (with a clear discussion of the significance of Hadrian's Gate). Philostratus, *Lives of the Sophists* 1, 25 records that the intellectual speaking at the opening of the temple of Zeus was Polemo, from Smyrna in modern Turkey; the star-struck writer is Pausanias, *Description of Greece* 1, 18. The dating system is discussed by Julia L. Shear, 'Hadrian, the Panathenaia, and the Athenian Calendar', *Zeitschrift für Papyrologie und Epigraphik* 180 (2012), 159–72. The role of the local elite in Athens is briefly reviewed by Dylan K. Rogers, 'Roman Athens', in *The Cambridge Companion to Ancient Athens*, edited by Jenifer Neils and Rogers (Cambridge UP, 2021), 421–36 (esp. 430–2). The portrait of Hadrian inside the Parthenon is noted by

Pausanias, *Description of Greece* 1, 24.

The standard work on emperors' travels in general is Helmut Halfmann, *Itinera principum; Geschichte und Typologie der Kaiserreisen im Römischen Reich* (Frank Steiner, 1986), but Halfmann also has a brief article in English, 'Imperial Journeys', in *The Roman Emperor and his Court*, edited by Kelly and Hug (above, 'General'), vol. I, 267–87. Various reasons are suggested by Suetonius, *Tiberius* 10, for his departure to Rhodes. The main literary accounts of Nero's visit to Greece are: Suetonius, *Nero* 19 and 22–24; Cassius Dio 62, 8–18; with good modern discussions by Susan Alcock, 'Nero at Play? The Emperor's Grecian Odyssey', in *Reflections of Nero*, edited by Elsner and Masters (above, 'Chapter 3'), 98–111, and Shushma Malik, 'An Emperor's War on Greece: Cassius Dio's Nero', in *Emperors and Political Culture in Cassius Dio's Roman History*, edited by Davenport and Mallan (above, 'General'), 158–76. The hostile essay is *Nero* (or *The Digging of the Isthmus*), attributed to the second-century satirist Lucian, though almost certainly not by him; it is cleverly analysed by Tim Whitmarsh, 'Greek and Roman in Dialogue: the Pseudo-Lucianic Nero', *Journal of Hellenic Studies* 119 (1999), 142–60. What survives of Nero's work on the canal has been traced by David Pettegrew, *The Isthmus of Corinth: Crossroads of the Mediterranean World* (University of Michigan Press, 2016), 166–205. The text of the speech giving freedom to Greece, and the reply, is translated by Sherk, *The Roman Empire from Augustus to Hadrian* (above, 'Chapter 4'), no. 71 and, in English with the original Greek, online at https://www.judaism-and-rome.org/nero-and-freedom-greece. Plutarch, *Flamininus* 10 records the earlier proclamation of the freedom of Greece. Germanicus's visit to Egypt is discussed by Tacitus, *Annals* 2, 59–61, with a recent dissection by Benjamin Kelly, 'Tacitus, Germanicus and the Kings of Egypt', *Classical Quarterly* 60 (2010), 221–37. Cassius Dio 54, 7 records the statue spitting blood; and an essay attributed to Plutarch, *Sayings of Romans*, 'Caesar Augustus' 13 quotes his anger with Athens. Augustus breaking the nose of Alexander is recorded by Cassius Dio 51, 16.

The Elizabethan minor aristocrat was Sir Henry Lee, who objected to the Queen's visit in a letter to Robert Cecil, dated 13 June 1600, although (or perhaps because) he had entertained her before. These entertainments (and refusals) are discussed by Sue Simpson, *Sir Henry Lee (1533–1611): Elizabethan Courtier* (Ashgate, 2014). Caracalla's demands are criticised by Cassius Dio 78,

9. The evidence for the upcoming visit of Alexander Severus is discussed by J. David Thomas and W. Clarysse, 'A Projected Visit of Severus Alexander to Egypt', *Ancient Society* 8 (1977), 195–207, and Peter Van Minnen and Joshua D. Sosin, 'Imperial Pork: Preparations for a Visit of Severus Alexander and Iulia Mamaea to Egypt', *Ancient Society* 27 (1996), 171–81. There is a useful introduction to the Panopolis papyri in Roger Rees, *Diocletian and the Tetrarchy* (Edinburgh UP, 2004), 33–6, with some convenient translations, no. 21. The original documents are published by T. C. Skeat, *Papyri from Panopolis in the Chester Beatty Library Dublin* (Chester Beatty Monographs 1, 1964); those concerning the imperial visit are in the first roll of papyrus.

The military role of the emperor is fully covered by J. B. Campbell, *The Emperor and the Roman Army, 31 BC to AD 235* (Oxford UP, 1984). 'Man-destroying war' is the phrase used in the Twelfth Book of *Sibylline Oracles* (lines 19–23); this unfamiliar genre of ancient literature, and this passage in particular, is discussed by David Potter, *Prophets and Emperors: Human and Divine Authority from Augustus to Theodosius* (Harvard UP, 1994), 71–97, 99–110, 137–45 (esp. 140–1). An old, not totally reliable, translation of the *Sibylline Oracles* is available online, at https://www.sacred-texts.com/cla/sib/index.htm. The background to particular military campaigns can be found in the general histories cited above, under 'General'. In addition to the military engagement (or not) of individual emperors referenced in their ancient biographies, note the following. Tacitus, *Annals* 1, 11 records Augustus's advice to Tiberius. The fluidity of frontiers is discussed by David Cherry, 'Frontier Zones', in *The Cambridge Economic History of the Greco-Roman World*, edited by Scheidel et al. (above, 'Chapter 6'), 720–40. The disputes over the function of Hadrian's Wall are briefly summarised in Richard Hingley, *Hadrian's Wall: A Life* (Oxford UP, 2012), 298–9. Jupiter's prophecy of 'empire without limit' is given at Virgil, *Aeneid* 1, 279. Roland R. R. Smith offers a clear account of the Great Antonine Altar at Ephesus in 'The Greek East Under Rome', in *A Companion to Roman Art*, edited by Barbara E. Borg (Blackwell, 2015), 471–95 (esp. 476–7). The phrase 'Grand Strategy' is borrowed from Edward N. Luttwak's once influential book, *The Grand Strategy of the Roman Empire: From the First Century CE to the Third* (revised ed., Johns Hopkins UP, 2016, originally published, 1979). The role of Britain in the Roman imagination (and politics) is well discussed by David Braund, *Ruling Roman Britain: Kings,*

Queens, Governors and Emperors from Julius Caesar to Agricola (Routledge, 1996). Cassius Dio 60, 19–22 gives an account of the invasion, including the hesitancy of the troops, the pep talk, the summoning of Claudius and the elephants. Tacitus's cynical assessment of the 'Romanisation' of Britain is at his *Agricola* 21. Ammianus Marcellinus, *Roman History* 16, 10 describes the impact of Trajan's Forum on the Emperor Constantius II in 357 CE, on his first visit to Rome. Trajan's Parthian campaigns are reviewed by Bennett, *Trajan Optimus Princeps* (above, 'Chapter 2'), 183–204. Cassius Dio 68, 17–33 covers the campaign, from start to finish, and its motivation – and is the main evidence for the details.

Pliny, *Speech of Praise* 15 congratulates Trajan as a *commilitio*; Dio Chrysostom's metaphor of the shepherd is at *Discourse* 1, 28. Virgil's image of Octavian/Augustus at the Battle of Actium is at *Aeneid* 8, 678–81; the realities are explained by Strauss, *The War that Made the Roman Empire* (above, 'Chapter 1'), 183–6. The stories of Trajan improvising the bandages and Septimius Severus and the water are told by Cassius Dio 68, 8 and 75, 2; the story of Caracalla's positive military qualities by Herodian, *History* 4, 7. The full text and translation of Hadrian's speech to the soldiers at Lambaesis can be found in Michael P. Speidel, *Emperor Hadrian's speeches to the African Army – a new Text* (Römisch-Germanischen Zentralmuseum, 2006). Details of the history and ceremony of triumph, including the fake versions, are fully discussed in my *The Roman Triumph* (above, 'Chapter 1'). Nero's ceremony is described by Cassius Dio 62, 20, as well as in the relevant section of Suetonius (*Nero* 25). The Roman satirist Persius, *Satires* 6, 43–7, jokes about Caligula's wife ordering the costumes for the so-called captives. Domitian's fake triumph is criticised by Pliny, *Speech of Praise* 16, Tacitus, *Agricola* 39, and Cassius Dio 67, 7 (borrowing from the stores). Trajan's posthumous ceremony is mentioned in the *Imperial History, Hadrian* 6.

Places to visit: Several of Hadrian's monuments in Athens are still visible. What remains of Hadrian's Library, near the modern Monastiraki Square, is open every day – though it needs some imagination to recapture its original glory. But it is impossible to miss the vast columns of the Temple of Olympian Zeus, just to the east of the Acropolis, even if you choose not to pay to get up close; the gate (or arch) of Hadrian stands just off the street nearby.

Chapter 9

Both 'emperor dreams' are from Artemidorus, *The Interpretation of Dreams* 4, 31; the prediction of death is at 2, 30. Peter Thonemann, *An Ancient Dream Manual: Artemidorus'* The Interpretation of Dreams (Oxford UP, 2020), 198–204, discusses the role of the emperor in this manual (with a good modern translation by Martin Hammond in the Oxford World's Classics series). Jennifer Trimble, '*Corpore enormi*: the Rhetoric of Physical Appearance in Suetonius and Imperial Portrait Statuary', in *Art and Rhetoric in Roman Culture*, edited by Jaś Elsner and Michel Meyer (Cambridge UP, 2014), 115–54, is a sophisticated discussion of the difference between the sculpture and Suetonius's descriptions. The long history of modern appropriation of images of Roman emperors is the main theme of my *Twelve Caesars: Images of Power from the Ancient World to the Modern* (Princeton UP, 2021), which also discusses in detail some of the questions about the identification of ancient 'portrait' statues treated briefly here (in particular, the different ancient images that have been thought to represent Julius Caesar).

The multiple statues of Julius Caesar are mentioned by Cassius Dio 44, 4; the pedestals are reviewed by Antony E. Raubitschek, 'Epigraphical Notes on Julius Caesar', *Journal of Roman Studies* 44 (1954), 65–75, and by Jakob Munk Højte, *Roman Imperial Statue Bases: From Augustus to Commodus* (Aarhus UP, 2005), 97. The authoritative catalogue of images of Augustus is Dietrich Boschung, *Die Bildnesse des Augustus* (Gebr. Mann, 1993). Jane Fejfer, *Roman Portraits in Context* (Walter de Gruyter, 2008), 373–429, offers an overview of the ideology, making, remaking and display of portraits of the emperors, with Caroline Vout, *Exposed: The Greek and Roman Body* (Profile, 2022), 235–68, and Susan Wood, 'Portraiture', in *The Oxford Handbook of Roman Sculpture*, edited by Elise A. Friedland et al, (Oxford UP, 2015), 260–75. Clifford Ando, *Imperial Ideology and Provincial Loyalty in the Roman Empire* (University of California Press, 2000), 206–45, focuses on the social and political significance of imperial images. The role of models and of their identification through details of hairstyle is discussed by R. R. R. Smith, 'Typology and Diversity in the Portraits of Augustus', *Journal of Roman Archaeology* 9 (1996), 30–47 (a response to Boschung's catalogue), Caroline Vout, 'Antinous, Archaeology and History', *Journal of Roman Studies* 95 (2005), 80–96 (raising some sceptical questions), and Klaus Fittschen, 'The Portraits of Roman Emperors and their Families', in *The Emperor and Rome* edited by Ewald and Noreña (above, 'Chapter 1'), 221–46 (a learned, but slightly grumpy, response to Vout). The friend of Hadrian is Arrian, in his *Periplus* (or *Circumnavigation*) 2 (translation by Aidan Liddle, Bristol Classical Press, 2003). John Pollini, *The Portraiture of Gaius and Lucius Caesar* (Fordham UP, 1987), 100 and 101, references the rival identifications of the two much contested statues. Different explanations for Hadrian's beard are canvassed by Paul Zanker, *The Mask of Socrates* (University of California Press, 1996), 217–33, Caroline Vout, 'What's in a Beard? Rethinking Hadrian's Hellenism', *Rethinking Revolutions Through Ancient Greece*, edited by Simon Goldhill and Robin Osbourne (Cambridge UP, 2006), 96–123, and Opper, *Hadrian* (above, 'Chapter 4'), 69–72 (focusing on a famous statue of the bearded Hadrian, which turns out to have been wrongly restored).

The portraits of Livia are collected in Elizabeth Bartman, *Portraits of Livia: Imaging the Imperial Woman in Augustan Rome* (Cambridge UP, 1999). The role of wigs in female portrait statues is examined by Helen I. Ackers, 'The Representation of Wigs in Roman Female Portraiture of the Late 2nd to 3rd Century AD', *BABESCH* 94 (2019), 211–34. R. R. R. Smith, 'Roman Portraits: Honours, Empresses, and Late Emperors', *Journal of Roman Studies* 75 (1985), 209–21, offers several examples of the portraits of imperial women being modelled on emperors (214–15). The whole group of dynastic statues at Veleia is discussed by C. Brian Rose, *Dynastic Commemoration and Imperial Portraiture in the Julio-Claudian Period* (Cambridge UP, 1997), 121–6 (with a plan in Kelly and Hug, above, 'General', vol. II, no. 5.7); the statue of Messalina by Susan E. Wood, 'Messalina, Wife of Claudius: Propaganda Successes and Failures of his Reign', *Journal of Roman Archaeology* 5 (1992), 219–34 (esp. 219–30), with discussion of the Greek prototype by Amy C. Smith, *Polis and Personification in Classical Athenian Art* (Brill, 2011), 110–12. The sculpture, and the history of the building, at Aphrodisias is laid out in detail by R. R. R. Smith, *The Marble Reliefs from the Julio-Claudian Sebasteion* (*Aphrodisias* VI) (Philipp von Zabern, 2013) – the panel with Nero and Agrippina is no. A1. The imperial reliefs are discussed more briefly by Smith in 'The Imperial Reliefs from the Sebasteion at Aphrodisias', *Journal of Roman Studies* 77 (1987), 88–138. The phrase 'signature conquest' is Smith's (in *The Marble Reliefs*, 142). R. R. R.

Smith (again) discusses the cameo showing Agrippina and Nero in 'Maiestas Serena' (above, 'Chapter 4'), no. 39. I explore further the constructive fudging between empress and deity in Twelve Caesars, 247–9. The gold plaque from Colchester (now in the British Museum) is briefly discussed by Catherine Johns, The Jewellery of Roman Britain: Celtic and Classical Traditions (UCL Press, 1996), 191. The gambling tokens of Livia are explained by Anthony A. Barrett, Livia: First Lady of Imperial Rome (Yale UP, 2002), 263–4. Dahmen, Untersuchungen (above, 'Prologue') reviews many of the imperial trinkets. The role and representation of emperors in Egyptian temples is discussed by Martina Minas-Nerpel, 'Egyptian Temples' in The Oxford Handbook of Roman Egypt, edited by Christina Riggs (Oxford UP, 2012), 362–82. The misidentification of the statue of Marcus Aurelius is one theme of Peter Stewart, 'The Equestrian Statue of Marcus Aurelius', in A Companion to Marcus Aurelius, edited by van Ackeren (above, 'Chapter 5'), 264–77.

The paintings (or painted statues) are referred to by Fronto, Letter to Marcus 4, 12 (included in Davenport and Manley, Fronto, above, 'Chapter 4', no. 24). Pliny, Natural History 35, 51 tells the story of the painting of Nero; Herodian, History 5, 5 explains the painting of Elagabalus. The surviving painting of Septimius Severus's family (including, rather unreliably, the papyrus evidence) is discussed by Thomas F. Mathews, with Norman E. Muller, The Dawn of Christian Art (J. Paul Getty Museum, 2016), 74–83, with a partial and accurate translation of the papyrus by Jane Rowlandson, Women and Society in Greek and Roman Egypt: A Sourcebook (Cambridge UP, 1998), no. 44. 'Relatively crude' is the judgement of Jaś Elsner, The Art of the Roman Empire (2nd ed., Oxford UP, 2018), 51; 'exceptional quality' that of Mathews, 74. The colossal statue of Nero is discussed by Barrett, Rome is Burning (above, 'Chapter 4'), 199–201, and Fred C. Albertson, 'Zenodorus's "Colossus of Nero"', Memoirs of the American Academy in Rome 46 (2001), 95–118. Pliny's admiration for the colossus is expressed in his Natural History 34, 45–47. Cassius Dio 65, 15 refers to the features of Titus (though suggests that the statue was actually first erected under Vespasian); the Imperial History, Hadrian 19 refers to its relocation; and Herodian History 1, 15, Cassius Dio 73, 22 and the Imperial History, Commodus 17 to the adjustments by Commodus. The colossal statue of Domitian is the subject of Statius, Silvae 1, 1, discussed by Newlands, Statius' Silvae (above, 'Chapter 3'), 51–73, and Daira Nocera, 'Legacy Revisited: Augustus and Domitian in the Imperial Fora and the Roman Forum', in *Domitian's Rome and the Augustan Legacy*, edited by Raymond Marks and Marcello Mogetta (University of Michigan Press, 2021), 57–75 (esp. 65–74).

Augustus mentions the silver statues in *What I Did*, 24; Marcus Aurelius and Lucius Verus's refusal is recorded in an inscription (*Die Inschriften von Ephesos* I no. 25) that is fully discussed, but without a complete translation, online at: https://www.judaism-and-rome.org/re-casting-imperial-images-ephesus-under-marcus-aurelius. The key question with colossal figures is whether they were erected in the emperor's lifetime. That is certainly the case, for example, with the larger-than-life statue of Augustus in the chariot in the Forum of Augustus, but others including some surviving fragments were only erected after his death. Martial, *Epigrams* 8, 44 may refer to a colossus put up during his reign. The complicated history of the colossal statue of Tiberius, now known from an ancient copy of its base, is reviewed by Ando, *Imperial Ideology and Provincial Loyalty*, 311. Rutledge, *Ancient Rome as a Museum* (above, 'Chapter 4'), 215–20, considers the monstrosity of the colossal. The 'cancellation' of images is discussed by Peter Stewart, *Status in Roman Society: Representation and Response* (Oxford UP, 2003), 267–90. The myth of the shit is dispelled by Mathews, with Muller, in *The Dawn of Christian Art*, 80. The Meroe head is explored in depth by Thorsten Opper, *The Meroë Head* (British Museum Press, 2014). Discussions of the Hadrianic reliefs on the Arch of Constantine are referenced above, 'Chapter 7'. Statius *Silvae* 1, 1, 84–7 jokes about the head of Caesar. The re-carving of imperial statues is a major theme of *From Caligula to Constantine: Tyranny and Transformation in Roman Portraiture*, edited by Eric R. Warner (Michael C. Carlos Museum, Emory University, 2000), esp. 9–14, with many individual examples explained in the catalogue.

The story of Otho being put on a pedestal is told by Tacitus, *Histories* 1, 36, and that of the plight of Callidromus by Pliny, *Letters* 10, 74. The perceived power of imperial statues is discussed by S. R. F. Price, *Rituals and Power: The Roman Imperial Cult in Asia Minor* (Cambridge UP, 1984), 191–205, and (focusing also on coin images) by Ando, *Imperial Ideology and Provincial Loyalty*, 206–39 (specific references can be found in the relevant ancient biographies). The collection of imperial portraits from Acqua Traversa is reviewed by Fejfer, *Roman Portraits*, 422–5, with a full discussion by Valentina Mastrodonato,

'Una residenza imperiale nel suburbio di Roma: La villa di Lucio Vero in località Acquatraversa', *Archeologia Classica* 51 (1999–2000), 157–235.

Places to visit: Most major museums have at least a few portrait busts of Roman emperors. One of the most evocative collections is the Room of the Emperors in the Capitoline Museums in Rome, a line-up of emperors, and their wives, from Julius Caesar on, first assembled in the 1730s. Both the famous statue of Commodus as Hercules and Marcus Aurelius on horseback are displayed elsewhere in the same museum. The Augustus from Livia's villa at Prima Porta is now in the Vatican Museums. Outside Rome, the statues from Veleia are in the Archaeological Museum of Parma, in northern Italy. The sculptures from Aphrodisias are in the museum on the site in south-western Turkey. The sculptured reliefs showing Augustus from the temple of Dendur are now in the Metropolitan Museum in New York.

Chapter 10

Christopher L. Whitton, 'Seneca, *Apocolocyntosis*' in *A Companion to the Neronian Age*, edited by Emma Buckley and Martin Dinter (Blackwell, 2013), 151–69, is an excellent introduction to the skit. The circumstances of death and the deathbed words can usually be found in the relevant ancient biography (where these are often a major theme). The bungled abdication is that of Vitellius (Tacitus, *Histories* 3, 68–70; Suetonius, *Vitellius* 15). The suicide of Julia Domna on receiving the ashes is one version of her story given by Herodian, *History* 4, 13 (different accounts are discussed by Barbara Levick, *Julia Domna: Syrian Empress* (Routledge, 2007), 105–6). The main evidence for Republican funerals is Polybius, *Histories* 6, 53–4 (translated in Beard et al., *Religions of Rome*, vol. II (above, 'Chapter 4'), no. 9.3, with a translation of Cassius Dio's account, 75, 4–5, of the funeral of Pertinax); the funerary ritual is discussed by Harriet I. Flower, 'Spectacle and Political Culture in the Roman Republic', in *The Cambridge Companion to the Roman Republic*, edited by Flower (Cambridge UP, 2004), 331–7. Augustus's funeral is described by Cassius Dio 56, 34–43, as well as by Suetonius, *Augustus* 100. Herodian, *History* 4, 2 elaborates on the funeral of Septimius Severus. Eve D'Ambra, 'The Imperial Funerary

Pyre as a Work of Ephemeral Architecture' and Javier Arce, 'Roman Imperial Funerals *in effigie*' discuss different aspects of funerals, in *The Emperor and Rome*, edited by Ewald and Noreña (above, 'Chapter 1'), 289–308 and 309–23. Imperial tombs are the central theme of Davies, *Death and the Emperor* (above, 'Chapter 2'). Boatwright, *Hadrian and the City of Rome* (above, 'Chapter 7'), 161–81, and Opper, *Hadrian* (above, 'Chapter 4'), 208–16, focus on Hadrian's mausoleum. The text of the imperial epitaphs can be found at *Corpus Inscriptionum Latinarum* (above, 'General') VI, 886 (and 40372) (Agrippina), 887 (Tiberius), 992 (Commodus) – 887 and 992 are known only from medieval manuscript copies; a translation of Agrippina's epitaph can be found in Emily A. Hemelrijk, *Women and Society in the Roman World: A Sourcebook of Inscriptions from the Roman West* (Cambridge UP, 2020), 304.

The consecration of emperors and the imperial cult in general has been a major theme in modern studies of the Roman empire. Beard et al., *Religions of Rome*, vol. I, 206–10 and 348–63, offers a general introduction to the topic. Simon Price, 'From Noble Funerals to Divine Cult: the Consecration of Roman Emperors', in *Rituals of Royalty: Power and Ceremonial in Traditional Societies*, edited by David Cannadine and Price (Cambridge UP, 1987), 56–105, was ground-breaking in its analysis of imperial funerals and the rituals of apotheosis – as was Price's analysis of emperor worship in the eastern empire, *Rituals and Power* (above, 'Chapter 9'), which also considered the precedents under the earlier kings in the region. Ittai Gradel, *Emperor Worship and Roman Religion* (Oxford UP, 2004) focuses on Rome and Italy. Tacitus deplores the sycophancy of deifying baby Claudia at *Annals* 15, 23. Witnesses to the ascent of the new god are mentioned by Cassius Dio 56, 46 and 59, 11 (on the honours to Drusilla); both passages mention the cash reward. Calendars of sacrifices to (or on behalf of) emperors and their families are translated in Beard et al., *Religions of Rome*, vol. II, nos. 3.3b and c, 3.4 and 3.5 (the calendar from Dura Europos). The nudge from the local governor is recorded in an inscription translated in Sherk, *Rome and the Greek East* (above, 'Prologue'), no. 101, and online, with full discussion, at https://www.judaism-and-rome.org/augustus%E2%80%99s-birthday-and-calendar-reform-asia. The role of the imperial cult in the rebellion of Boudicca is claimed by Tacitus, *Annals* 14, 31 (though Duncan Fishwick, 'The Temple of Divus Claudius at Camulodunum', *Britannia* 26 (1995), 11–27, explores some of the uncertainties surrounding this).

Useful overviews of the character of traditional Roman paganism include: Beard et al., *Religions of Rome*, vols. I and II; John Scheid, *The Gods, The State and The Individual: Reflections on Civic Religion in Rome* (University of Pennsylvania Press, 2015); and Jörg Rüpke, *Pantheon: A New History of Roman Religion* (Princeton UP, 2018). I look carefully at priests in 'Priesthood in the Roman Republic', in *Pagan Priests: Religion and Power in the Ancient World* (Duckworth, 1990), 17–48. Some of the tricky conundrums are discussed in detail by S. R. F. Price, *Rituals and Power* (above, 'Chapter 9'), 207–33, and 'Between Man and God: Sacrifice in the Roman Imperial Cult', *Journal of Roman Studies* 70 (1980), 28–43 (on precise conventions of sacrifice); by Price, 'Gods and Emperors: the Greek Language of the Roman Imperial Cult', *Journal of Hellenic Studies* 104 (1984), 79–95 (on terminology); by D. S. Levene, 'Defining the Divine in Rome', in *Transactions of the American Philological Association* 142 (2012), 41–81 (on the boundary between gods and humans); and by David Wardle, '*Deus* or *Divus*: The Genesis of Roman Terminology for Deified Emperors' in *Philosophy and Power in Graeco-Roman World*, edited by Gillian Clark and Tessa Rajak (Oxford UP, 2002), 181–92 (one attempt to pin down the distinction). I explore the awkward visual images of apotheosis with John Henderson in 'The Emperor's New Body: Ascension from Rome', in *Parchments of Gender: Deciphering the Bodies of Antiquity*, edited by Maria Wyke (Oxford UP, 1998), 191–220.

Fik Meijer, *Emperors Don't Die in Bed* (Routledge, 2004) is a popular book that describes the death of every emperor from Julius Caesar to the fifth century CE. The parody of Claudius's last words is at Seneca, *Apocolocyntosis* 4. Cassius Dio 77, 15 and 17 reports the last words of Septimius Severus, and 78, 2 the last words of Geta. Cassius Dio 56, 30 seems to interpret Augustus's dying words as a mockery of mankind. D. Wardle, 'A Perfect Send-Off: Suetonius and the Dying Art of Augustus (Suet. *Aug.* 99)', *Mnemosyne* 60 (2007), 443–63, sees his death as a perfect performance.

Places to visit: Although the mausoleum of Augustus in Rome is currently closed to the public, the mausoleum of Hadrian (the Castel Sant'Angelo) is regularly open to visitors.

Epilogue

The death of Alexander Severus is recounted by Herodian, *History* 6, 8–9 and the *Imperial History, Alexander Severus* 59–62 (canvassing Britain as the location of his murder). Kenneth Painter and David Whitehouse, 'The Discovery of the Vase', *Journal of Glass Studies* 32 (1990), 85–102, discusses the possible tomb in Rome. The events of the period after the death of Alexander Severus are laid out in some of the narrative histories cited above, under 'General'. The question of the 'crisis' of the third century (and even whether there *was* a crisis) has been debated for decades. *Crises and the Roman Empire,* edited by Olivier Hekster et al. (Brill, 2007) gives a good taste of different approaches and answers. A brief background to Shapur's relief can be found in Touraj Daryaae, 'The Sasanian Empire (224–651 CE)', in *The Oxford Handbook of Iranian History,* edited by Daryaae (Oxford UP, 2012), 187–207 (esp. 189–90). Christopher Kelly, 'Pliny and Pacatus: Past and Present in Imperial Panegyric' in *Contested Monarchy: Integrating the Roman Empire in the Fourth Century* AD, edited by Johannes Wienand (Oxford UP, 2015), 215–38, argues that the break with the 'one of us' style of emperor was not as sharp as it is often presented. I have based my remarks on the numbers of Christians on Keith Hopkins, 'Christian Number and its Implications', in *Sociological Studies in Roman History,* edited by Kelly (above, 'Chapter 5'), 432–80, with a useful afterword by Kate Cooper, 481–7 (I have also borrowed the phrase 'don't get too worked up' from there). Nero's treatment of the Christians is described by Tacitus, *Annals* 15, 44. *Roman Games,* edited by Futrell (above, 'Chapter 7'), 160–88, includes translation of some of the main accounts of martyrdom and Roman responses to Christians (the events of Lyon, 176–9). The short-term ruler was Decius (249–51 CE). The exact details of what he demanded are unclear, but some certificates to confirm that individuals had performed sacrifice have survived (a translation can be found in Beard et al., *Religions of Rome,* vol. II (above, 'Chapter 4'), no. 6.8c). The radical cultural and political revolution that came with Christianity is sharply and succinctly summed up by Kelly, *The Roman Empire* (above, 'General'), 78–94.

Places to visit: What is believed to be the mausoleum of Alexander Severus and his mother – now known as Monte del Grano ('Grain Mountain', from its shape) – is not far from the Villa of the Quintilii, between the centre of Rome and Ciampino airport; it is open to the public, but prebooking is usually required. The Portland Vase, a stunning piece of ancient glass, even if it did not hold the ashes of Alexander Severus, is a star attraction in the Roman galleries at the British Museum in London.

LIST OF ILLUSTRATIONS

Colour plates

14. Commemorative coin celebrating Trajan's defeat of the Parthians and the capture of Ctesiphon. Photo: © The Trustees of the British Museum
15 & 16. (Left) Augustus of Prima Porta, Vatican Museum, Rome. (Right) Painted cast of the original, Ashmolean Museum. Photo: © Azoor Photo / Alamy Stock Photo and © Ashmolean Museum/Heritage Images/Getty Images
17. The Great Cameo of France, Paris. Photo: © Pictures from History/ Marie-Lan Nguyen / Bridgeman Images
18. The ceiling of Domus Transitoria, Rome. Photo: Alessandro Serrano/ Photoshot/agefotostock
19. A ceiling design in the Antique manner, based on Domus Transitoria and attributed to Agostino Brunias. Photo: © Christie's Images / Bridgeman Images
20. Wall decoration, *horti* Lamiani, Capitoline Museum, Palazzo dei Conservatori, Rome. Photo: Roma, Sovrintendenza Capitolina ai Beni Culturali
21. Augustus as pharaoh, from the temple of Isis at Dendur, now reassembled in the Metropolitan Museum, New York. Photo: Robin Cormack
22. Mosaic showing racing in the Circus Maximus, Lyon. Photo: © Photo Josse / Bridgeman Images
23. Fayam portrait of a young man. Photo: © Pictures from History / Bridgeman Images
24. Gilded bronze peacock. Photo: © Governorate of The Vatican City State – Directorate of the Vatican Museums

Illustrations
1. Marble portrait bust of Elagabalus. Photo: © Bridgeman Images 3
2. The 'Table of Lyon'. Photo: G. Dagli Orti /© NPL – DeA Picture Library / Bridgeman Images 14
3. A replica of an ancient pastry mould. Photo: © Budapest History Museum, Aquincum Museum, Budapest, Hungary – Inventory no. 51595 15
4. Earring: portrait of Septimius Severus. Photo: © The Trustees of the British Museum 15

21. Canopus dining room, Hadrian's Villa, Tivoli. Photo: © Adam Eastland / Alamy Stock Photo 97

22. Tombstone of Titus Aelius Primitivus. Photo: © Governorate of The Vatican City State – Directorate of the Vatican Museums 103

23. Tombstone of Tiberius Claudius Zosimus. Photo: © Gabinetto Fotografico delle Gallerie degli Uffizi 104

24. View of the dining area and cave at Sperlonga. Photo: Flickr © Carole Raddato CC-by-SA-2.0 117

25. Detail of the blinding of Polyphemus, perhaps Roman copy after an Hellenistic statuary group, Sperlonga. Photo: © DeAgostini Picture Library/Scala, Florence 118

26. Scuba diver with statue depicting a companion of Ulysses, in the submerged Nymphaeum of Claudius, Baia, Naples. Photo: © BIOSPHOTO / Alamy Stock Photo 120

27. Fifth century BCE statue of a running Niobid from *horti Sallustiani*, now in Copenhagen. Photo: © Ny Carlsberg Glyptotek, Copenhagen / Ole Woldbye 127

28. Aerial view of the remains of Tiberius's villa on Capri. Photo: © Gianpiero Chirico 128

29. Pope John XXIII at his summer residence in Castel Gandolfo, 6 August 1961. Photo: © TopFoto 130

30. Lead piping from the *horti Lamiani*. Photo: © Roma - Soprintendenza Speciale di Roma/ Museo Ninfeo – Fondazione Enpam

31. The interior of the Auditorium of Maecenas, Rome. Photo: © Sebastiano Luciano 133

32. Hypothetical reconstruction of the Domus Aurea, from 'Staging Nero', in *The Cambridge Companion to the Age of Nero* (2017). Photo: Reproduced with permission of the Licensor through PLSclear 139

33. The octagon room in the Golden House. Photo: © Alberto Pizzoli/ Sygma/Sygma via Getty Images 141

34. Fresco restoration at Domus Aurea palace, Rome, 2014. Photo: © Marco Ansaloni/Science Photo Library 142

35. The Casino Farnese (garden lodge) in the Palatine palace. Photo: © Adam Eastland / Alamy Stock Photo 145

36. The Palatine stadium. Photo: © iStock / Getty Images Plus 151

79. Portrait bust of unknown emperor. Photo: © The Trustees of the British Museum 339

80. Portrait bust of Vespasian, Carlsberg Glyptotek Museum, Copenhagen, Denmark. Photo: © Prisma/Universal Images Group via Getty Images 341

81. Six empresses: Livia (© World History Archive / Alamy Stock Photo); Agrippina the Younger (© Fine Art Images/Heritage Images/Getty Image); Domitia Longa (© PHAS/Universal Images Group via Getty Images); Plotina (Flickr © Carole Raddato); Faustina (© DeAgostini Picture Library/Scala, Florence); Julia Domna (© Peter Horree / Alamy Stock Photo) 344

82. Three imperial women from a group of thirteen surviving statues found in Veleia, north Italy, now held in the National Archaeological Museum, Parma. Photo: © Mario Bonotto / Photo Scala, Florence 346

83. Life-size statue of Messalina, held in the Louvre, Paris. Photo: ©RMN-Grand Palais /Dist. Photo SCALA, Florence 347

84. Relief panel showing Agrippina crowning her son Nero, found in Aphrodisias, Turkey. Photo: © Paul Williams / Alamy Stock Photo 348

85. The earliest representation of Britannia, sculpture found in Aphrodisias, Turkey. Photo: © Paul Williams / Alamy Stock Photo 349

86. Relief panel showing Julia Domna crowning her son Caracalla, probably from Syria. Photo: © DCOW/EUB / Alamy Stock Photo 350

87. Statue showing Claudius as Jupiter, Vatican, Italy. Photo: ©INTERFOTO / Alamy Stock Photo 352

88. Trinkets showing emperors: finger ring with coin showing Caracalla. Photo: The Trustees of the British Museum; glass medallion showing Tiberius. Photo: gift of J. Pierpont Morgan, 1917 (17.194.18) The Met, New York; centre of ceramic bowl showing Augustus. Photo: gift of J. Pierpont Morgan, 1917 (17.194.1979) The Met, New York 354

89. Hand of emperor Constantine I the Great, Capitoline Museum, Rome. Photo: © Nevena Tsvetanova / Alamy Stock Photo 359

90. Finger ring with amethyst gem with engraved Nero. Photo: © bpk / Antikensammlung, SMB / Johannes Laurentius 360

91. Nero bust recut to depict Vespasian. Photo: © The Trustees of the British Museum 364

TIMELINE

LITERARY FIGURES	DATES	EVENTS	RULERS, PERIODS, WARS
		49 Caesar crosses the Rubicon	DICTATORSHIP OF **JULIUS CAESAR** AND ITS AFTERMATH
		48 Battle of Pharsalus; death of Pompey in Egypt	War between Caesar and Pompey
		46 Caesar's triumph	
		44 (JANUARY) Caesar is voted *dictator* 'for ever' (MARCH) Caesar's assassination	
CICERO assassinated	43	43	War between Caesar's assassins and Caesar's heirs
		42 Battle of Philippi: the defeat of Brutus and Cassius	
VIRGIL's *Eclogues*	39		
		37 Octavian and Livia marry	
HORACE active	from mid 30s		
		31 Battle of Actium	War between Octavian and Mark Antony
		30 Suicide of Antony and Cleopatra: Egypt becomes a Roman province	
VIRGIL's *Georgics*; possibly starts work on the *Aeneid*	29	29 Octavian returns to Italy	
		27 Octavian is given the title *Augustus*	THE JULIO-CLAUDIANS **AUGUSTUS**
Death of VIRGIL	19		
		8 The month 'Sextilis' is renamed 'Augustus' (August)	

		4	Augustus formally adopts Tiberius	
		2	Inauguration of the Forum of Augustus	
OVID exiled to Tomis	8			
		9	Battle of the Teutoburg Forest	
STRABO active		14	Death of Augustus	**TIBERIUS**
PHAEDRUS & VELLEIUS PATERCULUS active	20s			
		26	Tiberius moves to Capri	
		29	Death of Livia	
		33	Traditional date for crucifixion of Jesus	
		37	Death of Tiberius	**CALIGULA**
SENECA THE YOUNGER active	from 40s	40	Caligula's attempted invasion of Britain? Jewish Embassy to Caligula	
		41	Assassination of Caligula	**CLAUDIUS**
		43	Claudius's invasion of Britain	
		44	Claudius's triumph over Britain	
		48	Claudius's Lyon speech Execution of Claudius's wife Messalina	
SENECA, *Apocolocyntosis*	50s			
		54	Death of Claudius	**NERO**
		55	Death of Britannicus	
PLINY THE ELDER, LUCAN, PETRONIUS, PERSIUS active	60s	c. 60	Boudicca's rebellion	
Birth of PLINY THE YOUNGER	61/2			
		64	'Great Fire' at Rome Beginning of construction of the Golden House	

SENECA and LUCAN commit suicide	65			
PETRONIUS commits suicide	66	66	Nero's tour of Greece; grants 'freedom' to Greece	1st JEWISH REVOLT (66–73/4)
		68	Death of Nero	
		68–69	Civil war: so-called 'The Year of the Four Emperors'	CIVIL WAR GALBA, OTHO, VITELLIUS
		69		THE FLAVIANS VESPASIAN
		70	Destruction of the Temple in Jerusalem	
VALERIUS FLACCUS, STATIUS, MARTIAL, EPICTETUS active	70s–100s	73/4	First Jewish Revolt ends with the fall of Masada	
JOSEPHUS begins to publish *Jewish War*	75			
		79	Eruption of Vesuvius, destruction of Pompeii and Herculaneum Death of Vespasian	TITUS
PLUTARCH first active	80	80	Completion of the Colosseum	
		81	Death of Titus	DOMITIAN
		late 80s	Domitian's black dinner party	
JOSEPHUS, *Jewish Antiquities*	93/4			
		96	Assassination of Domitian	'ADOPTIVE' EMPERORS
TACITUS'S consulship	97		Nerva adopts Trajan	NERVA
		98	Death of Nerva	TRAJAN
PLINY, *Letters* Books 1–9	c.99–109			
JUVENAL, *Satires*	from c. 100			
PLINY's consulship and *Speech of Praise* to Trajan	100			
				1st DACIAN WAR (101–2)

					2nd DACIAN WAR (105–6)
TACITUS, *Histories*	109	109–110	Pliny governor of Pontus-Bithynia		
PLINY, *Letters* Book 10 (to Trajan)	110				
		113	Trajan invades Parthia Trajan's column completed		TRAJAN's CAMPAIGNS in the east, 113–17
TACITUS, *Annals*	117	117	Death of Trajan	HADRIAN	
		from c.118	Construction of Hadrian's Villa at Tivoli		
SUETONIUS, *Twelve Caesars*	120	120s	Construction of Hadrian's Wall		
		121–5	Hadrian's first 'tour' of the empire		
		128–34	Hadrian's second 'tour' of the empire Hadrian visits Lambaesis (128) Antinous drowns in the Nile (130) Hadrian's party visits the singing statue (130)		
		138	Death of Hadrian	ANTONINUS PIUS	
FRONTO, AULUS GELLIUS, LUCIAN, APULEIUS, PHLEGON active	140s–180s				
ARISTIDES, *Roman Oration*	144				
PAUSANIAS and GALEN active	c.160s –170s	161	Death of Antoninus Pius	MARCUS AURELIUS AND LUCIUS VERUS	
		167	Plague in Rome and the empire		
		169	Death of Lucius Verus	MARCUS AURELIUS	
ARTEMIDORUS active	from 180s	180	Death of Marcus Aurelius	COMMODUS	
		192	Commodus's displays in the Colosseum Assassination of Commodus		

		193	So-called 'year of the Five Emperors'	CIVIL WAR **PERTINAX, DIDIUS JULIANUS, PESCENNIUS NIGER, CLODIUS ALBINUS**
		193		THE SEVERANS **SEPTIMIUS SEVERUS**
				SEPTIMIUS SEVERUS'S CAMPAIGNS IN THE EAST, 195–8
CASSIUS DIO begins his history	c.202			
CASSIUS DIO's consulship	c.205			
				SEPTIMIUS SEVERUS'S CAMPAIGNS IN BRITAIN, 208–11
PHILOSTRATUS active	From 210s			
		211	Death of Septimius Severus Caracalla has Geta killed	**CARACALLA** AND **GETA CARACALLA**
		212	Citizenship extended to all free inhabitants of the empire	
		217	Assassination of Caracalla	**MACRINUS**
		218	Assassination of Macrinus	**ELAGABALUS**
		220s	Calendar of Dura Europos	
		222	Assassination of Elagabalus	**ALEXANDER SEVERUS**
		235	Assassination of Alexander Severus and his mother Julia Mamaea	
		238	Petition of Skaptoparans (reign of Gordian III)	
IMPERIAL HISTORY written	end of 300s			

ACKNOWLEDGEMENTS

In the long time that it has taken me to write *Emperor of Rome*, I have incurred many debts (intellectual and more). The germ of the idea for the book goes back to a course I taught in Cambridge in the 1990s with John Henderson and others, entitled, 'The Roman emperor: construction and deconstruction of an image'. I learned a lot from my fellow teachers and the students on that course, and more recently from the Cambridge Master's students who followed a series of seminars I coordinated on Suetonius. They sparked my interest in (and put me right on) many aspects of imperial biography.

In the course of writing, I have gratefully drawn on the expertise and generous assistance of many friends and colleagues: Christopher Burden-Strevens, Emlyn Dodd, Lisa Fentress, Roy Gibson, Christopher Kelly, Pamela Takefman, Peter Thonemann, Carrie Vout, Andrew Wallace-Hadrill and Peter Wiseman. The whole text was read through by Peter Stothard (who sometimes saw what I was trying to say, when I hadn't quite spotted it myself), by the wonderfully eagle-eyed Bob Weil of Liveright, and by Penny Daniel and Andrew Franklin of Profile. Debbie Whittaker double-checked everything and saved me from some embarrassing mistakes. Among my other Profile (and Profile-connected) friends, I am particularly indebted to Claire Beaumont, Catherine Clohessy-McCarthy, Peter Dyer (who designed the jacket), Alex Elam, Emily Hayward-Whitlock (of The Artists Partnership), Susanne Hillen, Ruth Killick (of Ruth Killick Publicity), Niamh Murray, Flora Willis and Valentina Zanca. Thanks too to Lesley Hodgson for the picture research and James Alexander (of Jade Design) for the text layouts. In the USA, I am also very grateful to George Lucas (of Inkwell Management), and Peter Miller and Haley Bracken (of Norton and Liveright).

As always, my family – from the oldest to the youngest (Robin, Zoe and Akin, Raph and Pamela, plus Ifeyinka, Ayodeji and Elijah) put up with a lot.

INDEX

Page references in *italics* indicate images
pl. indicates plate section

M

N

S

T

Y

Yourcenar, Marguerite: *Memoirs of Hadrian* 206, 212, 395

Z

Zenodorus 362, 366
Zosimus, Tiberius Claudius
104–5, *104*